The Unlikely Mr Rogue

The Unlikely Mr Rogue

A life with Ivan Pillay

Evelyn Groenink

First published by Jacana Media (Pty) Ltd in 2020

10 Orange Street
Sunnyside
Auckland Park 2092
South Africa
+2711 628 3200
www.jacana.co.za

© Evelyn Groenink, 2020

All rights reserved.

ISBN 978-1-4314-2946-2

Also available as an ebook.

Cover design by publicide
Index by Devi Pillay
Set in Ehrhardt MT Std 11/14pt
Printed and bound by ABC Press, Cape Town
Job no. 003715

See a complete list of Jacana titles at www.jacana.co.za

For those who keep carrying on

Contents

1	The voyage home	11
2	The imagining	111
3	Rogue One	193
4	Swimming with the crocodiles	269
	Where they are now	375
	Postscript by Ivan Pillay	379
	Notes	389
	Index	415

It's the days of apartheid in South Africa. The Dutch anti-apartheid movement, AABN, supports the African National Congress led by Nelson Mandela. In the latter half of the eighties, this support is increased to include disguises, safe houses and help with communications for an underground resistance project called Operation Vula. Dutch nationals, recruited by Conny Braam, chair of the AABN, take up residence in southern Africa to help Vula, while Vula coordinator Ivan Pillay, who operates from exile in Lusaka, Zambia, regularly visits Amsterdam.

Chapter One
The voyage home

Amsterdam, October 1989

My friend Bart and I lose our good seats for South African comedian Pieter-Dirk Uys's show in Amsterdam because of some high-up oke from Lusaka. 'We must pass our tickets to Conny. She is bringing him to the show,' Bart says resignedly. Conny is Conny Braam, chair of the Anti-Apartheid Movement of the Netherlands (AABN) of which both Bart and I are members, and if she is hosting a high-up oke from the ANC headquarters in Lusaka, there is little we can do.

That evening, sitting far away from the stage on the back balcony, I strain my neck to see what the high-up oke looks like. But I only see Conny's silver white hair and some curly black hair next to her. Do they laugh, I wonder. Pieter-Dirk Uys is irreverent. As much as he jokes about apartheid president P.W. Botha he makes fun of Bishop Desmond Tutu as well, portraying Tutu as a kind of clown. In our AABN events and campaigns, Conny usually keeps the irreverent jokes strictly among comrades: never criticise your own in public is her rule. We stand for unconditional international solidarity.

Our hatred of apartheid and our support for the struggle against that system is inspired by the Dutch experience of Nazi fascism that exterminated six million Jewish people, including over a hundred thousand in the Netherlands. Even if we are aware that there are important differences too – there are no gas chambers in South Africa, to name one – still, the black majority is deprived of any rights, banned to dry bantustan reserves and townships, often treated worse than animals. Activists are murdered, and children are shot and tortured in police cells.

We support the ANC and are guided by its Freedom Charter in the struggle for a South Africa – and also a world, we hope – that belongs to all who live in it. But no matter how much I try to monitor the couple in front, I can't make out the visitor's reactions. He sits still through it all. He may be a bit of an enigma. But since he has just arrived from a twelve-hour flight, he may also be fast asleep.

That evening in the theatre bar, around a big table with beer, gin and wine, I look for a black man to fit the curly hair, but I see no such person. There is only a small Indian sitting at the furthest corner of the table. He looks alert and content and keeps quiet as we loudly review and rehash Uys's jokes. He drinks tea.

That's a weird one, I think, and then for a year I don't think about the high-up oke from Lusaka at all. Not even when, suddenly, seven months later, a tense atmosphere of defeat pervades the rickety old rooms of the AABN office. Operation Vula is blown, I hear when I arrive that day. People have been arrested, computer discs discovered.

I don't know what that means, since nobody has told me anything about this Vula. I have no idea that the small Indian man from Lusaka had anything to do with it.

Back to the Future
Lusaka, late 1990

When I see him get out of a battered old Ford and walk down the sandy path to the balcony where I am waiting, I utter a surprised, 'Hey, I *know* you.' What are the odds, that among the thousands of ANC members and officials residing here in Lusaka, in exile, he is the one I meet?

Ivan, as he introduces himself, is indeed my contact. He will help me to carry out a new joint AABN and ANC project, which is to return two exiled freedom fighters from Lusaka to South Africa. They will be the first two MK (Umkhonto we Sizwe) soldiers to go home to what is still the country of apartheid. Mandela may be free now, having been released in February this year, and the ANC has been unbanned, but fighters are still in exile, prisoners are still in jail, and the white regime under President F.W. de Klerk is still in power. The new project, called Back to the Future, alternately The Voyage Home, is intended to speed things up.

I am excited. Finally, I can do something more than just write about the evils of apartheid. The mission fits in seamlessly with both my AABN membership and my communist background. I was brought up with tales about the struggles of the exploited, abused and downtrodden. Such revolutionary sentiments in my family go back to the early 1920s, when my grandmother who sold fish in the market and did domestic work for madams, danced with Soviet Russian soldiers in Amsterdam harbour on Saturday evenings. They had taught her all the Red Army songs and she had learned to sing them off pat, without knowing a word of Russian.

A decade and a half later, my grandfather joined the international brigades in Spain. He left my grandmother with two young children, my father being one of them, and had affairs both inside Spain and out. He was not exactly a hero. When he was home, he beat his wife and children. But even if my dad hated him for those things, still he inherited the spark of desire to fight somewhere, to fight for something, and he passed it on to me. My dad took me to marches against the Vietnam war, the Pinochet coup in Chile and apartheid in South Africa.

As an adult, I worked for the small Amsterdam communist newspaper *De Waarheid* (Dutch for *The Truth*) until 1985, when it folded under the weight of the uninspiring reality of Soviet socialism. In the late eighties, I travelled to central America, reporting on the anti-imperialist guerrilla wars that were waged there. I was in Nicaragua, and hoped that the Sandinistas would do better than the eastern European communists. They didn't.

In the end, as I find myself in Lusaka, only the worldwide anti-apartheid movement still inspires. The ANC's non-racialism, its uncompromising stand on human dignity for all, is exhilarating to me as the Russian songs and dances must have been for my grandmother.

In addition to the inspiration of the Back to the Future project itself, this is my first chance to get into South Africa to follow up on my investigation into the murder of ANC representative Dulcie September in Paris two years before.

The idea of the project is to assist the first two MK soldiers to go home to South Africa. We will do this together with a number of invited fellow Dutch journalists and Klaas de Jonge, a Dutchman famous for his participation in the armed struggle.[1] Together we will challenge the regime. If they want to arrest the MK soldiers, they will have to arrest us too.

Back to the Future is a small project, but it will challenge the status quo. It will probably make for some good media coverage in the Netherlands and in South Africa, and also hopefully internationally. It will add to the pressure on Pretoria. It may speed up things.

There is a second person here: a black woman with a limp, who emerges from the passenger side of the Ford as I get acquainted with Ivan. Nombulelo, she says her name is, and adds that she is 'in touch with the families inside'. She herself is from 'inside', as it turns out – legitimately in Lusaka, with a passport. Nombulelo will be the bridge, the only one who knows the exiles as well as their South African families. She has just travelled to their homes in the Transkei, to ask the families if they are happy to welcome them back.

It is not a strange question. There will be two more mouths to feed, two more unemployed and in need of care. One, a youngster known by his struggle name Zeph, is in a wheelchair. The older returnee, Morris, walks with difficulty, and is blind and mostly deaf. Both have been struck by land mines around the MK camps in Angola laid by Unita, South Africa's allied contra movement in that country. The decision to choose two disabled veterans to go back home was taken because the apartheid regime will find it difficult to arrest the two on charges of 'terrorism'. But their disabilities come with challenges too. 'I was worried that the families might hesitate,' says Nombulelo. 'But they immediately said they want them back.'

I ask Nombulelo about her limp, and she explains that she has had it since birth. 'It's because I'm a twin. After my bigger sister was born I was slow to come out because my leg was stuck somewhere. It took a while before my mother and the nurse realised that there was a second baby. I stayed behind in the womb for a while with my leg stuck and it remained crooked ever since.'

I will learn later that the older twin, Totsie, is an MK soldier who joined the underground in Swaziland having left Soweto to study in freedom. She left the country as she had the womb, leaving her sister behind. I will also learn later that Totsie was until recently part of Operation Vula, an underground resistance project aimed at infiltrating fighters, weapons and leaders into South Africa. Vula was a landmark shift in the armed struggle against the regime. Many ANC soldiers, like Zeph and Morris, had been isolated in camps in Angola, never getting to fight inside the country. Totsie linked up with Ivan in 1985 and operated from Swaziland. She became an expert at crossing border fences into South Africa.

The story of siblings ripped apart, one left behind and one propelled abroad, climbing over border fences, living a life alone in the resistance, is the story of many South African families who were torn apart. In time I will find out that it is the story of Ivan too.

Opening the path

Ivan was coordinating Operation Vula. The underground network was supported by internationalists such as Conny Braam in Amsterdam and other foreigners recruited by her to bring in weapons and manage safe houses. Totsie had jumped over borders, climbed back and forth, and linked with comrades in Natal, the Transvaal and the Cape. Vula, for the first time since the sixties, brought national ANC leaders into South Africa itself. Vula had been built on previous scattered experiences where small guerrilla teams had gone into South Africa to attack targets, and if all went well, escaped again. It now infiltrated ANC leaders into the country who lived in communities and had links to the mass democratic movement.

Strange as this may sound, this, besides being a good fighting plan, was also envisaged to bring about some healing. South Africa was bleeding and broken. Apartheid, with its bantustan homeland reserves, pass laws and forced migrant labour, had destroyed communities and families. Townships and villages were full of humiliated, wounded and angry second-class citizens. Many places had turned into war zones, ravaged by the police and the army, the only resistance coming from youngsters armed with stones and petrol bombs. The activists in the United Democratic Front (UDF), the unions and local civil society, worked day and night to channel the anger and pain into meetings, marches, mass protests and campaigns. They were stretched and under attack, under constant threat of arrests and bannings. Many were on the run. Church leaders, academics and teachers were being attacked by apartheid police, paramilitary gangs and vigilantes, even death squads.

Many on the front lines were children. Thousands of thirteen and fourteen year olds who fought in the townships were in jail, some tortured, some killed. Those who weren't were desperately seeking out the police informers in their own ranks, killing them before they could sell them out to the security police; sometimes targeting innocent schoolmates and neighbours on such suspicions. They clamoured for weapons, but how could they be given weapons just like that? Some bands of youngsters had even become criminalised, *tsotsi* comrades, as much to fear as the soldiers of apartheid. Gangsters and jackrollers, bands of schoolgirl-rapists who entered schools, picked you and you and you, and you had to come with them or else.

While local activists in the mass movement were beaten and jailed, young MK combatants who had been told to attack targets in the area were often left to their own devices, isolated from the movement, sometimes without shelter.

Solomon Mahlangu, the young freedom fighter for whose release we had campaigned in Amsterdam, was hanged in 1979. The movie *Kalushi* made much later about his life showed how the young man was unable to complete his mission; how he was arrested and sentenced to death after an unplanned shoot-out in Pretoria. 'This happened many times,' Ivan says when we later talk about the film. 'We did not have sufficient coordination among communities, mass protest actions, the armed struggle and the ANC leadership.'[2]

To bring about coherence between the four pillars of struggle, as the ANC called it – the mass movement, the political underground, armed struggle and international anti-apartheid pressure – was urgent for another reason, too. From rubble and mayhem, schools and neighbourhoods would have to be rebuilt, and civil society and democracy itself would have to grow once the war was over. Ivan feared that 'the way it was going, we would mainly have ruins and traumatised people left. With every passing day, month, year, from uprisings to massacres to states of emergency, the situation was running more and more away from us. During the 1980s forty thousand internal activists were jailed.'

Under the command of ANC President O.R. Tambo, senior leaders had finally prepared in 1986 to 'go inside'. Vula (Vulindlela or 'open the path' in Zulu) had established secret computer communication channels between inside and outside, patching up many ruptures in more ways than one: from Lusaka, Oliver Tambo could reach his erstwhile law firm and political partner, Nelson Mandela, all the way into his prison. As Ivan would later note, 'The communication was a leap forward by itself. Until then we had been couriering coded messages hidden in parcels and shoes, talking in brief phone calls from call box to call box, all painfully insufficient and inefficient. But in the late eighties, the first electronic communications technology was being developed. We started using that in Vula.'

Ivan had been in Amsterdam several times to coordinate the Dutch support for the operation. Conny Braam – who, in the course of Vula, was also the victim of an attack by apartheid's poison doctors[3] – had linked him to other Dutch comrades for whom solidarity was a given: They, like Conny, considered fighting apartheid as morally imperative as it had been for those in an earlier generation who had resisted Nazis. The foreigners were set to use their privilege – white faces, white passports, nice cars – in South Africa to end its white privilege system.[4]

In October 1990, as I land in Lusaka, I am not aware of any of this. Very deliberately, neither Conny nor Bart have told me anything besides what I need to know. Project Back to the Future is all that I am acquainted with. I don't even know that Vula leaders are in jail, that some comrades are missing or that in Lusaka Ivan has been busy shredding documents and wiping out electronic tracks. Conny's casual presentation of the new returnee project has masked her sleepless nights, her agony over those in danger, and her fear that some have been killed.

I am also ignorant of the fact that I am here precisely because Vula is over: Back to the Future is meant to be a new patch between inside and outside now that the previous connection has been closed. 'Vula Lite' Bart will call it, years later. Our job now is to bring an element of MK into South Africa, legally at least, in the guise of a media event around two disabled returning exiles.

It is no coincidence that the chosen returnees are from the Transkei. The Transkei is as close to liberated territory as you can get in 1990. The black homeland was created as an 'independent state' by the apartheid system as a reservoir for people not needed for labour in white areas. Now, to Pretoria's considerable chagrin, it is ruled by the ANC-friendly General Bantu Holomisa. Even worse for Pretoria, Holomisa has offered sanctuary in his own house to no less a person than MK Chief of Staff

Chris Hani, the regime's most wanted man.

Providing new connections is another reason why Klaas de Jonge is joining us. 'It's just because he knows Chris Hani and he is famous,' Conny had told me. 'It's good for publicity.' But of course Klaas is also part of MK. And – bar one of his eyes, blinded by what is suspected to have been yet another poison attack[5] – not disabled.

I am a fresh white face to help open this new path, legally, openly and under the spotlight of the media. I am useful also because I can't do any harm if arrested, since I know nothing worth talking about.

Arriving in Lusaka in the Dutch autumn of 1990, I don't even understand why people routinely keep referring to my temporary home as a safe house. I heard the term first from Lucy, the woman at the airport who drove me here. 'This is your safe house,' she had said. I had asked myself silently why I had to be in a safe house. Were there unsafe houses here?

The connections

Ivan drives his Ford up and down Lusaka as if the most important thing in the world is to find money, travel documents and Zambia Air tickets for our little party of a youngster in a wheelchair, a rather grumpy old deaf and blind fellow veteran, a couple of Dutch friends and colleagues and myself. In the coming days I find that getting the tickets and papers are certainly among the most difficult. During the empty hours and days as we wait for doors to be opened, paperwork to be finalised and people to come back to us, he invites me to come along to see places and meet people in Lusaka. There is always an interesting individual or office or shop 'just around the corner,' where, invariably, we end up meeting somebody else who is also interesting.

It makes me feel a bit uneasy: this man must surely have something better to do than show me around town. I will learn only later that he actually really doesn't have much to do now, now that Vula is over. But I begin to see that to him meeting with people is not just a chore. They are all important: the cashier in the dollar store, the grande dame at the travel agency who needs a lot of encouragement to finally process the tickets we need, the motor mechanic, the man at the fax machine in ANC headquarters. That first week in Lusaka, I get to know a trait of Ivan that has always been there and will remain: making connections. It's how he helped build the underground. It's what he does.

It is new to me though, not to mention scary. Although I eagerly trailblaze up and down unknown paths, I don't like meeting random people. Being a journalist suits me precisely because it shields me from having to deal with fellow humans. Never mind idealistic visions for all humanity: actual individual people whom I don't know do tend to scare me. If I decide I want to talk to someone I request an interview; for the rest I keep physical humanity at bay. But I can't be rude to the high-up oke – commander, I hear some people call him – who wants me to get to know the environment that I will be writing about.

As it turns out, many of the encounters are indeed enlightening, though there are boring ones too. Sometimes, they are enlightening and boring at the same time. The ANC Youth League guys, for example, four men in their thirties who lecture me about Marxism in a stuffy office with dark old furniture, are so bombastic and annoying that they cure me forever from any starry-eyed ideas I may have had about professional revolutionaries. The ANC Women's League members I am invited to spend a day with, though motherly and warm, are appallingly unfeminist. Most of them are social workers by profession and seem to be mostly preoccupied with youngsters whose behaviour bothers other people in the exile community. They talk of those who get drunk, start fights, hang out with unsavoury friends.

I know the trauma at first from the stories told by the mamas: about Freddy, who missed home so much that one day he stopped speaking, and about Thomas who 'stared into the glistening fields in the hot sunshine for hours on end, until he got blind'. The Women's League mamas show me a towering building, all dusty brick, on one side of one of Lusaka's main arteries: a home for people who have psychological problems, they tell me. Freddy and Thomas are there now. There are more stories about boys, so much that I have to ask what happened to the girls. 'Some girls commit suicide', is the bland answer from Mama Regina Nzo, the wife of ANC Secretary-General Alfred Nzo. Her shrug is even more unsettling than the statement.

Then I see it for myself: first in the guy who works at the ANC head office who misses a hand because of a letter bomb, then Ivan's colleague Reggie,[6] who drinks most of our whisky until he sheds tears talking about life in the military camps in Angola, where Zeph's legs were blown off and Morris turned into a blind, deaf, stiffly walking victim. 'So much waiting, so much hurt, so much waste,' he sighs. 'And for those who stayed there, little chance to actually fight the *boers*.' He nods obediently when Ivan reminds him that he, Reggie, has hardly been in the camps. 'But still.'

The trauma is in Morris, once a prince of the Ciskei royal family, now reduced to almost total incapacitation, his conversation mostly about the bad treatment he says he gets. He complains even as the youngsters who have been assigned to feed, bathe and clothe him wait on him hand and foot. They smile when I ask how they feel about Morris's sourness, and I think of Morris's family in Transkei, who have told Nombulelo they are ready to have him back.

It is in Eric,[7] who was part of MK's Natal machinery, and had to abandon his family, friends and comrades in order to not endanger them. He left the country because he was wanted by the police, and now whiles away time in Lusaka, in the clubs where he womanises, and in an apartment where he throws darts. You can get many girls in Lusaka if you are in the ANC, since it often means you have some dollars. He has got very good at darts, I learn when Ivan and I visit him and join in a game.

Like Reggie, Eric drinks, a lot. He confides that all he wants is to go back to the beaches of Natal and swim with dolphins again.

One evening at a party, where Eric has again had way too much to drink, he fights with his current Zambian girlfriend, violently pushing and hitting her. Then he pulls out a gun when people try to stop him. It is Lucia, the Dutch Vula communications operative (though I don't know that she is that, not yet) who stands up to him like a stern schoolteacher and takes the gun out of his hand. By then I have already learned that you do what Lucia tells you to do. She made me grate a full bucket of carrots and cabbage to make coleslaw for the same party.

In the end Eric takes off all his clothes and dives naked into the swimming pool, swimming up and down for a while until some comrades summon him and take him home. When another group of comrades, including Ivan, visit him the next day to tell him that women abuse is really not something a disciplined member of the ANC should engage in, they find the very same girlfriend sitting on his lap.

No one knows this yet, but Eric has AIDS. He will die of it a few years in the new South Africa.

The trauma is in Zeph from long before he lost his legs. It came from the mines where young rural men from the Transkei were expected to come and seek work. 'I had to pretend I had less schooling than I had, because the mine management doesn't want clever people. They say you are going to make trouble if you are educated,' he says as I meet him, lying on his bed with a book. 'I had gone to high school but I said I had only Standard Two.'[8] Playing dumb had been humiliating, almost as bad as the bullying Zeph had to endure from indunas, employed as tribal heads in the hostels. 'But the worst was the physical tests, where you had to run on the spot on a treadmill, naked in a hot room, then bend over for them to stick thermometers in your anus to see if you could stand the heat.'

It was the humiliation that had made Lizo Semane, now Zeph Mothopeng, want to fight. Zeph was actually happier in the camps in Angola than he had been in apartheid South Africa. The ANC encouraged his education, gave him political books to read, and made him a commissar, in charge of the political education of his fellow comrades. When he stepped on a mine close to the Viana camp, he didn't feel the pain immediately. Despite being in shock, he still directed his comrades to take the path back to the camp.

I didn't notice Zeph at first when he arrived at the safe house. I saw that a room was occupied that had been empty before, and greeted the nice young man who was reading on his bed, but didn't want to disturb him. It hadn't dawned on me that this was Zeph, the paraplegic MK cadre we were waiting for. Ivan introduced us in the evening, arriving with Nombulelo, to discuss the programme for the next day. 'He has just arrived from Zimbabwe,' Nombulelo said apologetically, when Ivan enquired why she hadn't told Zeph about me, or me about him. 'He has only been here a day.'

'Still, you should have made the introduction,' Ivan responded sternly, and suddenly, for the first time, I saw the MK commander in him.

'We are all traumatised,' he says the next evening. 'Morris and Zeph may physically look disabled, but we are all affected one way or another. Not just us in exile. I mean all South Africans. Look at the behaviour of the tsotsi comrades, look at the massacres between communities in Natal. With our history, it's not surprising.' I tell him the self-important ANC Youth League officials looked just fine to me. 'Maybe to be so full of yourself is also a kind of response to suffering,' he ponders. 'I didn't say that all traumatised people are *interesting*. We are flawed in different ways. The movement itself is affected by all these things too.'

The announcement of 2 February this year, regarding the unbanning of the ANC and the release of Nelson Mandela, has left exiled people uncertain. There has been no announcement, meeting or consultation: Those who could go back to South Africa as part of the negotiations simply went. All others stayed behind, and those in the underground remained fugitives. 'I have several passports,' Ivan says. 'But I can't use any of them.'[9]

What I do know, in the silence of Lusaka in 1990, is that asking Ivan for details about his own home somehow seems out of order, like asking his real name: Ivan is his struggle name. He did at one point make a remark about a crowded and polluted Indian township in Natal called Merebank, though, and it sounded like that could be where he was from. But 'What is home right, what is home?' asks another, elder comrade of Indian origin called Bobby, who visits one evening and reminisces about the place where he came from: the bustling community on the hills of Cato Manor in Durban. Bobby grew up there, but as a teenager saw it bulldozed to the ground, the families all removed to white rows of little houses especially built for Indians, far away from the city centre. 'Our mums and aunties were on the back of trucks and lorries with bags and their pots and pans. That is what I remember,' says Bobby. 'After that, I don't really know what home is anymore.'

Bobby is Sunny Singh, I later learn. He has served ten years on Robben Island. When he was released in 1974 – wearing trousers that were now way too wide for his skinny prison body – he had to make his way home from Durban Central Police Station, where he was dropped off by the state, 'holding up my pants with two hands until I had found a shop where I could buy a belt'. He soon went back to the townships to recruit more people for the struggle. That is how he and Ivan met.

The boy who looked for the ANC
Durban, in the beginning

The boy, who was not Ivan yet, but who shall be referred to as Ivan, jumped at meeting Bobby. By then, in 1975, he had already been looking for the ANC for ages. Though the community and family in the Indian township of Merebank, twenty kilometres from Durban, was warm and loving, it was also crowded and suffocating. It was where Indians had to be, away from the majority of South Africans, little pegs to fit in apartheid holes, buffers between white oppression and black rage. The boy felt fenced in in the small township, where way too many large families were jammed together in tiny houses.

At home he slept on a mattress in the sitting room after all visitors and family had retired to bed. There were visitors often, fellow Indians who were somehow related, all from families of formerly indentured sugarcane plantation labourers.

You could go out into the city, but, even there, there was limited space for you. As Ivan's friend Coastal would say some years later, in the city centre, any seat to sit in, have tea, have a cooldrink, was not for you if it was not specifically allocated to blacks or – as the term that was officially used – non-whites. Your mother would sometimes take you from the township in an Indian bus to the Indian part of the city around Grey Street to shop at the market. That was it. As soon as you strayed, you were told to 'move on, coolie'. Then you and your mum would be back in the crowded, boiling bus that took way too long, past many, many stops, at a snail's pace, to reach Merebank again.

It was what had made Coastal so very angry at a very young age: that in the city centre, where they sometimes had to be for an errand, his mother was not allowed to even sit down. If she was too tired, she had to sit on the pavement, sari and all, with feet in the gutter. That they would do that to his mother.

Coastal had become a fighter against apartheid even before Ivan had. He had met Coastal in school.

The boy Ivan just felt the need for space. One of his early childhood memories is about travelling in a small car crowded with relatives, so full that he was dangling, compressed between adults, his feet not touching the ground, crying for air and space at the top of his lungs. He would have nightmares for a long time still, in which he can't breathe and feels he is suffocating, then waking up and finding himself back in the same dream, suffocating still.

School was stifling too: Merebank Hillside was as infused with silence and fear as it had been when it was a detention camp for Boer soldiers during the Anglo-Boer War. As with all other schools in the country, discussion of politics was banned and questioning official history was not allowed. Actually, questioning anything was not allowed.

Their best loved teacher in primary school read the newspaper to them. Though censored, here at least, was real information about the world. That teacher, Ivan would later find out, had a brother who was an anti-apartheid activist and a member of the ANC. He was Kader Asmal, later to become minister of education. Ivan and his friends were soon to despise the servile behaviour of the majority of teachers who only aimed to please the principal. He in turn only aimed to please the white inspector.

One of the first acts of rebellion, led by Coastal, had been to resist the anthem, 'Die Stem' which they all had to sing: 'Uit die blou van onse hemel, uit die diepte van ons see', and, impossibly, 'Ons vir jou Suid Afrika.' Coastal stood up one day and said they were not going to sing it anymore. Others agreed. In the end thirty-five of them walked out. The boy Ivan, skinny and fragile, the sickly last-born of the family, joined the protest too. It was invigorating. Later, Coastal went even further, presenting a new text to the girls' choir to sing as a new anthem. 'From the mouths of starving children, To the malnutrition bound. From poverty-stricken quarters, To the depths of our black mind,' they sang defiantly. The teachers turned shades of pale and green when that happened.

After graduation, the youngsters began to look for real struggle connections. They had seen the potential of mass protest already in 1966 – they had still been in school, twelve and thirteen years old – when Robert Kennedy[10] visited South Africa and denounced apartheid in no uncertain terms. Thousands of South Africans were glued to their radios to listen to Kennedy's speech upon his arrival at the airport in Durban, and hundreds had come to listen to him in person. All the Verwoerds and Vorsters could do was gnaw their teeth, unable to stop him saying what everyone else would only whisper.

Ivan's brother Joe, who had been part of the huge crowd at the airport, could recite entire phrases from that Bobby Kennedy speech. Surely South African activists themselves could speak out as Bobby Kennedy had done, they thought, and more.

The first-year students, first-time workers and some unemployed friends started a community newspaper called 'The Sentinel'. The stencilled quarterly, funded with small donations from aligned souls in the community and carried in bunches door to door through Merebank, carried big headlines about lies and injustice, juxtaposed with big bold columns headed 'THE FACTS!' The boys – for they were mainly boys, in this traditional community where girls were either at school or indoors – also joined Merebank's community institutions, the Friends of the Sick Association, the Community Centre, the Child Welfare Society and the local ratepayers' association. They politicised these bodies, arguing that the TB and asthma that many in the township suffered had to do with pollution and therefore with apartheid. It was apartheid after all that had placed Indian families in an industrialised area. The people of Merebank *lived hemmed in between a sewage plant, a paper plant, a chromite mine and two oil refineries.*

For the most part they argued these things very nicely – with clean shirts on, politely and soft spoken – so as not to alienate those who were older, or afraid. Sometimes they made noise, though: For instance, when fake gurus of the evangelical churches came with their tents to hold events where they, loudly praying, pretended to heal people's sicknesses and sorrows in exchange for donations. It was Coastal – always Coastal – who would take the lead in disturbing the conmen, shouting that these so-called prophets were not going to help with their problems, only the struggle against apartheid would. They would all join in then and argue with the believers in the tents.

Once, when people queued for the stage where a guru was pretending to heal their illnesses, Coastal queued with them. On the platform, he declared that his problem was that he was black, and therefore could not get a good job because all the good jobs were for white people, and asked the guru to turn him white. 'These goons beat the devil out of me,' he would recall, chuckling, decades later.

'The Sentinel' – stencilled in the evenings in the family's garage, which was also where the teenage boys and passing relatives slept – insisted likewise that the lack of good books in the library, housing, bus shelters even, also had everything to do with apartheid. These were not just issues for a few Indian elders to write letters about to the municipality. 'The Sentinel' informed the Indian elders – who didn't like white oppressors, but sometimes liked black Africans even less – about non-racialism and Black Consciousness. The youngsters called themselves 'black', and told their relatives and elders that they were black, too.

Call it rogue if you like. Saying you were black as an Indian in those days was definitely not a fashionable thing to do. It was rebellious and scary. Besides the politics of it, such talk usually attracted the attention of the security police and many Indians were really rather afraid of blacks, especially of Zulu people in Natal. This was especially so after the 1949 pogroms in which Zulu impis razed Indian homes and killed many.

It was one of the things that apartheid did. Divide and rule. Some said that whites had whispered anti-Indian messages into the ears of the Zulu headmen, but it was difficult to find proof. What was very clear, however, was that white bosses and police did very little to disabuse the headmen and their impis of their notions and largely let them go on their rampage. It was reported that when police acted against the impis, and in some instances, shot instigators, white people were amongst those killed. This was possibly the earliest appearance of what would later be called the Third Force.

It did not take much to ignite racial war in South Africa. One only had to declare that some people were 'others'. Every Zulu could see for himself that, generally, Indians were relatively better off; the message that Indians were taking spaces and opportunities from blacks was received with approval by many. Blacks were indeed more disadvantaged compared to the Indian shopkeepers, bookkeepers, municipal bureaucrats and small farm owners. Indians were not even 'from here', indunas told the people. 'These makula should go back to India.'

Strangely, the indunas did not talk about whites in this vein. Was it accepted that whites were 'from here' and that whites were naturally bosses? Or was the issue not raised simply because even to think of raiding white areas was lunacy? The killing – 'I can still hear that thud thud thud of them coming,' remembers elder brother Suggie – had happened before the boy Ivan was born but many elders still talked about it, and gave it as a reason why they couldn't support the black struggle, much less consider themselves black.

The experience of his family was different, though. They were saved by old man Mdelwa, a Zulu neighbour who farmed nearby. Ivan's mother, highly pregnant – baby Loga would be born two days later – had hid below the bank of a stream with little Angie and Joe, half in the water, waiting for the impi to go away, and Pushpa, the eldest sister, found shelter in a nearby house with the boys Kisten and Suggie. Mdelwa and his wife then opened the door to the mob and convinced them that this house was theirs. They showed them that there were no Indians there.

The two families had been farmers together in a place called Sawoti in southern Natal. When the Pillay family moved to Merebank, Mdelwa and his wife had come too, under the guise of being Father Vadivaloo Pillay's farm worker, although Father had never owned a farm. But these were the days of the dompas, the hated domestic ID document that Africans were required to carry; Father signed Mdelwa's pass every month while Mdelwa farmed and did odd jobs around town.

Father, who was an insurance salesman, was good with paperwork, forms, and whites. 'He had his white shirt, his tie and his briefcase; he was polite and he understood all the relevant forms and the regulations,' remembers Kisten, the eldest son. 'He usually got the permissions he wanted because of that.' Kisten, who worked in a furniture shop then, narrates how one day Mdelwa came to visit him in the shop 'to tell me that I might think I was a big shot *with my desk and two telephones and copying machine, but had any white man ever pulled out a chair for me?' Apparently, during a visit to the pass office with Father, a white man at the office had pulled out a chair for 'Mr Pillay', inviting him to sit down. 'Of course, being black, Mdelwa was not even allowed to sit down at all. But Mdelwa was amazed that Father, as an Indian, had managed to impress a white man like that.'*

After Father became ill with Parkinson's, and unable to sign Mdelwa's dompas, Kisten took over, forging the old man's signature every month, even when Mdelwa worked for other employers and not for the Pillays. Later still, other employers had – for simplicity's sake – continued the tradition of forging Father Vadivaloo Pillay's signature and it is therefore quite possible that his monthly, live, signature far outlived Vadivaloo Pillay himself. Neither Father nor Mother were political, but, like Mdelwa and his family, black friends and comrades would continue to be welcome in their home, even if this caused increasing attention from the security police. With Joe and Ivan becoming more and more engaged with activism, and Father now bed-ridden, Mother and eldest sister Pushpa – who was like a second mother to the younger ones and usually simply called Sister – would bear the brunt of these visits. 'We knew that what the boys were doing was right,' Sister remembers. 'So there was no question.'

In those days the names of the ANC and Mandela were still only whispered; you would be in trouble and sent to the Island if you said such things out loud. But Black Consciousness was growing among students and the older youth and a multi-coloured community of comrades started to emerge again, for the first time since the early sixties. Hope permeated the lives of those aspiring to break down the walls. Ivan remembers the early seventies as a 'period of unfreezing'. A little later, released ANC prisoners from Robben Island would come in to play their role again, too.

African National Chaos
Lusaka, October 1990

Ironically, the fight had led to exile. In exile without your family and your lifelong friends, living clandestinely, you were always alert and anxious. There was silence and meeting people in empty houses, in the dark in strange countries. 'If I had had a choice, I wouldn't have gone into exile,' he confides during one of our Lusaka evenings. 'I would have stayed in South Africa and continued to work from within.' On that particular evening he has just stumbled over the mess of clothes pouring out of the open suitcase in my room, with the bed and the floor covered in books and notes. He smiles a little at it, but says nothing. Is he polite, or slightly amused at a chaos he would never allow in his own, tightly controlled life? I have learned by now that in his universe every crucial item has its own drawer, shelf, file, secret compartment or box. There is no crumpled paper, used plate or crumb anywhere. At his place, an apartment in a building in Lusaka's Kabulonga suburb, he always seems busy arranging, tidying, dusting, doing dishes. There is a suitcase in a corner, neatly packed and zipped, ready to leave at any moment.

Maybe it is just about security. Or maybe this is his way of dealing with a fragmented existence in a disorderly universe. 'African National Chaos', he often sighs and says, after sharing yet another tale of misunderstanding, mismatching, misplacing, mysteriously missing items and missed appointments. Fortunately, he manages to laugh at such things. By now, I think he must have laughed at Pieter-Dirk Uys's jokes in Amsterdam, too.

We talk in the lounge of the safe house about the plans for our group's departure in a few days' time. Meanwhile, in another corner, at the leather couches and fancy coffee table, a fat Zambian man is meeting a number of equally fat, equally male, ANC officials. They talk softly while a Zambian woman vacuums and scrubs around them on her knees, diligently emptying and cleaning the men's ashtrays as soon as they are even a little dirty. 'Some in the exile community call them Hoovers,' says Ivan, following my gaze. 'Vacuum cleaners.' He shakes his head.

He is more caring – always asking if I am fine, if I need anything, if I want juice, a phone call, if I need to go to the shops – than I am used to, coming as I do from hippie, punk and squatter environments in seventies and eighties Amsterdam. Not that my leftie freewheeling, sometimes communal living, way-too-much-drinking-and-smoking-anything friends are not good people. But we have not always exactly tried to be *comforting* to one another, engaged as we all always were with pressing personal issues, revolutions – sexual and otherwise – demons, parents, and the like. None of us had much space in our heads to worry about others.

I have had a few relationships lasting a couple of years and a green-card marriage with a friend from Mexico; we were together but would not have married if we could have lived in the same country without that formality. There have been calm enough times, but also lots of adventures, insecurities and problems. The sudden experience of being thrown together with someone who is continuously and visibly concerned with my safety and well-being is unsettling. In my Amsterdam activist circles, no male acquaintance has ever been this *nice* to me.

Being good
Durban, the fifties

His family was all about treating others with care. The community was a safety net, ranging from the practical – the extended family would come together whenever there was a need to pay study fees for anybody, or a funeral – to the simple, warm acceptance and security every human needs. The atmosphere at home was in line with what sociologists would call upper working class values: one would keep one's children clean, kempt, schooled, loved, fed and warm. One didn't drink, curse or gamble; one kept one's front porch swept clean. Meat was expensive but there were always vegetable curries and enough rice and bread to share. 'It's not difficult. You can curry anything,' Sister would say, pointing at the yard with the leaves and tomatoes and roots.

They always shared with those who had less: with visitors, poorer friends and comrades of the boys, with sickly relatives who lived far away – they would send one of the boys with fruit, or a tin with a meal. The family lived by Gandhi's words, 'Being good and doing good'; a portrait of Gandhi still hangs in second sister Angie's home.

Caring is what his mother and eldest sister did. It was as natural as breathing. They did it most especially for him, the baby of the family, always spoiling him with bits of food, smiles, hugs, simply and silently, without making a display of it. Caring was hardwired in Sister's own home too, when she moved in with her husband and Ivan moved in with them. Brother-in-law – babalaw, he called him – was one of those good men, traditional in his views but a responsible and dedicated breadwinner, and a warm and loving rock. Babalaw would come home with freshly caught fish and little presents. In the evenings, he delighted in switching on the radio and finding a quiz or music programme to listen to with the family. His wife, their kids Jenny and Morgan, and the 'third child' as the neighbours would know the boy Ivan, would enjoy the programme with tea and eats. Sister had been lucky – or clever – enough to get herself married to such a genuinely nice guy.

Sadly babalaw died in his forties of the asthma that so prevailed in southern Durban's industrialised area, now almost forty years ago. Sister still dusts his picture and lights the lamp for him every day.

She also still worries about her baby brother every day, even now that she is past eighty and he is over sixty-five. She'll get up – with the Parkinson's that has struck her, now, too – to cook all the curries he likes when he visits, even when everybody tells her to sit down, for goodness sake. She is still the same Sister who sternly told the security police to go away every time they knocked on her door; who had cooked pots of food for him and Joe in exile, travelling up and down to Swaziland for years. Recently she has been very angry indeed at the people who have hurt him, like Jacob Zuma, and Zuma's favourite tax boss Tom Moyane, who pushed a smear campaign and eventually a prosecution against him. She often says she'd like to shoot the both of them.

That's Sister, who is now my fierce wonderful Sister too.

Russian caviar
Lusaka, October 1990

After a week of marvelling at what is happening – now, of all times, when I have come here to firmly focus on work for a change and be professional – it starts to feel really good.

And then he has caviar in his fridge, too.

'Oh yes, the caviar,' he says, when I spot the jar with a Russian label that I think says Beluga. 'I don't care much for it myself. By all means eat it if you like.' Any qualms I may have about Moscow providing high okes in Lusaka with caviar – god knows in exchange for what in terms of loyalty and service to the world-dominating agenda of the Soviet Union – vanish. I eat a lot of it, with ANC-supplied crackers and a pimply lemon from the market. It is delicious.

Later he tells me about the Russian officer Vladimir Shubin who has been liaising with the ANC, especially in the context of Operation Vula. 'I don't think that Soviet support was a problem for us,' he says. 'Shubin provided real help.' Whether the Soviet Union will seek political payback from the ANC, once that party assumes power in Pretoria, remains to be seen. 'But if things go the way they are going with Gorbachev now, once that happens there will in all probability not even be a Soviet Union anymore.' As we come to know later, October 1990 will indeed be the last time the Soviet Union will ever hold its annual October Revolution Parade.

I prod a bit further after the first half jar of the caviar is well and gone. Has he ever been a devout communist who believed in the utopia of a society where all would be equal and happy and like-minded and everything would be shared? I know I did once, when I was fifteen or so, in the communist youth movement in the Netherlands. Ten years later I had resigned from the communist newspaper, together with colleagues. What about him? 'Of course we wanted to believe in a more just society. But I was concerned about reports that people were not equal in the communist countries either.'

I remember his comments about the woman on her knees cleaning around the fat men. He had had such concerns even way back then. 'I asked a question about it in a political class in Moscow once. If it was true that new elites in communist countries were driving around in fancy cars, had better homes and privileges, I asked, what was the response to be to that?' A smile. 'I was reported to the leadership for that divisive question.'

I ask who the tattle-tale was. Another smile. 'Jeff Radebe.'

Of course it was expected from him in that environment, but I still think about that every time I see Jeff Radebe on TV. He has been a minister in the ANC government for the past quarter of a century, ever since the Mandela presidency.

In the last few days in Lusaka, having a nightcap at his place becomes a habit and, each night, slowly, stark realism seeps into our conversations. I share my experiences with actual socialism in Cuba, where young people approached me not in the desire to get forbidden political books about democracy and human rights, but simply for chewing gum, Mills & Boon novels, pornography and jeans, and his eyes show hurt. 'It's sad – socialism was meant to create a society where people would be *better*,' he sighs. 'We spent time in Cuba. They trained us. We thought things might work out there.' I venture that most people probably just tend to respond contrarily when they are told how to behave. 'I guess so,' he says, and stays silent for a while.

Then: 'Some of us, last year, when watching live TV reports on the uprising in Romania – I was in London for meetings – cheered for the tanks of the communist dictator Ceaușescu. They actually wanted the tanks to roll over the protesting people. They never saw the contradiction with the very thing they were opposing in South Africa.' I remember the story. AABN people – Conny – had been in London too, had heard Ceaușescu's supporters cheering on the tanks. One of those present had been Aziz Pahad, with whom I had liaised closely for my research on the murder of Dulcie September. I tell Ivan that I have had lots of contact with Pahad, adding 'but he is not my friend'. 'I hope not,' is the answer. And for the first time, in this so very serious face, I see something akin to a twinkle.

I like that twinkle. I like it as much as I like the story about asking the communism question and being reported by Jeff Radebe. I recognise something rebellious in this skinny high-up oke who will not respect a leader if that leader turns out to be an awful person; who will not toe the party line if the party is wrong.

When the word 'rogue' is used to describe him, thirty years later, as part of a 'rogue unit,' in the most awful sort of way, I think back to these first glimmers of another, more benign meaning of rogueness. The rogueness of people who break rules if the rules are wrong, and who will walk away when walking away is the right thing to do.

Handling giants
Durban, the sixties

It's funny, though, that word 'rogue' being used about him. Because he always tried hard to be so very, very good. To do what his parents said, what the community asked of him. To conform to what was expected: be helpful around the house and in the yard, visit your aunties, do as your parents say. Be tidy and neat. God, he was neat. You'd almost hate him, that perfectionist little boy who would not leave the house if his shirt was not squeaky-clean and buttoned up, his shoelaces not perfectly tied. I hear about it, much later of course, from Sister. How he would take the broom and start sweeping whichever corner had been left not quite thoroughly swept, needing to take out even the minutest speck of dirt.

He was the goody-two-shoes, especially compared to eldest brother Dharma, who 'used to go to chase girls', in areas where girls were not as cautiously kept home as in Merebank. 'The girls are kicking you,' Sister had chastised him, noting bruises on his legs one day. But sadly, those bruises had not been from girls' kicks. They were from leukaemia and Dharma eventually died from the disease.

It is said that Father had his stroke when his eldest son died. Ivan, the youngest, was often given the task of helping the now bedridden old man, also suffering from Parkinson's, with his getting-up and washing. This was a change from the times when all had been in awe of Father, the traditional authoritarian in front of whom everybody trembled. The man who knew paperwork and always advised and helped others in the neighbourhood had been difficult to please at home, certainly towards Mother, who had served him and bore his children after entering what one would now describe as child marriage, straight from the farm in Sawoti. It had all been normal then, just as normal as it was that all the children would scurry to sit in corners with textbooks and observe silence when Father came home.

Now, the old man depended on his family for everything. He would still shout from his bed, but he didn't strike terror into anyone anymore. Even Mother didn't seem that worried about pleasing him now. Father would complain about a lack of salt in his food; the plate would be taken back to the kitchen and again be brought back to him 'with more salt', whereas in reality none had been added, since it wasn't good for him. He always ate without any problems after that.

Maybe that had taught the boy Ivan that even giants fall.

Sister had been a bit rogue, too, in that quiet way that said that you must not accept wrong things, even if others do. Excelling in her role of traditional wife and helped along by the fact that babalaw doted on her, she exercised her influence in the family nevertheless. At get-togethers in her home, she would send zinger-one-liners (muttered under her breath but felt like daggers) in the direction of some of the rougher individuals in the extended family and community. 'Two gun Charlie' she'd call the neighbours' boy, who was a good soul but a bit wild, proudly brandishing his pistol as he regaled mates with tales of his fights with criminals on the streets. She sheltered a depressed relative, simply known as 'sick-auntie', and supported sisters-in-law who had drunk and abusive husbands. She had stood by her daughter when Jenny had backed out of an abusive relationship and refused to get married; had taken in another young girl who had run away from home because of problematic parents. After babalaw's death she had been accused by evil tongues in the neighbourhood of 'running a brothel' because of that all-female household.

Funny how 'rogueness' and 'running a brothel' seem to go together in the minds of those with evil tongues. Forty years later, Ivan would be accused of the same thing.

Crutches and wheelchairs

One of the definitions of a 'rogue' in the dictionary is a 'playful troublemaker'. Funny that, too. A troublemaker for apartheid, for conservative elders, for the Marxist-Leninist political schooling class, perhaps. But *playful* – God, no. Later, after I get acquainted with his need to eat brown crackers regularly to appease ulcers and otherwise painful digestive system issues; after I become accustomed to his waking up at the slightest rustling of leaves at the window, and after I have got over the unsettling sight of a pistol in the underwear drawer, I finally ask him what he does for fun. 'I have never really thought much about fun', is the answer. 'I enjoy soccer, or a good movie. Lately I have started thinking that one should look for bright sides and humour in any circumstances. But that is still new to me.'

By then I have decided that I can probably help with that.

As he handles me and my project in the exact same way he has handled everything else in his life – meticulous in every detail, without noise, but with much attention – I wonder if I am not changing, too. That week in Lusaka observing his always neat pants and shirts, his careful handwriting and filing, his making of lists, the endless planning sessions and his continuous worry about there being enough supplies for everything and everyone, including me, I find myself thinking that all this is so not *me*. At some stage I even start, like a schoolgirl, to make lists of pros and cons about him. 'Caring' is on the pros and 'finnicky and crazy tidy' is on the cons side. The problem is that the two go together.

I am very different. Unconcerned about what I tread on, or whom I upset, I leave trails of dust and rubble like Pig-Pen in Peanuts. I am *loud*. Not to mention completely unsuitable for underground work. There is a reason why neither Conny nor Bart ever told me about Operation Vula.

'Hm, I hope I can remember. I've never kept any secrets in my life,' I respond, when he cautions me not to mention Lucia's safe house and the people who are there. 'Oh,' he says. 'Thanks for telling me.'

He uses a false South African passport in the name of an accountant called Yusuf Khan.

As we have a lunch of crackers and cheese on the last Sunday in the yard in Kabulonga, two little boys from the Mauritian family next door play a few metres away from us in the grass. Sammy has toy cars, while Paul has plastic soldiers with which he acts out a MacGyver story. He gives us a running commentary as we sit and watch: this is MacGyver, this is what MacGyver does now, this is how he escapes from the prison, this is how he jumps over the river, climbs the rock, fights the bad guy, runs away, surfaces and climbs and fights some more.

It goes on and on. I ask if the story will end at some point. He says no.

Sitting there together on the lawn and smiling at the little boys feels weird, as if we are living a normality that isn't normal, not here, not now. As if we are an old married couple in this yard of a flat in Kabulonga, home to neither of us, at a time when no one knows who is going where.

The very pressing thing on top of the to-do list, the next Monday, is to collect the plane tickets for Umtata in the Transkei. They should be ready now, but once again, we find contact persons untraceable and doors inexplicably closed. There are no mobile phones yet and the only way to check up on people in Lusaka is by driving around until you find them. It's midnight by the time we get back to my safe house. The lights are off, and no one answers our knock on the door. We spend the night in Kabulonga. 'I *did* think you were interested,' he says on that first morning, with a smile.

In the way that things always seem to turn out, we finally get the tickets just in time.

At Lusaka airport the next morning, all the trauma of apartheid, war and exile seems to be visible just by looking at our little group: Zeph in his wheelchair; Morris with his dark glasses and stiff limbs, professionally supported by Nombulelo in spite of her own limp; Klaas with his poison-blinded eye. Completing the picture, as if in an effort to blend in, I too, lean on a crutch. I tried to jump over the gate to Ivan's apartments' yard after dinner the previous night, when we found the compound locked and the security guard keeper of keys gone AWOL. I enthusiastically tried to scale the fence, just like Ivan, and had landed out off balance, twisting my foot.

To get to the boarding gate, Ivan pushes me on a luggage trolley. For the rest of the trip I'll have to find a way of hopping along, supported by the crutch once used by Operation Vula commander Mac Maharaj when he pretended to be severely ill as part of his cover story.

Landing safely at Jan Smuts Airport in Johannesburg, in transit to board our next flight to the independent homeland of Transkei, Klaas gives me a little folded-up piece of paper. 'I was only allowed to give you this when we were safe,' he says with a shy smile. It's from Ivan. 'I don't want to say too much,' it reads. 'But I think of your effervescence and explosive laughter and hope I will see you again.'

Winnie

'I would like to know if you are all right,' says a nervous blonde girl in a trembling voice. She wears pink lipstick and a blue beret and stands in the transit hall at Jan Smuts Airport in Johannesburg. At first, I have no idea what is going on. Is she referring to our respective disabilities and asking if we need some extra help? I wouldn't mind a wheelchair for myself, come to think of it. That sprain is hurting badly. But before I have gathered my thoughts the *Suid Afrikaanse Lugdiens* ground staff girl continues: 'Because there is a *lady* here, you see. Upstairs. In the hall. It's *her*. *She* is asking if your group is all right.'

The blonde girl looks positively terrified. I call Klaas, who is standing with Zeph and Morris at the transit hall windows. A lady? What is this about a lady who is scaring the heebie-jeebies out of this young woman? As Klaas walks towards me I suddenly remember. It's Winnie – it has to be. Winnie is here!

Ivan made a phone call from Lucia's safe house to a contact, last week, asking to make Comrade Winnie Mandela aware of the project. By then I had understood that Lucia, somehow, was crucial: she was in charge of the phone, which was located in an outhouse in the yard. She stood outside, wearing her blue fluffy morning gown, looking watchful, while Ivan dialled. After getting through, I heard him ask if Comrade Winnie could be present at the airport, perhaps, for our arrival. 'They will be in the international transit hall so maybe she cannot enter there, comrade,' I had heard him say. 'But perhaps it will help if she can be around at the airport.' He did not explain why he was making this call, but I understood it was about protection for Zeph's and Morris's voyage home. You can't get up to nonsense with Winnie around, so much was clear.

I asked Ivan if he knew her. 'Not personally,' he said. I also asked him about the bad things we had heard about her. The alleged misdeeds of a security unit of young men around her who called themselves the Mandela United Football Club, their alleged reign of terror among activists in Soweto, the disappearance of a youngster called Stompie Seipei. 'Winnie is problematic', was his response. 'She has always operated as a force on her own and not as part of the structures of the mass democratic movement. But she is powerful and she'll be effective on this matter.'

It is precisely because Winnie answers only to herself that we weren't at all sure that she would in fact come. Even without her changing her mind or her priorities, there is turmoil in the country, and much danger and insecurity, for her too. She is busy, making appearances with the recently released Nelson Mandela. And even though they are met by adoring crowds wherever they go, apartheid still exists. The security police and their henchmen still spy and provoke and kill.

But she has come.

I can see Winnie in my mind, surrounded as always is by her guards from Soweto, maybe dressed like them, as she often is, in military camouflage. I see her standing in the middle of the main arrivals hall, being her customary formidable presence, and refusing to go anywhere unless her queries are answered, right there, right then.

'Please tell the lady that we are all right,' Klaas tells the ground stewardess. 'And that we are very grateful.' The young woman smiles, relieved, and scurries away as we queue to board.

* * *

In 1975 Winnie came to Durban.[11] *In between banning orders, she had energetically taken the opportunity to visit. The cavalcade of about a dozen buses snaking through the townships was almost like a ticker tape parade.*

People were out on the streets in the usually subdued Indian townships, and in Umlazi cheering masses joined them. Mother, Sister and Sister's daughter Jenny, still a teenager then, had gone too, excited to be out among fellow South Africans, happy just to feel part of multicoloured humankind. Even the slightly drunk bus conductor, who had been kept in the dark about the identity of the celebrity on his bus, was in a party mood, shouting and exclaiming 'I know that lady! I know her!' Ivan still doesn't know for sure if the conductor actually really knew who Winnie Mandela was, or whether he just knew he had seen that lady's picture in the papers. But he remembers clearly how the joy of her visit, the almost physical ripping through barriers, caught everything and everybody that day.

Being damaged

But Winnie is damaged now. War, pain, fear and paranoia have been her universe for decades: banned, arrested time and time again, jailed in solitary cells, her little daughters yanked away from her, without her knowing where they were, not knowing if they were even alive. Kept naked, beaten, without pads during menstruation, smeared with her own blood, for days. 'Now I know how to hate,' news reports quoted her, and also, 'I am the product of my enemy.'[12]

By the end of 1990, many in the anti-apartheid struggle are concerned about Winnie and her 'boys' in the Mandela United Football Club, especially their penchant for weeding out traitors, impimpis. Impimpis were a real problem: Conny Braam would, at times, talk, with tears in her eyes, how this or that person was no longer alive today because they had been betrayed. You had to kill or somehow silence impimpis before they killed you.

But you didn't really know who they were. The security police were skilled at manufacturing fake impimpi trails while protecting the real ones. There were also comrades who would point and shout 'impimpi' at someone else to direct attention away from their own activity, or to obtain more power, or just because there was a frenzy all around.

An article published in 2019[13] by a friend and activist in the Eastern Cape during the eighties invokes the atmosphere.

'Long, long ago, there was a teacher in Cookhouse, a railway junction town in the Eastern Cape. He was a drunk. Every Friday he'd be arrested and released on Monday. Everyone in town knew him and knew that about him. My mother, being a nurse in that town, knew him too. On a certain Friday, he was arrested and you'd think it was "as usual". But this time around, it was by the Security Branch of the police. Thereafter, they went from one activist's home to another, arresting every activist they could find. They also went to hideouts and arrested those they could find. This being a small town, everyone 'knew' who'd pointed out the houses. Word spread quickly to the surrounding towns – Somerset East, Bedford, Adelaide, etc. Comrades went into hiding. For the UDF activists this had become a habit. As soon as you heard of a raid in a nearby town, you knew they were coming for you. You hid.

By Monday he was released. But, on the same day he was killed – by an enraged mob who put a tyre around his neck, doused him in petrol and lit the fire.[14] He died amidst the shouts of "impimpi"! – the "informer", the 'collaborator'! In South Africa's dubious parlance for the gruesome killings of suspected collaborators, this was known as "necklacing". The cunning plan had worked: Who else would have known who the activists were and where they'd hide but their teacher?

He didn't know. He wasn't an informer. But the Security Branch knew that "the community" would go for an obvious target.'

My friend the activist who lived through this will write this in a reaction to an effort by (then ex-) president Jacob Zuma to revive the spectre of the impimpi accusations.[15] Testifying before Judge Zondo's Judicial Commission of Inquiry into Allegations of State Capture, that was looking at events during Zuma's corrupt reign from 2009 to 2017,[16] Zuma will, rather than answer questions about his own actions, blame 'spies' for his downfall. The activist writes his account as a warning not to go down this path again. His name is Yolisa Pikie. I will write more about him later.

***

In Lusaka, we talked about Winnie and other damaged people. Ivan explained that he felt he was lucky. Growing up in a mostly cohesive family, having a relatively happy childhood was a 'privilege when compared to the lives of many black people', he said. 'Most families classified "black" were broken up through migrant labour, pass laws, forced removals. As an Indian family you were also harassed and humiliated, yes, and suffered, but not to that extent. Apartheid inflicted severe pain upon millions of completely ordinary Africans.'

I had read reports about fathers strip-searched in full view of their wives and children by white train conductors; parents slapped and mocked by random whites; elders called 'boys' and 'girls' by white bosses; women obliged to mother white babies instead of their own. Most black kids could look forward only to a life of 'tea boy' or cleaner, or working in the mines, as Lizo Semane had done for a few months until it became too much and he ran away to look for a machine gun, and became Zeph Mothopeng.

'We have no idea what we are going to be up against just now when we are in charge,' Ivan sighed. 'This country needs *truckloads* of therapy.'

The porcelain cabinet

'I always wanted a white woman,' Lizo Semane's cousin or a comrade activist attending the party says drunkenly, as he holds on to a cabinet that displays porcelain dolls on glass shelves against the wall in the family's four-roomed house in Ngangelizwe township, Umtata, Transkei. 'Oh?' I ask. 'Why?' He doesn't respond. But everybody knows why, of course, also the relatives and friends who quickly busy themselves chatting with one another to avoid embarrassment. They all know that white women were off limits, always, which is precisely why you'd want one. Just to take one from the white men, to break through the walls and barbed wire that separate you in your desolate bantustan homeland from the plush and pretty white areas.

Now, in 1990, Lizo's cousin or the comrade activist can hypothetically visit a white area if he wants to, since pass laws were abolished four years ago. It is also no longer a crime to have a dalliance across the colour bar. But in practice, the walls around his unemployed drunken self and the rest of the world are as high as ever. You cannot visit the rest of the world, certainly not the white parts: You don't get a visa, not if you are black without a steady job and sufficient financial reserves clearly displayed on your three months' bank statement. Not if you are a drunken Ngangelizwe comrade or cousin, holding on to a porcelain cabinet to stay on your feet.

Semane senior is tipsy, too: he has danced and laughed and hugged Lizo and cried ever since we stepped on the tarmac, not wanting to let him go, crying and kissing him all the time, way more than Lizo's mother, although she is also tearful and happy, even as she keeps a watchful eye on the other boy and her porcelain figurines. It isn't long before Lizo's father falls fast asleep and is carried away to his bedroom.

Lizo, in his wheelchair, with the fiancée he met in exile by his side, tells me he has plans to uplift his community, 'with projects and a shop'. He seems very content to be here. Maybe that is because he always had other options, even if his legs are gone. He has studied. He can apply for things. He doesn't have to be in Ngangelizwe and, in a strange reverse parallel to his comrade or cousin, that is precisely why he wants to be.

The other returnee, Morris – Dugmore Mthimkhulu – has been taken home to his wife Veronica, a nurse. The couple are part of the royal Dalindyebo family and when Morris/Dugmore was helped out of the little plane and Veronica, resplendent in a blood-orange dress and sunglasses, stepped on the tarmac to meet him, she immediately put her arms around him to indicate to the helpers that she would support and help to carry him from then on. The helpers stepped away in silence as if it had been rehearsed. The crowd whispered, 'Nkosikazi, nkosikazi' – the wife, the chieftainess.

'I know he is difficult,' she confides in me later, as her husband-chief is led away by male relatives to rest. 'He was always demanding, even before he got wounded. So I had to think. Can I cope with this? The social worker told me about all the things I'll have to do for him. And I know he'll still be demanding and complaining more even after I do all that. But you know what? I could not say no. I could not be like that. So I said yes.' She straightens her sunglasses on her forehead and looks wistfully. 'So here we are.'

Here we are. South Africa in 1990: a place of broken families, wounded returnees, and a youthful population that swings between determination and despair. A cabinet of porcelain dolls, where some will still break and some will remain on their shelves and stay together, under the watchful eye of mothers who keep hoping.

Later, back in Amsterdam, someone at AABN tells me that Dugmore Mthimkhulu is demanding a car. 'He says you promised him one,' the colleague who took the phone call says with a puzzled look. I wonder how Dugmore Mthimkhulu could have heard me say that when he was never able to hear me say anything at all.

Holomisa's palace
Transkei

The following day I get a glimpse of the promised country's splendour. On our way to join Chris Hani's convoy, which is to visit the town of Lady Frere, Comrade Ezra, who is assigned by the Umtata ANC branch to this project and is now my driver, and I drive over endless hills and through villages where all the huts are pink, perhaps, I imagine, because all the neighbours got together to buy buckets of paint in bulk, and the grandmother or tavern queen who wanted pink got her way. We pass skinny free-roaming cows and goats and a few meandering horses.

We lag far behind as we see the shiny black cars of Hani's convoy far ahead of us negotiate the dangerous winding mountain roads of Satan's Nek. Besides Hani and his bodyguards, the convoy also carries old struggle mate Klaas de Jonge, whom I imagine might now be a tad more frightened than he was when driving cars full of weapons through apartheid border posts. 'The boys like to drive like that,' Ezra laughs.

When we finally stop at a field where the others are waiting for us, we find them raucously laughing and shooting at little poles next to the road. 'For practice,' grins one. Hani himself walks around relaxedly, eating a sandwich, smiling. He turns back to his vehicle to continue his talk with Klaas.

We stop at Lady Frere for Hani to talk to the people in the village. It is clearly not the first time: 'He is our boy,' an old lady says, beaming. 'We are so happy that he is here with us now. We had to miss him for so long.'

Hani doesn't speak for long. The sun is harsh and there are only umbrellas for him and other guests; someone has appeared and holds one over my head, too. But the crowd is still excited, humming approvingly after every sentence, sometimes with recognition. I only catch 'Shakespeare' and 'ANC' from the isiXhosa, but am told later that he likes to use a few quotes from the great bard's kings dramas to explain how leaders who don't have the support of the people will inevitably fall, and how good rulers prioritise the welfare of their citizens. Apartheid's 'kings' are falling, and the people, this very people here in Lady Frere, will vote for good new ones. The ANC will make sure that these new leaders will be good and will stay good. And amongst cheers of 'ANC!' and 'Umkhonto we Sizwe!' the small village meeting breaks up.

When photographer Pieter Boersma takes out his camera, dozens of youngsters, boys and girls, flock towards him. Many are brandishing what seem like guns and rifles and I move back in fear, and then see that the weapons are made of wood: Transkei handcraft has taken on special characteristics in this district, soon to be renamed Chris Hani Municipality. As the children jump around grinning, yelling, happy, proud, clamouring to be photographed, Pieter Boersma beckons me to come into one of the shots. And so, somewhere, exists a picture of me sitting in the sand, surrounded by excited Xhosa teenagers with wooden guns.

'But they must also know Shakespeare,' says the old lady from before, who has suddenly resurfaced next to me. She sits down on a plastic stool next to the stage in front of which we posed for a picture. 'They must take all of Chris Hani as a role model. Not just the gun part. Also the school part. And the politics. Our children need all three.' She then carefully takes a black, green and yellow ANC membership card from a stack in her handbag and tells me I must now become a member. Ezibeleni branch, she writes – the name of the ANC branch in Ezibeleni township in nearby Queenstown – because that is clearly her branch; the village of Lady Frere doesn't have an established one yet. Not even waiting for me to consent, she goes on to fill in the annual membership fee: twelve rand. 'But it will be valid until the end of next year,' she says reassuringly.

It's not the money: In 1990, twelve rand is worth quite a bit more than it will be in time to come, but still only about five US dollars. However, as far as I know, ANC rules forbid membership for non-South Africans, and I try to explain that to my recruiter. But she will have none of my objections. 'That's not important,' she says casually and now that I'm out of excuses, she proceeds to write my name on the card, carefully copying the spelling from my passport.

Nobody ever bothered to make me pay the fee after that first year, but I still have the card displayed on my bookshelf in Amsterdam.

My recruiter and I have a longer conversation after that. About white people who came from the sea to conquer, and who had more modern technology and ships and guns. The old lady doesn't begrudge abelungu, white people, that much. 'They invented more than we did, and that was clever of them. But why did they come here not to share what they had, but instead take what we had from us? They even moved us away from our rivers. Those rivers were not theirs. Nobody can justify that. So their apartheid must go, it must be finished now. That's clear, isn't it?' I nod. It's very clear.

It's late at night when we arrive back in Umtata, but the food in General Bantu Holomisa's state residence is hot, there is music, and plenty of wine and whisky too. Holomisa and Hani speak briefly, welcoming Klaas, and hugging Lizo Semane and Dugmore Mthimkhulu, who have been brought from their family homes by Holomisa's men for the occasion. Armed guards shield the palace entrance against any eventuality, but it is unlikely that the apartheid military would try anything now. Holomisa rules here. And even if the event does irk the white minority regime in Pretoria – the Xhosa general is, in struggle speak, supposed to be an apartheid regime puppet after all – there is very little they can do about it. Ironically, the uniforms they wear and guns they carry were supplied by Pretoria itself.

'I don't want to call you a homeland dictator,' a foreign correspondent defers to the general politely in a radio interview shortly after our visit. To which Holomisa cheerfully responds: 'But you must. I *am* a homeland dictator, you know.'

That evening, as underground whispers are exchanged between Hani, Klaas de Jonge, Holomisa and perhaps others, the rest of us party. Drink flows, food is eaten and music plays, and we all mingle as we would at any social occasion. Until a recording of 'Nkosi Sikelel' iAfrika' starts to play. All stand, raise fists in the air and sing the ANC's struggle hymn. There is also a photograph of me doing that: a seriously passionate expression on a wine-flushed face, the nose both sunburned and snotty, tears in the eyes.

A white glass bowl

Cape Town is so white that it feels like a different planet. After Transkei, the glitter of white buildings, blonde white people, pink lipstick, white beaches and that white-reflecting mountain hurt my eyes. I think of Conny Braam telling me, once, after a months-long stay in the black frontline states and border areas, that she was startled at seeing herself in the mirror. 'Jeez, I am white!' It is funny not only to have a similar experience, but even stranger to realise that most people I see here, on Heerengracht and Strand, or most other white people I know, will never have such an experience at all. White is normal to them, the same as it has been for me, for most of my life.

Black people live so far away that it takes a two-hour bus trip to get to the family I want to see in Gugulethu. It takes even longer to visit a new friend, Sandile Dikeni, in Khayelitsha. Dikeni[17] works at *Die Suid-Afrikaan*,[18] a progressive Afrikaans publication that is committed to ending apartheid and building a new South Africa. The collective of white and coloured progressives plus the one Xhosa is only hampered by the fact that Sandile often misses editorial meetings because there is a strike, or the buses don't run, or someone has set something alight, or the apartheid-puppet mayor of Khayelitsha, a murderous warlord called Hoza, has disappeared a comrade again. Chris Louw, editor of *Die Suid-Afrikaan*, knows all this and still he grumbles when Sandile doesn't show up on time, because how are we going to get this paper out? But, sometimes, Sandile just oversleeps.

Their worlds are so far apart it hurts more than just the eyes. The Cape, with its history of indigenous Khoi and San peoples, and later slaves who were brought from Malaysia, should at least be a little brown. But Khayelitsha is light years away, and even coloured Lansdowne and Hanover Park are more than an hour by bus from Oranjezicht, where I stay. You only meet the 'others' when you venture out to get a saloomie – in Durban they would say roti – in Long Street, where the coloured lady serves customers of all colours. Outside, back in the shiny white streets in the suburbs, the only ones who stay in your face are the bergies – the name resplendent with slave rebellion history, because runaway slaves used to hide out on the mountain – now drunk and homeless. They beg and stink. 'When you've had them vomiting on your stoep for a couple of nights you sort of lose that feeling of revolutionary comradeship,' says Chris Louw.

There must be political platforms, artists' haunts and jazz cafés where colours mix and the discourse is exciting and full of hope. Sometimes the arts sections of the progressive *Weekly Mail* carry reports on such things, but I don't find them during this short stay when I live between white Cape Town and Gugulethu, where the granny who rules a household of herself and two grandsons – the comrades who invited me – pours my gift of a great old single malt whisky down the kitchen drain when she thinks I am not looking, because who brings liquor to a decent house?

I start to hate that mountain that stands in the way of wherever people would want to go or could mingle. I walk through Cape Town looking for a city centre, but besides the more or less lively looking Long Street and its parallel, Loop, it doesn't seem to exist. 'I don't understand,' says a white lady when I ask for it. 'Do you mean the beach?'

Then I see the poster. Ronnie Kasrils, it reads. Janet Love. A few other names. In big black letters, it says they are wanted for terrorism in connection with an illegal operation called Vula; they must be considered armed and dangerous. In my memory, Ivan is also there on that poster.

In reality he wasn't, though: My mind must have projected the image from another wanted poster, distributed years earlier in Swaziland, that I would see later in Ivan's own documents. That image shows him as from a dark mirror: the eyes hidden behind sunglasses, the curly hair bigger than I know it, almost an Afro, the mouth set downwards, almost angry, an outlaw. The poster on the Cape Town lamp post shows the 'wanted' Vula faces similarly as sinister. Operation Vula. Illegal. Terrorist. Armed and dangerous. *l'Affiche Rouge* flashes through my mind, that red Nazi propaganda poster that once warned the public in France against a group of resistance fighters.[19] On that poster, too, the wanted ones had looked dark-bearded, dark-browed, 'black with beard and night, dishevelled, threatening,' as the poet Aragon had written.

The rogue factor
Durban, early 1970s

Finding himself on the wrong side of the law – rogue, so to speak – was a slow process. For most of his young life in Merebank, he had worked within established normality in spite of the authoritarian system at school and the occasional outbursts of protest by the group of friends. He had followed the lessons and written his matric. The biggest rebellion then had been to refuse to learn Afrikaans, the oppressor's language. He chose Latin instead and was pleased to learn that 'Vis', the name he was called at home, meant 'force' or 'strength'. It was a pleasant discovery, bearing in mind how thin and weak he had been for most of his youth.

After matric, some went to university, but Ivan was content to be where the community and the workers were. For a while the family had tried to find the money for him to study overseas in Ireland, where many young South African Indians went, but he wasn't disappointed when that plan didn't work out. He told his older brothers that he wanted to be home so that he could be part of the struggle. Suggie had once almost smacked him for that, but was appeased when the young one went to work, first at a construction company, then, like his elder brothers, in a furniture store.

Supporting non-racial sport in the face of the regime's efforts to segregate even that – by colour-coding facilities and competitions into segregated units, barring black South Africans from representing the country internationally and pressurising businesses to sponsor only apartheid sport – was rebellious too, but in a way that was shared by many. Like multitudes of South Africans, Merebank loved soccer, and its fans were hardly likely to stop doing what they had done for decades – organising teams and going out to play others, irrespective of colour – just because the regime wanted them to. At high school, Coastal had called his soccer team the Peter Hain Five, after the sports boycott activist Peter Hain, and had got into quite some trouble for it, too. Ivan also had a team, called Freedom's Children, but they largely played unnoticed 'because we didn't win'. However, since the Hain Five won, and the winning teams' names were to be displayed on the score board, the principal had insisted Coastal remove the 'Hain' part. Coastal had pretended to concede and told them he'd rename his team 'The Band', only for the school to discover that, come the day when the champion team was announced, it was proudly displayed as 'The Banned'.

The sports fan base grew as a non-racial sports movement precisely because *of the viciousness of the regime. Apartheid had that strange way of not leaving people alone to do as they pleased. By interfering with sports fans, it created its own opposition even among those who did not see themselves as political at all. In 1973, hundreds attended a mass meeting in Merebank to garner support for non-racial sports. Well-known sports luminaries[20] spoke at the meeting; Ivan chaired it. In the following years, support would grow from a few hundred to thousands of spectators who would watch amateur soccer at Curries Fountain in Durban's grey area, which became a Mecca of non-racial sports.*

The movement was soon to be headed by seasoned sports officials[21] and became such a thorn in the flesh of the apartheid regime that some of its protagonists would be hounded, denied passports and banned. South African Council of Sports secretary Manikum Pather's home was petrol bombed and sprayed with bullets, and his two-year-old granddaughter sustained an injury to her ankle. By the 1980s, non-racial soccer had grown so big that even some white soccer teams would leave their apartheid league and join the non-racial federation.

The struggle in the community advanced similarly. They addressed the issue of poor transport, high cost of living, pollution and unequal amenities at meetings where even mothers and grandmothers in their saris joined in. By the eighties, and on into the early nineties, residents would picket and march, with Ivan's mum Dhanam and Coastal's mum in front, carrying placards and posters saying 'Listen to us' and 'Let us live'. They won some small victories in that way, the main one being to prevent an unjust municipal decree that would have Merebank's residents buy their houses at inflated prices.[22]

Whiffs of protest were already permeating the air when the banning order of the (now late), well known activist Mewa Ramgobin expired in 1971. He immediately launched a campaign for the release of political prisoners, which was met with enthusiasm, and the inaugural meeting of the politely named Clemency Committee in Merebank was attended by hundreds. When Ramgobin called a little later for the revival of the Natal Indian Congress (NIC), the Indian counterpart of the ANC, Merebank responded again: a branch was founded and Ivan became its chairman.[23]

* * *

The non-racial principles of the Freedom Charter had by then already become Ivan's north star, as he said: 'Human equality and rights and justice for all are obviously the right principles. But more than that, they are also a strategic imperative. By adopting these principles, you welcome everyone, black, white, brown, Indian, coloured, whatever, into your movement. The issue is not where you come from but your sharing of the same values. If you work together like that, each contributing what they can, you move forward towards your goal. With every single person who joins you, you weaken the enemy.'

Being inclusive meant that you could make alliances with those who thought differently. They worked a lot with the Black Consciousness movement gathered around Steve Biko, even if BC, with its emphasis on black unity and black psychological liberation[24] did not fully align with the non-racial Congress ideals. Roy Chetty, a Merebank friend who had become a national office bearer of the Black People's Convention, asked Ivan to accompany him on a trip to Johannesburg and the Eastern Cape. They drove at night, with a thermos of tea and cover stories ready. In a building in King Williamstown, Ivan recognised the host without any hesitation. It was Steve Biko.

Yet, the clampdown was still to come. Returning to the furniture store where he had just started working, Ivan was told that he was fired. The security police knew of their trip and had told the boss. The boss understood the message. It was one thing to lie to your boss, telling him you were sick when you weren't, that could be forgiven. What could not be forgiven was to cause trouble for the boss, to bring the security police.

It increasingly seemed as if you could not live your life and not be on the rogue side of things.

A cloud of loss and regret

As I move around Cape Town, visiting the coloured areas, the further ones still more desolate than those nearby, and the eerie white sparkling houses of Khayelitsha with their towering stadium lights so nobody can hide and the wide streets so the Casspirs can get through, I hear the stories of people whose normality is not the normality of others. The family that was ripped apart, with family members of different colours forced to live in different locations. The uncle in the workers' compound for factory labourers, the grandmother who was white moved to a white area, while other relatives disappeared into drugs, or jail, or other countries. Now some of them lived in the same little house again, but without any joyful reunification: they did not know each other anymore and were universes apart, sharing a space under a cloud of loss and regret.

Sandile Dikeni's grandmother Emily was burnt in her house by comrades who had accused her of being a sell-out. They locked the old lady in the house and the family heard her scream and watched her burn while the comrades cheered. The leader of the gang of comrades was named Justice and Sandile doesn't know, he says, how he can hear the word 'justice' again without thinking of this.[25]

'I learned an important thing though,' he tells me. 'There is a right and wrong beyond politics. Never mind that your cause is right and the others are wrong. There are universal laws that are above all that. You don't burn somebody's grandmother alive. That's just something you don't do.'

Was it necessary for Sandile's granny to be burned alive for him to learn this lesson, I wondered. Even more importantly, perhaps, would Justice and his crowd experience misgivings later? Would they ever accept the universal laws that say *don't burn gogo*? Or would they remain as they were, scarred, not feeling anything beyond their own pain or gain, capable of doing it again?

There is trauma even in the white Oranjezicht household of Chris Louw. Their hospitality is a very nice gesture from him and his wife Johanita, made in a context of solidarity with the anti-apartheid movement and the struggle, and Bart and I had met Chris in Amsterdam a few years back. Chris Louw is rogue, too, in a way. He grew up white and Afrikaans but was sympathetic to blacks and so-called terrorists, having been a member of the group of Afrikaans intellectuals who met the ANC in Dakar in 1987. He is on one side of a schism now. On the other is much of his family, their heritage, the farm, the mainstream media colleagues he had abandoned to found and edit *Die Suid-Afrikaan*, together with poets and authors, who included Hein Willemse and Sandile Dikeni.

Die Suid-Afrikaan is a band of dissidents: even the verligte among the mainstream colleagues – the more liberal Nationalists – are only verlig in terms of smiling at black people and providing charity every now and then. They would certainly not support giving them the vote, as the 'terrorists' demand. This disturbing political side to Chris Louw is why fellow parents at the kids' schools are wary of him and Johanita. There is torment below the surface of Chris Louw's cheerful, politically mature demeanour.

Outwardly he holds it all together, sharply penning critiques of Afrikaner intellectuals who still defend, maybe not apartheid but something very akin to it and laughing heartily at comedian Leon Schuster's pranks on 'boere' who easily fall prey to his hidden camera because they are just so authority-minded, it's hard-wired. One of the clips shows Schuster masquerading as a traffic cop trainer. He makes young – so naïve, so blue-eyed – recruits imitate traffic sounds: motorcycle revving, sirens. They must make the sounds loudly to pass the test, show that they recognise what is what, he tells them and, foeitog, they do. They even spin around like the blue lights on the police car and Chris Louw almost falls of his chair laughing. 'That's us, I am telling you! Afrikaners gehoorsaam! We obey without question!'

On the same evening, after a couple of brandies, he shouts in response to my – in hindsight rather glib – whites-blaming discourse: 'Well, you try it in Europe then! Abolish your borders, dethrone your queen and start talking German!' In 1990, we have no clue that in decades to come Europe will indeed be facing a similar conundrum, with a refugee crisis, people dying in their hundreds in the Mediterranean and a choice between openness, tolerance and uncertainty or authoritarian white, Europeans-only politics.

That evening I start to understand, ever so slightly, the feeling of having to give up a lot in exchange only for an awareness that you must do what is right. I think back to that when I hear the shouts, nowadays, of the UK's migrant-fearing Brexit voters and the terrifying populist masses' cheers for narrow, ethnic, authoritarian leaders – Trump in America, Putin in Russia, Orbán in Hungary, Modi in India and Geert Wilders in the Netherlands.

In 2000, Louw will write an angry open letter to the famous verligte Afrikaner elder Wimpie de Klerk, brother of F.W. de Klerk. *Boetman is die bliksem in, This young man is angry*, he headlines it. In the letter he recalls how in the 1970s, when Louw was a young journalist at *Die Vaderland* and De Klerk a senior editor at the Perskor conglomerate, there was nothing verlig about such elders. The men with 'wrinkles on the face and grey hair on the temples, a conservative pair of specs on the nose to create the impression of someone with status, someone with insight, whose judgement can be trusted, whose words carry weight,' he wrote, told boys like himself, in school, in church, in their newspapers and on radio, that all was just fine and dandy, that blacks were happy in their separate areas with their huts and that the only ones making trouble were communists.

He recalls in the letter how the *boetmannetjies* were sent by De Klerk's generation to war in Angola to fight the communists, then furiously notes that the same elders, after the war was clearly lost, both in Angola and in the eyes of the world, postured as progressive and well-intentioned men. Willem de Klerk would become a respected think tank member advising a future F.W. de Klerk government, while the conscripts found they were hated and would get beaten up in bars overseas by not-very-brave people who had heard about bad white South Africans.

They played his generation for fools, Louw feels, like Schuster's traffic cop instructor, except that in the real world, it was not a joke at all. An entire generation was betrayed by evil old men masquerading as civilised benevolent leaders, who ran death squads and ordered massacres in townships while using their own boys as cannon fodder.

One evening Chris Louw says we must go for a drive because he wants to show me a few places. I worry because he has had at least two tots already, but I say nothing. I don't want to offend him and his tone tells me there is something serious going on. After the first few minutes, I bitterly regret my acquiescence as we drive furiously down the sharp curves of Chapman's Peak, the winding road along the boulders of the Cape where Chris Louw's forefathers, and mine, landed centuries ago. Those sailors, who must have felt fear on the high waves of the ocean as they were exploring the unknown, with big wind bursts whistling and rocks looming everywhere, must have been really adventurous – or desperate – to embark on such journeys. Because if their fear then was anything like my fear now, as we hurtle down and through hairpin bends, ravines, rocks and waves beneath us at over a hundred kilometres an hour, I would have stayed at home without any colonialism, thank you, and eat bland porridge in the cold forever. I am convinced that we are both going to meet our end right here, which is a pity because I have just found true love in Lusaka.

Miraculously, we end in front of a large gate in Noordhoek. Chris points and says, 'Here, can you see?' All I see is a big gate and a driveway and a rather big white building in the distance. 'This is a house,' Chris says. 'A *house*. You'd think it was a cross between a castle, a fortress and a palace, right? But this is a house. The businessman who lives here has made billions. Out of apartheid, out of blacks, even out of his own people. He has more houses elsewhere, and yachts, mistresses, holidays. The only thing he does not have is a conscience.' Louw may have mentioned the name of the businessman, but I have forgotten, if it registered in my mind at all. All I think of at the time is how I can persuade Chris to take a different route back.

'It's much more difficult for whites, you know,' Ivan will say, later, back in Lusaka, when I tell him about the encounter. 'Those who joined the struggle like Bram Fischer[26] and Joe Slovo[27] really had to abandon homes, families, privileges, career opportunities. For blacks in a way it is natural to come to the ANC. Even exile may be tempting, it might give some a better life. Whites have to think a lot harder before they choose the struggle. They have a lot to lose.' When I ask how it was for Indians, he smiles. 'A bit of both, I guess.'

A workers' buzz
Durban, 1974

For a while he had the best of both worlds. The community of Mother, Sister, relatives and friends in Merebank, and the network of activists, was all-embracing. The universe of whites, blacks, coloureds and Indians, all opposing apartheid and working together in community organisations in Durban and throughout the country – he was now the secretary of the Southern Durban Civic Federation – made him see what was possible. It made him believe in it. He saw what the ANC had intended South Africa to be from 1912. It was to bring together all the people in pursuit of a joint vision for a better country. The movement was growing. It was not a pipe dream. It was real. It could be real.

He had found really close comrades in Pat and Jabu Msomi. Pat, with his rollicking laugh, big belly and six fingers on each hand, had once been a bouncer at the Paradise nightclub in Durban. Now he worked for Sudan Herbalists, a traditional medicine postal order business in Victoria Street, and was the chair of the Natal region of the Black Consciousness-aligned Black Allied Workers Union, BAWU. Jabu, his wife, was a BAWU organiser.

There was a workers' buzz in the early seventies. A turning point in the atmosphere of silence and oppression was reached in labour relations, and wild cat strikes erupted in Natal. In 1973 more than a hundred thousand black workers marched with red flags, some carrying illegal ANC pamphlets. From the furniture store where Ivan then still worked he saw masses of strikers march by, singing. That had been just before he had gone with Roy Chetty on his Eastern Cape trip and had got fired as a result.

The voyage home

Ivan had come to know of BAWU because, on the return from that trip, Steve Biko had asked them to give a lift to a Black Consciousness comrade who needed to be dropped off there. BAWU, located on a small dark fourth floor in Beatrice Street, also in the multiracial area, was not formally recognised as a union, since black workers could not belong to registered trade unions. It was set up as a supportive home for all black workers, whose exploitation was after all not limited to labour issues.

Pat Msomi[28] easily recruited and convinced black workers to come to BAWU. They came in their dozens to learn about the struggles of the international working classes, the teachings of Marx and Engels. 'We had rooms of twenty people, sometimes fifty,' Ivan recalls. 'Some could barely read and write. But they were excited about the stories of the international union movements against capitalism. There was plenty to tell of how in Britain, the US and Germany, workers had risen to free themselves from hunger, slavery, and alcoholism.' The workers who attended were often people who 'had grown up thinking that their fate as black men and women was pre-determined and unchangeable, and that white bosses were forever. Now they were told that change and freedom and a better life, as citizens next to citizens, with the same rights and living conditions, was possible. It had been achieved in other countries. They wanted to hear more, learn more.'

Pat and Jabu often brought their baby daughter to work. The little girl, Nomzamo,[29] was kept in a makeshift cot made out of two armchairs facing each other in a corner of the office, while Jabu assisted workers who came for help and advice. It was often difficult to help adequately, since apartheid was the law of the land. But some rights violations, such as retrenchments and summary dismissals, underpayment, being made to work without registration, being denied sick leave, abuse – workers were often physically hit by bosses – and victimisation, could be fought by using some laws which did not specify that they did not apply to Africans.[30]

At the same time, democratic activists in Durban were challenging the formal unions that organised white, coloured and Indian workers because of their usually apolitical stance. Ivan recalls an event, around the mid-seventies, where activists came to attend a gathering of the mainly coloured and Indian, Natal Liquor and Catering Employees Union.[31] They planned to tell the workers that the struggle was wider than just wages and that, with struggle, a better life could be built for all. 'It was not to the liking of some of the moderate union bosses. As the students spoke, conflict erupted and one union VIP in particular objected to a very vocal student who had long hair –

he objected to the long hair itself. What was that young man up to, with hair like that? Was that even decent?'

The move backfired. Many in the audience, excited by the buzz – and perhaps, he suspected, slightly under the influence of the liquor that was so central to their trade sector – booed the VIP. Why was he going on about the young man's hair? Why was that an issue? The long-haired student was given the space to say what he wanted to say, and indeed some of the workers cheered, in another small victory for the anti-apartheid struggle. That activist with the long hair was Pravin Gordhan, a fellow member of the Natal Indian Congress.

The workers' organisations, gatherings and advice offices would grow into a tapestry of many unregistered unions, winning important victories on the factory floors and in the courts. They eventually gathered such strength that in 1986 – four years before the changes in 1990 – the rights of African workers to belong to a union was recognised. A year before that, in 1985, most activist unions that identified with the struggle against apartheid, registered or not, BAWU among them, had already unified in COSATU.

* * *

After being fired from the furniture store, Ivan found another job as an accounts clerk at a Roberts' Construction building site. He made friends there with Clifford Mabaso, a time clerk with dark-rimmed glasses. Mabaso, like many Zulus then, was a member of Inkatha. Inkatha had a difficult relationship with the ANC. It called for Mandela's release but also accepted a homeland partnership with the apartheid regime, while its leader Chief Mangosuthu Buthelezi artfully suggested that his movement represented the ANC inside South Africa. But a lot of Zulus were members of Inkatha simply because it was the only organisation for them that was permitted to exist.

In the friendship between Clifford and Ivan, it didn't matter. During breaks the two, together with other workers, played marabaraba: a game in which squares are drawn in the sand with a stick and you have to fill in your squares with stones or bottle caps, trying to make an uninterrupted line, much like noughts and crosses. Marabaraba always came with a lot of enthusiasm and loud cheering. Though Ivan was not as boisterous as the others, he enjoyed it.

The workers also shared a deep aversion for a black supervisor, a 'boss boy' named Khumalo, who was based at Roberts headquarters nearby and often visited. Khumalo was the supervisor for all the black time clerks, called 'mabalans' in everyday parlance. It was Khumalo's job to keep his fellow blacks hard working, meek and quiet. 'An awful man, short and fat with loose flappy hands, who looked so much like a seal you'd expect him to start honking and clapping at any time,' as Ivan remembers him. The man was always trying to ingratiate himself to the white bosses by pushing those below him down as much as he could. Clifford Mabaso disliked him with a passion, too.

But even if Mabaso was a man of decent values and secretly receptive to unionist ideas, he would not participate in any strikes when these were called. 'He was a family man. He could not afford to lose his job. And Khumalo would have victimised him really badly if he had joined.'

A few years down the line Clifford Mabaso's friendship would nevertheless prove to be invaluable.

A path around the mountain
Cape Town, November 1990

'They killed all the red squirrels,' says an old white lady in Company's Gardens as I meander past the flower patches and look at the squirrels in the tree. 'But the squirrels are here,' I respond, puzzled. 'No,' says the lady. 'These are the grey squirrels. They are the bad ones. They killed the red ones.' Googling it many years later, I find out that that old lady was right. Invasives.org.za lists grey squirrels as an invasive species that 'outcompetes the red squirrels' and even carries a virus that 'affects indigenous species'.

Wherever you go in South Africa, you find a war.

Every now and then I walk by that wanted poster. It speaks to me every time, not because of the grainy black-and-white photographs and the terrorism threat, but because of the word 'Vula' that is there and because of what 'Vula' means. Not 'let's bomb the unbelievers', not 'all whites must be chased into the sea', but 'open'. Vulindlela, open the path.

After a week in Cape Town, it becomes unfathomable that anyone here would *not* feel the need for it. Let the path be opened, for goodness sake, break down these damned colour barriers, bring healing. Bring Mandela's leadership to Lansdowne and Gugulethu, Oranjezicht and Khayelitsha. Make buses go faster and more regularly, get communities together to shake off their puppet mayors and murderous ghetto warlord bosses. Have a decent town council that connects all people to the city;

maybe you'll then create a real city centre, too. Bring the Freedom Charter's creed that South Africa belongs to all who live in it to places of despair, so that there will be no more traumatised killer justice that burns grannies to death.

Walking alone in Adderley Street, I imagine myself explaining to white police officers and soldiers who are looking for Ivan that they are mistaken; that armed resistance is not only a good thing, but very necessary for the future of this country, too. That you, policemen and soldiers, must be fought as long as you are still rolling through townships in Casspirs. Don't you know that your Stability Unit, as you call your troops in Soweto, is called the Instability Unit by residents? That this is not a question of wordplay but that they actually think it is called the Instability Unit?

I think of the white intellectual men Sandile Dikeni told me about: who invited him, the township comrade poet, to a literary event in a letter addressed to 'Mr Guavajuice'. This is funny, but darkly so. Guavajuice is the township word for petrol bombs. Dikeni adopted the name because of the fire-filled uprisings about which he wrote his poems. The alias was both apt and necessary, since publishing under your own name could bring arrest. But now that it is 1990 and the ANC is unbanned, the intellectual white men thought it a nice idea to bring a young firebrand from Khayelitsha to their festival. They wrote to him as Mr Guavajuice thinking that that was really his name. Black people have weird names after all.

There is a gap between blacks who think whites named their paramilitary force the Instability Unit and whites who think an African poet's real name is Guavajuice. Can it ever be bridged? The question leaves me breathless for a few moments, then desperate. Possibly it never can. Not in decades, maybe only in generations. But one shouldn't say that, not even think it. One should try. Keep trying.

I don't tear the poster down, afraid I may be seen, because of course I am not going to argue with apartheid policemen. I continue on my path through this scattered, broken, scarred city with that malignant carbuncle of a mountain rising up everywhere I look, feeling painfully how even the landscape stands in the way of uniting people.

When I finally get to Johannesburg, I hand Klaas a note to give to Conny. It is a letter I have written to tell her that I understand now, and how beautiful it has been, and how much we must still work to try and come together and do more Vula operations in any way we can.

The clampdown

As the activism intensified, the clampdown did, too. The days of driving as far as the Eastern Cape, armed with no more than plausible stories you could tell the police if you were stopped, were over. Roy Chetty was arrested after they – Ivan and his brother Joe – had tried to help transport him to a meeting in town. With Roy huddled in the back seat of Joe's car under a blanket, they hadn't gone far before a convoy of security police cars intercepted them, one stopping in front and one behind. They bundled off Roy and detained him for some days. He would go into exile in Botswana shortly afterwards.

Coastal, who now worked at the library in Merebank, and was as loud and combative an activist as ever, was constantly visited by the police. But Coastal was Coastal. He would face anything rather than tone his activism down. Ivan admired Coastal, ever since the latter had shown up in school wearing purple shoes instead of the regular black school ones. He liked people who visibly took a stand; whose passions were in your face, even if he wasn't one of those people himself. Quiet and contained by nature, he preferred the background.

But he still had to come to the forefront sometimes. When in 1974, certain NIC leaders proposed that the organisation should participate in the South African Indian Council – an apartheid structure, which had previously been appointed by the regime, but would soon be elected – he was part of those who fought that idea. Becoming 'racial' went against everything the Congress alliance stood for: besides violating the 'north star' principle of inclusivity, it was also strategically wrong, he thought. The more you excluded people, the more you weakened your own side.

Progressive Indians had always boycotted any apartheid elections premised on 'own local affairs'. Now, suddenly, the supporters of this proposal advocated working from within the system, as the Coloured Labour Party (CLP) did and Inkatha in KwaZulu. At the NIC meeting in question, Inkatha's Buthelezi was guest of honour and Sonny Leon of the CLP was a speaker.

Ivan and friends deliberated on how to counter this push. 'We knew that there was no barrier to membership of the NIC, so we used that to create a dilemma for those who wished to participate. Pat and Jabu Msomi registered as members. Our group then challenged those present: if we work with that Indian Council, it will be Indians-only. Then these African comrades will not have the vote. You want to deny these comrades the vote? Just like the apartheid system does? And that was that.'

A safe house
Johannesburg, November 1990

'Hear this,' says Mac Maharaj as he tunes the car radio. He means a strange high tone like the flatlining signal from a heart monitor. 'I think they are still listening.' He laughs because he likes the implication that they still consider him dangerous, even now that he has just been released from Section 29 emergency detention in police cells in Johannesburg. He was detained there for the past four and a half months, ever since Vula had been uncovered. 'I am not doing anything illegal now, but it's interesting that they think I still *might*.' Another grin. 'I applied for a gun license, too. Not that I'll get it. But think how many hours they will spend having meetings about it.'

We enter an empty, dark house to do an interview about his life. Only a couch, a few chairs and a bottle of brandy await. As the seasoned strategist of the ANC underground, and commander of Operation Vula, moves around to find glasses, it strikes me how natural his life in the shadows seems to him. He even seems to enjoy it, much more than Ivan. Or is it bravado, an act, meant to reassure everybody – perhaps himself, too – that he is really fine? They are still trying to kill him, even now: a few months after our conversation, a bomb will be placed in his car.[32]

As we talk and the bottle empties, he rubs his glass left eye, saying it irritates, but he won't take it out because he says, 'it might scare you.' He lost his eye long ago, when he was a teenager, in a knife fight with gangsters. 'It was primitive rebellion. I was into smoking dagga, marijuana, hanging around on street corners.'

Somehow, he made it to university, but it remained difficult. 'I kept getting in trouble, but now because of politics. You'd call me a firebrand, I guess.' The administration used every excuse in the book to get rid of him. 'My marks were late, I was absent, my registration documents were not in order. Each time I kept coming back. Until the registrar cried out, exasperated: 'Don't you get it? We don't *want* you!'

Then came the early days of MK, Mandela and the underground ANC reaching out, concocting home-made bombs of sulphuric acid you could buy in nurseries, blowing up railway lines and pylons. He was arrested and landed on Robben Island, where he, Mandela and others cemented friendships and trust that would survive for decades. This included Sunny Singh, who later recruited Ivan. It was thanks to Sunny

Singh that Ivan and Mac met, and I now have met Mac because of Ivan. I carry a bundle of hand-written notes from him that refer me to contacts inside the country, Mac most prominently among them.

We talk about Operation Vula and about how the De Klerk government and most media portrayed the underground network – with its arms caches and its operatives jumping border fences in disguise – as a flagrant betrayal of peace negotiations between the government and the ANC. Nothing less than sabotage by fringe elements in MK, rogues, as it were. 'They made it seem as if it was a project of some communist Indians and whites,' he says. 'As if it had not been led by Oliver Tambo, which it was. As if there had not been African leadership in Vula.'

This was always the apartheid story, he explains. 'They would consistently pretend that communists, not blacks, were the enemy. Communists were poisoning the minds of nice, friendly, happily working and peace-loving blacks. In their narrative, communists were mostly Indians and whites; rarely ever black people themselves. When they arrested us for Vula they paraded Billy Nair,[33] Pravin Gordhan and myself, but hid the fact that they were hunting for at least six African comrades and that they had arrested two Africans already.' He tells me to write down their names: Charles Ndaba and Mbuso Shabalala. 'They have disappeared. I think they have killed them.'

In his view, Vula can still be a pillar of strength for the ANC in the negotiations. 'There is a reason why they clamp down on us, continue to prosecute us and look for comrades they haven't found. This happens in tandem with their sowing of violence in the black communities and unleashing Inkatha.' The Zulu movement, having fallen under the influence of apartheid security forces during the eighties, is increasingly causing mayhem in ANC-aligned areas. 'A week after my arrest a thousand lives were lost in the Transvaal. They want chaos and despair to push their agenda through. The network of progressive activists and the ANC are the only things we have to counter that.'

When he was arrested, Mac Maharaj had just proposed a way forward for the negotiations to the ANC's National Executive. It centred on a suspension of the armed struggle: an armistice between MK and the underground on the one side and the South African security forces on the other. He had carried the proposal in his briefcase at the time of the arrest and Police General Basie Smit had grinned widely when he found it. '"I got you now," he said. He wanted to use that as proof that I was talking peace on the one hand while engaged in sabotage of peace on the other. But are they demobilising the South African Defence Force? Because if they keep their army intact, according to their own line of reasoning, then they are sabotaging peace prospects, too.'

Basie Smit may not have been the only one to see and portray Vula as a betrayal of negotiations. The ANC itself has been silent on Vula. I have even heard whispers of disparaging remarks, reportedly made by those in the forefront of the talks with the regime, about 'those cowboys who want to play underground'.[34]

The biography of Thabo Mbeki, written by Mark Gevisser in later years, seems to confirm, if not the disparaging remarks, then at least the attitude. The book, called *The Dream Deferred*,[35] details Mbeki's deep dislike of Joe Slovo – who led Vula next to O.R. Tambo – and the armed struggle in general, which Mbeki, according to Gevisser, saw as only supported by naïve hawks who were 'quixotically focused on military conquest'.[36] *The Dream Deferred* also details how Mbeki was convinced that he was a prophet in the wilderness, as well as the head of a government in waiting, who could almost charm the apartheid regime into accepting the ANC.

Besides staying silent on Vula, formal ANC structures have also done little to help Mac and the others. O.R. Tambo would have been the leader to spearhead such action, but he has suffered a stroke recently and cannot stand or talk. In his absence, the ANC hasn't even demanded an investigation into the arrests, the hunt for 'fugitives', or the disappearance of two cadres. I have been told Mac has resigned from the National Executive Committee because of all this. He sighs. 'If they genuinely think that we do not need an underground anymore, that's fine. Let's then discuss that. How are you going to deal with Inkatha, the death squads, the Casspirs in the townships, the divide and rule tactics? Give me your views. But there doesn't seem to be such a discussion.'

Clearly, the painful division between fighters on the ground and a group of established ANC leaders from exile, ready to become a new government, hurts quite a bit. But even with the bottom of the bottle in sight Maharaj won't bite when I talk of anger and regret. 'I prefer to talk about life lessons. If you are angry, buy a punch ball. What we must learn from our experiences is that leaders must always be questioned, not cheered. And that ideologies may come and go, but that values remain. Truth, humaneness, passion.' A pause. 'Those three are it. One, you must not lie. Two, you must stay true to humanity, protect the rights and dignity of all. And three, passion, for fighting for these things.'

He is preparing to be a house husband now, he says. 'As soon as my wife and kids are back from London, she can earn the money and I'll stay home and rest.' I ask if he seriously expects that a one-person income – not likely to be on the level of a minister's salary – can provide for a family that has to start from zero, with practically no savings, in an uncertain time and place? There is no social welfare safety net and he still needs to pay lawyers. How will he live? There is a glint in his eyes – I seem to see it even in the glass eye – when he answers. 'Live? One can always live!'

Hopkins Street, later

'Well, of course, Mac stayed here,' says Jasper Cook, the only white member and trombonist of the African Jazz Pioneers. 'He didn't tell you? This house has been a thoroughfare for all of them.' I had wondered how Mac, tipsy and at night, and with only one functional eye, had been able to find this place so swiftly, 20 Hopkins Street, in the vibrant and bohemian suburb of Yeoville. So this house, where I now stay thanks to Bart and Conny's introduction, is a kind of activists' den.

Which is exactly how Colleen Cook, Jasper's sister and the owner of the house, wants it. Colleen is an organiser, a woman with computers and skills and flowing colourful robes who works for human rights lawyers, activist committees and an ANC trying to establish itself in the city. She has housed and continues to host scores of persecuted, homeless, rebellious individuals in her house with many rooms. There is Barbara Hogan, ex-underground and ex-prisoner, who has found temporary shelter here, an unemployed actress called Thandi Vilakazi and three white girl students who have abandoned their authoritarian families because they are 'just too Calvinist,' says one, and 'just too racist,' says another. Also living here is Adrian, a coloured doctor who is busy setting up a practice in Yeoville, and of course Jasper Cook himself.

Jasper has not made much of a success of any established profession – or his several marriages for that matter – but he has found music and that is what really counts. One evening he tells me, with his loud and boisterous laugh, that even though he earns the same pittance as the other members of the band – Sowetans most of them – they still expect him to pay for their drinks when they go out. 'I am white so I *must* have money.'

I reside in a former maid's room built on the side of the house, overlooking the front yard. With its bed, a shower and toilet, a tea kettle and a hot plate, it is perfect. The house in Hopkins Street comes close to what I have been looking for ever since my first day in Cape Town: here are people thrown in from waves of struggle and change, all different, all in various ways orphans from the old and hoping for the new. The house and its inhabitants echo a sentence from *Alice in Wonderland*, which occurs just after Alice has cried a great lake of tears: 'They were indeed a queer-looking party that assembled on the bank.'

Finding Philip
September 1974

It was clear that the regime would ban the Frelimo rallies that had been planned across the country. The Black Consciousness Movement (BCM) was eager to celebrate impending Mozambican independence, the current hasty departure of Portuguese colonisers and a certain victory for ANC ally Frelimo. The BCM intended the rallies to send a clear message to the South African settler government. And indeed predictably, the Minister of Justice, Jimmy Kruger – who would three years later infamously declare that Steve Biko's death in police detention 'left him cold' – soon announced that consequences would be faced by anyone who dared to show up at any of the planned events, especially the main rally at Curries Fountain.

Ivan wasn't sure that it was a good idea to openly defy the police squads that would be waiting. But other comrades and fellow activists were determined to go through with it and eventually he decided to go too.

Showing up on the day, hundreds – some reports say thousands – found the stadium gates padlocked. The police contingent commanded the crowd to disperse, which they refused to do. Then police dogs and their handlers hidden inside the stadium were unleashed. There was pandemonium, with the crowd running in all directions, away from the stadium. Coastal and Ivan ran too, barefoot in his case: he had lost his sandals.

They made their way to the South African Students Organisation (SASO) offices, close to BAWU in Beatrice Street to link up with the others. But they found the office hectic, with close to twenty people in outrage mode, making phone calls to the media and supporters abroad, and issuing statements. He said to Coastal, 'Let's get out of here' and Coastal agreed. They left the office, but stopped downstairs at the exit to talk with a group of journalists, one of whom was a progressive reporter[37] they knew from Merebank.

Then heavily armed police arrived. They set a cordon around the precinct and asked the group what they were doing there. 'We are journalists,' they replied. Thankfully the police did not notice Ivan's bare feet. He then saw the comrades from the office being dragged down the stairs, and later heard that they had all been arrested, as were comrades elsewhere in the country.[38] Thirteen would be charged with treason shortly afterwards, charges that depended on police witnesses who stated they had heard the accused talking of 'violent overthrow' and so on. Nine would eventually be convicted under the terrorism act and imprisoned on Robben Island.

After the arrests, the core of Black Consciousness activists in Durban was decimated, and the families of those arrested were harassed by the security police. The wife and two children of Aubrey Mokoape, one of the detainees, had had to leave their home, and moved into the Merebank house with Mother for a while. Their furniture just fitted into the same garage where 'The Sentinel' had been printed. The older brothers who had slept there before had left by now to set up house with their own families.

BAWU was left without the necessary staff too, and so Pat, Jabu and Ivan travelled by train to Johannesburg to link up with activists there. That is how he met Philip Masia, a comrade whose family was originally from Giyani in the far north, but who had grown up in Alexandra, the northern township in Johannesburg, where blacks were then still allowed to own land. Masia's family was forcibly relocated to Soweto after the freehold title was revoked. He was now part of BAWU in the Transvaal.

Philip Masia was short and wiry, but as Ivan got to know him, he started to think of Philip as larger than life. Phil was certainly larger than the life that blacks were supposed to live. He resisted the torment he experienced as a clerk at an insurance company on a daily basis, refusing to yield an inch to patronising bosses, and standing up to humiliating treatment – which he would get even from receptionists and secretaries – every single time. Once he threw the leftovers of a birthday cake that the black workers had been given after a whites-only party on the ground, stamped on them with both feet and delivered the creamy mess back to the madam who had sent the crumbs over. The madam cried and they fired him of course, but took him back again after all his black colleagues walked out in solidarity.

In his free time, Philip worked Soweto's Mzimhlophe neighbourhood, explaining the Freedom Charter and the social justice aspirations of the movement to neighbours in their houses. Together with his studious wife

Thabisile, with her glasses and her love of books, they distributed ANC pamphlets that came hidden in stacks of Sudan Herbalists promotional material. Philip was arrested for being in possession of such a mixed stash once.

Thabisile and he had met in church, but Philip was anything but a good sheep in a flock. Always a rebel, difficult to pin down one way or the other, he was not totally ANC, nor was he totally Black Consciousness. He would simply not follow any leader besides himself and even rebelled against being identified with black culture: his four-roomed house in Naledi, Soweto, was more likely to blast out Pavarotti than Miriam Makeba. At some point, partly because Islam had become the religion of choice for African American activists like Malcolm X and the boxer Muhammad Ali, and partly to rile his conservative Christian relatives and neighbour, he had become a Muslim.

Always ready to stand up against anything that was wrong, Philip had once got into a fist fight with a white Father Christmas in a department store. Whether the fight started because Philip smoked at the entrance, tried to get into the store, or talked back at Santa Claus has become unclear over the years. Probably it was all three. What is still remembered by those who were around at the time is that rolling around on the pavement with the surprisingly muscular man in the red suit on Eloff Street, white passers-by had come to help Father Christmas, while black ones had sided with Philip. Thabisile recalls how the story of the 'bad Father Christmas' had put off eldest daughter Shoki, who had been a toddler at the time. She had not wanted any presents from that Father Christmas who had hurt her dad.

Philip and Thabi hosted Ivan at their four-roomed house in Kgaye Street, Mzimhlophe. Hosting individuals from another race group overnight was illegal, of course, but still Ivan was always safe there. The neighbours got to know him and the community provided a friendly shield. He took the township trains alone to the BAWU office in Johannesburg and back, without experiencing any problems. In turn, Philip would stay in Mother's Merebank home sometimes, during the months he was later to spend in Durban, helping out at the BAWU office there.

In short, even if it was sometimes an absolute hazard for Ivan to have pugnacious Philip with him when he would prefer to be diplomatic and courteous, the colourful Sowetan and the quiet Indian activist from Merebank became great friends.

Politics

Johannesburg, November 1990

Johannesburg may allow for some breathing space after Cape Town but it is not safe here either; not yet, not for the likes of Barbara Hogan, whose car burnt out last night. Only a smouldering carcass is left. Was it meant to explode with her in it? Was it just a warning? What is she suspected of, what do they think she is doing? She has just been released after eight years in prison for 'acts of terrorism' committed in the late seventies and early eighties, but maybe the security police think that those just released, like Mac, like her, might soon go back to their old habits.

Barbara Hogan has gone to the police to report the wilful destruction of her car. 'Is there anybody who bears a grudge against you, ma'am?' a police officer taking her statement asked helpfully. 'Yes,' Barbara answered. 'You.' The policeman says she mustn't be like that. 'You mustn't bring politics into it, ma'am.'

Politics is a dangerous thing in South Africa, always has been. It is the reason why, when you talk about current affairs to a white person who is not a comrade, they are always a little startled. Politics is not nice. It brings discord. The whites-on-the-margins in the activist house in Hopkins Street have this in common: when they asked uncomfortable questions, they were always told that it was politics and they should stay away from it. They should not ask why can't they invite the domestic workers' child to a party, even though that child lives with them in the same house; or why the students are angry; or who that man Mandela is; or why some houses have been bulldozed with the families who lived there standing outside?

The difference between white and black people in South Africa was that for white people it was, of course, completely *possible* to stay away from it. As long as you didn't insist on asking questions, it could be done. There were no problems in the places where you lived; everybody was normal and nice. The TV showed mostly reassuring presidential speeches and lovely flower shows and cheerful banter between men and women who looked like they were from the Brady Bunch. There were black maids but they, too, would smile at you and pretend they just loved your family to bits. As a white South African, you could always easily live your life without ever confronting it. You just had to dumb down a bit.

Stay far away from politics.

It was what had made Chris Louw so angry when he found out that it was all a lie.

Living in still largely white Yeoville, but spending days in Soweto, is like moving between make believe and reality. In Yeoville, you can lash out at a policeman with a white madam voice. I hear Colleen do it sometimes, when there is one at the door to ask about Barbara. 'Do you have a warrant? Where is your paperwork? Can I phone your commanding officer? What is his name? What is *your* name?' In Soweto's Naledi, where Philip and Thabisile Masia and their children now live, you don't have a chance to ask anything. They don't knock. The bedroom door has a large hole in it, still from when a police boot kicked it in, some years ago. Phil being Phil, of course, has never had it repaired.

I have visited the Masias in Naledi a number of times, sometimes spending the night cuddled up behind Thabisile's nightgowned body in the one big bed in the matchbox house. Asked if this was not an imposition, what with Philip having to sleep on the couch on those occasions, Thabi laughed that it had always been like that. 'In Mzimhlophe, Lindiwe Sisulu[39] stayed with us too like that, and Jabu Msomi, and so many others.' If the visitors were men, they would go in the other bedroom, with Shoki and Hassan who were small, brought in to sleep with the parents. Likewise, the later Naledi house would also make room. 'Once we had a boy here who was chased by the police because they wanted him to give state evidence against the Sharpeville Six.[40] We hid him for a long time, telling Philip's family that the boy – Joe – was my cousin, and telling my people that he was from Philip's side.' Joe, now in his fifties, still rents a room in that house.

Meeting the ANC

In 1975 he found Sunny Singh. Singh – the Bobby I meet in Lusaka – had been released from Robben Island in February 1974, after serving his ten-year sentence for MK activities, and was still under house arrest and security police scrutiny.

Ivan was told about Sunny by a former school friend of Sunny's, whom he knew. 'The person was trying to warn me that activism would land me in jail. He said he knew someone who had been an activist like me, who was ANC and who had spent ten years on Robben Island. The story was meant to scare me but all I wanted now was to meet that person,' he recalls. 'I was knocking on his door the next day.' Sunny Singh remembers that he 'was prepared to do a lot of political convincing to recruit people to rebuild the underground, but these boys from Merebank handed themselves to me on a platter.' Besides Ivan and Joe, a third 'boy from Merebank' was Krish: Krishna Rabilal of Hubli Place in the township,[41] who had become Ivan's best mate over the years both in school and at 'The Sentinel'. Like the Pillay brothers, he was ready to go underground. Coastal, since he was a high-profile activist, would continue to operate at an overt level.

There were other ex-Islanders in the leadership, connected to Sunny, too: Judson Kuzwayo and Shadrack Maphumulo had been released at the same time and were now working as research fellows at the University of Natal. Like Sunny, they had immediately started underground ANC activities again. They operated on a need-to-know basis and the boys did not physically meet them, but coordination, on the one end with Krish, Joe, and Pat and Jabu Msomi and on the other with the ex-Islanders and through them with the ANC in exile, was now in place. Together, they formed one of the first functioning ANC units in the country since the 1960s.

It was happening. He had never felt so filled with anticipation in his life. Being together, breaking free, was air, water, sunlight. It was escaping a polluted, cramped, fenced-in existence in more ways than one. He had longer hair then, curled almost into an Afro, and tried to play guitar, a Bellini he bought in town for seven rand: Joan Baez, Bob Dylan.

Sunny and Krish opened a shop, Dayglo Stationers, in the grey part of town. Apart from selling political books under the table, and for earning some income from the stationery sales, it was also a meeting place. The Msomis would hang out there, and others from Merebank, like Coastal. They all read voraciously now: books about Vietnam and Algeria; Amilcar Cabral, Basil Davidson, Marcuse, Frantz Fanon, Paulo Freire, Robert Taber's War of the Flea, *Mary Benson's biography of Nelson Mandela. Sunny Singh got such books by ordering them overseas and having them delivered to post offices in South Africa under untraceable names.*

Sunny was already organising books when he was still on the Island, either secretly, through visitors, or openly, by careful checking what was and what wasn't banned. You could get a lot. 'You could not have Newsweek, *for example,' he explains, 'but you could receive the much more conservative sounding* Economist *for a while.' Grinning, he narrates how there had been confusion around the* Economist *once. 'One of the common criminals who was imprisoned with us – he was trying to curry favour with the warders, and also confusing some spelling – ran to a warder after seeing us with the* Economist. *'Baas, baas!' he shouted. 'They got comonist!'*

The neighbouring shop owners, who might otherwise have been suspicious of the music, the African visitors and the meetings, remained friendly because the boys were still just as nice and neat as they had been when distributing 'The Sentinel' in Merebank. They kept the place clean, they greeted people politely. These things were important if you wanted to bring the community with you. It also helped to avoid unwanted attention from the security police.

But there was more to being polite, clean, friendly and quiet than just safety. For them, to behave properly was a value of the struggle in itself. Whether a neighbour, client or passer-by was a comrade or not, was known or not, agreed with your politics or not, you still had to respect them and treat them right. A quarter of a century later, the ANC would be lauded for its inclusivity and lack of vengefulness, for being decent and kind towards every single human being, but it had already been in the old books then and in the Freedom Charter, always. 'It was in the DNA of the ANC.'

Besides that inclusive humanity, it was also the bread and butter issues, like organising for more bus stops and clean air, and housing protests that continued to root them in the communities. These distinguished them from Black Consciousness supporters, mainly students, who focused on political debate, often centred in and around the universities. They participated there too, often walking from Merebank to the University of Natal Medical School and back – there is so much walking when he talks of activism in those days – but kept coming back to practical community needs. 'Black Consciousness made important contributions to black psychological liberation, but did not clarify how, beyond being proud and an independent thinker, you could actually bring down the racist regime over time,' he says. 'To us it was important to fight daily discrimination and oppression very practically, not only because you wanted the bus stops, but also as a strategy. If you focused on people's needs you could mobilise them for national liberation. Every step in that direction also indirectly weakened the enemy. The community structures would help build up the country again after apartheid, too.'

When the Umgeni River flooded a shack settlement called Tin Town, in 1975, activists from different areas and civics all came to help, Pravin Gordhan and his group of activists among them. Ivan appealed for humanitarian assistance from his bosses at Roberts Construction, telling them there was a need for a safe place, a roof where donations of clothes and food could be stored and civic activists could meet to coordinate. The bosses were amenable and agreed to donate a prefabricated office for that purpose. The experience, like his friendship with Clifford Mabaso, taught him that formal employment had a value far beyond simply earning a salary. He built up a network where he met some good people, and where people valued him in turn. Some of these connections would remain for life. He remembers one boss named Symington, whom he would meet again in Swaziland. Symington, finding him then a refugee, promptly offered him a job.

Some of the activists who responded to the flooding of Tin Town were to become a strong organising core for the future. The activist organisation led by Pravin Gordhan and others moved with the affected people when they were relocated to a new Indian township called Phoenix, north of Durban. Their community work, mass mobilisation and organisation there led to the formation of several youth and civic organisations in the greater Durban area, and in the following years, together with similar formations across the country, their efforts helped to start what was to become the United Democratic Front. In parallel, keeping away from the surveillance of the police state, the group around Pravin Gordhan would join the African National Congress and become part of its underground structures.

The hurt of comrades

Maisy[42] regularly has to fight to defend herself. Her neighbourhood, Tladi, just one sandy road away from Naledi where the Masias live, has been attacked by an Inkatha impi militia from nearby Merafe Hostel three times in the past six months. Every time, people have died and houses have burned, she says when I visit. 'It's a routine now: you see them coming, you sound the alarm, comrades prepare to fight them, everybody else hides. In the end you count the damage and the dead. The police never do anything to help.'

I met Maisy at Malibongwe, a women's anti-apartheid conference held recently, in January 1990 in Amsterdam. Maisy had come there to speak about women and the struggle, and I had been in awe of her. Maisy was serious about the race and gender question and could speak to it, and quote elders like UDF leader Albertina Sisulu and Helen Joseph, the union activist who co-founded the Congress of Democrats, the ANC's white ally. Laughing uproariously, Maisy could also make fun of old chauvinist ANC leaders and their silly wives who would defend traditions, for example women being obliged to bring men tea and food on their knees. (Later, in December 2013, President Jacob Zuma will refer approvingly to this tradition. 'I like to be here,' he will say, visiting the northern Venda region where the custom is still practised in some places. 'Women still lie down to show respect.')[43]

Maisy is completely unapologetic about being a comrade and a feminist. If she could fight the security police, she told me, she could also take a stand against the rape she had suffered, and against the violence so many women were suffering at the hands of partners, relatives, comrades. That your own men would hurt you, sometimes even more than the whites – of course more than the whites, you did not *love* the whites – was something that she needed to address. It was one of the reasons why she had wanted to come to Malibongwe.

She broke down and cried when reliving how the 'kitskonstabels', hastily trained auxiliary black police, who seemed to delight in beating you up even more than the whites did, kicked her and broke her arm just before she departed for the conference; how a black policeman at the airport, on her way to Amsterdam, had jerked her arm for no other reason than to inflict more pain. It was a fight in itself to remain human, she said, telling me how much of her struggle was about precisely that. She had a son as a result of her rape, but made a project of loving him. 'We have enough children who grow up without love already,' she had said, pensively, when she told me that. I was left to fathom how much energy, pain, time and agony she must have invested in that alone, in addition to the daily struggle for survival.

'I catch myself still at risk of becoming dead inside,' she says, when we meet up in Tladi. 'Sometimes the atrocities are so normal that I don't even recognise them anymore. The other day some comrades caught an Inkatha spy – or at least they said he was a spy. Some held him while another comrade broke all his fingers with a stone. I was watching it and then suddenly I realised my son was watching it too. My god! He is eight years old! And he is growing up thinking that this is just part of daily life. I scolded him and made him go and phone for an ambulance.'

There may not be a mountain here blocking black pain from white comfort, but there might as well be one. The border here is the concrete highway which you cross by minibus taxi, out of Naledi, past the Kae Kapa Kae 'whoever you are, you are welcome' shop, towards the high rises in the distance. Egoli, it is called, the city of gold, where you can stay away from politics if you are white. But for how long will white comfort remain isolated, as black pain is moving to town? Some of Maisy's friends live in slowly blackening Hillbrow now, and Maisy and I visit them as we do a story following up on Malibongwe, on abuse of women. Meet Maisy's friends: burned women, women with broken knees, a woman in bandages from top to toe. They may have got out of the township, but pain has followed them here.

I ask some neighbours in Tladi and Naledi about Winnie, the iconic heroine who, like them, suffered. Maybe in a different way, but probably just as intensely. What does Winnie mean to them? 'She is brave,' says one. 'There is no question about that. But we are scared of her, too.' 'Especially her boys,' says another.

Killing Zulus
November 1990

In the evening, as Maisy shows me around her neighbourhood, we observe the Merafe Hostel in the distance, and the area in between that separates Tladi from the hostel grounds: the war zone. A comrade we meet tells us that Inkatha is now getting guns; he supports this assertion by fetching another comrade, who dutifully confirms having seen a van with men unloading guns at night close to the hostel.

Another youngster in Naledi confesses that he is not just scared of Inkatha, though. 'If you walk past comrades and they see you as Zulu' – he is Swazi, but that's close enough – 'they'll necklace you. If you meet Inkatha and they see you are from a township, they kill you with a knife or beat you to death.' His solution is to carry both a red comrade headband, and a white Inkatha headband, and interchange. 'But that's not always safe either. Because if they search you and they find the other headband, you are dead, too.'

I also hear, when asking around, that when the impi comes, its members shout that 'khongolose' – Congress, meaning the ANC – must stop killing them. Which is puzzling, because everybody in the township says that the impis always start the fighting. Do they mean 'killing' figuratively? Inkatha leaders have said that urban township blacks want migrant workers to leave, intent on keeping all the jobs and salaries for themselves. Or is there more? We can't go and ask the Zulus in Merafe Hostel; in the current atmosphere, that would be close to suicidal. But

Philip Masia says we can go to Nancefield, another hostel, ten kilometres to the east next to Klipspruit. He has some contacts there. Philip is perhaps the only comrade who would, in this time of killings, burnings, stone throwing, kidnappings, torture and massacres, even contemplate visiting a Zulu hostel.

He goes alone first to prepare the ground: 'I'll just tell them that I am looking for a friend of mine - I'll make up a name like Amos Magadla or something and say he moved here from the mines in Welkom. Magadla is such a common name, there must be Magadlas there. And when it turns out they don't know my Amos, we'll still have a nice chat.'

As Philip and I enter the hostel on a Sunday morning, sun warming the benches where men are having beer, we find the Zulus a rather sad bunch, sitting hunched over and looking depressed. At first, a chief with big holes in his ears called Madondo does all the talking. He is pleasant enough, having received Philip with his 'Amos Magadla' story again as an old friend. Then it turns out that part of his enthusiasm has been triggered because Phil has brought a white woman. Such a visit doesn't often occur here, I gather, and just like that he wants to marry me. 'He says I brought you as a gift for him,' Philip says after some banter in Zulu. Grinning, the chief says: 'We must now negotiate lobolo – how much you will cost.' Five BMWs, I say quickly, because I have heard somewhere that nowadays bride prices in some urban areas are measured in luxury cars, not in cows, and Madondo laughs a loud hearty laugh and abandons the subject.

Having had a few beers, the others become more talkative, and start complaining about how 'khongolose' comes at night to shoot them while they are sleeping. They have lost several of their own like that, they say, one after the other, in recent months. They can't explain why anyone would venture close to the hostel at night and shoot workers in their beds – beds being a grand word for the narrow sleeping spaces, cramped next to one another and covered with filthy blankets – but they are adamant that it has happened, at least four times. Comrades gone crazy for vengeance? Or apartheid police agents, Third Force as they are called, out to provoke the impi?

A young worker with a fur headband explains with his eyes looking downwards that he used to have a fun social life with township friends, and even with township girls, and that he doesn't understand why now they all want to shoot him, if he simply wants to get bread, or cigarettes.

We ask his name. Bizzah, he says and when Philip asks him to spell it, he writes it on a paper napkin. Philip laughs: that is a township tsotsi name! Bizzah shrugs and repeats that he used to be at home here, but now he is not. He moves to the little radio in the corner, tuned to some mix of gospel and rhythm and blues, and dances a bit.

Talking more with the men around the table, sharing beer, I start wondering whether the war in the township is only a matter of Inkatha's belligerence, fuelled by the police's divide and rule tactics, or whether real class and ethnic tensions between the established Soweto community and the migrant workers play a role. The Zulus certainly seem to feel mistreated by those who, compared to them, are perceived as middle class, and the ANC comrades who rule them. 'They think they are superior because their ANC is going to be the next government and then what?' one of the men says. 'They will chase you away after you have slaved here for years, decades. But we won't go. We must work and save up for a tractor for the village back home.'

As we leave the hostel, shaking hands and embracing like old friends, we know that many more will still die in this war zone and that it is doubtful that any of these men will ever return back home, triumphantly, with a tractor.

The soft white men
Pretoria, December 1990

'I have been in the townships. I have seen how they murder their own people. Their councillors. With necklaces. Hack them to pieces with pangas. So bloody. It's pure horror.' The man on the swivelling leather lounge chair pulls on his pipe, looks thoughtful. Then concludes, 'This is not a people that is mature enough for democracy. Surely you must see that. They say "one man, one vote", but we fear that it may become "one man, one vote, one time." So we must build in protections for our rights as well.'

Another swivel on his monster chair, then a few clicks on a computer. 'We have it all here now. The scenarios. What do you get when you merge a standard bill of rights with the protection of minorities, with qualified votes, with property rights. We feed all the considerations in, we get the blueprints out.' Puff, swivel, smile. 'We can even protect the rights of communities who like opera. And' – with a smile – 'I am not part of such a community myself, I assure you.'

The man in the chair is Human Sciences Research Council (HSRC) head Tjaart van der Walt, a member of F.W. de Klerk's think tank, or so I am told. Van der Walt would not describe himself as such exactly: 'I don't know that there is a think tank and how many members there are and whether I am a member or not. But this institution – the HSRC – plays its part and I play my part. And yes, I know F.W.' The interview takes place because, on assignment for a new story, I try to understand how South Africa's white rulers are preparing themselves for the inevitable transfer to an ANC government – or, as Van der Walt and his fellow advisers around De Klerk would have it, a government in which the ANC also 'has a role to play'.

They all like Mandela, of course, the soft white men whom I interview these days, one after the other. They are accessible and friendly and well-meaning, the men 'who know F.W.', with their sweet blonde secretaries and pastel-coloured offices in architectural masterpieces like the HSRC building with its waving pale-pink Star Trek décor, and the very white aesthetic of Pretoria University, where Professor Willie Esterhuyse, Afrikaans thinker and philosopher, resides. Esterhuyse explains how skin colour really doesn't mean much, that it's all about culture and good manners after all, and that white South Africans will eventually understand that. Even NIS, the National Intelligence Service, already consults him on 'the meaning of current changes', he says, with a self-deprecating smile.

As an example, Esterhuyse tells me about a student who was Indian, 'but whose manners were impeccable'. When travelling together with her to a conference, he suggested she use a whites-only toilet at a garage on the way – 'You look Italian, you can pull it off' – but she had come back saying she could not use it because it was so dirty. That story had taught him how human she was. Imagine a brown person rejecting a dirty whites-only toilet. It had changed him, he says.

Obviously, things mustn't move too fast. The white men have good advice to offer on how we must go about this transition. One mustn't really think, for example, that Mr Mandela can control his own people: those ones you see daily on TV, destroying things and killing one another. Human rights are all well and fine but we have to be careful, see, we can't have death and destruction, not here. I am from Holland, right? They know Holland so well. They have been there often. Delightful country. A bit too much red-light district and drug using, perhaps, *hm, hahaha*, but who are they to judge, they are broad minded enough not to get worked up over such things, everyone has their culture and their quirks after all. But as a Hollander I must surely also appreciate that it's easy for me to talk. Holland only has a small black minority. Compare that to our South African numbers, they say.

Five or six faces, says F.W.'s brother Wimpie de Klerk, the former Perskor editor who attracted the rage of my friend Chris Louw in the 'Boetman' letter, and whom I meet in his rustic Cape Dutch cottage in Orange Grove, Johannesburg. There will be five or six black faces added to the white government. 'We can't accommodate more than that. It will be sufficient for now. There may be chaos if we just get a racial overhaul. We must protect our institutions.' I listen and note five-or-six; it becomes a tune in my head that makes it difficult to ask more questions. He is so calm too, on his couch with his grey hair and glasses under the old Dutch painting above his couch and the books he has written on the shelf beside him. He sits and shrugs as if it's a minor inconvenience that you must now add some darkies to your government, but if they want it so badly, what can you do?

I wonder if this man even knows about anything like Maisy's broken arm, the Zulus in the hostel, or the whites taking the rivers in the Transkei for themselves. Has he ever heard of Mayor Hoza and his Khayelitsha Gestapo, or of how, after another arrest of Philip, Thabi and their kids were transported between Mzimhlophe and Diepkloof in the back of a police combi with a set of dogs? How Thabi was then taken away from baby Leila, breasts painful and needing to feed, but without being given relief; and how medication prescribed by the district surgeon was not given to her as she sat in her cell? How Lizo Semane, aged fifteen, naked in the mines, was made to run on a treadmill and had a thermometer prodded into his backside, to see if he could stand the heat?

At some point in the interview, I become speechless, as to talk of these things seems incongruous and pointless. There is no way that I am ever going to dent this man or even provoke a reaction; his flesh is as invulnerable as it is soft – he is made of pure comfort. I am the one who might end up crying, not he.

Only former Broederbond chair, Dr Pieter de Lange (small-rimmed glasses, crow's feet around benevolent old uncle-eyes, who self-deprecatingly calls himself an 'old schoolmaster' and receives me at his home with a motherly wife and her home-baked cookies), shows a crack in the otherwise impenetrable exterior. It happens only once, after I finally muster the courage to ask him about the snipers who are killing the Zulus in the hostel and ask how he can use the violence of black people as an argument to withhold full human rights, when they – whites, the Broederbond, amabhunu – themselves have started the violence?

Pieter de Lange's face changes then and he almost drops the plate of cookies. 'There is nothing like that,' he says sharply, with raised voice, a warning contained in it. 'If you start like that ... there is *nothing* like that. Nothing.'

To get back to Hopkins Street from Pretoria, I take the train past Irene and Olifantsfontein. A sign at Irene station has been painted over: there are now only black streaks where it once must have read 'whites only'. Barely legible are still parts of 'w' on the left and 'ly' on the right. The blacks still queue on one side, the box where they sell the third-class tickets hasn't changed. Five-or-six, goes the train rhythm. Five-or-six.

The Swaziland route
Natal, 1975

They knew by now that the only way to resist the police state was clandestinely. Almost never bringing their activities home anymore, they kept to the Dayglo Stationers bookshop that Sunny and Krish had opened and to other safe places where they would meet mostly one on one, and never together. They learned how to check if they were followed, kept away from blabbermouths, checked for informers. 'Africans have navigated the system similarly for ages. If you don't want to be arrested you dress well, carry a briefcase, don't attract attention, don't have a big mouth, say "my baas" if a white asks you a question. It was a bit like that.' They reduced their public profiles little by little. They saw less of family members and school friends, and if they ever had contemplated dating, this was certainly now off limits, too.

Pat Msomi, travelling for Sudan Herbalists, used his country-wide meetings with herb suppliers to drop and receive communications. He would go north, via Empangeni and Richards Bay towards the Swazi border, then cross the fence on foot. He would meet ANC members, get pamphlets, funds and instructions. Over time, he would help comrades across, too: Mac Maharaj, Stephen Dlamini,[44] Sunny Singh.

The others also kept their daily work routines, to make sure they were seen as unremarkable citizens. Ivan still worked for Robert's Construction; Joe resigned from his teaching job in Illovo and opened a second-hand furniture store in Beatrice Street, which happened to be opposite the SASO offices. It provided some income and a cover story.

Taking people to meet others was complicated. Beside the secrecy and the security police, there were also no mobile phones then. They had a network of pay phone booths, at which they would be present at an agreed time, and waited. They reserved the phone by pretending to make a call, but kept their hand pressed down on the lever until it rang. To develop systems for that alone was part of building an underground.

It was not just about blowing up things, certainly not in the beginning. They first set up the infrastructure: safe houses, covert links with the community. They made contacts in the public protest movement, groomed potential recruits for the underground, established safe communications. Ivan would talk, frowning, of how at times that necessity was overlooked; how, for instance, from exile, MK would put youngsters over the border fence 'with two thousand rand, a few weapons and the instruction to attack'. Modest organised support within the country was needed, but in many instances was absent.

Solomon Mahlangu was captured and hanged by the apartheid state after operating in a similar void.

An impressive man

Working on a need-to-know basis, Ivan, Krish and Joe did not know who their ANC contacts were. The connection with Shadrack Maphumulo was kept a well-guarded secret. They got to know him later in Swaziland, though, the soft-spoken, caring, mature comrade who impressed all in the unit with his resilience, humanity and his ability to communicate with practically anybody. He could explain Marxism in Zulu; get rural people to understand what it meant to organise for social justice.

Maphumulo, they learned, had once been first and foremost a family man, who would never have taken up arms if the regime would just have let him be. Shadrack had practically been forced to join the struggle after, from a young age, he had just tried to make a life for himself and his family, but had found walls, kicks and cruelty everywhere he turned.

In a while, Joe would become so fascinated with Maphumulo that he started writing his biography. Reading the – now finalised, but as yet unpublished – manuscript, one wonders how those who did not take up arms managed their existence. Would they not have hit back, like Shadrack did, the white son of the madam owner of the café where he worked, after the brat had humiliated him, kicked him and dirtied the place on purpose, for months on end? Maphumulo had subsequently been denied a taxi license he had saved hard for; the license had been given to a rich Indian person who had bribed his way instead. Then a shop run with his aunt in KwaMashu had to close when it was suddenly declared to be in a non-business area.

It was as if apartheid wanted Maphumulo to fight. He had been among the first to join MK, had been arrested, tortured and spent ten years on the Island like Sunny Singh. Just released, he also had immediately gone back to the struggle.

Burning veldfires
1977

When Ivan read in a newspaper on a Saturday morning that someone had been arrested in Durban for terrorism, he did not know it was Shadrack Maphumulo. 'But something told me that it was our contact,' he recalls. He found Joe and told him; he phoned the BAWU office and said he urgently needed to see Pat Msomi.

Shadrack had been arrested after a weapons transport from Swaziland had gone wrong. A car loaded with guns and ammunition on the Swazi side had successfully crossed the border unnoticed – it had been well-timed to coincide with heavy festive traffic prior to a Swazi royal wedding – but had run into a roadblock nearing Durban. To avoid a search, the driver sped through it and the police set out on the chase. The driver, a comrade called Ngwenya, managed to outrun them, but drove so fast that he lost control of the vehicle on the hilly roads and it overturned. The accident injured Ngwenya and one of the other two comrades who had been in the van. The third one escaped, but police caught up with the two injured ones and arrested them. Torture of the detainees led the security police to Shadrack Maphumulo, who was arrested the next day.

In his biography of Shadrack Maphumulo, Joe Pillay quotes him: 'I stuck to my story that I had had nothing to do with the weapons transport and they could not link me. But the problem I had was that they had found R450 in my bag and they did not accept my explanation that I had earned it selling vegetables. The notes were in sequence, meaning that the stash had had to come from a bank. This was true. It was given to me by Pat Msomi, who had brought it from Swaziland for the needs of our unit. My biggest challenge over the next few days as I was tortured by the Security Branch was to find a story that could explain the money from the bank.'

Maphumulo finally managed to think of such a story and told them that Mac Maharaj had given it to him to give to fellow ex-Robben Islander and unit member Judson Kuzwayo. It was a neat tale with a neat ending, impossible for the police to follow up, because Mac had by now left the country. They had to let Shadrack go after that. He did not name any names, and betrayed no one. But searching Shadrack's office, they had found the rental papers for the Toyota Hiace they used, which had been signed by Joe.

When Ivan read about the 'terrorism arrest', and thought that that could be Pat's contact, he also thought that the police might find the car rental contract. He met with Pat, who had by now adopted the struggle name Nzima, and Joe, that same afternoon, one day after the arrest, in the bushy area off Higginson's Highway. At the meeting, Pat/Nzima confirmed that it was their contact who had been arrested and that there was indeed a risk to Joe because of the rental contract. It was decided that Joe should skip the country with Pat. Ivan would stay to pick up the pieces and inform Jabu.

Jabu was livid. Her sister's wedding was the next day. Pat had been tasked with logistics; he was the one with a vehicle, after all. He was also the best man. They did not even know for sure if there was any danger, she yelled at him. Couldn't they at least wait one day? But Ivan was adamant. The risk was simply too great. Jabu and the kids should stay put for now and go through with the wedding as if all was normal. Jabu relented and after a few days, asked that she be assisted to exit the country too.

Ivan then travelled with Jabu and her young daughter to Philip Masia's place in Mzimhlophe, from where it was arranged that Philip would take them out of the country across the fence near the Ramatlabama border post to Botswana.

In Durban it seemed safe again for a while, but then Joe crossed back into South Africa some weeks later to tell him that the ANC had decided Ivan should leave too. Staying was too risky, they had said, since he was Joe's brother, and still known as an activist. He was not happy about the instruction, but did not object either. The struggle was the struggle; you went where it called. He spoke to the family, to Sister. They decided that it was better if Joe and he did not travel as two single men, but as a family, together on an outing. Sister agreed and talked to Suggie, who could drive and had a car. Then started cooking.

***

The car with Suggie at the wheel, cousin Pal in the passenger seat, and Jenny in the back with Joe and Ivan, dropped them near the Golela border post just before ten in the evening, when it would close. They could see the lights of the border post in the distance as they walked with their knapsacks alongside the railway track. Looking at the veld fires that burned around them all the way to the villages on the other side, he thought of it as a sign of the war that was to come: a slow-burning, unofficial, grassroots war it was to be, in which you had to find your own way in the dark. A ramshackle war of individuals just like him and Joe, walking alone in the bush with their duffle coats, with identities and lives petering out to be rebuilt on the other side.

A war of outcasts. Or rogues, whatever you prefer.

Chainama Golf Course
Lusaka, December 1990

Smart Mike drives fast in his shiny red car and he is proud of it too. 'Never slower than 140,' he grins, looking sideways at me. Living dangerously is what he does. 'I drink and I drive,' he confirms happily. 'I speed. I deal. I gamble. I do what I like and I do it as fast as I can.' I ask him if he isn't scared, if not of the traffic police, then at least of physical injury or death. He laughs loudly now, throwing his handsome shaved black head back, not looking at the road again, and says he knows how to cheat death, too. 'I am called Smart Mike for a reason.'

After South Africa, I am back in Lusaka again and Ivan, worried that I might get bored since he now has some work to do, has asked a close acquaintance, car mechanic Pattan,[45] to introduce me to some other friends. One of these friends is Smart Mike, and indeed, one might feel a whole lot of things with Smart Mike, but boredom isn't one of them. From Cairo Road we speed on to the east, to the Chainama Golf Club, where he will introduce me to the others. We sit and order beers at a spotless white table in the luxurious club house. It has beautiful views of lawns and trees through wide, impeccably clean windows. Thirty years ago, the likes of Smart Mike and his friends could only enter here in white uniforms to serve the colonial masters.

The servants are still black, but now some of the masters are black, too. Anecdote after anecdote, beer after beer, Smart Mike and his friends impress on me just how masterfully they operate in their many deals that often seem to centre around spare parts. One of the men runs a warehouse for spare parts in the industrial area to the west of town. Another imports spare parts for Fords and Land Rovers from the UK and boasts that he owns a Bentley. Smart Mike himself deals in spare parts for anything, from photocopiers to tractors to mining equipment. When I ask why spare parts are so crucial, they don't seem to understand the question. 'You need spare parts for anything,' one says. And no, Zambia doesn't make any machinery or equipment itself. 'We just sell the copper,' one says and the group laughs uproariously. I ask if it ever happens that they can't get spare parts. Yes, that happens quite regularly. And then what? 'Then nothing works', is the answer and again there is mirth around our table.

Just as I start feeling I'm at a Mad Hatter's tea party, Smart Mike elbows me in the side, telling me to look at a group of guests that has just arrived at the club. 'The man in the middle is a Greek tycoon. The others are the government officials he deals with.' A white man in a white suit takes a seat at a large table, right under the chandelier. An entourage of black men in suits seat themselves around him. Smart Mike mentions a name but I don't catch it. He continues in a conspiratorial whisper: 'He buys emeralds and ivory and other stuff. He brings in things too – different things each time. Once it was sewing machines.'

Sewing machines could be sewing machines. From the arms trade research I have started in connection with the murder of Dulcie September,[46] I know that they could also be guns – same weight, same metal clanking when the crates are transported. Zambian customs are not known for their thorough checking.

Pattan says he doesn't think that will ever change. One, everybody is just too happy to cut in on a deal, including border control and police officers. Two, the government would collapse if they didn't make themselves and the foreign businessmen happy, because that is all they know. Three, to stop making deals serves no purpose. He needs spare parts for the cars he fixes from Smart Mike, the Greek needs emeralds, the officials need their share. 'How can you stop making deals? You can't.'

The way Pattan explains it, it begins to sound quite logical.[47] It is simply a particular operating system. You might call it Pirate Planet. It has plenty of treasure and it's all about who gets there first. Then you bargain. The treasure-seekers from outside get your copper and ivory and emeralds and in exchange the crates with spare parts and other things come in. It's never all you need and many times it's not what you need at all but you make do. Pattan's Zambia is a country that hangs together like one of his cars: with some rope, some ill-fitting parts that squeak and strain when they are forcibly made to fit, some rubber bands.

That afternoon Pattan takes me to a compound where, between huts made of planks and straw, with an open sandy place in the middle, artisanal miners seated on stools and crates clean their little green emeralds. The stones look unimpressive: dusty, dirty and small. Pattan proposes that I take some to South Africa and sell them there for him. If the government can do it, why can't he?

While I politely reject the offer, I can't help thinking of Philip Masia. He would love an opportunity like that. He would love Pattan too, with his car-fixing skills, his network and his improvisational talents. And why am I really not even considering helping Pattan? If government officials can sell out the country's resources to fill their own pockets, then why not Pattan, who is a Zambian citizen and definitely in more need, not to mention more deserving, than they are? What do you do when your own country pushes you to operate your own networks, rogue, as it were?

It's not underground. No one is chasing you, arresting you, torturing, killing, jailing you. The government is not an evil machine, not even an ineffective evil one. It's simply not there. And if there is no formal legality, then your network may be rogue, but it can't be illegal, not really. It is simply what is.

This opportunistic jungle doesn't work for everybody, of course. In the lounge of Pattan's two-bedroomed house, where his mother welcomes us with lemonade, a young woman lies on the couch. She smiles and greets us, but it's clear that she is fatigued; her eyes close all the time and she doesn't move at all. She wheezes and coughs. 'My sister,' says Pattan. 'She is sick.'

Pattan does not go into detail, but HIV-related tuberculosis has peaked in Zambia. Fifteen per cent of the population is infected, and it is still spreading like wildfire. Pattan nods when I mention TB. 'That's probably what it is, but it doesn't really make a difference to know. There are no good medicines in the hospitals. You get paracetamol. Antibiotics only sometimes.' Despite his extensive network, it is doubtful that Pattan could lay his hands on the strong antibiotics needed for his sister, nor can the family, if she does have AIDS, even dream of accessing the first-generation antiretrovirals that have recently been developed in other parts of the world, let alone ensure the regular, continuous supply she may need. Even Smart Mike can't make that deal.

'That's why it's not a viable operating system,' says Ivan that evening when I tell him about Smart Mike and the visit to Pattan's house. 'Deal making alone can't sustain a country. You can be the smartest trader but you still need a government that can deliver medicines to hospitals. You also need to maintain the roads to get there.' I think of the many potholes Smart Mike has swerved around with squealing tyres today, but then the many beers I've had in the Chainama Golf Club kick in and I fall asleep.

Corruption
Lusaka, the next day

'Of course we write about corruption,' the editor of the *Zambia Daily Mail* – another friend of Pattan's – says passionately.[48] 'The opposition is *very* corrupt.' That may be so – indeed many rumours circulate about opposition leader Frederick Chiluba's dalliances with dodgy businessmen[49] – but surely the ruling party, which the *Daily Mail* supports, cannot really claim to be doing a sterling job of governing the country? I tell the editor about the Greek tycoon and the government officials in the Chainama Golf Club, but he just shrugs. 'I understand what you say. But the way we do it here is that we look at the corruption of the other party, and the other party looks at ours.' It is a media system that I will recognise in many other countries in decades to come, and not only in Africa.

'We always thought we would do better than Zambia, or Angola, or any of these other places where a ruling party simply replaced the old colonial elite with a new one,' Ivan says that evening at the flat in Kabulonga. 'And maybe we still will. We have examples to learn from; we have seen what others were doing wrong. We also know by now that political rhetoric won't help us. That there is no such thing as a socialist Utopia.' I think back to a conversation I had had with Zeph Mothopeng in the Lusaka safe house, before leaving for Transkei. The youngster had narrated how he had been taken to tour a model factory in the Soviet Union once. 'Everything was so perfect there and everyone was so happy that you just knew it was not real,' he had said, smiling.

Also, precisely because of apartheid and white settlers, South Africa might be in a better starting position than the countries where colonisers just packed up and left, Ivan ponders. 'The Portuguese in Mozambique smashed the place up in anger; they literally shattered windows and furnishings in government offices and institutions. In one high-rise building they poured concrete down the lift shaft.' The building is still there, he says, looming over the beach, still unusable. 'But the majority of South African whites will probably not do that. They will stay. They have an interest. The country must also work for them.'

I note that he has partly been talking in the conditional tense. We thought we would do better. Does that mean he doesn't think that anymore, now? He sighs. 'Now I am not so sure. We are damaged. We have been outside functioning systems for a very long time.'

Over the border
Swaziland, the late seventies

After being met by Nzima in the Swazi capital Mbabane, Ivan was taken to Maputo in Mozambique for debriefing: Because of impimpis, the movement needed every newcomer to go through this. His temporary lodgings there were the servants' quarters at the back of a house which, he found out, belonged to a former diamond smuggler named Khuzwayo. Khuzwayo had been wanted in South Africa and had fled to Mozambique, where he joined the ANC. He had now gone for military training in an Angolan MK camp; his son and his nephew were already there. His family remained in the house in Maputo and hospitably housed ANC guests.

Ivan got on well with the Khuzwayo family. Though a bit surprised about Khuzwayo's diamond smuggling, he understood it. On the run from the police, crossing fences to escape South Africa, you would rub shoulders with other people who had run away from the police, too. Not all these people were necessarily bad. He had known for a long time how apartheid criminalised black people in general, simply because living itself often transgressed some law or other. For decades, drinking spirits had been an offence. You could be jailed for being in town, or for being rude to the 'baas'. It stood to reason that some had reached the point of not caring about the law anymore.

Those who broke the law most strongly sometimes achieved hero status. Philip Masia was fond of narrating how gangsters with their sharp suits, cool hats, money and revolvers were respected in Alexandra. Ivan had found the situation to be similar in Mzimhlophe, where Philip lived when Ivan met him. Local gangsters used to see the politicals as kindred spirits and even admired them since, as they would say, they were not scared of the police. In Merebank, Ivan himself had learned some ducking and diving, as he calls it, from a bootlegger called Chindeva, who was a local celebrity: He had even spent time in jail for attempted murder because he had attacked a Merebank businessman who, he believed, had set the liquor and drugs police onto him.

Chindeva had helped Ivan once when he, aged eleven, had found his normal way to school over the railway line blocked for some reason. Chindeva had seen the boy looking for a way to cross, and had beckoned him to his nearby house and showed him a way through the basement. A tunnel led from the basement to the other side of the railway line, which Chindeva had built as his escape route from the police.

In Maputo, he had to tell his life story several times. 'They called it your biography. You were made to tell it – and write it – again and again, and your debriefer would try to catch contradictions and gaps that would flash warning lights: that here was an impimpi, a spy.' He dutifully told and retold, wrote and rewrote, but also, uppity as he was, said a whole lot more, too. He criticised the ANC for not being in the country, and harped on about how it should be there. How there should be an underground and how it should be political. How it was not enough to bring in pamphlets and explode a bomb somewhere every now and then. That you were not going to bring the masses along, destroy apartheid and build a new country like that. Very good, they said. Write it down.

Eventually, the veteran Mozambican ANC representative and Umkhonto commander Lennox Lagu – well known for his participation in the joint ZAPU and MK Wankie campaign in Zimbabwe[50] – gave him the struggle name 'Surly'.

He was also taught how to assemble and disassemble a gun.

Good people

They could not get him back into South Africa after these first few weeks in Maputo and Swaziland. It was frustrating to have to stay put in the house to which he had been taken in Swaziland's second town, Manzini, waiting for the sign, for transport, while there was so much work to do. He had to start tightening the network around Durban, bring in more people for training and send them back with clear assignments. Now he was doing nothing for days on end; Nzima tried his best but he could not make the connections.

One day he asked Nzima if they could not just take the car and drive around in the border areas, because there might be South African companies working there. He thought that Roberts Construction might be one of them. Nzima had said of course. After driving for two and a half hours they indeed passed a Roberts Construction site sign. He got off, found the office of the 'mabalans' and asked if, perhaps, one Clifford Mabaso was there.

He was.

On hearing that Ivan needed to get back into South Africa, Clifford Mabaso did not ask questions. He organised a seat for him in the truck that took workers back on fortnightly paydays to their homes in South Africa. At first they considered hiding him in the back of the truck, but in hindsight they were extremely lucky not to have done that. The border agents had shone a torch under the tarpaulin and he would have been discovered. Instead, aware that this was regular transport, that the border agents knew the company and key people, and hoping this would lull official alertness, Mabaso simply collected everybody's passports and took the pile to the immigration office. Ivan walked with the workers and waited at the gate. There, all were handed their stamped passports back by Mabaso, plus a vaccination certificate for Ivan. The empty truck crossed over into South Africa and they all climbed in.

Back in South Africa he felt relief, but also worried even more. It had been a crazy risky plan. What did it mean that, in the fight for South Africa's future, one seemed to have no choice, but to depend sometimes on crazy risky plans?

One lesson was learned from the experience, though: the best, safest connections were with the best, safest people. Clifford Mabaso was not a political activist, but he was a friend and – more importantly – a good man. In turn, Clifford did not question what Ivan was doing, because he had come to know him as a good man too. If you worked with good people, you could get things done. It informed all that he did then, and it still does today.

The wonderful thing was that there were plenty of good people. Often they came from very close by. He linked with his niece Jenny, in Chatsworth, who burst out laughing when she found that the contact she was told to meet in a church was her childhood friend and youthful uncle. 'It's you!' she had squealed in delight, then went on her way with the parcel Ivan had delivered. He also linked up with Krish and talked to Coastal, inviting both to come out because the security police were going to come for them, too, but Coastal was the only son left at home to care for his aging mother and could not go. Coastal was to be arrested and tortured repeatedly after that, with his head put in the toilet and electric shocks to his genitals, but he never betrayed Ivan, Krish, or anybody else.

Krish and he spent some time contacting other possible recruits. 'We were incredibly nervous,' he recalls; if caught, they would not get off lightly. Around Durban they moved from safe house to cheap hotel to cheap hotel, at one point booking into a place to which they did not go, fearing it had been compromised. They then travelled to Johannesburg to meet with Philip Masia, who took them out of the country again, this time through Botswana, to the west, since going back via Swaziland again would be risky.

They could not, of course, avoid all mishaps. Crossing into Botswana, the two Indian youngsters had blackened their faces with stage makeup acquired and applied with the help of an actress Philip knew. They had also donned woollen caps to make themselves look more like migrant labourers. The plan worked well to get across the border. But on the other side, as he was bending over a tap to wash his face, Ivan noticed a pair of boots. Slowly he stood upright. The boots belonged to a policeman. With hearts sunk, terrified they were going to be delivered into South African hands, the two had no choice but to enter the Botswana police vehicle.

Fortunately, held overnight at the Ramatlabama border post, they were able to convince their captors that they were South African refugees and the policemen were amenable to process them as such. 'Do you know anyone here who can vouch for you?' they were asked and, again fortunately, Ivan remembered a Non-European Unity Movement émigré who had set up a shop in a town called Lobatse, 55 kilometres away. The next day they were handed over to the care of the émigré in question and asked to register as refugees.

The two then had to await transfer at a smallholding in Mogoditshane, to the west of the capital. There, they found themselves in the company of about 25 young men – teenagers mostly, some as young as thirteen or fourteen, sleeping on the floors at night. Botswana is hot and dry as it is, but the Mogoditshane farm, located on flat rural land, and with no running water, was suffocating.[51] Boredom and fear pervaded the atmosphere, with the fear exacerbated further when they heard on the radio that Steve Biko had been murdered; it reached fever pitch when, a few days later, the South African minister of police said that he was aware of an 'ANC terror camp' in Mogoditshane.

They implemented a watch roster then, but even those whose turn it was to sleep hardly did. One night, they saw headlights approaching on the sandy road leading to the farm, and all ran out, only partly dressed at most, to hide *in the bushes. Coming back into the house after the danger had passed – it had been a passing car – they discovered that the bushes were prickly and itch-inducing, and they scratched for days.*

At Mogoditshane Krish and Ivan realised that many of the MK recruits were traumatised, petrified boys. Jacob Dlamini, in his book Askari,[52] *would later identify these 'new members of the ANC's military wing from the 1976 generation' as responsible for MK's growth from about a thousand to around nine thousand in that period. The boys, often high school students, had been so terrorised by their arrests, beatings and torture they had experienced, and killings they had witnessed, that they had run from the country, desperate to take up arms. Dlamini describes, partly quoting Ivan, how such youngsters 'lacked (the) life experiences' and 'useful regimes,' to be able to make it as soldiers who could look after themselves and remain stable under pressure.*

The context is used by Dlamini to explain young Glory Sedibe's conversion from a militant youth to a notorious traitor, the askari 'September', the subject of his book and a scourge of the ANC machinery in Swaziland. September's treason would later help the security police abduct and kill comrades.

The term 'lack of useful regimes' makes me think back to the Transkei where the old lady who had recruited me into the ANC told me that the local youngsters needed 'school and politics and books' as well as guns; and that they should not just try to emulate the fighter Chris Hani but also Chris Hani the mature and well-read politician, who emphasised education and lessons from Shakespeare's tragedies. 'Education still doesn't compensate for the lack of growing up in a stable environment,' says Ivan. 'Many children from the uprisings suffered disrupted family life, too. They would never learn to do chores at home, spend time looking after smaller siblings, even hold a weekend job. How were they going to make decisions, plan and implement organisational activities in an underground army? Come to that – presuming they would survive to see liberation – how were they going to build up a new country?'

It was also questionable whether others in the farmhouse were equipped with sufficient stability and core values to mentor and guide the new recruits. Besides Krish and Ivan, there was only one other seasoned activist there.[53] One older man looked like a rough fellow, and used a shard of broken bottle to shave. They suspected he had a criminal background.

For three months they waited for arrangements to travel to Angola for military training. When the call finally came to board the plane they found O.R. Tambo travelling with them. 'It made such an impression,' Ivan recalls. 'You had joined, and waited for so long, and then finally here was the legendary leader. And he was just so nice. He talked to all of us.' In the ANC transit camp called Engineering, their skins were tormented again, this time by very large mosquitoes, not at all deterred by mosquito nets with even larger holes in them. He met Khuzwayo there again, the diamond smuggler in whose house in Maputo he had stayed. In ill-fitting uniforms captured from Unita, they learned basic drill and marching.

After a few days he got the message that he was to go back to Swaziland to receive the contacts he had recruited in South Africa. The recruits would need to be thoroughly debriefed with regard to their life stories. They would also need to familiarise themselves with the ANC's history and politics, its Strategy and Tactics document and other basic literature they would have been unable to get back home. Then their role and tasks would have to be clarified and a work plan agreed to, for which they would need to be given rudimentary but appropriate training.

All this would have to be done within two or three days at most, a long weekend, so as not to raise suspicion in the police state around the recruits' absence. Many South Africans used to go to Swaziland for long weekends: you could party there, mingle across the colour bar, even gamble a bit. They would use these activities as a cover, having the recruits check in at a tourist hotel and at times visit the casino.

He said goodbye to Krish, who would complete his full military training in Luanda, repeat it in the German Democratic Republic, then come back to enlist with MK in Mozambique, Swaziland and the Natal command. The two friends would sometimes meet later, but only when necessary and always very carefully arranged.

Building the underground

The ANC command in Maputo had decided that Joe and Ivan — as he was now called — should declare themselves to the authorities as non-aligned refugees. They did so, received refugee permits, then moved into St Joseph's Mission, a boarding school in Manzini, where Joe had found a job as a teacher. They were to avoid contact with known ANC persons and only to meet with members of their MK unit in secure environments. Such units were to recruit for MK in South Africa, send in trained cadres, weapons and explosives, and carry out armed attacks. Nzima — who would later run a number of informants within the security police — was assigned to the ANC's Security and Intelligence unit.

Ivan still felt that a focus on military action was not enough. The ANC needed to create a political underground that would popularise the movement, he thought, inter alia by communicating the ANC's positions in response to the events of the day. The underground should guide the mass democratic struggle inside the country, while also shielding and assisting the MK operatives in the police state. He had communicated these views verbally and in writing on every occasion when he was debriefed in Swaziland, Mozambique, Botswana, Zambia and Angola. He continued to put them to the relevant structures. No doubt, others also did so. Sunny Singh certainly did.

Two years later when in Angola to undergo the military training that had previously been cut short, he was visited by MK headquarters member Cassius Maake, who was also in the ANC's National Executive Committee (NEC), and in the Revolutionary Council, which was in charge of all operations. Maake told him that there was to be a new structure, called the IPRC – the Internal Political Reconstruction Committee – that would set up a political underground. Sunny Singh was to join the relevant unit in Mozambique and Ivan the equivalent unit in Swaziland. He was to return at once.

The IPRC was to 'insert the ANC into the lives of South Africans', as Ivan put it. The cadres would paint slogans, distribute leaflets and pamphlets. They would operate in civil society organisations and recruit others, then form cells that would function under the command and control of the ANC. They would also recruit new cadres for MK, as well as build infrastructure for MK and support its operations. When it was formed, the IPRC mirrored the four regional military commands: urban and rural Natal, and urban and rural Transvaal. Each region was now covered by both a military and a political structure.

Since Swaziland was a small place, they would run into each other, like Ivan often did with Nzima. He also became good friends with Archie Whitehead, who was in the Transvaal political command of the IPRC. Nevertheless, with the military and the political sectors connecting vertically, but in silos, to their own hierarchies in Maputo and Lusaka, there was still little synergy. This was understandable in terms of protection against information leakages and penetration by the South African security forces, but it was also a problem. Sometimes they really needed to put political, intelligence, underground and military heads together to increase impact of a specific operation, or to build a connection with a mass protest.

Although the establishment of an underground infrastructure in the police state was welcome, he did not think that creating the IPRC as a new structure in itself was the best solution. The lack of synergy still remained between the military and the political, as well as between these and other functions. This was not addressed partly because the ANC would rather leave what already existed in place and preferred to graft on a new structure on the side.

'We always do this,' he will reflect later. 'When something is not working properly we set up something new. Even nowadays, instead of fixing the hospitals, we think up a health insurance system. You end up with several structures requiring even more coordination. Eventually it can all become hugely dysfunctional.'

Despite these complications, together they started building a lasting underground capacity of comrades in South Africa who had day jobs and a limited political profile; who lived in the country legally and, therefore, could successfully pass most scrutiny. In that way, they had huge advantages over those who were sent into the country without any legal status or home base.

Decades later, reading a book about the resistance against the Nazis in Holland, I come across the case of a woman who had had to shoot a collaborating policeman on her doorstep, because he was about to discover a Jewish child hiding inside. To get rid of the man's body, she ran to the baker in the next street who had a van. The two of them had then carried the body in the van to the local undertaker, who was the baker's friend. They put the corpse in a coffin together with another departed soul who was about to be cremated. Both were burned together and nobody was the wiser, least of all the grieving family of the person who had received company.[54] *'It is precisely such situations you were dealing with,' Ivan comments, then. 'They were not all so dramatic, but all successful work needed such rooted infrastructure.'*

The regional chair of the IPRC, Jacob Zuma, operated from Maputo, but Ivan did not see much of him except at meetings. There were always queues of people outside his apartment, subordinates who needed to talk to him personally. 'Though he wasn't actually royalty, he always behaved like he was,' Ivan says. 'He had "subjects," hundreds of individuals, and he dealt with all on a one-to-one basis.' It was very different from the way Judson and Shadrack operated, and the two usually kept their distance from him.

The tightened connections with South Africa on one occasion had the effect of thwarting a large-scale infiltration attempt by the security police, which had got its hooks into a project called Maluti, the mountain, an initiative from Winnie Mandela to form a legal pro-ANC organisation inside South Africa. A two-person delegation from Winnie – it turned out that she, unaware of the infiltration, had indeed sanctioned their mission – had come to Swaziland to ask the ANC for its go ahead to set this up. But Nzima had sounded the alarm: he had information that the entire project had been leaked to the security police. The most likely source of the leak was one of the two members of the delegation, whom Ivan calls X: a person who was then in the national leadership of the Congress of South African Students, COSAS.

Now aware that this was most likely a trap, 'we decided to stretch out the discussions with the two persons so that in the meanwhile we could persuade X "to go to Angola for training",' he recalls. 'As we had expected, since the security police would be happy with the opportunity to infiltrate ANC camps and perhaps MK, X readily agreed. He was taken across to Maputo and told to wait there for a 'flight to Angola'.' By pure coincidence, however, some weeks later, while attending a workshop in Maputo with Shadrack Maphumulo, Ivan had found X in the same flat where he and Shadrack were accommodated. Checking with relevant structures, he found that X was still not aware that the ANC knew that he was an infiltrator.

Shadrack was not aware either, which meant that he 'liaised with X normally, in his usual commissar mode, which was somewhere between a political mentor and a counsellor. During the next few days, every evening, after the daily workshop sessions, Shadrack would have deep discussions with X – about politics, but also life in general. On the fourth night, X confessed to Shadrack that he had been sent by the enemy.' It is possible, Ivan considers, that the approach might not have worked with a seasoned spy. 'X was probably a newish informer, still conscious that he was doing something wrong and stressed about it. But Shadrack could get most people to take to him like that.' Since X had confessed even without being confronted, he was not incarcerated and, after training, he was deployed in the logistics department of the ANC in Angola.[55]

They worked from person to person, on the basis of personal acquaintance with and recommendations by tried and tested comrades. One such new member was Elvis Govender, a youngster in his early twenties. He had crossed the border illegally, was trained over three weeks, then crossed back into South Africa to go home. He was eager and brave – I will later learn that he had asked Ivan for an RPG[56] 'to take down the Merebank oil refinery' – and also a bit of a hippie: Ivan was puzzled to find, after a few days visiting him in his quarters while in Swaziland, a lot of little silver foil cones attached to the ceiling. Upon closer inspection he had found these were little, improvised, marijuana pipes.

But dagga and all, Elvis in his underground cell[57] worked well and remained undetected, save for one time when he had a car accident while transporting a roneo machine. With his damaged car and roneo machine on the side of the road, he was fortunately not encountered by police but by another comrade.[58] The comrade knew Elvis, saw the roneo machine, drew the correct conclusion, and ensured that roneo, car and Elvis were removed to a safe place where the injured youngster received appropriate care.

Others weren't so lucky. Every now and then, they heard that someone did not come back from 'inside', or about a comrade killed, wounded, or arrested. He felt the losses were too high. In guerrilla warfare, the enemy losses are supposed to be greater than your own. But they rarely got any more than the stock response: 'You don't know what losses the enemy is experiencing.'

Ships that pass in the night

While trying to avoid the authorities, it helped sometimes to work with others who were also trying to find ways around apartheid law enforcement. Smugglers, for example, were good at getting vehicles across the border and making them untraceable. One of these comrades who could access stolen vehicles was called 'General' because of his daring exploits.[59] Another was Paulus, the son of trusted car mechanic Baba Nsibande, who serviced vehicles for Ivan and Judson.

In 1979, father and son Nsibande had helped to get the ANC's Stephen Lee out of the country after a sensational escape, together with Tim Jenkin and Alex Moumbaris, from Pretoria Central Prison.[60] 'We spent hours with Baba Nsibande and his son in planning Lee's extraction, trying to ensure that every risk was identified and managed. Eventually the two said that we must just relax. They would do it, they said. And they did.'

Ivan and I went to Swaziland after 1990, to look up Baba. 'Such a nice man, Baba,' he reminisces then. 'His other son stole my car once.' He hastens to explain that Baba had been very angry at the young man for that, and very embarrassed and apologetic, too. 'The Swazi police followed up and I got the car back.' Having found a trigger mechanism for an incendiary device in the boot and – erroneously – thinking that this was left there by the car thieves instead of by Ivan, the policemen reported the find to him. 'I told them I was shocked.'

Discussing the implications of using criminals, Ivan emphasises that 'most comrades were ethical, moral people' and that encountering criminals was like 'ships passing in the night'. He tells the story of a rendezvous in a Swazi border area that was disturbed by the sudden sound of a truck engine firing up on the South African side. 'We were with Pravin Gordhan and another two comrades[61] from his underground unit, waiting for transport to take them back to Durban, hiding in the bush, careful not to make a sound. When the noise started, we almost jumped, fearing that we had been discovered. But then truck lights flicked on, and we saw it reverse towards the border fence. Simultaneously on the Swazi side a truck was backing towards the fence, too. When positioned back to back, men on the South African side started to throw bags from their vehicle onto the Swazi truck. Then it hit us: they were vegetable smugglers!'

Swaziland had then just restricted vegetable imports from South Africa due to a cholera outbreak arising from floods. 'The smugglers must have bought off the border guards because they were not even trying to be quiet. Fortunately, everybody there kept their cool.'

There were also mistakes, clumsy arrangements and risks taken that could have been avoided. Archie, who was in time to join Operation Vula, would later tell stories about undercover mishaps like wigs falling off, thick makeup running down faces in the heat or moustaches falling in glasses. It would also happen that when meeting clandestinely, quite often, comrades who were supposed to act as if they did not know one another, could not help winking or surreptitiously waving. Or someone would simply be left at the border fence in the middle of the night because someone else had not remembered the collection time accurately, or had forgotten about the whole thing altogether. It was all extremely dangerous and nerve-wrecking and possibly disastrous, but also funny. When Archie started telling these stories he would have comrades rolling on the floor in no time.

More seriously however, underlying the faults and hiccups and mistakes was a lack of preparedness. 'Even if the cadres were formally trained,' Ivan says, 'sometimes the trainings weren't appropriate for police state conditions. Also there was often a lack of maturity; nowadays you'd call it emotional intelligence. Comrades like Shadrack Maphumulo and Judson Kuzwayo were mature, but there were not enough Shadracks and Judsons to mentor this new generation.' He often thought that the country, when liberated, would be impacted by the large number of scarred adults.

***

In spite of all the challenges, the community of comrades in Swaziland by now almost felt like a family. There were Pat, Jabu and their children, three daughters and one baby boy; Shadrack and his wife; Judson and his wife Beauty and their young daughter Fezeka. Joe still lived and worked as a teacher at St Joseph's College. At some point, Ivan would move out of those premises: His refugee permit withdrawn without explanation, he was now in hiding and moved between safe houses, but the connection with St Joseph's remained. They had made friends among Dutch, British and American expats teaching at the University of Swaziland too: they all abhorred apartheid and were happy to help the ANC underground.[62]

Sister, Mother, Jenny and other family members – often Angie's daughters, Kogie, Sendi, Prani and little Seshni too – kept visiting come Christmas time. In the beginning they would come to St Joseph's to see 'the boys': they got to know the community there and contributed whatever they could, bringing food and doing much cooking. Later, with Ivan no longer there, and with police activity intensified, they started meeting in holiday chalets.

The visits were much needed and welcome on both sides. They offered at least a brief respite from missing and worrying about the boys; the boys themselves found breathing space from the unrelenting pressure. They tried their best to attract as little attention as possible, making such occasions look as much as a normal South African family holiday getaway as they could. But, again, they couldn't guard against all dangers. In 1987, seventeen-year-old Sendi caught malaria during one of their reunions in Zimbabwe. Back home, it was misdiagnosed, and not treated, and the girl died as a result. Her picture – long black hair, soft sweet face, smiling, with a book in bed in the holiday chalet where they met then – is still on Ivan's desk.

Ghosts on the road to Ndola
December 1990

Dusk is falling around us and I am worried about the long drive ahead on this narrow and unlit road, which requires nimble driving to avoid potholes. We are to attend a wedding in Ndola, 300 kilometres north of Lusaka. Comrade Goldberg, who named himself after Rivonia trialist Dennis Goldberg and works for the South African Communist Party (SACP), is preparing for a future back home with his fiancée Jowela, a Zambian seamstress. I have agreed to the outing because it is, well, an outing. We can do with one. But there are no shops or petrol stations anywhere around here. And as it gets darker all around the winding road, the telephone poles that lean skew, with loose hanging cables, start to look less like telephone poles and more like tentacled shadows.

There are long minutes of silence as we drive in the dark, with fog steaming out of the fields and an increasing number of shadow formations and mysteriously shaped objects appearing on the side of the road. I recall Conny Braam saying – in a conversation about southern African border zones – that even running into a South African Defence Force soldier would be a refreshingly solid experience compared to other scary encounters one might have there.

I mention that in medieval times the Dutch believed that whiffs of white fog on the fields were dancing witches and Ivan laughs: 'If you were a Zambian you'd believe in ghosts and witches, too. Many powers around here are intangible and untraceable to the common citizen.'

As we drive past more dark shapes of crooked trees and loose telephone wires dangling in the fog, I think of witches' victims. Those who were tortured and still live with the nightmares, those who were hanged and massacred, the burned women. At least in South Africa, the history has been written. The witches have names. There will be a reckoning, I think. It will be a just and non-violent one, since the ANC rejects violent revenge and wants to bring human rights violators to legitimate courts – but it will happen, hopefully soon.

In Ndola there is cake on plastic tables under umbrellas outside on a lawn, and a speech by the father of the bride, who says that he and his wife 'entrust their daughter to this young man and his movement', to go forward to 'a brighter future in South Africa'. Jowela herself walks around in an enormous white dress with an equally enormous white bow on her back, looking rather serious. I mustn't think that she is unhappy though, says Ivan. He has met and talked with Goldberg and Jowela, back in Lusaka, and they are really eager to make a life together in South Africa and full of hope.

She is, I think, probably also happy to get out of Ndola.

Ndola was once a vibrant town, the centre of the copper belt, full of bling and wealth. Then, suddenly copper prices fell and Ndola suffered, as had the rest of the country, with its lack of manufacturing capacity. The Kaunda government, which ran the nationalised mines, still battled on, but there was not much success and most people in Ndola were back to rather unshiny poverty, the town a dilapidated ghost of its former self.

Would Zambians blame the trauma of the copper belt on President

Kaunda or on witches, I ask Ivan on the way back. 'I don't know what the people in Ndola think', is the answer. 'But why do you think Kaunda is always waving that trademark white handkerchief of his?'

Bombing the Republic

Witches and ghosts was why no one had opened the door for him and Joe, way back in 1977 when they had walked through the fields on the Swazi side, after crossing the border. Witches would come for you at night. You stayed in bed, with everything – even windows – tightly shut, hoping to see the morning. The young men had slept in the veld then, and brushed off the burned grass from their duffel coats as well as they could, before finding a bus to Manzini: the kind of bus that had lots of bags on top, and chickens and goats. Witches or no witches, you simply carried on.

Witches, or rather the belief that you are powerless against them, would bother them on another occasion again, much later, when Sunny Singh had to be taken by comrades from Swaziland to Mozambique once. He had arrived almost at his destination when a deer jumped over the road from left to right, or from right to left, Ivan can't remember which. The event had been interpreted as a bad omen by the comrades in the mission, who had promptly turned back and delivered Sunny where he had come from. Sunny had been fuming.

Nevertheless, over the years, the political-military fight against the enemy started taking shape. Increasingly, attacks on police stations were accompanied simultaneously by the release of pamphlets, or coincided with protests in the communities around these stations, such as in Soekmekaar, where a community resisted forced removals. In June 1980, Sasol, a facility that converted coal to petrol and diesel, lost eight storage tanks to an MK attack.

Apartheid forces retaliated, of course. On 30 January 1981, the South African Defence Force raided a safe house in Matola, close to Maputo, assassinating twelve ANC members, among whom was Krish Rabilal.

Then slightly more than two weeks after the death of Ivan's best friend, Nzima informed him that a South African Security Branch team was on its way to Swaziland to kidnap comrades. He had obtained a list with the names of a number of them, including the Pillay brothers. That afternoon, Ivan met Joe at a rendezvous point and passed on the warning. Joe, however, shrugged it off: having become more involved with teaching and less with armed activities, he assumed that he would be safe.

It was a mistake. They went for Joe anyway – perhaps because it was too difficult to get Ivan, who was always changing houses, never telling anyone where he was or was going to be. (He still acts to avoid risk, all the time, instructing our daughters and me to be alert for this, that and the other, even when just going to the cinema in the mall. He checks everything about the car, tyres, water, oil, every time we go somewhere. Any unexpected noise or movement seen, anywhere, anytime, must be quickly checked out, too. We indulge him, smile and shake our heads. But it may have saved us, too, from bad fates on dark roads, who knows?)

When they knocked at the door of the cottage at St Josephs in Mzimpofu, it immediately struck Joe that these were the security policemen Ivan had warned him about. He cleverly outwitted them at first, saying he would take them to 'Joe', but instead led them to the home of close colleague, David Manyatsi, who was a Swazi. But once the door opened and Joe posed his question to David, the visitors realised that they were being played. They grabbed Joe and bundled him into the boot of their vehicle.

During the scuffle witnessed by David Manyatsi,[63] *one of the attackers fortunately lost his dompas. Ironically, the apartheid-era ID for Africans was still obligatory, even for black members of death squads on their missions.*

While an international campaign by the Swazi-based expat comrades mobilised Amnesty International and progressive forces in the Netherlands, Nzima worked his contacts to find out more about the man who had dropped the dompas. Then David Manyatsi, walking in Manzini, recognised another one of the kidnappers. He turned out to be Mozambican, a member of the South African-supported Renamo movement that collaborated with the apartheid security forces. Nzima and Manyatsi succeeded in getting the Swazi police to arrest him. After a few weeks, and a hushed swap arrangement, a blindfolded Joe was taken out of his cell, bundled into the boot of a car, driven into Swaziland and unloaded onto a dark street in Mbabane in the middle of the night.

How did Ivan still carry on after losing Krish, and having endured weeks of fear for Joe's life? Maybe he was even more determined, his body running on adrenaline? 'Are you sure that it was only two weeks in between? It feels like it was a much longer time,' he answers when I ask about these events. Later, he will tell me how, at times of pressure, he has a habit of slowing down, going through the seconds and the minutes very deliberately, one breath, one step, one thought at the time.

I know it now, too. Whether there is a traffic emergency, a tray of dishes falls, or a child scrapes her knee, I mustn't shout, or make any quick moves or panicky suggestions, or do anything to break his focus. He is set to handle it.

Others who experienced similar losses and anxiety somehow pulled through as well. Ninety political MK attacks rocked South Africa in 1981, the year of mobilisation against the twentieth anniversary of the apartheid republic. Celebrating the two decades since 1961 when South Africa declared itself a republic, it was to be a year of flags and anthems in white schools, of cadet training for white boys, speeches by President Balthazar John Vorster, and parties in white dorpies and suburbs. But between April and November, police stations, power lines, railway targets, military bases and recruiting offices were reduced to rubble.

'*In that year we got it right. The political message was clear: We were attacking the apartheid republic as it celebrated itself. We had started working well together with MK, particularly with a commander, Inkululeko, who was running a network of legal military cadres inside the country.*'

The ANC attacked symbols of apartheid that affected people's everyday lives: the Indian Affairs building in Durban and the Bantu pass office in Langa, Cape Town. Voortrekkerhoogte, the military base in Pretoria, was hit in August. Just into the next year, on the ANC's birthday on 8 January 1982, the Koeberg nuclear plant was attacked, too.

In June that year they murdered Pat and Jabu, with explosives wired to their car. Comrades took their four children home to relatives in Pietermaritzburg. They mourned briefly, but there wasn't time to fully digest or feel, there never was.

What did you do, I ask, just close yourself up again?

Yes.

He did not rage about such things. The enemy struck back, he says. What else does one expect?

He spent some time inside the country the following year, linking up with UDF comrades, extending the political ANC underground. 'We had people. Combatants inside. We were moving disjointedly, but we were moving.'

Wanted

Suddenly, it was all-out war. On 16 March 1984, the Frelimo government in Mozambique, succumbing to growing South African pressure, signed an armistice known as the Nkomati Accord. The agreement limited the number of ANC people in Mozambique first to eight, then just to a small ANC chief representative's office. Non-combatants were hurriedly moved to Zambia, but most involved in the armed struggle, including MK regional commanders, flooded into Swaziland.

Inevitably, the large number of MK combatants in the small country was noticed by both South African agents and Swazi security forces, who were now actively working with the South African regime in the fight against the ANC. Sporadic firefights erupted. Newspapers requested their readers to report suspicious activities, such as large numbers of males living together, staying indoors during the day and only moving out at night. Impimpis were so many that, according to one interviewee in Jacob Dlamini's book Askari, *'we were running away from impimpis instead of them running away from us.'*

South Africans suspected of ANC activity were arrested, detained and interrogated, sometimes in the presence of the South African security police, and thereafter deported to Tanzania. Scores of ANC members who had legal residence papers were detained for a while in Mawelawela, an old army camp. Among them were also Shadrack Maphumulo and fellow IPRC member Chief Mampuru, who were still registered UN refugees.

Of the many wanted photographs published in all newspapers during that time Ivan still has one – a full page with a dozen pictures, including one of him: all dark and sunglassed, a terrorist. Theophilus 'Viva' Dlodlo, of the Transvaal underground machinery, was on it too, and Siphiwe Nyanda of MK, also called Gebuza, whose brother Zwelakhe had been assassinated by a security police squad the year before.

Ivan had taken to sleeping with a pistol and a hand grenade on a nightstand next to his bed by then. He intended to take a few of them with him, to ensure they couldn't take him alive, ensure that he couldn't talk and betray others. Perhaps the suffocating nightmares started then, too. They are gone now, but he still wakes up when a leaf brushes the window, or when I stir.

The retaliatory assassination of a high-ranking local policeman, a Colonel Hlubi who was notorious for working with the South African security branch, worried the Swazi forces.[64] *Several Swazi policemen approached ANC members they knew to plead for their safety. 'By pure coincidence, Baba Nsibande knew the new commissioner of police, Majaji Simelane. Early one Sunday, Baba and I drove up to his house unannounced. When we knocked at the door, the commissioner was in his dressing gown. He started to tremble visibly when he saw us, and quickly ushered us in. We sat down and I then told him that since our fight was not with the Swazis, MK and the Swazi police needed to reach an understanding. He quickly agreed to our proposal that both* sides should hold back our forces, and Baba would be our go-between. The whole discussion took less than an hour. When we parted he begged me to not give his address to our cadres.'

Upon leaving, they drove away sedately until they were out of sight, then floored the accelerator.

A period of calm ensued, even if it was short lived. Simelane was dismissed when there was a shift in Swazi politics and repression intensified again.

Another blow came in 1985 in the form of a traffic accident. Some comrades suspected foul play, but Ivan says that the car crash that killed Judson Kuzwayo in Zimbabwe probably really was an accident. Nobody ever provided any evidence to the contrary. It was nevertheless another personal loss of a good friend.

Asked again what he did to deal with the fear and pain of death that was there every moment of every day and night, Ivan still can't think of much. 'But other guys drank too much, partied, had dalliances with young girls,' I prod, having been informed of this by Totsie, who had shrugged as she told me about the men, including her own, doing these things. 'Of course they would always deny it, saying they had merely gone to secret revolutionary meetings, but we knew better. We just carried on,' she added, with a look that said women always just carry on: it's the way things are.

'I heard about parties,' he says. 'But you know, I tend to limit public exposure. I watched sports on Saturdays, with Archie.'

In early 1986 Ivan was to spend three months in South Africa where, in many instances the situation still threatened 'to run away from us', as he puts it. Street committees and self-defence units in townships were chasing suspected impimpis and engaging in necklacing. MK combatants who had been sent to liaise with local comrades found themselves drawn into such battles, too. Moreover, the so-called Third Force created mayhem in Johannesburg, Natal and Cape Town. But in spite of all the mishaps and obstacles, the underground in the country was growing, and the ANC cadres who were rooted in communities were by now well connected with the UDF. Ivan met key individuals, listened to everything, read everything. In those pre-internet days there were many things you could only know if you got your information directly from inside.

'I did not know it then,' Ivan remarks, 'but the stay was good preparation for my work in Vula.'

While still preparing to travel inside, he had been contacted by Chris Hani, who requested that on his return he travel to Lusaka as soon as possible, but *didn't tell him what it was about. When he arrived in Lusaka in August that year, he was told that he was appointed as the Operation Vula coordinator.*

Days of September

Ivan was in Lusaka when, on 12 December 1986, Shadrack Maphumulo was kidnapped, shot and beaten so hard that he died in a police van en route to South Africa. Shards and snippets of news about other abductions and assassinations followed. Comrades were being killed like flies now. In many cases this was because of Glory Sedibe, known as September, the former head of MK's Transvaal structure who had turned askari after having been kidnapped. His treason — rumoured to have come about rather easily — enabled the security police to almost completely destabilise the Swazi-based underground.

Three days after Shadrack's murder, on 15 December 1986, IPRC Swaziland head and Zuma deputy Ebrahim Ebrahim and two colleagues were abducted, then jailed on Robben Island. Then in May 1987, Viva Dlodlo was murdered in an ambush in Manzini, together with two passengers in his car. In July it was the turn of Paul Dikeledi and Cassius Maake. On 8 June 1988, MK cadres Lindiwe Mthembu, Makhosi Nyoka, Lenny Naidu and Ntsiki Cothoza were shot dead when their car was ambushed near the border town of Piet Retief. A little later that month Phumla Williams, who went by the struggle name Flo, was arrested while underground in Soweto. She would later recall that, alighting from a minibus, she had seen September among the plainclothes men who dragged her into a security police vehicle

Phumla survived. I will meet her later. I will also learn later that Lenny Naidu, one of the four murdered in Piet Retief, had been the boyfriend of Ivan's niece, Prani.

In July 1988 they kidnapped, tortured and then executed Emmanuel Mzimela; in October that year Phila Portia Ndwandwe was also executed, the young courier who would later be known for making herself panties from a blue plastic bag she found in the police cell where she had been kept naked. Neither Emmanuel nor Phila Ndwandwe had talked under torture. 'That was a brave one,' one of Phila's executors would later recall before the Truth and Reconciliation Commission (TRC). Totsie had met her even if she didn't know her well. 'She did the same work as I. I kept thinking: that could have been me.'

We visited Swaziland, later in the nineties, with Joe and the family, Kogie and her husband Dhavan, Suggie, Sister, Jenny and our young daughters. *We would drive around towns and Ivan would point: There is this flat. There is that flat. I stayed in that yard once. Our girls were a bit bored. What was this pointing at buildings for? The flats were mostly greyish and unimpressive. Asked what it was all about, he had not – would not – evoke the bad things that had happened, the killings, the disappearances, the fear. But he had spoken, as he still does, of Shadrack, and Judson, and Pat and Jabu, Krishna, Indres, Sunny and Archie and the alliance of black, white, coloured and Indian that existed, that fought for justice, in the face of much fear, pain, death and sorrow, in the underground.*

South Africa, 2020

As we live the post-apartheid years we wonder what happened to those values. Why are white comrades, who have been comrades all their lives, suddenly called white again, and 'Stratcom',[65] and 'Monopoly Capital'? Why are corrupt black politicians protecting themselves by pointing fingers at other races? Why are dubious white and Indian businessmen suddenly better friends of the ANC than Indian and white struggle comrades from the trenches? Why is the bantustan puppet Lucas Mangope mourned by the ANC when he finally kicks the bucket,?

Ivan tries to explain – 'as far as I understand it' – what happened to the ANC. 'Firstly, the leadership of the Congress alliance was decimated in the sixties. In exile, there were mainly leaders from that sixties' generation who had not been in the country for decades, and many of whom were really not in touch with what was happening there. Then after 1976, thousands of high school and university students came, all of that generation that had experienced massive violence and disruption. We in the ANC found ourselves with an acute lack of experienced middle cadre throughout the late seventies and eighties.'

For the post-1990 period, this meant that a very large but poorly managed ANC came back into South Africa where it still had little internal organisation. 'We had worked hard to bring it all together, particularly under Vula, but it was perhaps too little, too late. Then, all of a sudden in 1992, the newly legal ANC claims a million new members. Where do these members come from? They may be very eager and well meaning, but they have certainly not grown up in the ANC. At the same time, many of the organisations' most senior leaders are aging and frail. How do you expect this concoction to speedily grow into an effective mass organisation and still remain true to its original values and principles, in the midst of the chaos and hurt in the country? No business organisation would consent to grow its employee base or even its customer base from say fifty thousand to one million in a year or two.'

The internal disarray would necessarily impact on the ANC's capacity to take over the government. 'The ANC in exile had some good organisers but not nearly enough. The idea that the exile structures were akin to a government-in-waiting was ludicrous; it was a fragmented and rather small bureaucracy. In South Africa itself, how many black people had experience in designing and running public administration? The UDF and the unions had capable organisers, but the people with experience in managing government institutions were collaborators. Apartheid, mostly, kept black people from running anything at all.'

I think of Shadrack Maphumulo, who wanted to manage a taxi business and a shop, but who was stopped from doing either by the regime's rules and officials. I mention him and Ivan nods. 'You could say that apartheid actively worked to *not* prepare black people for power. Nonetheless, if we honestly acknowledged the gap, we would have made more progress. But we pretended we could do it all and we consequently stopped learning.'

He still carries Krish's picture, has put it on the wall in every office in which he has worked, SARS being the most recent; now it is displayed in his study at home. He wrote a newspaper article about Pat and Jabu Msomi,[66] and requested that they be considered for medals, an effort that was successful in 2015 when Pat and Jabu, through their daughters Lindiwe and Ntombenhle, posthumously received the Silver Order of Luthuli.[67]

He has also kept close to Beauty Kuzwayo and, of course, young Fezeka, through the years, until Fezeka died, and then until, three years later, Beauty died.[68]

And to Rae.

Rae
1978–1990

Rae had been there too: a hero and a victim like so many. She lived and worked with Ivan from 1979 in Swaziland, at St Josephs, then in a series of safe houses and flats, and later for about a year in Zambia. Whatever he did, he did with her, for years, he says, but they had become estranged as danger and loss surrounded them. She had developed paranoia, sometimes perceiving even close comrades as threats.

They had met when he had come to help her, a comrade needing to exit illegally over the border. Recruited by Judson Kuzwayo, and part of the underground ANC network, she had been exposed after the arrest of a contact and needed to leave urgently. Remarkably, she had had no problem doing the risky work, or even leaving her family. This was unlike many women – especially in the close-knit Indian community – who were counted upon to keep family households, businesses and traditions together and going. There was a certain rogueness in her too, in that way.

Ivan often says that those who join the struggle are often not 'normal', in the sense of 'not average'. An average person can certainly be concerned about injustice, but most well-adjusted, functional citizens have such strong ties to family, education and work that they will seldom abandon it all for an uncertain existence in an unknown place. Even less so when there is physical danger involved. 'We are all a bit crazy,' he said once and I had asked him what was crazy about him, other than being monosyllabic and always awake and suffering from stomach ailments. He laughed and said that he was on the other end of the spectrum: so normal that it was crazy again.

For a long time, Rae had remained stoic throughout the weapons handling, the transports, the fear, the killing around them. But eventually, something gave way. Maybe the trigger was the hand grenade that had exploded in her hand during military training in Angola, some time in 1982. She recovered from the injuries but had experienced immense pain. Some pieces of shrapnel in her body had not been removed, and she had had to be operated on again in Swaziland.

They would move together to Lusaka in 1986, for Ivan to coordinate Operation Vula from there. By 1988, however, it was decided she should be moved to a safe environment, away from threats and risks. She was taken to live with relatives in Zimbabwe and once the ANC was unbanned in 1990, arrangements were made for her to return home to South Africa.

He felt guilty because she had been so damaged. Being a woman, she had had more obstacles to overcome than he had; being taken seriously, trusted and respected was already much more difficult for her. 'I always felt I should have done more to help,' he says.

Vula
1986–1990

Jacob Zuma played no direct role in Operation Vula, that has to be made clear. Ivan still gets irritated when journalists write that. Vula was led by O.R. Tambo. Joe Slovo was the second in command.[69]

The ANC's National Executive Committee had given Tambo and Slovo the mandate to send high-calibre leaders into the country as early as 1985. The two had appointed Mac Maharaj as the head of the first contingent. He was to go in together with MK's Gebuza, Siphiwe Nyanda. They were to be joined by others.[70] *From 1986, those who were to be based in the police state had been taken in several batches to the Netherlands, and provided with disguises by Conny Braam's network.*

Conny, through friends in the very wide Dutch anti-apartheid movement, had immediately and efficiently accessed all sorts of helpful skills: from theatre people who specialised in makeup and costumes for the disguises, to craftspeople who made small bags with small compartments to conceal things, to a stewardess who would carry the computer discs needed to set up the communications in South Africa. A dentist was to work on comrades' teeth to make them look different. Vula communications operative Lucia had had all her teeth pulled out and replaced by implants. Conny Braam tells the story that, to those who felt that was taking the good cause a bit far, Lucia would respond that 'at least I got all my teeth done for free'.

Lucia was to be based in Lusaka, close to Ivan, to take charge of the post office. She would route encrypted communications between Lusaka, Johannesburg, Amsterdam and London: always with a detour, never directly between Zambia and South Africa.[71] *Messages from O.R. and Slovo, communicated to her by Ivan, would reach the inside operatives through computer whiz Tim Jenkin in London; the messages from inside would also first go to London and from there back to Lucia, Ivan, Slovo and O.R.*

The communications were crucial. 'Mac had determined from the beginning that the key to success would be a modern computerised messaging system. He and his wife Zarina worked with Tim Jenkin to develop it.' From 1986, the early versions used electronic bulletin boards; later, digitally encoded messages were sent to and from call boxes. The signals would be received and copied on tape at the call box and later decrypted. Similarly encrypted messages were sent to predetermined public call boxes in South Africa.[72] *In South Africa, a satellite mobile phone was later used for greater control and security.*

Mac, who was the most senior high profile leader to go in, had had to create his cover story first. He was purported to be seriously ill and was sent to Moscow for 'long term medical attention'. When the time came to enter South Africa, Mac and Gebuza, who had both travelled from Europe under false papers, were met by Ivan and Totsie in Manzini, Swaziland. Mac had been made to look fatter with padding, and was fitted with a wig; Siphiwe had adopted a dignified grey old man look, with wigs, false moustache and beard (with the option of later taking all that hair off again and dressing differently, looking then like 'a young coloured' as he would put it). Totsie had taken them to be ordinary cadres, but had at some point suddenly recognised Mac's voice. She says she nearly had a heart attack then.

Of course, something still went wrong. The border transport team from inside South Africa did not turn up to a preparatory meeting in Manzini. After some head scratching and deliberating, they resolved to wait while Totsie and Ivan went to the border area and talked to their contacts to see what the security situation was. They confirmed that the selected day and time was in fact the end of the month, and border patrol soldiers would all have gone into the nearest town to cash their pay cheques. They should cross during the day, as originally planned. Mac said he was determined to go ahead, and so was Gebuza.

In Manzini, Ivan called on an Irishman called Kieran, with whom they had linked on occasion when in need of a safe house, and on Dutchman André Ravesloot, who had been placed in Swaziland to support the ANC. Both, approached for help, agreed. Being white and legal, they crossed the border separately with no problem. One travelled ahead to signal any danger. The other moved to the pick-up point for Mac and Gebuza on the South African side to drive them to their destinations.

Having come back safely after crossing the two men over the fence and handing them over, Totsie felt relieved. Surely the hardest part was over now. She and Ivan drove back to the Swazi capital Mbabane, then to the airport, from where they were to fly out to Zimbabwe. But, when queueing at immigration, the official, seeing their passports, sternly remarked that he would have to arrest Ivan. 'I almost jumped out of my skin,' she recalls. 'I did not know whether to start running or crying.' Fortunately, she did neither; she simply froze as she heard Ivan quietly ask why. 'Because you are taking our beautiful country's beautiful daughter away from us,' the official merrily joked.[73]

To this day, Totsie says, she can't get how Ivan can 'always be so calm and dry'.

'It is that thing of slowing down,' he repeats. 'I just start to see everything in slow motion.' He remembers how Totsie was still trembling after the plane had taken off, and for quite a while afterwards.

※ ※ ※

As Vula took root in South Africa, 'O.R. was kept informed of whatever the regime was trying to discuss with Madiba in prison. Mandela, in turn, was also able to make inputs to Tambo and the National Executive in the preparatory talks about talks.' Mandela was also sent information the apartheid authorities were likely to keep from him, like the Harare Declaration, the Organisation for African Unity document that urged South Africa to abandon apartheid and embark on a democratic process, he adds. 'It is therefore not true, as is sometimes alleged, that the white government talked with Mandela alone. Lusaka did know what was happening there, and Mandela knew what Lusaka thought. Make no mistake, O.R. was in charge.'

Lucia guarded the communications in her well-hidden house, away from the ANC community in Lusaka, sometimes literally with her life. Once, at night, she had noticed noises: burglars, kabalala, were approaching, rustling around in the yard. They had even whispered: 'kabalala, we are the kabalala', in an attempt to scare her into letting them take what they wanted. But she had taken a machine gun and started shooting out of the window, shouting at them that if they were kabalala they could die for all she cared. They ran away.

Lucia would later tell us how after Vula was broken and the security police were on the prowl, she had to burn notes with instructions from O.R. and had done so with tears in her eyes, but had still saved a few because she simply couldn't destroy them all.

Ivan too still cherishes what Vula did. 'At a crucial moment in our history, Vula brought coherence to the political underground and alignment with the mass struggle. The communications broke through Mandela's isolation and provided important links between the ANC and the internal democratic forces.' Then the watershed announcement of 2 February 1990 came, even though he had not expected Mandela's release and the ANC's unbanning so soon. 'Vula strengthened our position in the negotiations process that was about to start.'

Months later, the arrests of some of Vula's operatives would be used by the apartheid government to accuse the ANC of sabotage of those very negotiations. Ironically, while the accusation of foul play was loudly blasted in all its media and the regime plastered wanted posters all over the country, its forces threw the bodies of Charles Ndaba and Mbuso Shabalala, wrapped in hessian sacks and tied to concrete poles, into the Tugela river.[74]

Being a safety risk
Lusaka, December 1990

Upon my arrival back in Lusaka after six weeks in apartheid country, I wondered about Ivan's tension, which seemed more prominent than I remembered. He had asked me questions, not normal conversational ones, but interview-type questions. It was like an interrogation. Whom had I met, whom had I spoken to, had I written anything? It took all of twenty minutes for me to get pissed off. Why was this man interrogating me? What had I done?

He relented and explained that 'people' were really worried that I might have talked about Vula while in South Africa. He had received alerts about it, asking him to do something about me, because I might be unwisely leaking information and endangering people. I understood then. This was about the little note I had given to Klaas to give to Conny. 'Viva Vula!' I had written, explaining that I understood how important it all was. Conny must have been concerned on receiving that admittedly foolish note.

The assumption was correct. 'You and Ivan also seemed to be a bit love-struck,' she would explain to me later, when all disquiet has died down and we meet back in Amsterdam. 'At least that was what I heard from the others who had been with you in Lusaka.' I was unable to withhold a grin. 'I thought you might go around saying things. Or that they might even arrest you. That was a real concern.' But I had not mentioned Vula to anyone, except in the note that I gave to Klaas.

'It's OK,' says Ivan as we sit on the couch as we would have before my trip to South Africa, though I suddenly feel much older. 'I told Conny that I didn't think there was any damage.'

'Well, thank you very much,' I say, still cross about this man interrogating me like he is my boss. And think to myself that one day I'll be interrogating him.

Chapter Two
The imagining

A broken foot
January 1991, Amsterdam

It's cold, with winds that make you shiver and ice on the streets. My mother doubts the wisdom of waiting for Ivan. She doesn't think that he will ever be able to fully separate from Rae, his life partner in the underground. 'Two soldiers stuck in trenches,' she says. 'That's a bond you cannot break. And even if you could, would you want to?' Rae, the wounded fellow fighter, the comrade. What do I know of shared war, shared pain, missions, sacrifice? Maybe my mother is right. If I continue to hang on, I might remain in limbo.

Abandoning my green-card marriage to my Mexican former partner – one failure to connect with a world different from my own already – I moved back home with my mother the previous year, months before going to Lusaka. In doing so, I invaded her own new beginning in an Amsterdam apartment, just after she reclaimed independence after a second marriage that lasted twenty-five years. My mother loved me, but was not ecstatic to have a homeless daughter knocking at her door again almost simultaneously with that important step in her own life. There was some relief when the Lusaka exiles project came up, but now I am back in the attic again.

Ivan has written that it may take a while before there is clarity on if and when we might be together. Rae is not in a good state. He is taking it one day at a time.

He is in the Soviet Union now, being treated for his stomach ailments, courtesy of the communist comrades from way back when. Without indemnity papers to shield him from arrest for terrorism, he still can't go back home to South Africa, and since Operation Vula is essentially over, having this health break seemed like a good idea. A bonus is that he can pass through Amsterdam on the way back from Moscow.

Waiting for him at Schiphol, I hear an announcement: 'Can the person waiting for a 'Swazilean' gentleman please approach the office?' I contemplate several scenarios, none of which are good, as I make my way towards the information booth and, from there, move with a woman to a border police point in the entrails of the airport building, along passages I never knew existed.

My heart sinks as I see him, looking so very thin and small between two burly blond uniformed marechaussee, immigration policemen. With his tasselled woollen hat and big winter coat he looks a bit like Mehmet Pamuk, the famous Turkish migrant worker character from a Dutch TV show. 'I am sorry. I didn't know Swazis needed a visa for the Netherlands,' Ivan says calmly, looking in my direction. He never actually tells a lie.

Fortunately, the marechaussee turn out to be rather friendly, not intent on sending back or imprisoning anyone. 'Just deposit 4000 guilders as surety,' one says. 'You'll get it back when you leave again.' I quickly say we can do that, hoping fervently that between all my relatives we can come up with such an amount. Some phone calls later, we find my brother Maarten able and ready to post the money.

These days are still very different from the maximum security style – and racist – processes we will come to experience at airports globally in the near future. With the marechaussee smiling, my younger brother is allowed through to our location. He is told where the airport bank branch is, and jumps – which he does with great agility – over turnstiles back to the hall to get the cash. After he returns with the required amount, we shake hands, smile, wave and leave.

We spend a week together in my mother's attic room, much to the chagrin of the landlord, who keeps reminding us that people may not reside in the attic of this third-floor Amsterdam apartment. He has given my mother one stern warning after another already, but somehow he never comes back with police. In Amsterdam in 1991, all authority seems more jolly and relaxed than now. Maybe some of the free spirit of the seventies still seeps through. In our current time of authoritarian leaders, populists, refugee-haters and white supremacists, those days seem so long ago.

Even though Maarten has said he can wait to get his 4000 guilders back from the border police, Ivan wants to refund it as soon as possible. He phones Barbara de Leeuw and Rens Trimp, a former Swazi-based expat teacher couple and helpers of the underground, who are now back in Limburg province. They immediately access their savings and transfer the amount to Maarten. 'You do what Ivan asks you to do' is their simple explanation when I ask them, decades later, if they hadn't hesitated, 4000 guilders being a lot of money after all.

And then I break my foot.

Ivan organises the ambulance by alerting the police in the icy Warmoesstraat where I slipped and fell, even though it is risky. He briefly hesitated: what if they would ask to see his papers? But they don't. He stayed with me in the hospital and – shy, soft spoken, walking around nervously trying to find someone who is not too busy – gets me painkillers from nurses when the foot starts to hurt badly. It turns out that quite a few bones in and around the ankle are broken. At night, alone in the hospital after the operation, I sigh mentally. The fact that he is so caring will prevent him leaving Rae, but I want that care, too. Maybe all this foot spraining and breaking means I should stick it out for a while.

'It's like the whole return process has a broken foot,' smiles Mac Maharaj over the phone. 'We are still in limbo. Can't get anyone back from Lusaka yet.' I ask him about progress towards the multi-party negotiations that South Africa is expecting with bated breath, the negotiations that should open the country to the return of exiles, the release of all remaining political prisoners, non-racial democracy and a hopeful future, perhaps even for me. He sighs. 'The regime is up to its old tricks,' he says. 'It may still take a while.'

Painting flowers
May 1991

'We cross the colour frontier', we headline in our paper, *Anti-Apartheid*

News. 'Presenting a South Africa as you've never seen it before!' It is propaganda for our newest project: a tour guide book to a more colourful South Africa than its wildlife and lilywhite beaches. We will evoke the yellow, pink, orange and purple of the flowers in Namaqualand; the blue and white painted houses of the BoKaap; the red sunsets in Merebank, the rainbow buzz of Yeoville, the violet, green and blue of the Wild Coast and, most importantly, all the shades of all the people. We will invite readers – dreamers like us, fascinated by South Africa and its ideals of social justice and democracy – to see how much more exciting this country is than they had thought possible. How much more it is than Camps Bay villas, luxury lodges and truckloads of servants. We'll show our fellow foreigners the way.

We don't need to think long to find a name for this endeavour. It is Vulindlela, of course, open the path, once again. It is the sequel. A peaceful, enjoyable, fascinating opening for the whole world to see what we see. What we have dreamt. A small publishing house has agreed to contract Bart and myself to do such a tour guide. My foot is better. We are on our way.

An incentive is, of course, that Ivan is now back in South Africa too.[75] It will be good to be there at the same time, even if we cannot be together. Living with his family in Durban, he has written to me how he is getting reacquainted with his own past, places, relatives and friends. With Rae reintegrating with the same community and the same past at the same time, that relationship is still paramount. But maybe I'll see him every now and then.

At least his letters have exuded excitement about the idea of community tourism. He seems to see it as something he could be involved in in the future. He would like to get to know his own country, he has written, for real this time, not just by climbing over fences in the dark. On a more practical note, he simply needs to find a real job, too. The ANC has offered him a position in the internal organising committee that must set up the organisation anew, as a legal political party, but he has refused it. He has not explained why. Maybe he doesn't like the set-up, I think, or the people involved.

After some prodding I find that the second guess was right. The new committee is supposed to be led by former MK commissar and ANC National Executive member Steve Tshwete. From the little that he says, it is clear that he doesn't want to work under Tshwete, who appears to be a rather bullish man. Moving from a pro-reconciliation stance in 1987 when meeting Afrikaner progressives in Dakar, he had shortly afterwards become a proponent of landmine attacks by MK, even if these hurt innocent civilians, announcing that such attacks would be 'ruthless and sensational'. He is, however, not on record as recognising any of the problems bedevilling activists or MK operatives in the country. I check to find if the ANC's new national organiser, for that is his title now, has said anything in defence of the underground, or the arrests and disappearances of Vula operatives, but there is nothing.

For the moment, Ivan sells (mainly ladies') garments, like tops, skirts, dresses and underwear in Swaziland, Lesotho and South Africa. Ivan has some knowledge of Swaziland and also Lesotho, after all. Textile manufacturer Shirish Soni, who was part of the ANC underground in Durban – he was arrested and badly tortured by the security police around 1988 – has given him this sales job.

He wrote to me about it in a matter-of-fact way, as if it wasn't weird or terrible at all. Bart, Conny and I were unsure whether to laugh or cry at the news. The coordinator of Operation Vula, commander in MK and the underground, a ladies' garment salesman? But he seems fine with it, calm as ever. It is not a pose or a brave face. He often says that even sweeping garbage off the streets is an honourable job, as long as you do it well. Doing useful things the best you can is always a step towards a better world. Even if that useful thing is providing women with quality underwear.

In his last letter, he described a visit to a botanical garden in Moscow. The garden was little more than a quiet place full of naked trees and bushes in the snow, with no flower or green leaf in sight. But the guide described the full glory of the garden as it was in summer, vividly painting the blossoms on the fruit trees and the flowers in their beds with so much passion and enthusiasm that Ivan could imagine the beauty of it. He was impressed by the woman's ability to share her vision of a blooming garden in the midst of winter.

Of course he also knew that this woman was not really using her imagination; she knew what the trees looked like in summer. She was also an apparatchik of the state, and she was simply doing her job. But the point, perhaps, was that she did it well and that in that way she helped *others* to imagine something beautiful.

He likes to imagine how things could be better. How that continuous, relentless, imagining of improvements has fascinated, but also very often vexed, me in the past thirty years! The continuous remarks on how things in the house could be worked on, where we should build, should paint, which repairs are urgent. How people – including himself, and me, and everybody – could do their jobs better or more properly maintain their places and assist their children. In what ways the government could do better, and the ANC, of course. Sometimes I have sympathy for those at the receiving end of all the analysing, nudging, judging and suggesting. Especially when I am one of them. He often asks me, ever so nicely, if I should not be going to the gym.

Trauma country
Winter 1991, South Africa

Bart and I try to imagine a new South Africa as we drive through it with a number of local comrades as guides, but it's difficult. We mostly encounter situations where people are stuck in the old, with the new so far away that it is impossible to reach or even see. While visiting Brandfort in the Free State to see Winnie's dilapidated house[76] – the one in which she was internally exiled for years – we meet a man named Bosman who has spent his whole life trying to build his very own house. He has done that consistently, brick by brick, but still only has foundations. He explains how every time he wanted to build more there was a problem with some official or regulation and I think of witches and how Shadrack Maphumulo ended up in the armed struggle.

Elsewhere, too, people seem to remain where they are. In the Molemela Hotel in Phahameng township near Bloemfontein, we have a beer with Mike Pieterse, a black man with an Afrikaans name, who boasts of a 'very long drinking experience'. In the Eastern Cape we meet Griqua[77] community leaders for whom hiding from their own particular demons has become a way of life. 'We think we will survive as chosen people as long as South African governments don't find out where we are,' says one, who predictably wants to remain anonymous. The better beaches of violence-ravaged Natal, now formally open to all races, remain mostly as white as they were before, simply because they are far from public transport routes.

Damage is everywhere. The area around the settlement where Mohandas Gandhi once tried to build a caring community is now the crumbling shack- and violence-riddled Inanda. The bulldozed Cato Manor from where Sunny Singh's mother and aunties had to move by climbing on trucks with pots and pans and toddlers in tow is University of Natal property. The university may have been a hotbed of progressive activity when Shadrack Maphumulo and Judson Kuzwayo were fellows there, but the large and empty tracts of land, obtained through forced removals of African, Indian and coloured people still lie there. On Natal's south coast we hold our breath at the blue-green waves of the Indian Ocean and gaze at the rocks from where Shaka Zulu once threw his captured enemies to their deaths. In adjacent Ifafa, the main landmark is the bottle store, where unemployed men sit on its stoep, bottles in hand. It's trauma country and also breathtakingly beautiful. But is it ready for tourists? Who will take them by the hand, who will be able to explain it all? I see Ivan briefly in Durban, but we have no time together.

Makgoa

Philip Masia guiding us in the north, from Bophuthatswana to Venda, is an adventure for more reasons than the fact that he knows the way and how to drive (both of which Bart and I don't). Used to operating underground, he bluffs his way around, like he did in Nancefield hostel with his Amos Magadla ruse. He gets us into the Bophuthatswana bantustan casino and pleasure resort, Sun City,[78] without paying the parking fee just by chatting a bit with the brother at the boom gate. We spend some time in the complex with its high-rise hotels, giant swimming pool and elephant statue. We don't spend a lot of time here though: this is imagination of the worst kind, painful kitsch in the desert, a casino like so many casinos, and way too hot. When we see two women dressed, like the complex itself, in gold foil, sweating and heaving their way up a set of marble stairs, we call it a day.

On the way out, Phil's geniality then helps to make contact with the occupants of a Bophuthatswana government limousine parked next to us at the petrol station. As Philip jokes with the driver, a man in suit and golden watch joins us from the back seat. As it turns out, he is the Bophuthatswana minister of foreign affairs. With Bophuthatswana recognised by no country in the world, save South Africa, this is an odd thing to be and the minister himself has a good sense of humour about it. 'I call myself the Minister of Nothing,' he says, and laughs uproariously.

But maybe it was a mistake to leave Sun City so soon, we realise when we are refused accommodation a few consecutive times at tourist lodges. At least the black homeland resort traditionally accommodates unconventional behaviour and relationships; even porn and strip clubs are allowed here. Back in South Africa, however, our trio is an anomaly. Bart and I are welcome, of course, but 'Oubaas Malan' must come and say if it's allowed for 'him' – pointing at Phil – to stay, too, we hear at the first place we try. With Oubaas Malan not showing up, we knock on doors at a few other places, but not one accommodates him. 'We are for *makgoa*,' a shy black receptionist tells Philip at the last one, and he explains: makgoa means whites, or 'those strangers who bother you', in Sotho. Abandoning our plans to stay in idyllic, forested northern landscapes, we settle for the Holiday Inn in Pietersburg

The next day a friend of Philip's, who is a lawyer in that town – now called Polokwane – explains how the word 'makgoa', also came to mean 'witches' in some places in the north. Philip laughs as the lawyer – a friendly man of Muslim Indian heritage whose name I have sadly forgotten – shows us a research report he did on the use of the term in the eighties, during the anti-apartheid uprisings. The report details how, in explosions of mob justice, apartheid spies were hunted and burned as witches. 'Of course you whites were witches,' Philip says after he finishes. 'With your evil and your fire-spewing machines.'

'Only mostly it was not whites but apartheid collaborators, black policemen and city councillors, who were attacked and burned,' the lawyer corrects him. 'Because they were seen to be damaging their own communities. It was very rarely that a white person was attacked.'

'But that changed later,' says Philip, stubbornly. 'Later we attacked them directly.'

For the first time, Bart and I, who grew up with Cold War narratives about the bad witch hunts directed at communists in the United States during the 1950s, as well as with stories of how original witch hunts in medieval times in Europe murdered thousands of women, are presented with a scenario in which witch hunts might have been justified. Were they not akin to witches, these alien beings who came here to take the best land and rivers, to ban the natives from the splendid forests, to kill and cause disease? Were the locals they enslaved to do their bidding now not witches, or at least witches' helpers? Abundant stories tell of 'zombies', once normal individuals, who were turned into witches' slaves through evil magic.

I think of askaris and September.

We keep trying to find a beautiful place in the country that will accept the three of us as guests. To our delight, after another few attempts, we find ourselves in a welcoming lodge in Magoebaskloof. That evening, in the lodge's restaurant, drunk with relief, helped along by really good wine and whisky, we start making Magoebaskloof puns. Saying 'Mugabeskloof', after Robert Mugabe, is good fun, since it seems to rile a company of male makgoa in safari attire at the bar who observe us in disgust. In turn, they start talking loudly among themselves in Afrikaans. We hear words like 'kaffir' and some obscene references to what Bart and I would be doing with Philip, and, presumably, they with me. Bart just thinks it's funny and I am way too happy with the bath and the clean clothes and the food and the drinks to bother at all, but Philip gets incensed. He wants to get up and fight them, upon which we quickly say no; we are going, we are very tired, come on, Phil, let's go. Back at the rondavel, however, Philip still wants to go back 'just to discuss with them', he says. Bart and I look at each other. It is not a good idea. He is drunk, like we are too, but he is also very angry, and these men may actually shoot him. It has happened more than once that the angry lekgoa, once provoked, shoots you dead. More often than not, such a lekgoa will only get a slap on the wrist from the courts.

'No, I am going,' Philip says, unimpressed with our pleading, and he starts to put on his jacket. There is only one thing left to do. 'Take the car keys,' I hiss at Bart, in Dutch. In this resort one drives between the central buildings and the chalets. Philip can walk that distance, but may find the men gone when he arrives. Or he might have sobered up. Bart grabs the keys from the nail on the wall, passes them to me and I go to my room with them, knowing that, as drunk and angry though he is, Philip won't come after me. I hear Bart go into his room and Philip pacing, up and down the passage and lounge of our chalet, until he gives in and retires, too.

We don't mention the incident at all in the morning.

Changing as soon as possible

Driving south, near Nelspruit, a sign says 'Come Together'. It points to a holiday farm: small advertising boards popping up on the road mention Christianity, community and sharing. It is almost four o'clock, and we are ready for some of this: if not for Christianity, then at least for some community and sharing. But when we have booked into the chalet and prepare to sleep on the wooden camping beds under the soothingly cool, shady thatch roof, a black employee comes to tell us, hesitantly and softly, that 'he' may not sit on the beds. 'He' is Phil of course, again. 'I am not sitting,' Philip says, stretched out with his head on the pillow and a newspaper on his chest. 'I am about to fall asleep.'

'But that is not allowed,' whispers the man, clearly terrified, upon which Bart and I righteously make our way to the reception room where the Come Together Christian Farm boss, a blonde woman in her thirties, resides. We demand to know what is going on. Can't we even come together on a farm called Come Together? 'I know what you mean,' says the woman, taken aback. 'It is perhaps not right anymore nowadays. But it's still the rules. I am sorry.'

When we ask who makes the rules and can we speak to them, she vacillates. 'Well, I guess it's me, actually,' she replies with a slight smile. 'I am the manager.' I say that in that case we are speaking to her in her capacity as manager. Surely she can change the rules? Suddenly, there is anger. No, she can't. It is simply not going to happen. As we pack our bags and strut back to the parking and into the sun outside, the manager yells after us: 'We'll change as soon as possible!'

After entering Nelspruit, Philip parks the car on yet another Voortrekker Street, close to the mall. 'The ANC office is right here,' he says, calmly. 'Let's get you another driver.' Another driver? Where is he going? 'Home,' he says. 'There are plenty taxis to Soweto here. I need to go home now. For an important meeting.'

We don't argue. We get into the ANC office, where a boisterously welcoming comrade who introduces himself as Jackson Mthembu embraces us. Though he does not know us at all, the mere fact of us mentioning the anti-apartheid movement is enough. 'Comrades! It's good to see comrades from far away in Nelspruit!' he booms and calls others who are around at the office to come and greet us. We don't know who he is either, save for the fact that he works for the Nelspruit ANC, and don't have an inkling that one day he'll be a minister,[79] but it's heartening to once again experience the unquestioning bond that characterises those in the liberation struggle.

But even the warmth of this encounter can't move Philip to continue on our tour with us. 'Let someone else take over for now,' he says, with a serious face. He is not angry, but also not grinning. 'I'll see you in Soweto.'

We continue for a bit with a young comrade called Thabo for a driver. It is satisfactory, but only up to a point.

'White people are witches,' I tell Ivan over the phone when we are back.

'I know,' he says.

The Kingdom of Peace and Happiness

Johannesburg's winter chill still engulfs the maids' room in Hopkins Street. Every now and then Ivan visits, almost continuously shivering, since the small electrical heater doesn't really warm up the draughty wooden outbuilding. In my memory we stay in bed in the freezing cold, huddled under blankets.

We do talk about some kind of a future, sometimes. Maybe when things are better he'll settle in Swaziland or Lesotho, with his textile sales. Maybe we'll do community tourism. Maybe the ANC will do something useful and want him to be part of that, and pay him a salary. But he doubts it. He is still as much at a standstill politically as in his personal life. We agree that I should try to come to Durban for the ANC conference to take place in two weeks' time.

* * *

Meanwhile, change is definitely coming on the small black-and-white TV in my room. The South African Broadcasting Corporation, the SABC, nowadays continuously bellows togetherness-themed jingles. Sunrise-filled commercials show adorable children of multiple races walking hand in hand, singing and smiling, towards said sunrises. 'South Africa, we are one,' sing the jingles. '*Simunye!*' After our traumatic 'Come Together' experience, I feel like investigating the source of so much hope and vision and, since I have some time before the ANC conference, I go to report on the changes in what was always propaganda city: the SABC headquarters in Auckland Park, Johannesburg.

At least here not all blacks are servants. Resolute, blonde and friendly PR lady Bess Bredenkamp, born in Bethlehem in the Free State close to thirty years ago, introduces me to several black colleagues with whom she works in good harmony, she says, assuring me that she has always got along well with black people 'from when we were kids on the farm'. She even thinks some of them, particularly the suave Thabo Mbeki, and the rough-ish charmer Tokyo Sexwale,[80] are quite sexy. 'But my mum would have a heart attack if she heard that.'

She speaks fluent Northern Sotho, too, a language she learned when she was assigned to the Qwa-Qwa bantustan division of the SABC. 'Sewing, cooking,' she says when I ask her what content she and her colleagues produced there. 'And you should see the responses I used to get – and still get – when they find I can speak their language. They get so happy!'

In these tall and large-windowed offices, people, for the most part, really do seem happy. 'This is the kingdom of peace and happiness,' Bess Bredenkamp announced when we entered through the heavily secured glass cubicles at the entrance: everybody smiles, everybody welcomes visitors, everybody offers time, explanations, coffee. 'Of course we are happy here,' grins the black DJ in the studio where music is selected for the black channels. 'How can we not be happy? We play nice music for nice people!' Together, he and Bess explain that the SABC has programmes for every population group in the country, from Tswana to Tsonga to Zulu to Xhosa, to Radio Lotus for the Indians. I ask if Afrikaans and English are not preferentially treated, with most airtime, but that is logical, they say. It has always been like that. Those channels get the most advertising anyway.

The DJ shyly shakes his head when I mention some South African tunes that are by now famous all over the world. No, he does not play Hugh Masekela, Johnny Clegg, Jasper Cooks's African Jazz Pioneers, or Abdullah Ibrahim. 'We don't do agitating language. We don't want to rile people against one another,' he says, a bit sheepishly, and Bess Bredenkamp defends the notion. 'It is actually our policy,' she says. 'We can't be *inflammatory*.' The second rule, probably linked to the first one, seems to be no mixing of races in content, except in the sunrise-children-hand-in-hand commercials. The different ethnic channels bring family dramas, uplifting talks, sports and music tailored for each separate population group; if there is any actual news they get it over and done with as quickly as they can, most often in the form of some powerful or official person who says something.

'If someone in your tour group asks a political question,' says Bess's PR colleague Sue-Marie Smith, who is leading a tour of white wives through the studios – their businessmen spouses are at a conference in town – 'the trick is to palm it off – ask another person in the group for their view.' Smiling broadly: 'Then they start arguing among themselves and you carry on.' She adds that the current batch of ladies won't be thus inclined 'but sometimes you get *students*'.

Bess Bredenkamp then introduces me, together with Sue-Marie and the ladies' club, to current affairs talk show presenter John Bishop, who – urbane, charming and only slightly greying on the sides – asks if it is 'signature' time again. 'I am told that my signature is worth more than Pik Botha's,' he says with a self-deprecating smile. Pik Botha is the famously easy-going, verligte, long-serving minister of foreign affairs of this country. 'But I already *got* Pik Botha,' responds one of the ladies cheerfully. John Bishop presents the new flagship current affairs programme Agenda, the existence of which, Bess Bredenkamp says, is the surest sign that times are in fact changing.

Agenda *does* talk politics. Only the way it does that is eerily reminiscent of Sue-Marie Smith's diversionary tactics. Agenda puts 'everybody together,' John Bishop explains, 'from Joe Slovo to Piet "Skiet" Rudolph. You know Piet Skiet? The trigger-happy right-winger? Slovo, you'll know of course.' He winks, having already identified me as 'probably one of those'. As he shows me the previous episode of Agenda, I see that Slovo hardly gets a word in edgewise as Rudolph shouts in a low voice, with a typical Afrikaner frontal R, that 'you are going to destrrrrroy the country'. The white public shouts approval.

'But communism is a real danger, surely,' Bishop answers with raised eyebrows when I ask him how a viewer is expected to distil any actual information from such pandemonium. 'I asked Slovo what South Africa will look like when it's fully communist. Of course, Rudolph is going to respond to that. And the audience.' I understand that Agenda is mostly about such vehement disagreement. Digging into actual current affairs – the quickly expanding HIV/AIDS epidemic and continuing Third Force massacres, to name just two burning issues – doesn't seem much of a priority. Neither is interrogating white minority government ministers: Bishop has had only one minister in the hot seat in past weeks.

Asked what he did in the old days, when communists couldn't even be quoted, let alone interrogated, he shrugs. 'We accepted government control, I think. I am a family man and not one of those journalists who risk losing their jobs. And then what is wrong with reporting that there is rioting, that there is fire, that the police needed to act?' I suggest that he could ask *why* there is rioting and fire and he thinks for a while, then shrugs again. 'All that background, all that asking ... if they didn't allow me to do that, I wouldn't turn it into a make-or-break situation. So my scripts have been censored, so what? All politicians have secrets.' As we sit in his comfortable office sipping tea brought to us by a black tea lady, he continues. 'But I am telling you, once we are faced with a totalitarian communist system in this country, with state unions and Marxist censorship, then I'll fight!'

Oh, *then* you'll fight, I say. He laughs delightedly, as if this really is a fun conversation.

At the end of our chat John Bishop phones his colleague, Afrikaans fellow-presenter, Freek Robinson. 'Come here a minute, will you,' he shouts cheerfully. 'There is this woman here from Holland. You should meet her. She is absolutely free. Free like you won't believe!' I ponder if John Bishop's view that I am free means that he thinks he isn't, and wonder how he can live happily with that thought. Then Freek Robinson enters the office. He is another white man with good hair and a chiselled face, and pleasant enough. His banter is on par with Bishop's and, likewise, for the most part instantly forgettable. 'See, I do work with other population groups,' John Bishop says, happily. 'Freek Robinson is Afrikaans. Only we call him *Freak*.' They laugh, again.

As Bess reappears, ready to take me to the news sections, we pass through a studio where the Afrikaans children's programme *Wielie Waalie*[81] is recorded. The visiting ladies queue around the set and explore the fuzzy animals who talk and play in the programme. Suddenly a heavy baritone voice breaks the chatter on the ground. 'Children, today is a beautiful day in Wielie Waalie land,' it thunders from a speaker in the ceiling. It is so sudden and loud that I jump, but I am the only one; the ladies carry on as they were. As if they are used to voices coming from above.

Velabahleke they call that power in the north, when witches make you believe all is well. They sing you to sleep, mesmerising you, while they empty your house and take your children. There was a paragraph about that in the witches report we had been given in Polokwane.

If makgoa were witches, it made sense that their radio and TV would have that power, too.

Two sides of the story

By now very curious about the black current affairs programmes, I enter the editing room of the newly established Contemporary Community Values channel, otherwise CCV, with something akin to hope. It is intended, for a change, to provide programming for the black population in general, without specific ethnic time slots. Music plays here: the 'South Africa We Are One, *Simunye*' jingle I have heard so much on TV recently. Bess looks for someone for me to interview, but they are all busy. One of the black producers seems to be dealing with an emergency. 'We need Inkatha,' he yells into a telephone. Don't come back to me until you have found someone from Inkatha! We only have two hours left!'

After he has slammed down the phone and sits with his head in his hands, I approach him to ask what that was about. He is startled. 'It's OK,' says Bess, clarifying to him that I have come from Holland 'to do a story about us and the changes'. With her go-ahead, the man welcomes the opportunity to vent. 'We need a Land Act specialist from Inkatha,' he says. 'Otherwise the minister for land and agriculture won't come on to the panel discussion. But Inkatha tells me they don't *have* a Land Act specialist!' Asked why he must absolutely have someone from Inkatha, he answers that it is a question of balance. 'Otherwise we would only have an ANC person to debate with the minister. And we have to have Inkatha. It's the policy.'

CCV programme director Mike Mxasana – 'a former KwaZulu homeland spokesman,' says Bess Bredenkamp – agrees. 'If you have the ANC, then you also have to have Inkatha. Or the right wing. As long as you have people from the left and from the right of the government. The government is always in the middle.' Sue-Marie Smith's tactic – 'get another person to argue with the difficult person so that you can carry on' – is evidently the main policy mantra here in Auckland Park.

Head of in-depth programmes André Geyser confirms this. 'Inkatha and the ANC are the ones fighting one another over black issues, so we must hear from both of them.' The overall managing director of CCV, freshly appointed, grey, bearded and sage-looking Madala Mphahlehle, tells me that it is indeed good journalism, and CCV's policy, to 'have two sides of the story'. Asked how his reporters get to what the story is in the first place, he seems puzzled as to what that might mean. He shakes his head, hands firmly slapping down on his desk: 'I don't *care* what the story is. As long as we have two sides of it.' This new policy of ping-pong reporting may be a small improvement after decades of censorship, but I'm not really sure if it is.

Walking to the Brave New Towers' exit I notice, in the lobby, a display of an educational leaflet about politically correct terminology. 'The word "sakemanne", businessmen, is now discouraged,' the leaflet says. 'There is after all also such a word as business people, "sakelui".'

When I phone days later with a few last-minute questions, I am told that Mike Mxasana is not there. Nor is André Geyser. 'They have gone to Ulundi,' the friendly secretary tells me. Ulundi: that is where the headquarters of the KwaZulu homeland government and Inkatha are.

Khomanisi
Durban, July 1991

Could I move further away, please, asks a man who comes out of the marquee on the lawn of the University of Durban Westville, where the ANC conference is being held. He explains, apologetically, that 'Comrades don't trust reporters generally', and I might overhear. Only muffled noises can be heard from where I sit on the grass, but with the SABC experience still fresh in my mind I fully understand why comrades might not trust reporters, and move further away. Ivan will later introduce the same man to me as Moe Shaik, a close comrade whose underground unit had supported the Vula leadership.

Wandering about, I find Chris Hani, standing in front of one of the university buildings, characteristically upright and calm. He does not recognise me from Transkei. Thinking I am trying to interview him, he tells me he is not here to answer questions. 'They told me I must wait here, so that is what I am doing,' he says. 'There is going to be some workshop or other.' Deciding that there is no point in reminding him about the time we met, I walk on until I am waved into what seems to be a VIP tent by Mac Maharaj. He offers me a soft drink. 'You?' I ask after greeting. 'Didn't you say you were going to be a house husband?' A grin. 'Maybe not.'

When I'm finally allowed into the big tent to witness the first free elections in South Africa for the ANC National Executive Committee, I see that Mac is on the list. Many vote for him, too, and he comes walking down the corridor between the seats with his fist in the air as his name is heard and the conference cheers. 'The people called,' he will shrug later, when I ask him about it. The remark is made with a half-smile, but it is true, too.

Chris Hani has received even more votes, almost as many as Nelson Mandela. There seems to be great passion for comrades who are known to have fought in the trenches. Former mass action detainees and MK stalwarts are elected; among them a sizeable number of people who are seen as communists, or khomanisi in township lingo.

They come in all colours, the khomanisi: Hani, Slovo, Mac. The honorary title has at times been whispered around our Dutch solidarity people too. Lucia, now working for a civil society organisation in Port Elizabeth, had repeatedly been called by that epithet. 'These are not just friends', were the words used in a welcome to a group of AABN visitors in a black township, a while ago. 'They are khomanisi.'

In contrast, the diplomatic London-friendly bubble around Thabo Mbeki doesn't seem to get much grassroots support at this first free ANC gathering in South Africa. The diplomats who were based in safe Western countries, or associating with the political elites in places like Ethiopia or Russia, are applauded too, but not as raucously. A slight tinge of fear creeps down my spine as I participate in the cheering and applause for Chris and Mac. The title khomanisi may be a badge of honour, but the other side sees them as communists, too, I think suddenly. I try to suppress the memory of John Bishop's raised eyebrows, but don't succeed.

They won't want any communists.

I don't know it yet, but the Durban ANC conference of 1991 is the last time I'll ever see Chris Hani.

Afterwards

'Come,' says Ivan. 'My niece will drive us.' I will be staying with comrades Janey and Ish in Merebank. Ivan's niece Kogie, also here at the conference because she is the secretary of the ANC branch in her neighbourhood, will drop me off at their place. At the time I only note handsome young Kogie's eyes, dark and bright at the same time, curiously peeking at me in the rear view mirror. I will learn later that Kogie lost her sister Sendi to the conditions of exile – malaria in Zimbabwe – just over two years ago, and that Kogie's other sister Prani's boyfriend was killed by the security police.

Lenny Naidu had been a local idealistic youngster the sisters had met in the neighbourhood youth association, UDF-linked Helping Hands. He had joined the ANC and MK shortly before he was shot dead in a hit squad ambush of June 1988 in Piet Retief, just over the border from Swaziland. The Truth and Reconciliation Commission will, later still, find that the activists were unarmed at the time, and that the hit under the command of death squad captain Eugene de Kock was thus outright murder.[82]

There is now a Lenny Naidu road in Chatsworth.

On the way to my hosts' house, I break the initial silence by telling an anecdote from Bethal in Mpumalanga, where Bart and I had interviewed a white municipal official in charge of liaising with the local Indian township. The official had assured us that the Indians there were very comfortable with the way things had always been. They were even upset about the recent abolition of the Group Areas Act that kept all the race groups separated. The Indians had petitioned the city council rather to fill the public swimming pool in their neighbourhood with sand than have blacks come swim with them. We didn't have time to go into the Indian area and interview any residents, but we thought it a tall story.

Kogie also doesn't believe that an Indian community would be that averse to black families wanting to swim. 'Just after the Group Areas Act was gone here in Durban, a few black kids came to put their feet in the water. It wasn't a big deal for anybody.' Then, frowning: 'But that doesn't mean there will never be problems. We have been used as a buffer between blacks and whites. We are still seen as privileged. A few months ago a youngster told me in the street that after apartheid was gone, he would own our fridge, with everything in it.' Kogie didn't really fear losing her fridge; the youngster seemed relatively harmless. But what was frightening was, she says, the assumption that obtaining a wealthier family's fridge would somehow solve structural poverty and inequality.

Merebank, later

Talk of khomanisi. Janey and Ish's quiet, clever daughters are nine-year-old Nikita, named after Krushchev, and her elder sister Yuri (age twelve), after Gagarin: Their mother is a teacher and deeply committed to real existing socialism. The family – Janey Juggernath, her engineer husband Ish Ramkissoon and their two girls – have welcomed me in their home and at their table, for weeks on end on various occasions, and I will remain forever grateful. Despite their genuine hospitality, I once again note Ivan's pull. 'You do whatever he asks you to do,' Janey says, with a smile, just as erstwhile comrade expats Barbara de Leeuw and Rens Trimp had said.

Decades later I will hear, with great amusement, how Ivan's way of influencing people has come to mean danger for some. 'He can make you disappear in less than an hour,' whispered, I am told, a lady who works in finance to another, in terror at the idea that Ivan was now working at the South African Revenue Services. And as much as I don't know of anyone who disappeared after meeting, being around, or even annoying Ivan, the 'less than an hour' part puzzles me no end. Are there people who make other people disappear very slowly and over long periods of time?

Stories of exile, hardship and sacrifice resonate within Merebank's community, as well as the hope for a better life and a better world. As I get to know the neighbours and comrades, the story of Ivan and Joe Pillay's exile and struggle regularly evokes talk of the Ramayana, the Hindu epic that describes the travails of the hero Rama who spent fourteen years in exile, beating demons, to return victoriously back home along a divine lighted path.

There are plenty of heroes in Merebank. The neighbours all remember Krishna, Ivan's friend from high school, who was shot by apartheid soldiers in Matola, and Coastal, who never talked, no matter how he was tortured. From 'The Sentinel' community newspaper rebel group, there is Spider, Janey's brother, who worked with Krish and Ivan in the early days. The community also remembers Vijay Ramlakan, who blew up the post office, as well as the MK contingent that fired a rocket at the oil refinery in 1984. That group was led by Robert McBride, who grew up in neighbouring coloured township of Wentworth.

'I told Ivan to just get me an RPG and I would do it,' says Elvis Govender. 'You know, a rocket-propelled grenade launcher? But he never did.' Elvis Govender is the Merebank comrade who had come out to be trained by Ivan and Judson, who had had Ivan puzzled by his little balls of silver foil stuck on the ceiling, and who had met the car accident with the roneo machine. Now he is back here and takes me around to see the former Indians-only beach with its dangerous Dead Man's Pool, the industrial environment that induced asthma and other ailments, the sewage plant and oil refinery that MK attacked. But there is also a spot on top of the hill from where you can look beyond the industrial area and see the houses and gardens with their avocado and mango trees below, and the Indian Ocean in the distance. 'This is where we like to hang after partying,' says Elvis. 'At night, under the stars, the sea is dark velvet. Merebank is beautiful here.'

Indian government

It is 7 July 1991, one day after the ANC conference has ended and the leadership is all here in Durban, to address the people at King's Park Stadium. We are all here, too: Ivan; his mother, with silver white hair, dignified walk and piercing eyes; his elder sister, sweet-faced with a long black ponytail; her energetic and cheerful daughter Jenny, niece Kogie who drove us to Merebank from the conference; one of the brothers whom I can't place yet; and Rae. She must be Rae, this tall, long- and strong-limbed, curly haired woman with glasses. We all sit quietly in our row.

The young black man in the Mandela T-shirt who opens the proceedings is clearly happy with the opportunity to be heard. Ahead of the political celebrities, he starts to make a speech too, listing all the things – one man, one vote, et cetera – that the ANC demands. He reads his list out with passion, until he pauses, reading something again, then shouts it anyway: 'Forward to an Indian government!' There are chuckles all around as we realise that the youngster must have stumbled on the word 'interim' in the demand for an *interim* government.

I remember very little else of the speeches or the event at King's Park. Etched on my memory, however, is the picture of Ivan's mother, sitting rigidly straight in her sari, all satisfied smiles and calm eyes, with her silver hair outlined against the bright blue Durban sky. She told a radio interviewer earlier that she is fine now. Her baby is back.

Back at the Merebank home for tea – Rae has been driven to her family's home – I realise that no one in this house seems to wonder about me. There are no questions, just silent warmth and acceptance. Do they know? It can't be. Ivan doesn't say things if not absolutely necessary. They probably, like all comrades here, just accept everything Ivan does, including whomever he brings.

His mother beckons me, I must come and see something. 'You are journalist.' Her English is still an Indian English, a second language after Tamil. She removes some trays of cups and containers out of the bottom of a cupboard and takes out some paper from under it, wriggling it carefully so that it doesn't tear. Going down on my knees and coming closer to the cupboard in the small dark room I see it is a copy of 'The

The imagining

Sentinel'. 'You kept this all this time,' asks Ivan, with a catch in his throat. 'You said I must keep it,' his mother says, shrugging slightly.

Years later I will be told the story of how Ivan's mother scared away the security police, by telling them she would kill herself the next time they came knocking. 'Why would you do that, Granny,' an Indian security policeman said, trying to calm her down. 'Then you would be dead, what good would that do?' Mother replied, 'It would do good because before I kill myself I tell my sons who did that.' They bothered the household significantly less after that.

Later

Back in icy Johannesburg I prepare to be alone again but not yet: we still have a few days before Ivan, who accompanied me here, has to return to Durban. Paging through newspapers to see if there are any good movies or plays, I look for a pen to jot down some ideas and telephone numbers. 'Pen, pen, pen,' I mutter looking around and notice a shiny golden pen in Ivan's jacket's breast pocket. I will discover later it is a gift from Shirish Soni, the textile manufacturing comrade. 'Give.' He gives me the pen, I do my jotting and give it back. 'Oh,' he says. 'I thought you wanted it.'

'Yeah, for a quick note,' I respond. 'I wouldn't expect you to just *give* me such a posh pen. It looks expensive.' He puts the pen back in his pocket and says shyly: 'I'd give you anything.'

Wait for him forever I will.

That evening I discover two things. Firstly, on our way to the Market Theatre, it turns out that the taxi driver doesn't know where that is. Walking the twenty minutes from Wolmarans Street to Newtown I realise once again how far this country is from even a shared understanding of reality. The Market Theatre is for intellectual progressives; the imagined South African society that is nurtured and reflected there – the versions of Pieter-Dirk Uys, Athol Fugard, Ronnie Govender and John Kani – clearly do not touch the life of a South African who drives a taxi in the city. The theatre is largely an elite pursuit in many places. But here, especially here, with its separated realities, its fake surfaces and the pain underneath, we need to tell each other our stories. It is becoming painfully urgent. If we don't meet at the Market Theatre, then where?

The second thing is that Little John – or Bricks, or Christopher Manye as his real name is – Swaziland underground Little John, Totsie's husband, is in trouble.

Bricks was one of the bravest. He led numerous missions into South Africa and carried out many armed attacks against the regime. Together with Cassius Motsoaledi and Jabu Shoke, the three cadres had formed the nucleus of the Transvaal urban command under Siphiwe Nyanda. Ivan had met Bricks numerous times before he even met Totsie, always in the dark of night, crossing to and from Swaziland and Mozambique. Short of stature, Bricks made up for his lack of height in physical strength and determination as he carried heavy loads of weapons and explosives over rough terrain. When Vula started, Ivan found both Bricks and Cassius in Lusaka, and felt they were underutilised. He requested that they both be allocated to work with him. After training in Cuba, Bricks then worked for Vula in Cape Town, remaining undetected until the unbanning of the ANC. For his part, Cassius became part of the Vula Lusaka team, travelling often to the forward areas to meet couriers and provide them with armaments which he concealed in their vehicles.

At the Market Theatre in 1991, Totsie meets us, and tells Ivan about Bricks's current misery, and his alcohol-filled life. She fears he may not last long anymore. She and Ivan speak only briefly – eyes darting around, a habit from the old days – trying to think of rescue plans, but options seem few. There is no money for rehab and even if there was he would not agree to go. Surrounded by friends who are just as drunk and miserable as he is, one more South African life is petering out.

The Market Theatre, site of artistic protest and struggle, sometimes is about such experiences, but, as is the case of most theatres, most of its audience is not. The gap between people on the ground and the new struggle elite is wide, and may be widening still. You see Aziz Pahad a lot there and MI6 spook Anthony Rowell, and the others from the London bubble. Anton Harber of the anti-apartheid *Weekly Mail* is often spotted, as is British ambassador Robin Renwick, who supports the free press and has given the *Weekly Mail* a bag of money for their good efforts,[83] and the entire Johannesburg leftie jet set with its foreign correspondents and its parties and friends from way back at the Dutch AABN, too.

They are all honourable, good people, here in Newtown's imagined South Africa-to-be, but just so very far away from Totsie and Little John.

* * *

Later in the year, Colleen kicks us all of us out of her house in Hopkins

Street. 'I have had enough of people using my space,' she says, and it's true, even if I pay a modest rent, I too have used her office room with its many computers, without offering to pay extra for that. Our little society here may have been an illusion. Thandi the actress has been booted out for defaulting on her rent already, and now it is our turn.

Colleen is right, of course, but she also seems tormented, more emotional than the situation would warrant. Has the end of South Africa's uncertain transition, the gradual slowing down of the merry dance of the civic organisations in Yeoville, the creeping bureaucratisation, become too hard for her to bear?

It is of course depressing that the ANC, preparing to govern, is busy snuffing out the lively universe of the UDF with their 'you can sit down, we are back now' attitude – the bustling movement was disbanded in March this year – but as it turns out, that is not it. Or not entirely it. A few months later, we hear she has died and Jasper tells me that she had a brain tumour: besides feeling ill she also felt desperate and enraged. 'But she did not want anyone to know what the problem was.'

With Colleen Cook's death, the safe haven in Hopkins Street dies too.

Privilege

Back with Maisy in Tladi, Soweto, I stay with her and her family. 'Is it wise?' asks Ivan over the phone, when I tell him of the move. 'There is still a risk of violence.' I tell him that I feel little danger here. Merafe has been quiet and neighbours have been protective, fussing about me disproportionately as I walk everywhere. Passers-by and even taxi drivers incessantly impress on me how I must be careful about criminals, and offer to walk with me 'because it's not safe'. 'It's because they know you are with the struggle,' Maisy says at first, earnestly. 'There is a lot of respect for those whites who join us.' But though that may be so for those who identify as comrades, I feel that there is also another, more basic concern for me as a white person. The way people worry about me is as if I am a princess in a fairy tale: I must be careful with the glass and bricks on the road, my dress mustn't get dirty, don't shake hands with that guy, he is a drunk, are you sure you can drink from this plastic cup? I had hoped for new comradeship and discussions about such things, joint moves towards that rainbow nation we have so far only seen in commercials, but all I get is white privilege.

Maisy shrieks with merriment when I tell her what I think. 'You are not made for the hard life, my dear,' she chuckles. 'It's true. My mother got such a shock when she saw you do the dishes. She told me. She had just come home from work for a white madam in town where she was doing the dishes. She comes home and there is a white madam doing the same thing in her kitchen! She had to lie down on the bed and pray, she told me. Hahahahaaaa!' Even now, I still can't imagine Soweto without Maisy's laughter.

It is a protective shield, of course. The young girls and women I meet in the neighbourhood also laugh a lot, even if their lives are at risk every single minute of every day. The last time I was here, Maisy took me to meet friends and comrades who were dealing with violence in their relationships, some of whom barely survive beatings and even burnings. The girls I meet now are still at home with their parents, but abuse and unwanted sex are already part of their normality. There are such things at home as well as in the street. 'Men are just like that,' they shrug.

A small group of friends invite me to see how they handle danger. Again joking and laughing, they show me how they dress up as boys when they need to go out after dusk, with woollen caps to hide their hair, and baggy pants. Most have also learned how to fight, even though they admit they won't win 'when the boy brings friends'. Except for a tall, tough-looking girl with scars on her face, who carries the tsotsi name 'Mangko', which means 'the nose'. There is nothing wrong with her nose and I don't know where the name comes from, but she is something of a hero to the others. She can handle a knife. 'You try to attack her, you will regret it,' smiles young Pamela.[84]

Living with Maisy for four months, I experience the domestic normality of a township woman's life. Even if I am discouraged, particularly by Maisy's mum, from actually doing anything myself, I see how both Maisy and her mother, like all the neighbours, continuously lug heavy shopping bags and babies around, alternated with mopping, sweeping, polishing, child minding, washing, chopping vegetables, and of course cooking and cleaning again afterwards. Men hang around; it seems to be all they do. 'We have to keep our hands free,' Philip grinned once, when I asked him about the division of household labour in the neighbourhood. 'If I carry the baby, how can I protect you and the baby from the lion when it comes?'

It's true that the danger of attacks by Inkatha still exist and that many

The imagining

men in Tladi would probably fight the impi when needed, but other than that, you almost never see a man do anything useful here. In Maisy's house, her unemployed brother Andy [85] does nothing, while his mother even shines his shoes for him. His baby, a cheerful but often filthy two-year-old, develops a habit of greeting me in the morning after Maisy has gone to work in town with his nappy bursting at the seams with sharply stinking shit. I change him once or twice, but, thankfully, Maisy's mum usually comes running to take the burden away from me.

The automatism whereby the women in Tladi continue to accept the idleness of men puzzles me as much as the special treatment that I receive. Why do some humans automatically get the benefit of privilege – or rather certain types of privilege, because let's face it, Andy is still as poor and miserable as they come – and others don't? Why is it so ingrained? Why am I treated as if I'm made of glass, even in this post-apartheid time, why can I not even do dishes, and why must the other women clean up after their sons and brothers, as well as their husbands? Do we subconsciously take the load off those we somehow see as special and more deserving? How long will it take before that unquestioned acceptance of privilege will be erased from our hard drives?

Of course things are not fully black and white. Not all men are idle. Beside Andy, there are other brothers: Comfort is employed and Lucas is in MK, and there is also Charlie, I am told, though I will remain unclear about what he does.[86] There is another brother, Enver[87] too; but I'll find out about him only much later because now he is temporarily in jail. Likewise, the women are not all martyrs. They can be harsh and cruel, especially towards their own daughters, whom they condition to their own experience of suffering and hard work. After seeing it everywhere, the housework and the extra burdens and the harshness dished out to daughters; the lack of understanding when they ask for some patience, some warmth, I start feeling that the women just think that this is it. That a daughter must just get used to it. That it will be harder if she rebels.

But while rebellion is precisely what Maisy does, others seek relief in submitting, closing their eyes and hoping for a sign from God. Quite a few neighbours here follow prophets who promise them heaven, and on Sundays I witness groups of women in their long dress uniforms – green, white, blue – in the yards and streets, crying out their pain as they sing and wave their hands in the air, all looking at the preacher, waiting breathlessly for words of comfort.

Others – or maybe they are the same, for why shouldn't these groups overlap – try to find material ways out of the hardship. You see them at the shebeens and taverns, taxi ranks and Baragwanath hospital, cajoling men for handouts, jewellery, meals. How much you get depends on what you look like, how you market yourself, how savvy you are. At the Baragwanath taxi rank the poorest girls will go with men in exchange for a cooldrink.

Or any drink. Men drink themselves into stupors, but there are plenty of women who do so, too. One evening in the local shebeen, where Maisy takes me so that we can both have a beer after a hard day, a drunk woman rants at Maisy, using what must be the most obscene expletives in Sotho, aggressively addresses her as a 'slut' who 'has forgotten where you come from' and 'sleeps with comrades in town'. Maisy translates for me quietly, until she finally loses it. Rising slowly from her plastic chair, she takes an empty beer bottle from the plastic table, breaks it against the wall, then points the sharp-sharded half in her hand at the woman. She whispers something in Sotho, in a low, dangerous voice I have never heard, and the woman meekly gets up and slides away, out of the plastic curtain-covered rectangular space in the concrete walls of the concrete block that is this drinking hole.

'I get so angry with such women,' Maisy tells me later, when she is calm again. 'They are like crabs in a basket, all angry, all ready to pull one another down.'

I ask where the comrades are in all this. All I can see of ANC activity is an old 'Viva MK' slogan painted on a wall nearby the shebeen. She sighs. 'We don't get together. Some of us work in town, with the NGOs. I try with the Women's League. But somehow we are not together in the community.'

We agree that we should get away from here.

A glimpse of the new

Hillbrow is freedom. The friendly white woman who gives me a lift from the airport ('Ooohhh, but I can't drop you there! It is dangerous! We'll get raped!') may not see it that way, but it is. Even if gangsters live where we do, in a flat called Smits Hof, and the main glass entrance door sports a bullet hole, they don't hurt us. Barring the eventuality that one might be in a wrong place when bullets fly.

'They rob whites,' laughs Maisy. 'Just stay close to me.' She is right. We pass gangsters in the street and, somehow, they seem nicer and less threatening here than they were in the township. They even smile at us, as do the tomato and cabbage vendors outside in Kotze and Jeppe Streets. Often when we pass the vendors they shout that they *love* us. 'Marry me! I adore you!'

It is here, even more than in Colleen's house in Hopkins Street that a sentence from *Alice in Wonderland* comes to mind: 'they were indeed a queer-looking party that assembled on the bank.' In this case that may have something to do with the fact that there are actual queer people here. Just around the corner, the comrades from the Township AIDS Project, headed by Simon Nkoli, can be seen daily collecting their boxes of condoms and educational leaflets from the clinic in Esselen Street. Simon Nkoli is dead now, but this is how I remember him: thoroughly sweet and with bright eyes, carrying boxes of condoms that are so desperately needed by so many, gay and straight, working incessantly to protect as many people as he can.

I get to know Nkoli a bit also because Bart, who spends more and more time in South Africa, and he are now dating. As we talk about life and politics, Simon shows great depth and maturity, as well as the kindness I have come to note as a sure sign of character and courage among comrades who have suffered, but who have overcome their bitterness. For the past decade Nkoli has been through violently oppressed protests with police beatings and arrests; a trial for 'treason, terrorism, subversion, murder and furthering the aims of the ANC' as one of the Delmas trialists; and jail time for four years, sharing a cell with comrades, some of whom gave him a hard time because he was gay. He was released on parole in 1988, and has worked since then to fight for gay rights within the ANC.

He giggles and embraces you when he greets, and dances with great joy in the Skyline on weekends. Still selfless and hardworking and passionate and pleasant, he is one of the many impressive South Africans who together form the wonderful mystery of this country: so much pain, yet so much warmth, while still facing incredible odds and disaster, and the ubiquitous threat of AIDS. Why does it have to be this way? Hasn't this country suffered enough? Why this new nightmare, after emerging from the old one? What have these people done to be punished thus? *Senzeni na*?

The virus spreads through blood, and this country is bleeding, often literally. Among hurt, dislocated and fragmented people, broken men and women, lost loved ones, violent relationships and ruptured communities, the epidemic infiltrates everywhere, martyring thousands who have already been martyred before. Chris Hani saw it coming from exile: he warned at a recent AIDS conference in Maputo that this new scourge may 'ruin the realisation of our dreams'; and 'result in untold damage and suffering by the end of the century'.[88]

Simon Nkoli himself will die of it, six years from now in 1998.

But now he is alive, and we meet him and Bart for lunch at the Three Sisters restaurant, or paging through subversive and foreign literature that is now freely available at Exclusive Books, and in the Skyline disco where Raymond Matinyana does his drag Miss Thandi act. Even though we are surrounded by new and old disaster, we all become liberated here, in Hillbrow in the early nineties, where white and black, women and men, gay and straight, are envisioning a new country. There is a lot of sex across colour lines, as well as the gender bar, here, too.

It has been a trend in Hillbrow, says flashy Solly Rametsi, owner of the Razmatazz nightclub, when Maisy and I are having drinks on his terrace. Throughout the eighties, he dated only white girls, who would come to dance and fornicate here with him, escaping Calvinist backgrounds, living dangerously. His present girlfriend however is black, he confesses, pointing vaguely at one of the amazingly pretty and lithe creatures who hover inside his club. 'I feel more at home with our girls anyway. White ones, that was nice when it was not allowed.'

Solly Rametsi is not just a gemstone-studded nightclub owner who broke apartheid mores and laws. In conversation with him, nightmares still break through the cracks when he tells of his father who had been cheeky to his 'baas,' and then been forced to dig his own grave. Solly was then a little boy, growing up on a farm near Rustenburg. He watched his father digging the grave, then being shot and falling into it. There are few places in this country where you can scratch the surface without unearthing terror.

I indulge in my bit of crime, unscrewing the 'Whites only' plates from elevator doors and confiscating them. I also indulge in the luxury of the swimming pool in our flat, which is equipped with one like many flats in Hillbrow. They were for whites once, after all.

The cabal

Ivan has, meanwhile, been busy rebuilding his life as an activist in Durban. He now works at the Durban Housing Action Committee (DHAC), a formerly UDF-linked civic organisation that defends the interests of residents in the city. When I visit him one day, I meet Pravin Gordhan, and two other friends, Vish Sewpersadh and his wife Vidhu. I learn later that they were steadfast and incredibly courageous members of the Durban ANC underground too.[89]

The activists who are his friends here are all Indians. Some, including Pravin Gordhan, are involved in preparations for the multi-party conference CODESA, Conference for a Democratic South Africa, that must map out the transitional future. I ask Ivan light-heartedly if he remembers the speaker at King's Stadium who called for an Indian government instead of an interim government. Are we on our way there?

The response is irritated. 'We lived in segregated areas and went to segregated schools. That was not because we wanted it. It was what apartheid did. Of course Indian activists mainly know Indian activists, just like African activists mainly know African activists.' I don't know yet, at this point in time, how hard they had worked to change precisely that. Krishna, Pat and Jabu, Judson and Shadrack sacrificed their lives for that ideal. Pat and Jabu had even been members of the Natal Indian Congress. Had they survived, would they ever have expected that the architecture of apartheid would simply remain in place after liberation, a guilty and immovable landscape? 'The day after liberation is essentially the same as the day before. We have a long way to go,' he says. 'We knew that.'

I discover only later that to his ears, my remark about Indians carries echoes of the anti-Indian invective spewed by some in the UDF and the ANC recently. Peter Mokaba, now the rabble-rousing leader of the ANC Youth League, and an activist who puts down others as a tactic to advance himself, is its most vocal proponent.[90]

Pravin Gordhan's name is the first one mentioned in an anonymous report doing the rounds recently, 'The Undue Influence of the Cabal', dated 14 March 1990. It was supposedly drafted for the ANC by an anonymous Commission on the Cabal, which in all probability included Peter Mokaba, since a draft version mentions Mokaba in various capacities as the designated individual to follow up on and 'deal with' the cabal.[91] The report states that this cabal, a group of 'certain Indians and whites' (...) 'manipulates strategy, lacks democratic practices and stifles free and open debate by strategising for all and sundry (…) and imposing their will on others. (…) Those who disagree with such strategies are often labelled as nationalists, mavericks, old guard, etc.'

The report concludes that cabal activities have 'led to the ousting of senior activists', and that to counter this, the ANC's 'strategy should be aimed at isolating certain individuals and at the same time undermining their power base'. The report has remained in the shadows though, and has never been presented as an actual ANC document.

Most activists on the ground have ignored the cabal report; yet, the narrative lingers, to be resurrected every now and then as power struggles and factional fighting rear their heads in the ANC. Prompted by such an instance in 2016, journalist, editor and former UDF activist Cyril Madlala will attempt to explain the anti-cabal resentment in the late eighties. Indian activists, he writes, coming from relatively privileged areas, happened to have 'more access to basic resources: printing facilities, typewriters, suitable venues for meetings, vehicles and offices, some cash to spare for the struggle, and so forth' than black comrades did and that created bad blood.[92] Nomboniso Gasa will later write that a subsequent resurrection of the cabal story was intended to 'protect the looting project' by some in government.[93]

It is a logical assumption that better resources and networks could result in greater influence in mass campaigns and public meetings. However, when I research details of the cabal accusations I can't find examples of 'imposing their will on others', nor any suggestion that bad decisions were taken as a result, good decisions thwarted, nor descriptions of cases whereby good comrades were unfairly treated. The document claims that some individuals were 'ousted' after having been called 'nationalists, mavericks and old guard', which seem to be things activists may indeed have called one another in debates. If there was any unfair ousting, this might be problematic, but the Commission on the Cabal doesn't seem to object to that practice, as long as it is the commission itself that does it. The report concludes that 'we prepare to finally rid our structures of them'.

'Every time activists come to the fore, there is this talk of a cabal,' sighs Ivan. 'They did it in the UDF and they did it with Vula.' Mac Maharaj too complained about how the security police had tried to portray Vula as a conspiracy of Indians and whites, a ploy of evil lighter-coloured communists to manipulate a black majority. It is unsettling, though, to realise that one's own comrades would do the same thing. The disowning by the London bubble – Thabo Mbeki, the Pahads – of Operation Vula also centred around the narrative that Vula was a plot by a few, not something carried by the ANC as a whole. I did not realise that the anti-communist, anti-Vula narrative intersected with the noise about an Indian cabal.

'But these intersections are not ideological,' says Ivan. 'At different times, different factions will try to advance own interests by name-calling and wedge-driving. Only some, like Mokaba, will openly advance accusations; others may just quietly support them because they benefit. Yet others, for the same reason, will simply condone and say nothing. The common denominator is that it is never about principle. They could not find anything wrong on principle with Pravin.' Pravin Gordhan, who was in the movement since the mid-seventies, was strong in the leadership, at grassroots level in the communities, and in the ANC underground. 'So they would attack him simply for being strong, and mobilise on the anti-cabal, anti-Indian thing. They were not engaging with progressive goals and values. They were only talking about how so-and-so had power and so-and-so was side-lined.'

He never understood, he adds, why certain leaders would not see the destructive consequences of that focus. 'Why not be pleased that there was such a strong group on your side? Why not make that work for the movement?'

The cabal accusation is to be mixed with a general anti-Indian narrative, I note in 2018, when vocal populist Julius Malema, a new incarnation of the Mokaba type of activist, starts mentioning racist Indian employers in the same breath as Indian comrades in the ANC. Indians mistreat their workers; they don't want to marry Africans; they won't vote for political parties led by black Africans, he says, while stating that 'an Indian cabal' led by Gordhan has come to power in the ANC and the country.[94]

The two categories of Indians are obviously very different: a racist Indian shop owner would not have died for the struggle, as Krishna Rabilal had done, or go through detentions, prison, torture, like Mac Maharaj, Pravin Gordhan and Billy Nair. But Malema, and others who use racial invective to increase their own power base – the apartheid regime did it very successfully too, of course – blend the two different types of anti-Indian sentiment.

Them and us

The struggle has failed to snuff it out then, this knee-jerk sentiment of 'them and us'. Whites versus blacks, Africans versus Indians and coloureds, even within the Congress movement. In some areas in Natal and the Transvaal – even, scandalously, in some international media – there has been talk of a 'war between Zulus and Xhosas' instead of between ANC and Inkatha, never mind a Third Force. It is exactly what apartheid wanted. Don't think about what you stand for or what you jointly work for. Rather align with your group, make it all about your group, and fight to keep out those who are not like you: others, foreigners, strangers. The ANC was founded on opposing racism, but maybe it is too much to ask to find these values already rooted in South Africa, when ethnicity still pulls so strongly everywhere, from Congo to China, India to the United States, Kenya to Brazil, and Poland to Italy.

It strikes me, however, that anti-Indian accusations have rarely been levelled in the ANC against certain other high profile Indians, like Thabo Mbeki's allies, the formerly London-based Pahad brothers, for example, or Indian businessmen like the tycoon Vivian Reddy, who never appeared to oppose apartheid but is now cosying up to the powers that be. Do ethnic divisions stay dormant as long as one is not perceived to be a problem? 'Anti-Indian sentiment is used to sideline those who think independently,' Ivan says. 'Probably because they appear to pose a risk to those seeking power. They even use the label against principled African comrades. They call them puppets of Indians and whites.'

In years to come, Vivian Reddy and fellow Indian businessman, race horse and security firm owner Roy Moodley, will emerge as good friends of then President Jacob Zuma. Beside three other Indians, that is. The Gupta brothers from Uttar Pradesh[95] even look the greedy, self-advancing and shady part to the hilt, with their shrewd-looking eyes and Bollywood-style moustaches. But though they do operate like a mafia, and are Indian, from actual India, they will never be accused of being a 'cabal'. 'Populist politicians don't fear crooks,' shrugs Ivan. 'They welcome them.'

It is ironic that though the cabal rhetoric accuses Indian ANC comrades of accumulating power and privilege, the Indian activists that I know don't seem to be very good at attaining wealth at all. Mac Maharaj stays in Yeoville, Pravin in a flat in Durban. Sunny lives in a dilapidated part of Durban that will soon be redlined. Ivan is still selling textiles door to door. His family continues in the old house in Merebank, and Coastal still stays with his mum.

The advantage that still benefits many in the Indian community, however, is its social capital: a history in educational advancement, community structures and management. Indians established and ran their own schools even before apartheid; some are in professions or are employed in the manufacturing and service industries; some own small businesses. In this community you actually do have uncles in the furniture business, as the jingle of the now defunct furniture chain Joshua Doore used to go. It will be used jeeringly, to great laughter from his sycophantic audiences, by Julius Malema later, when attacking Pravin Gordhan, calling him 'Joshua Doore'.

Some Indians are pharmacists, that profession that creates something powerful out of knowing what to put with what and in what dosage. Pravin Gordhan is a pharmacist. The Hillbrow pharmacy in Kotze Street is run by fellow Indian comrade Joe, who takes messages for both Mac and Pravin. 'They call pharmacy studies Indian studies at my university,' a white girl tells me at some occasion. 'Sometimes activists say it's racist to say that, but it's just true.' Philip has had great fun telling me about black fear of – real or imagined – Indian knowledge. One of his stories had been that in the north, people believed that you could buy 'bottled lightning', a magical weapon with which to target a rival or an enemy, from Indians.

Ivan talks of the old non-racial ANC a lot during the days when he prepares for CODESA, as if that old ANC is at risk. 'We were taught about inclusivity,' he shakes his head, reading in the newspaper about yet another public event in which Mokaba – in spite of criticism from more sage leaders like Mandela – has riled crowds with his 'kill the boer, kill the farmer' slogan. 'Why must you kill boers, or white people at all?'

It's when we are together with comrades like Totsie, or the late Victor Molefe[96], the leader of the attack on the Voortrekkerhoogte military base, or Dipuo, or Flo, who is Phumla again now, that we talk about our diverse backgrounds without judging each other. Having Jan van Riebeeck for an ancestor comes with a great responsibility to help put things right again, we all know that, so I guess I am expected to do my bit as Totsie gets into people's banking, pioneering home loans for the lower incomes, Dipuo organises the ANC in Alexandra, and Ivan joins a new campaign against polluting practices of the Mondi paper mill in Merebank.

I don't know if it is enough that I just write but our comrades don't stress about that. They have all been struggle leaders in their own right, most often also hailing from strong families who stuck together during the harshest of times. They have grown in the Congress of Mandela, Tambo, Dadoo and Fischer, a universe in which Mandela was a Xhosa royal, Tambo a teacher from an incipient African academic elite in the Eastern Cape and Johannesburg, Fischer a comrade lawyer from an old-fashioned 'boer' Afrikaner family and Dadoo a UK-educated medical doctor. In the non-racial universe, all four were eminently useful and worthy, precisely because of the value they added from diverse backgrounds.

In 1991, the very idea that the best friends of ANC President Jacob Zuma will be a mafia of Gupta brothers from India, while Pravin Gordhan will be haunted by a former apartheid cop from the Transkei,[97] seems unthinkable. Or that white comrades like Barbara Hogan will be called servants of a morphed apartheid demon called white monopoly capital. Maybe if one knows everything that is going to happen one will not be so cheerfully moving forward. Maybe it is best that one does not.

Breakfast at the Holiday Inn
October

It is 1991 and the country is preparing for CODESA; all-party negotiations are to be held at the World Trade Centre close to Jan Smuts Airport about a new Constitution to replace the apartheid framework. The ANC negotiating team is headed by Cyril Ramaphosa, Thabo Mbeki, Joe Slovo and Mac Maharaj, while Chris Hani and Nelson Mandela deliver opening speeches. The NIC is here, led by Pravin Gordhan, and Ivan is part of the delegation too. He will take part in a working group on the subject of an interim government and an interim Constitution.

I haven't planned to report on CODESA. There are dozens of journalists from Europe, including the Netherlands, to do so already. I have already missed the opening when I decide belatedly to attend the talks anyway. I tell myself I might interview Mac and Ramaphosa, and maybe Mbeki if I get a chance. But, of course, it is really about Ivan. After months, he is finally in Johannesburg again, and I haven't seen him yet. I can't not go.

After emerging from my Hillbrow Maxi Taxi, wandering around the maze of little rooms where sub-committees and sub-sub-committees sweat out myriad things, and waiting at reception areas and at water coolers, the only known face I see is Mac's. He narrates how, in one committee, the Nats have tried to sell the idea of a senior parliamentary house in the new dispensation. 'They proposed it should consist of "established structures in society" like the Dutch Reformed Church, the private school governing bodies, landowners' associations, and the like. They meant a white senior house, of course,' he grins. 'They even wanted it to have a veto over all parliamentary decisions. So I told them it was a fine idea. And that we should also add the black taxi associations, the burial societies, the township churches and the stokvel savings clubs. They never mentioned it again.'

There is only one way to find Ivan. At the airport Holiday Inn where all the delegates sleep, I ask for him at reception and he comes down the stairs, surprised and a bit alarmed. I am half expecting to be told to go home, but he says I can stay if I want.

Much later, I find out that Ivan has already discussed our personal situation with his peers in the activist networks in Durban and asked for guidance. The local comrades understood his position. The verdict, as far as I can fathom, has been that all in the group, including Ivan himself, will continue to care for and liaise with Rae, while he is also entitled to start a new life.

When I hear about this, years later, it's from Mac, of course. I ask him on that occasion how difficult that decision was. Three people, two traumatised by war, of whom one is severely damaged. The third is a newcomer from outside, a disruptive, alien element. How do you decide? 'It's not that hard,' says Mac, in his measured negotiator's way, in which compromise is a given. 'Two out of three can be happy.' I still hear him say that in my mind.

Privilege II

Back at home in Hillbrow, I learn how a white person in South Africa – particularly one who knows the way in the white rule system – can be useful. When Lucas, the most political of Maisy's brothers, disappears after having been arrested, the police at the Hillbrow station just keep telling her he is not there. There is as yet nowhere to go for Maisy to complain, or insist on an investigation, and she now just sits, her skin all grey, under a blanket next to the phone while, at intervals, ANC comrades from Soweto visit to discuss the case. They inform us that

Lucas should be freed from wherever he is, since he did not commit a crime and the weapons in the car he was found in – sleeping, while the driver and others had gone on an errand – belonged to a self-defence unit, and were meant to resist Inkatha.

Sadly, the clarification doesn't really help much. When after four meetings no way forward has come up, I phone Ivan. You should contact Stephanie Kemp, he suggests. 'She is the head of the ANC branch in Yeoville and she knows everybody.' He gives me a phone number.

It works. Kemp has clearly dealt with more such cases after her return from exile. She is well connected and authoritative. She knows how to find the colonel in charge of peace-keeping in the Johannesburg East region and knows how to make him feel *personally responsible* for whatever fate Lucas might be facing. Lucas surfaces the next day in the holding cells at Hillbrow police station. He has been there all along.

The second thing I learn is that the centres for street children in Hillbrow are virtually all for boys. After my third visit, for a story, to a 'lost boys' care home, I ask the black male social worker where the girls are. 'Girls can take care of themselves,' he assures me. 'They always find a place to sleep.' He means girls can go with men, they can be magosha, hookers.

The one project Hillbrow has for homeless girls, on only one afternoon a week, discourages girls from going that route though. They are invited to tea and a meal, and to learn how to crochet, but are also told 'how to be a proud and good woman' by the project leader (whose name I have sadly forgotten). 'We teach them not to be magosha. Rather sleep in the cold than sell yourself,' she says. I ask about the danger of rape and death in the streets. Should the project not rather campaign for help for the girls? The project leader nods, with sad eyes. She knows. She is not a bad person. 'But as women we must learn how to suffer. In Sotho we say the woman holds the sharp end of the knife.' And she thinks that is a good thing? She thinks, then shrugs. 'It is how it is. We better get used to it.'

Or not.

Maisy's laugh, long-lasting bursts of loud laughter, provide much-needed relief from the victim narratives, from the 'stand by your man' ones to the 'hold the wrong end of the knife' ones. 'When they talk to me about my culture,' she says, wiping the tears from her face after one of her laughing fits, 'I tell them my culture is sitting in a jacuzzi for hours and doing absolutely nothing.'

Still, every time I think of the hostile universe so many continue to live in in this country, amid fear of death and pain and messages of how they must die for self-respect and hold knives so they can bleed some more, I see Maisy's tears that come when she laughs. They are only partially of laughter.

Valentine's Day, 1992

I am at Bart's place at the Mercatorplein in Amsterdam, where South African friends often stay for holidays and periods of respite from their lives of struggle and disease. We try to make sense of who we have become, from very Dutch communists to individuals politically and personally intertwined with this new South Africa, although nobody knows what it is or what it will become. We seem to be changing with it, with everything and everybody in it, too. We drink vodka, Bart's daily evening comfort, and today also mine.

When the phone rings, it is Ivan, and I am surprised; he got Bart's phone number from my mother. I wait to hear news, how it is going, when I can return, if I even should return. But he says nothing besides asking how I am doing and I get irritated. Why is he even phoning if he has nothing to say? I ask him about developments, he says 'none'. It tell him that maybe it's better to call it quits, in that case, because these phone calls about nothing are not helping anybody, let's be honest.

'I just phoned because it's Valentine's day,' he says and I hear it, but only half, because Valentine's Day is not celebrated in Holland. Worked up and tearful I hang up the phone, and after a few more vodkas fall asleep on Bart's couch.

Red lights

It is June when we meet again, in Amsterdam's red light district. We meet here because I am living in my friend Liesbeth's apartment, which borders the district, while she is in Germany. Ivan has written to me to say that we will relate in whichever way I want, as long as we can relate. If I want to break off, we can do so. He is not ready to make any concrete promises but he still wants to see me. I have said yes. Of course.

Ivan is probably just a little surprised to see the neighbourhood as he arrives, but he says nothing after he rings the bell and I open the door and we stare at one another for a while. He then walks up to me and puts his arms around me, awkwardly, and then says that I must know that he wants a family and children with me and that he still doesn't know how to move forward but he is trying. He intends to stay a couple of weeks, if that is alright with me. Rae is stable. It is all he says about her. He also says he has put everything else on hold.

It is that night – using the calculation of hindsight – that Devi is conceived.

'I can't say I'm excited,' he responds when I tell him about the pregnancy test. 'It is a bit soon.' It is soon. I am surprised too. Who knew this would happen as soon as you relax on the precautions, just once, just a little bit? Excitement is also not what I feel. It's nice to know that the body procreation things work, for sure. But we both have no house, no steady jobs. We don't even have a country. Of course, there is abortion. But neither of us want that, for now.

We revert to taking it one day at a time after he leaves. WhatsApp and email don't exist yet. His last fax came two weeks ago, typically with very little information in it. He only asks when I will be coming. I faxed back a date and a time, but had no response after that. As I approach Hillbrow in the Maxi Taxi with my nearly three-month-old foetus and my South African visa 'alsook vir die nuwe baba' in my handbag, I still don't know what will happen.

If I hear nothing, I must go back. I then will probably consider ending the pregnancy before it's too late. But I have felt movement inside my body already and I love the experience, so I really would not want to do that. But what if he has decided this – me, this new thing, this new universe – is not a good thing after all, then what, you don't want a baby amid homelessness, partnerlessness, bitterness. Then what.

I have no idea why Maisy is laughing as she opens the door to the flat at 101 Smits Hof on the tenth floor. I ask her what is funny as I put my bags down, and then the bathroom door opens and he comes out, as he has come out of the bathroom so many times per day during the days I have known him with his messed up digestive system, only now he comes out of the bathroom in the Hillbrow flat as I stand here with my little belly. I look at him, and he looks at me, and Maisy has a bottle of champagne.

Which I can't drink now.

***

We visit Swaziland, where he shows me where Shadrack, Pat and Jabu were killed, where Joe was kidnapped. We go out to the movies in Mbabane, and a group of men in the street surround us asking for a light, but clearly intent on appropriating our wallets and my handbag. He handles the danger by telling me to stand on the side of the pavement while he proceeds, calmly, to light the cigarette. I can see the confusion on the men's faces as they open the circle to let me stand on the side, then meekly wait for the cigarette to be lit and let us on our way.

You do what Ivan asks you to do, I remember, and I think how extraordinary this actually is, with this man being so small and thin.

'They must have thought I had a gun,' he laughs, later.

In Yeoville

While Ivan prepares his Durban environment for our upcoming changes I am back in Hillbrow, still in the flat with Maisy, but spend time mostly in neighbouring Yeoville. One cannot but enjoy Yeoville, with its orthodox Jews, communists, dreadlocked Ethiopian filmmakers and butch women who wear T-shirts that say 'Nobody knows I'm a lesbian', even if it's clear that everybody does, and the comrade at the chicken outlet who exclaims 'Whoa, three continents in one stomach!' when he gets to know me, my background, the fact of my Indian partner, and our plans for a future in South Africa.

I love the jazz places, the second-hand bookshops and restaurants, and meeting friends at our regular haunts for coffee or drinks, but I am also often here just to get out of the flat in Hillbrow. We now share the place with two friends Maisy has taken in to help pay the rent, but Linda and Corlia,[98] both trying to make it in town, are not the most cheerful company. Corlia is desperate to find a job because her savings are running out and Linda mostly sits around with a sullen expression on her face. There is probably also trauma where these two come from, but I haven't got the mental space to ask them about it – even assuming they would want to tell me – and chances are I can't help anyway. So I just get out.

In the mornings I report on the Goldstone Commission, just established by the De Klerk government to investigate what is now routinely called the Third Force. Thanks to intrepid journalists, and in spite of the regime's efforts to destroy and hide records of its murderous activities, many reports and documents have recently surfaced about army and police support to Inkatha impis and death squads. The regime can't pretend anymore. The commission led by Judge Richard Goldstone sits in the Dutch Reformed Church Synod in Pretoria and I go there almost every day, with my belly in the minibus taxi, to hear testimonies about detention, torture, murder and mayhem carried out by impis and faceless regime operatives in the areas where black people live.

But then suddenly, the Third Force is in Yeoville, too.

It comes in the shape of a Mozambican kitchen help who works at Scandalo, a Greek restaurant in Rockey Street. I am told about him by the owner, the portly, friendly George Milaras. 'Don't worry, I already got the press on it,' Milaras says excitedly when he spots me at his takeaway counter. 'But I thought I should tell you too. Maybe you can write it for overseas.' As we sit down and I am offered a cooldrink, Milaras narrates how he recently employed a Mozambican named João Cunha, who had come recommended for the kitchen cleaning job by two white policemen, whom Milaras knew, 'because of my liquor license issues and so on'. Soon, however, the restaurant owner discovered that Cunha was much more than a dish washer: he was an ex-soldier, a deserter from Mozambique's Frelimo government army. 'He was still involved in dangerous activities,' Milaras continues. 'After a few months he came to me to ask if he could be transferred to a restaurant elsewhere in town, because the police were paying him to spy on an Indian man who lives here in Yeoville, in Muller Street, and he did not want to do that anymore. He wanted to get out.' I can talk to João Cunha if I want, Milaras says. He is in hiding but he can organise it.

I don't know what to say. My instinct, pregnant and looking at places to build a family in and around the very same Muller Street, tells me to stay far away from this. A bomb was placed under the bonnet of Mac's car here last year.[99] And the Indian man in Muller Street is probably Mac. He lives there with his wife, Zarina, and their two kids.

We must warn Mac, of course, and pass on the message that there is still foul play afoot. But getting involved with this story, just as we are trying to find some peace, is quite another thing. I don't want to see João Cunha and, more importantly, I don't want him to see me. I ask which local newspaper is on this at the moment and am relieved to find that it is in very good hands: the intrepid Pearlie Joubert at the progressive *Vrye*

Weekblad is working on it.

She will soon unearth the fact that, apart from Cunha having an interest in Mac, the man has also identified sites of massacres in KwaZulu.[100]

The João Cunha affair is not the only fear-inspiring feature of this clearly not very new South Africa. There are also regular train murders, in which men with assault rifles spray commuters from the townships with bullets. Dozens fall victim to it, and no one knows why. It is unlikely that these cases will ever get solved, shrugs Goldstone advocate Torie Pretorius. 'The perpetrators who got caught won't talk,' he explains and when I ask if they cannot be turned to talk in exchange for lighter sentences, he responds indignantly. 'We can't do that, we live in a regstaat, we need to respect the rule of law.'

In September, in Bisho in the Eastern Cape, soldiers kill 28 participants of a protest march against the corrupt bantustan leader Oupa Gqozo. We see it on TV and Corlia stands up and screams because relatives and friends are there. In December, when we bury struggle veteran Helen Joseph at Avalon Cemetery in Soweto, people start running and shouting during the ceremony because a bees' nest has been disturbed; immediately afterwards stories do the rounds that the security police put those bees there like live, remote-controlled weapons of makgoa.

And who can blame one for being suspicious, when the records of the supposedly neutral Goldstone Commission are kept in the Air Force building in Vermeulen Street, as I discover one day, while the company that types the sensitive witness statements is called Vlok Transcripts? 'Certainly, our Mr Vlok is the brother of Adriaan Vlok, the minister,' replies yet another friendly smiling receptionist when I ask. Until July the previous year, Adriaan Vlok was the Minister of Law and Order.

The spokesman for the Goldstone Commission is similarly comfortably unaware of the demons and nightmares that keep resurging from the old. 'The government is neutral,' he insists. So what if the military safeguards the Commission records?

Demons also surround the formerly heroic, now dangerous Winnie Madikizela-Mandela, who is openly friendly with a diamond smuggler named Hazel Crane ('We share much, we both have had trouble with the police,' she has said about her) and a French arms trader ('He helps us.'). And while we gallivant in Yeoville, there is a rapist on the loose: a disturbed black man who forces white single young women to pretend they are his girlfriends. ('The whites hanged my father,' Wonga Ndungane will say when he is finally arrested.)

In our Hillbrow flat, depression reigns as Corlia drinks Old Brown Sherry in the afternoon when she comes back after fruitlessly looking for an office job, and as time progresses, also in the mornings, while Linda sits around hygiene-challenged and obviously depressed. Do they ever pay their share of the rent, I ask Maisy, and she just sighs.

At the end of our working days we watch soapies. *Days of Our Lives* is the one moment of the day that despite our exasperation, we rest and identify with a strange town in Salem, once town of witches in the United States, where at this point in the series one of the main characters, a blonde doctor named Marlena is possessed by a demon and talks in a terrifying low voice.

Somehow, imagining the demons far away makes it better.

* * *

One of the last stories I do before going back to Holland to give birth concerns the annual police ball in Pretoria. The Dutch newspaper I write for is curious to know, as I am, how the police in Pretoria can do fun fairs and tiekiedraai at a time when people are being gunned down in the trains.

I speak to a Warrant Officer Schreuder who sounds genuinely puzzled when he says he knows nothing about murders in trains and that he can't imagine what such things would have to do with the police ball. 'Minister Pik Botha is the guest speaker,' he offers helpfully, steering me back to the issue at hand. 'I can send you his speech.' I briefly contemplate asking him about the Pik Botha-authorised military raids in neighbouring countries, that killed Krish in Mozambique as well as the artist Thami Mnyele and over a dozen other people in Gaborone, Botswana. But I say nothing and put down the phone while Warrant Officer Schreuder is still talking about the youth programme, the choir and the sports auction.

'I don't know what is going to happen,' I tell Bart over the phone, exhausted after the police ball interview, telling him about it while feeling my tense belly and painful back. 'There are things going on around me and inside of me. And I don't know what it is and whether it will turn out well or not. With all this insanity, the baby might even come out crazy or whatever.' 'As long as it doesn't come out as a Warrant Officer Schreuder,' says Bart.

A pink lounge suite
Amsterdam, 1993

'I have set aside a pink lounge suite,' Ivan says as he carefully cuts Devi's nails on the sleeper couch in our temporary apartment in Amsterdam. Tiny Devi's fingernails are long from having been kept too long in a womb that took too long to do its job of birthing, and she has scratched her cheeks. She is also still a bit red from the heat lamp that the cautious nurses put on her because she was just so small, and bony, and bald, a red little river crayfish. Ivan switched that lamp off after a while because, frankly, she was almost getting baked. 'And a pram. It's all waiting for us. Suggie helped.' As per the Joshua Doore jingle, 'You've got an uncle in the furniture business', Devi does have one indeed, and a good one, too.

Actually, it is two uncles in the furniture business, because both Kisten and Suggie work for Beare Brothers' furniture shops, just as Ivan and his brother Joe did, for a short while in the past. It is a wonderful thing for us to have uncles there too, because we had nothing and now we are going to have a second-hand pink lounge suite and a pram.

The family knows all about us now. There was loud cheering in Chatsworth, from the other end of the phone line just this morning when Ivan told them the news. It was so loud that I could hear it on the sofa where I was lying down with the baby, with her big eyes that she fights hard to keep open because she is just so curious, even if she really needs to sleep. 'They like the name,' Ivan said, smiling, as he held the phone in my direction.

That little bald red bony creature will brighten and grow considerably more beautiful in the coming weeks as she manages to keep her eyes open for longer periods, and the dark brown hair grows and her skin becomes a good beige. But even that first day, with all her redness and scrawniness, Ivan holds her and gazes at her with soft eyes, and there is no lack of excitement anymore. 'It almost makes you believe in God,' he says.

* * *

Ivan has just gone back to South Africa to rent a Yeoville flat and transport our pink lounge suite there when Chris Hani is killed. Devi and I, still in Amsterdam because she is too small to fly, watch the murder scene on TV. Chris is wearing the tracksuit I think I remember from Transkei, but now it is full of blood and he is lying face down in his front yard in Dawn Park, Boksburg, which is a place I do not know. I also don't recognise the man who is crying beside him and shouting that Chris was his friend, until the TV commentator names him: Tokyo Sexwale.

A little later the TV shows thousands of angry and crying South Africans in the street, with one after the other commentator expressing concern about violence, even civil war. I panic a little. What will happen to our plans to live in Yeoville with our furniture and our pram? But then the culprits, two racist white conservatives, are caught and I sigh with relief so audibly that Devi briefly wakes, looks around, sees that everything is soft and warm around her and smiles.

We are preparing to go back when O.R. Tambo dies, too.

It is a second disaster. Chris Hani had held the combatants together. They loved him fiercely, as much as they disliked the actual head of MK, Joe Modise, with his lack of caring, his expensive whisky and his penchant for sending cadres to buy shoes for him in white apartheid towns. Just as Chris Hani was the commander of the principled MK, so had Oliver Tambo been the principled president of the ANC, with his humility, humanity and stamina. He had kept everyone and everything together in exile. He had his first stroke in 1989, but this second one, on 24 April 1993, kills him. 'The murder of Chris must have been a terrible blow,' says Ivan over the phone.

South Africa still has Mandela, of course, the wise leader, the statesman, the connector, the powerful magician, but will it be enough?

Landing blindly

I try to keep my anxiety down in Amsterdam, as I take springtime walks with Devi in our sea explorers' neighbourhood, from Vespucci, Bartholomeus Diaz and Vasco da Gama streets back to James Cook Street. I looked up James Cook, an explorer who was killed while trying to kidnap a local ruler in Hawaii. The others, even if they were trade route trailblazers rather than outright colonisers, were sometimes violent too. I read that Da Gama massacred people in the Muslim ports on the East African coast to force them to make way for European shippers – like a taxi war, perhaps, but with boats. The Dutch are split between a right wing that is proud of the 'heroes' who conquered parts of the world, and the left that is deadly ashamed of the slave trade, the Dutch East India Company, the wars and the exploitation.

We were especially terrible, of course. Apparently, Karl Marx himself singled out Dutch colonialists as among the most cruel in history. In *Genesis of the Industrial Capitalist*, he cites British colonial administrator Thomas Stamford Raffles as saying that the history of Dutch rule in Asia was 'one of the most extraordinary relations of treachery, bribery, massacre, and meanness'. Marx also quotes a report from Makassar, in Dutch-colonised Indonesia, that describes the place as 'full of secret prisons, one more horrible than the other, crammed with unfortunates, victims of greed and tyranny fettered in chains, forcibly torn from their families'.[101]

The Dutch brought slaves and political exiles from Indonesia and Malaysia to work in the colony that Jan van Riebeeck established too. A Muslim community of fishermen in the early 18th century erected a shrine for exiled noble, Sheikh Yusuf of the Sultanate of Gowa, who was credited with founding the Islamic faith in the Cape. Since the Sultanate of Gowa was situated in Makassar in Indonesia, the site is now a township named Macassar, with a C.

At the AABN we had done our best to make our compatriots understand that there was little to be proud of. Yes, we had got rich as a country, and the daredevil adventurism and curiosity of the early explorers could perhaps be admired. They risked their lives after all, sailing on only a compass and a sextant, landing blindly. But after that, it was just greed and violence, and the sowing of nightmares.

We had used apartheid South Africa as the most poignant illustration of the evil our ancestors had done, and our current government still did by trading with the regime. We had renamed streets and squares in the Transvaal suburb in the east of Amsterdam from Pretorius and Piet Retief to Luthuli and Steve Biko. We had shown films of public speeches made by O.R. Tambo to foreign trade associations and union's international committees as part of the Boycott Apartheid campaign. On one such occasion a large harbour worker had nodded in approval and said that 'that Mr Tomba really had a point.'

And now, after Chris Hani, Tambo is dead.

On a more personal level I also worry about what this means for Ivan. Now that both Chris, the leader of the guerrilla army, and Tambo, commander of Operation Vula, are no more; now that Vula has been rubbished, played down as a cowboy game, without Tambo there to set the record straight, will Ivan be discarded? Those who know Ivan will trust him with any assignment – it is why he was invited to CODESA – but he has no formal qualifications, no more schooling than matric. In the underground, he has always kept personal relations to a minimum. And he will not lobby for a job. The ANC is all he knows. Will he have to remain in textile sales? He thinks it will be alright. 'We have some networks. And we have our family.'

Chatsworth, later in 1993

Boy, do we have family. Walking up the twenty-something concrete steps that lead to the front porch of Sister's house in Unit One, Chatsworth, with Devi in my arms, I am greeted by more family than I have experienced in my entire life. Again, there are no frowns, no whispers, nothing but elated, hearty, happy wishes and embraces, from all the aunts and uncles and cousins and the odd neighbour who has come to witness. First the youngest brother, the one who stayed away for fourteen years, has come home, and now there is his new family too. I feel insecure and I look at Sister, with her long black braid and beautiful face and soft eyes – Ivan's eyes – looking kindly at me and I ask something, half spoken, not clear, and as she looks back at me, there are only softness and offers of sweets, and her voice saying I must be fine, all is fine. The baby goes from arm to arm, welcomed and hugged by everyone in the tiny lounge in this township home. 'This surely is the whitest Devi I've ever seen,' grins cousin Indran.

It's also the most hugged and embraced this particular Devi has ever been. After a while she is all hugged out and exhausted, and as we retire to a Durban beach-front holiday apartment for the night, she cries out her distress at all these new strange arms enveloping her, and cries for an hour as the sun sets into the Indian Ocean over this new and strange South Africa.

People on the roof

There are people on the roof in Yeo Gardens[102], the flat where we now live with our baby and our lounge suite. I'll get to know them over time: a washer woman named Alida, a policeman whose name is Buthelezi but he doesn't really like Inkatha, and Sunday.[103] Sunday scrubs the stairs in this building and does cleaning for our neighbour, Mr Weber.[104] She has two young children: Mandla, who is four or five years old, and baby Thandi, of crawling age.[105] They use the fire escape to get to the roof where they live in a tiny room because the lift and internal staircase don't go all the way up.

Let me say this again. A five-year-old and his crawling baby sister move up and down to their home, via the fire escape, to a cupboard-size room. Up metal steps with huge gaps between them and no safety rail. With the street five floors below. 'I have to trust Mandla to keep her safe,' says Sunday, with her straight serious face. 'What must I do? I must work, I can't be with them the whole day. No one will build safe steps for me.'

And indeed, no city safety department, no landlord, no building caretaker seem to think anything remotely wrong with this situation. All I can do is offer to have the kids play here, in our flat, when Sunday is working, and she happily accepts. She was thinking about this already, has imagined it as a solution, I realise afterwards, remembering how she said good morning to me a week ago, rake-straight, carrying baby Thandi in a colourful shawl on her back. She looked straight at me in a piercing, unsettling way, as if she had come to call on me.

And now Devi has friends. She and Thandi shriek with laughter as Mandla pushes them around in the cardboard box that came with the washing machine. They also watch kiddies' programmes on TV, mainly *Pumpkin Patch*, which Mandla and Thandi love, with animated talking donkeys and cows. Devi is fascinated too, even if she is still too small to get what the toy animals are up to. She cries bitterly every time turtle Timothy Traddle sings his regular sad song about the thorn stuck in his foot, but apart from that, 8 Yeo Gardens, in rapidly blackening Yeoville, thankfully starts out as a place of warmth and laughter. Even Sunday laughs when she visits and watches Pieter-Dirk Uys on TV in his Evita Bezuidenhout attire, announcing herself to the help in the staff quarters at the back as 'Comrade Madam from the big house'.

Oliver Tambo and the fun

Laughter is what I remember most of the Yeoville days. It was there from the very first day, that crisp morning when we tried to enter the place prepared for us by Maisy. Or rather, under Maisy's supervision. Her brother Enver and his girlfriend, Pamela, had helped clean and prepare the flat found by Ivan. I remembered Pamela from Soweto: she was one of the girls showing me their survival strategies, part of which was dressing up as men to avoid sexual violence in the streets. I did not know that Maisy had a brother Enver then, nor that Pamela was Enver's girlfriend, nor that Enver was in jail at the time. But Ivan and I were informed by Maisy that Pamela was now our babysitter and cleaning lady because she needed a job.

It took a while before we got to the point of having this conversation inside our new apartment, though, because at first we couldn't get in. In one of those very South African mess-ups which you can't help laughing at, as we stood there with the baby and our suitcases, we realised that nobody had the key. Looking at one another and at Maisy, she had suddenly remembered that her brother Charlie had it. And Charlie was at home in Soweto, fast asleep, we had noticed, when he groggily answered the phone.

After Maisy had bellowed at him and we waited the hour that it took for him to get here by minibus taxi, he had come panting and heaving up the stairs to join us. Only to say 'oh' when we asked him for the key, and sheepishly confess that he had forgotten to bring it. The key was still in Soweto. We had laughed, jeez Charlie, and Charlie had dutifully travelled back up and down again to finally get that key.

Perhaps there was a meaning even here, a reason for Charlie's absent-mindedness, a reason why he had been sleeping late in the middle of the day, and then was so distracted that he forgot to think where he was going and for what purpose, only feeling vague alarm and a pressure to hurry. Everybody here was still battling to create a little normality in their lives.

It was still funny though.

The mornings since then have been full of laughter too, beginning when Devi, full of anticipation, pulls herself up in her cot under the portrait of O.R. Tambo and excitedly awaits what this new day will bring. She continues to enjoy herself when I place her in front of the TV after feeding and bathing her so that she can watch her favourite newsreader,

Leslie Mashokwe. She loves Mashokwe, and hops energetically in her baby seat, chuckling whenever he appears. She doesn't do this for any other newsreader and we wonder why. At one point I notice that Mashokwe's hair and facial shape are similar to Tambo's, and he also has a similar big-toothed smile like Tambo has in our portrait of him. Could that be it?

Maybe not, because she also has another favourite: Clientele insurance ads show a grey, clean-shaven and avuncular Lasting Dignity man, who tries to convince us several times a day to take out his very good funeral cover. Besides these two – and Uncle Philip, whom she adores – the only other man who gets the full hopping, feet-kicking and chuckling treatment is her father. She goes through the roof when Ivan gets home, with wide-eyed and excited outbursts of laughter, as if to say here is that delightful, *hilarious* man again.

Maybe she just likes fatherliness. A reassuring, caring look and a kind, gentle smile are the only characteristics her father has in common with Mashokwe, Tambo's benevolent face, Uncle Phil and the Lasting Dignity man.

A normal life

Ivan has found a job in the internal audit department of the ANC, on the twelfth floor in Shell House,[106] in a storeroom with wooden partitions, where he deals with businesses who want to sell supplies to the ANC. 'They try to make me order stationery and furniture by giving me presents,' he smiles when he tells me about the salespeople who visit. It all still sounds rather harmless, but he worries about the desks, chairs and couches for leaders' offices, especially when some of the new Shell House occupants order really expensive ones. 'It's not just that there is a danger of corruption,' says Ivan. 'Why do we need expensive furniture and equipment if many of us will soon be in government? We risk spending more than we have unnecessarily.'

As we are having conversations about furniture, we have no idea that, without Chris Hani to stand in the way, the South African military, British Aerospace and Thabo Mbeki's MI6 advisors are already best of friends with upcoming Minister of Defence Joe Modise, and are preparing for a R60-billion arms deal. We have no idea at all, as Ivan drives a second-hand Opel Kadett and is home at 5 pm every day to help cook dinner and put the baby to bed.

One day he tells me he is surprised at the 'guys at the office who don't want to go home, who stay out for drinks as late as possible', and shakes his head at how terrible their home life must be. He continues to be adorable in that way, even as I see my feminist plans for full-time co-parenting go up in smoke over the Yeoville rooftops. I had planned for us to each spend half the time with Devi and half the time doing paid work. What use is it that he has agreed to be there for Devi three days a week, four days every other week, if that is impossible to implement? The ANC financial department where he works under Gill and Tessa Marcus's father, Natie Marcus, wants him every day. And we need the R 2000 he brings home monthly now.

I still write freelance, but it is not a regular income, and international interest in South Africa has receded. It will pick up again in the run-up to elections next year, I tell myself, as I settle into my new life of motherhood.

We regularly have our small network of friends over during weekends and then we laugh again, with Maisy of course, and Philip Masia who is now Uncle Phil, and Bart, and Jasper Cook, who is still trying to get by as a musician in a life where the rewards never measure up to the fame he enjoys. He tells tragicomic tales of his failed and sometimes violence-ridden marriages, then also, in the same breath, of the abuse he himself experienced as a small boy. Maisy will talk about abandoning yet another boyfriend, a Pedi-boy as she calls him, who has beaten her up quite badly, and Philip of neighbourhood abusers he beat up himself. We laugh again when Maisy tells us how even more determined she is now scouting for a really good candidate to ensure a *proper* supply of tender loving care.

It's not that we are all insanely cheerful, it's that somehow we are all linked through humour. I have heard that humour kept people going even in the Nazi concentration camps. 'You must make the stories funny because you don't want to make the children cry,' Sunday will tell me later, when I ask her why she laughs as she tells me her life story full of control, beatings and shouting.

One evening Archie tells us more spiced-up stories of the past. This time he includes one about a warning that circulated among women in exile about a certain top ANC official. Let's call him Alfie. Apparently, you should never open your door when Alfie knocked, asking you if you're up for a game of Scrabble. 'Next you are being chased around the bed by Alfie with his Scrabble board,' the story concludes as we roll on the floor laughing. No, violence and racism and mortal danger and sexual harassment are not fun, and yet you can make people laugh with stories about precisely those subjects, too.

It is how our newly normal South African existence has started and how our first daughter has passed her first year. Amid tragic tales of trauma and hurt, there is laughter under the gentle smile of Oliver Tambo.

Dressing properly

Sunday reminds me of my grandmother. Dirt poor but dignified, she left a cheating husband and made it on her own with two small children, washing stairs and cleaning houses, doing whatever was necessary to feed and clothe herself and her family. Like my grandmother, she never loses sight of what is also important: her posture, her hair, her well-scrubbed and polished looks, her dresses, cheap but exquisitely chosen, well ironed and well sewn, her earrings – the only ones she has, but golden they are – and her beret placed just so, with the angle that frames her face best. Then there are her good name, her reputation and status. Don't let anyone pull your dignity down, always be straight up, always look people in the eye, my grandmother's words, are echoed by Sunday: you may be poor but you are a human with dignity. And a comrade.

My grandmother's name was Helena Meersschaert. Coming from a communist working class family in Holland early in the last century, she knew poverty, bucket system and all. She knew what it was to work for madams in houses where luxury and delicacies abounded, yet never having money to buy chocolate for herself. She would recognise what Sunday narrates: standing, mouth-watering, in front of shop windows featuring pastries or roast chickens. Sunday had walked the mountains of the Eastern Cape, complaining to herself how unfair it was that white children were driven around in soft warm buses while she had to go fetch water from the river on winter mornings. Like my grandmother and her phonetic Russian songs of revolution, Sunday knows South African struggle songs in all the country's eleven languages. Helena Meersschaert had been gorgeous; plenty an admirer had hummed along to the then popular song 'You are like a wild orchid' on seeing her. Thanks to her international communist connections, she had even once had an Indonesian independence fighter beau. Of course I am beautiful, Sunday says, when complimented on her looks. Black is beautiful.

Sunday's humour is also much like Helena's was: medicine to elevate you above daily sorrow, in a way similar to Maisy's, and Archie's, for that matter. My grandmother would tell stories of her family until she would tear up with laughter: about the uncle who never had time for the even poorer street musicians who came to beg for a five cent coin, and told them straight he'd 'rather hear a dog bark'; or the cousin who disliked dogs with a passion, countering dog owners who told him, 'He is only sniffing you', with, 'What if I smell nice, he might just want a taste.' My *oma* had inherited that humour, unlike her two sisters, who – or so the family's stories went – were more prone to envy and badmouthing others, thinking themselves the most done-in and mistreated creatures who ever lived, with resentment over time having become etched on their faces. Legend has it that their sourness irked my Oma Lenie so much that one afternoon she refused to let them into her house.

Sunday has no time for those who can't see the sunny side of life, or their own nonsense. 'Yho, life is too short,' she will say. 'You can't be proud of suffering.'

My Dutch grandmother Lenie was undoubtedly imbued with racist notions about African people. Growing up in a country, the Netherlands, that was mostly whites only, she would have only heard of Africans as primitive people, wild and hostile, or alternatively hungry and sick, incapable of looking after themselves and in need of education and civilisation. She had felt uncomfortable when such alien individuals cared for her and washed her in the home where she spent her final years, afflicted by multiple sclerosis, that terrible disease that stopped her from dancing, then walking and later even from using her hands and arms. But I imagine that if she had got to know her, she would have liked Sunday.

When I meet Sunday, for her, whiteness is still a different planet. She will later confess to me that she was curious about us precisely because we were in the white world but not white: the first such family she had ever seen. Of course you are white, she explains, but you are not the first person she saw moving into the flat. She saw Ivan and Maisy, then Maisy with her brother Enver, doing the place up. Then she saw Pamela, who came in to clean but who was also clearly Enver's girlfriend. She only saw me for the first time when I had showed up with Devi in my arms. She later noted our diverse visitors: Philip and Archie, Bart and Jasper Cook. It puzzled her.

She had wondered also about what I saw in this Indian man because he didn't seem to have a lot of money. 'Those Pep Stores pants of yours, those flipflops,' she will tell me later, still shaking her head. What madam wears that? It was almost an affront, not just to me but to her, who wanted to associate with me: How can she be friends with me or do piece jobs for me when I take so little care of myself? Maybe it was Ivan's fault for not giving me enough money to dress well.

Later, when she started to babysit for us in the evenings after Pamela had gone home, she examined Devi for colour, then took her in the pram to her 7th Day Adventist church around the corner in Cavendish Street to show her off, and to declare to everyone: 'People, this child is *brown*.'

Critical as she may be of my lack of sense when it comes to dress and status, there is also a positive side to our unusual demographics: it makes it easier to talk about whites. Not to complain about how bad we were with apartheid and dispossessing people from their land, and causing so much pain. 'That is just what they do. It's like lions,' she says. 'You don't hate lions for wanting to eat you. Lions are lions. You have to watch out for them, that's all.' No, there is something *really* wrong with white people because she thinks we have sex with our children.

'So, will Ivan sleep with Devi when she is big?' she asks me one day during those first months, with what appears to be studied casualness. 'No! What in the world would give you that idea?' I shriek. 'But white people do that, isn't it?' she replies curiously. 'The boss in the house where my mother works does that with his daughter. And Mr Weber does it, too. He doesn't have kids but he does it with our kids.' Gasping for air I don't know where to start. How can I explain that two sordid, illegal, abusive, terrible but anecdotal experiences don't mean that an entire race or culture engage in such behaviour? Can I ask why her mother has not gone to the police? Or why *Sunday* has not laid a charge against Mr Weber?

'Thank God,' she says when she understands that this is not normally something all whites do, and is certainly not seen as acceptable in white society. 'I expected that Devi might be safe anyway because Ivan is not white. But I had to know.' She explains that she has dealt with Mr Weber by not taking Thandi and Mandla along when she cleans there: 'After I noticed he wants to take them into the bathroom with him.' It was a lucky coincidence that we moved in, as an alternative day-care facility for the two kids at roughly the same time.

Still, the police, I say. And what about that poor girl in your mother's bosses house? She shrugs: 'You think we can go to the police? You have to give your name to them if you complain. They will tell the boss. My mother will lose her job.' She promises to at least tell her mother that this is not normal, not for white people and not for any people, that the girl in her house is being abused, and she should advise her to tell someone like a teacher. 'I don't know if the girl will listen to the maid,' she says. 'But I'll try.'

Little by little, Sunday acquaints me with the black rooftop universe. We often chat with Alida, who needs support in her eternal fights with the boyfriend who also lives on the roof, and Buthelezi, the policeman, who can't help with rape and sexual abuse cases as his job is just to patrol the city centre; but he does help Sunday when clients refuse to pay her for doing their washing. She can't go through regular police channels when she needs the law on her side – they won't help – but good old Buthelezi will just go with her in the evenings and show his uniform and flash his badge and gun, and the clients get scared and pay.

But he can't do much beyond that, especially not with the main headache both Alida and Sunday face, which was what my grandmother faced sixty years ago. It is to get their wayward ex-husbands and boyfriends, fathers of their children, to pay maintenance. I understand there is something like a maintenance court, I tell Sunday one day, shouldn't she try that? She responds that she knows, but that it doesn't work. She has wasted enough time there already, waiting amongst throngs of women, for clerks who set appointments for you and your ex, who never shows up. 'Only some white women with cars and lawyers get anywhere,' she says. 'Us, we are kept running in circles. And you need to take off work and then you don't earn money. It just takes too much time.'

Sunday lives in a world where things don't work. Never have. She only has her church, her network, her individual connections. They are mostly powerless to get anything done in white structures, but they do provide warmth and a safety net of sorts. Devi adores being taken around Yeoville by Sunday, in the evening in the pram, Thandi on her back and Mandla by the hand, attending the church where uMfundisi preaches and the congregation shouts, 'Yebo, Baba!' This South African child of mine still likes fatherly benevolent men, it seems. She ecstatically shouts 'Abo, Baba!' when she gets home, little arms waving in the air.

At the same time Sunday is very well aware, of course, that she needs

The imagining

a connection to the white universe where things *do* work. It is, beside her curiosity, why she approached me with her piercing greeting a while back. Not that she had any defined plans, but she knew, as any penniless black woman does, that a connection to a white, or in our case semi-white, household can save you when you have children but no proper job, no help, no father for the children, no breadwinner. It can mean the difference between starvation and just scraping by.

My grandmother used to stick with her madams, too. My father, as a young revolutionary student, used to get annoyed with her betraying the family's communist roots, as he saw it, by incessantly ingratiating herself with the women she worked for: smiling at them, bringing them home-baked cookies on their birthdays, telling them they looked so very chic today. He would tell her to tell them to get lost with their fat rich faces. But of course he also knew that he was able to study medicine precisely because of what his mother did.

I would love dearly to have Sunday as Devi's full-time caregiver and pay her a lot more than she is now getting as a cleaner and washer, but I already have Pamela. Which is not the best deal I ever had. Not that Pamela is a bad caregiver: she is sweet and affectionate and plays games with Devi, who loves her to bits. But her hard life at home, about which I soon learn, often makes it difficult for her to come to work. She is the eldest of five siblings, who live together in a shack somewhere in Soweto. Their parents are deceased, and all care for her younger brothers and sisters falls on Pamela. The income from our household is all they've got; it's why Maisy organised it for her. Her partner, Maisy's brother Enver, is unemployed and can't help much.

It is a classic madam's conundrum: I am aware that the job is all she has, and you'd have to have a heart of stone to take it away from her, but she regularly fails to show up. It's when one of the smaller children is sick, or the ramshackle day care at a neighbour's place is not operating, or there is a problem at school for one of the older ones. Pamela is often sick herself, with viruses and bacteria making a meal out of her exhausted nineteen-year-old body. She does make her way to work when she is sick to make up for other absences; but then of course I cannot have her working, with her skin so hot, her eyes red and watery, and moving so heavily that it's painful to watch. I tuck her in bed on those occasions and feed her orange juice. I pay her double the salary she has asked, but I can't afford more and it's not enough.

'We must get involved with the community,' Ivan said when we moved here, and I agreed energetically. Yes, involvement with the community in the new South Africa, that is what we are all about, but I imagined it a bit differently. I had envisaged exhilarating meetings with comrades in Yeoville bars and jazz clubs and bookstores, Newtown all over again but everywhere this time, with late evenings, debates and initiatives to march forward towards a non-racist, non-sexist rainbow country. Not this.

Mbokodo
Late 1993

Besides the still-present apartheid landscape and social injustice, the demons of the past are also still here. August has seen the release of the Motsuenyane Commission report on the ANC's mistreatment, torture and murder in their camps in surrounding states of people suspected of being apartheid spies. Sometimes, the victims were labelled as spies because someone wanted them out of the way, for example when the victim had a girlfriend who was the target of the camp commander's affections.[107] The report contains chilling descriptions of conditions in the camps and camp prisons in exile, and talks of 'staggering brutality'.

As the revelations make headlines for a few days, Ivan helps me to get in touch with Samuel, who was tortured by the security police and then later by the ANC because they thought the security police had turned him into a spy – which in fact he hadn't been. He returned to the ANC and truthfully told his commanders that he had been caught and tortured, and that he had talked and agreed to work with them just to get out of there. He confessed it all to the ANC. He *hadn't* spied.

Samuel tells me that he doesn't bear any grudges, though. 'We are liberated thanks to the ANC. I can't be bitter,' he says, but I come away from our interview with a feeling that he may be too forgiving. Mbokodo,[108] the ANC security department responsible for these atrocities, has never apologised to him. There might have been mitigating circumstances because it was war and the ANC did not have much capacity to deal with the danger of impimpis, but there should be at least some accountability. How can we move on with the likes of Samuel never being given an apology? Especially when it is accepted that there might be some among the current leadership who really were spies? What does that say about the current ethics of the movement?

'O.R. and Chris are the ones who really cared,' says Ivan. 'They went out to investigate and did what they could to improve the situation. But it wasn't enough.'

Ivan once personally rescued a young man from imprisonment in ANC's Angolan Quatro camp. 'I heard that they had jailed him on suspicion of being a spy. I knew he wasn't a spy, he was just someone who loved to shoot his mouth off, demonstrate his brilliance, ask questions and criticise, even make accusations. But he wasn't a spy. Spies avoid attracting that kind of attention to themselves.' On his assurance, the young man, Bheki Jacobs, was released. But there were no structures to retry or filter out others like Bheki.

Besides the ethical implications, there is another question not being faced here. If the ANC, even under Tambo and Hani, was not able to manage and supervise its activities in the camps alone, how do we expect it to manage a country? And now O.R. and Hani aren't there anymore. And Joe Modise is.

In October we marry in front of a surly Afrikaans lady in the Johannesburg magistrates' court. 'You must say "I do",' she admonishes Ivan when he only says 'yes' to the crucial question, true to his habit of using as few words as humanly possible. Our witnesses and full party consist of Philip Masia, Maisy, Jasper Cook, Pamela and Devi, who, later at Zoo Lake, sticks her whole arm in the cake we bought at a corner café and delightedly licks the cream off.

In the wrong place
January 1994

We have moved to a house nearby, also in Yeoville, in Muller Street, as it happens. We can afford this because Ivan has been called by the ANC to serve under the new TEC, the Transitional Executive Authority, which oversees the transition to the new South Africa. He is going to earn a fortune: R5000 per month. His job in the TEC is to be part of a team that supports the formation of a National Peacekeeping Force (NPKF) in the run up to the elections. The force is needed to keep the South African army and police in check, quell armed scuffles between Inkatha and ANC self-defence units in urban townships, and hopefully prevent any further massacres by the Third Force in townships and on trains. In its ranks, old apartheid army structures must merge with units of MK combatants and former bantustan army troops. The mixed force is to be deployed in the areas where they are most needed and, in so doing, ensure a peaceful climate for elections.

The question is whether such a huge endeavour can be successfully completed in the four months, from the start of the merger in January to the elections in April this year. 'We in the TEC support team are just to provide bases, training and logistics for it,' Ivan explains. 'Not to lead it, thank goodness. But I doubt that it can be done well in such a short time.' Already, he says, there are difficulties with the ministry of defence saying that there isn't an army base available to provide a home for the peacekeeping force. The issue is being escalated to upper levels in the TEC now. He adds that 'the usual polite atmosphere' that reigns there is now pervaded with the suspicion that the old apartheid defence force wants to see the NPKF fail.

Fortunately, just in time, information comes that there is a new unused air force camp in Hoedspruit, not far from Phalaborwa in the north east. The tip-off has been picked up by Ivan's new partner in the support team, a good-natured South African correctional services colonel who lives in the residents' quarters at Kgosi Mampuru, the Pretoria prison named after Ivan's Swazi IPRC comrade Chief Mampuru's grandfather or grand-uncle.[109] The colonel, eager to help do good things for the new South Africa, has broken through the obfuscation of the SADF through his contacts and found the camp. He and Ivan fly to Hoedspruit, inspect the site and find that it will fit the bill. 'Crisis averted, but valuable time lost,' Ivan sighs when he gets home.

The colonel is very friendly towards us personally, too. He invites us to visit his prison residence sometimes and I get my first impression of an old-fashioned white Afrikaans household as his wife, Mavis,[110] nervously flutters about with koeksisters and tea for her and myself, and drinks and biltong for the men.

To find out how the defence force mergers materialise in practice, I attend a joint racial sensitivity training of former MK combatants and SADF soldiers, given by a white ANC-supporting psychologist. Amazingly, as they sit in a room and discuss how they should get along in the future, the black and white men all positively seem to bubble with friendship, good feelings and a forgiving attitude. Mandela magic? Or simply a reflection of the reality that there is no other way to go? It's only later in the training that old wounds appear that are not totally healed, especially on the black side. While the whites continue to go overboard in calling the black mates their 'new best friends' and loudly explain how they were always following orders and never 'agreed with racism', the black soldiers start showing noticeable signs of exhaustion and sometimes prickliness.

Remarkably, the merged group eventually finds an equilibrium, but it isn't in discussing the past, or any hurt feelings: It is in a new brotherhood in the most masculine sense of the word. On the last day of the exercise any and all conceivable grudges are drowned out in cheery and boisterous talk of girls and where you can get them, preferably for not too much money. Some groups then divert into a session of joint gay-hating, with one – suddenly very angry – black guy pointing at people's butts and shouting that they have 'sex in the wrong place'. Beside the instructor, a white woman who now looks slightly alarmed, there are no female soldiers here.

There may be a need for far more sensitivity training, I tell Ivan that night: the potential capacity of the new army to defend human rights might still be limited. He asks if I expected anything different. 'The NPKF's operations are a bit disastrous already, too,' he remarks. 'There is chaos and infighting and sabotage.' As so often in the ANC, the idea was held together by good intentions and make-believe, not supported by proper design and planning. As a result, 'the implementation is once again far short of the aspiration,' he concludes his report of the day as we put the baby to bed.

Sometime later, Totsie's sister Nombulelo, who had helped return Zeph and Morris to their families in Transkei and is now called Ntsiki again – and is an army officer – tells us that female soldiers are being raped by male counterparts in the makeshift new South African Defence Force integration camps. 'And nobody will do anything about it.' She tries to keep her cool as we eat dinner, but fails and her eyes tear up. 'I am talking to our superiors but to them it's not a priority.' After another silence: 'I thought we were comrades.'

Noise in the street

In the run up to the April 1994 elections, it turns out that, besides the impimpis, the human rights violators, the less than ethical, the traumatised and the total machos, the ANC in exile also counted some politically volatile individuals in its ranks. Three former MK members are now a crack unit that campaigns for the National Party.

The three, who go by the names of Vronda Banda, Desert and General, have left the movement, according to themselves, because of the ANC's 'cruelty in the camps of exile'. Quoted in newspaper reports on the NP's windfall, Vronda Banda, a cheerful bearded fellow, says that he is concerned that the ANC 'wants to force the country into one party socialism'. The second one, Desert, is mainly sad and doesn't talk much. The leader of the unit, a large, loud and cheerful man, is indeed the same General who was in exile in Swaziland, who dabbled in car rackets. He gets excited when I ask him if he knows Ivan: 'Yes! My buddy! We got along! Say hello to him for me!'

When, after a day of driving around with the crack unit in a minibus, distributing pamphlets about the ANC's misdeeds and the NP's promises at shopping centres and bus stations, I get home to tell Ivan about the encounter, he smiles. 'It's true, we got along well. Even though he was always more about his own gain than about any politics.' That hasn't changed then. The first thing General had bellowed out, when discussing the unit's programme for the day, was 'First, we are going to party headquarters to get some money!'

27 April 1994, Yeoville

As I wait, with Devi in the pram, to cast my vote too – which I can because all who happen to live in the country at this point in time have received once-off identity documents – I observe how some in the queue appear to fear that whites may spoil it even now. When Sunday arrives, carrying little Thandi, she looks around furtively and whispers that she is hiding from Mr Weber, also here, who wants to help her to vote. The idea that such a sordid man wants to help Sunday to cast her vote makes me laugh out loud. She shushes me, frowning: 'I don't want him to spot us, please.'

Then another woman in the queue seems hell bent on avoiding my questions as I ask a number of fellow voters about their views and feelings. She repeats time and again that her son will come to advise her. A reverend will do the same, apparently; she is waiting for either the son or the reverend or both and doesn't seem to have any opinion of her own. But after the voting, as we stroll home, the same woman runs after me. 'Now I can tell you! I voted Mandela!' Without son, without reverend?

She smiles shyly. 'I just said that. I had to guard my secret vote. But now it's done and I can tell you. ANC! Mandela!'

'One must be careful with whites,' grins Ivan. 'They still have strong muti.' Muti is medicine, but this includes magical materials such as the herbs and concoctions used by witches.

Sunday is louder and more confident after the voting than she ever was before. 'I was singing and laughing with my friends in the street,' she tells me when she comes to take Devi out on one of her evening church excursions a few days later. 'Then a white man leaned out of his window and shouted at me to be quiet. That we were making noise in the street. But I shouted back! I told him I was not going to be quiet, I was not going to be quiet ever again!'

The evening of the 27th itself we spend in Soweto with Philip, and it is an almost other-worldly affair as groups of elated people roam the streets, singing and cheering, but their voices drift away in the dark evening chill and they look like spirits and ghosts because there is mist on the ground that engulfs the crowds. It looks like a choreographed ritual. As we enter a shebeen to get out of the cold, Ivan, Philip and I with little Devi in my arms are greeted with a chorus of 'Viva Mandela! Viva Buthelezi! Viva de Klerk!' Soweto is clearly happily looking forward to peace, unity and an end to the massacres, whether by Inkatha or tsotsi-comrade, or impimpi-fuelled. Tonight we are one big happy family.

Then somehow Devi is being passed around as if she is a token of all that is new and good and receives sloppy kisses from quite a few of the drunk men in here. I don't think this is a good thing for a barely one-year-old; this place must be positively teeming with germs. But we can't stop it, everyone is just too happy and while Philip and Ivan look at one another and at me as they consider getting into the thick of things and dragging her back, I am paralysed.

Devi doesn't seem to mind, though. She looks around with big eyes, curiously absorbing this interesting and clearly joyful environment, before one of the more mature men, smiling, gently hands her back to us.

Baked pudding

Sadly, the elections do little to release me from my white housewife existence. Now that they are over, the demand for journalism from South Africa dwindles again and I find that baby and household take up more and more of my time. Often, I think back wistfully to earlier times when I earned more than Ivan did. Before we married, I had even insisted on signing an ante-nuptial contract which was, all my friends and mother and aunts said, the wise thing to do. One aunt was divorced but still paying off her ex-husband's gambling debts, after all; and Ivan had told me that he liked to gamble a little at times too.

In hindsight, community of property would have been much better for me, but there you go.

After the TEC, Ivan is back in the private sector, this time in a medical rescue ambulance business started by a comrade and former chair of the Detainees Support Committee, Dr Paul Davis. But then a phone call from an old comrade in Shell House comes. 'We need you here.' The secret services of the former regime and the ANC are merging now, and he must, they say, come and join the amalgamation team. He has never been in intelligence,[111] and his experience with Mbokodo has not at all been good, to say the least. But it is a challenge, and he goes.

He probably does have a talent for intelligence work, though, since he is an expert at not being noticed. He *likes* not being noticed. There may be no more underground nowadays, but the flashy cars, impressive introductions or winning smiles of today's politicians are still not for him. Mostly you don't see him at all, a quiet small man dressed in grey tones, much more John le Carré's Smiley than James Bond. I walked straight past him in the street in Port Elizabeth on holiday once, after he had gone out to do some shopping and I somewhere separately. When on holiday much later with teen daughters, obnoxious men would often whistle and catcall them, which they probably wouldn't if they had seen their father standing right there. The Monty Python sketch 'How Not To Be Seen' is one of our favourites. He worries sometimes in the morning, asking whether a plain light blue shirt is not too loud.

So now Ivan works in a structure where old and new intelligence services meet, under the chairmanship of Deputy Intelligence Minister Joe Nhanhla. After the amalgamation preparations he will be assigned to the new National Intelligence Agency, the NIA. Later he will move to the foreign service, the SASS. He tells me little about it while I run the household, deal with repairs, cook at set times and run around between supermarket, electricity offices, the bank and appliance shops.

Seeing Devi trying to run before she can walk, falling flat on her face every time and giggling about it is worth a million foreign news articles.

But be that as it may, I still don't enjoy being a stay at home mother. I desperately continue to look for assignments and work hard to do them, even when they pay little, hoping to get back on track again. Pamela should be helping to take care of the baby but she continues to arrive late, calls in sick every so often, and now she is pregnant too. One morning when she shows up at eleven, and I have missed a deadline because of baby vomit and a call from Tokyo Sexwale just as I was changing a very bad nappy, and made a mess of both the phone call and the cleaning operation, I burst into tears. I can still see the thoroughly puzzled look on Pamela's face. Surely spending some time with your own baby isn't *that* bad?

I think of Mavis, the wife of Ivan's colleague, the prisons boss. She has been living this life forever and seemed happy with it. She was simply traditional, I had thought and considered that there was nothing wrong with that in principle. So what if your husband works all day outside, and you work all day inside? As long as both parties agree to such an arrangement, it's obviously fine. I also found her endearing, the way she eagerly explained how she had done the potatoes just so, and the *gebakte poeding*, baked pudding, just so, with cream instead of custard. She added jokingly that a husband's love is triggered through his stomach. The colonel was a large man.

I also smiled when she softly poked me and whispered, 'What does your husband drink at 4 pm?' Shame, I had thought, it is part of the carer's job, of course, knowing the husband's routine and anticipating all his needs. She is very good at it too. But one day when clearing the dishes I had noticed in the kitchen, under the wooden '*My klein kombuisie*' (My little kitchen) plaque, a small rack filled with antidepressants, and sleeping and anxiety tablets, all made out to Mavis.

Privilege III

In Durban, though the atmosphere in Sister's house is lively and warm as ever, I notice that there too a housewife's existence isn't all sweetmeats and garlands either. Especially now that Ivan's mother is ill and needs lots of care and prayers and family get-togethers. Sister looks pained at the end of the day after she has carried enormous dishes filled with ingredients from the yard (where she cleaned and chopped them), to the kitchen (where she braised and cooked them) and then to the table (where she dished them up), and afterwards cleans them all again. She is helped by other women, but the men always just sit and talk.

Being there for the get-togethers I also hear stories of wayward uncles who drink all the time, never do anything to help, and sometimes don't bring money home. Some uncles are known for beating their wives – not in Sister's house or the direct family, though; these are all dears, with the men working hard in the furniture business and elsewhere, and always handing over most of their payslips to the wives. But still the stories are there, and no one who behaves badly is ever held to account beyond a shaking of the head and silence.

As Sister chops and cleans and washes and carries pots, I realise my choice is to help and be nice, like the other women, or not to help at all. I could sit with the men to make a statement. But Jesus, that would be awful. People would believe that I think am too good to work, too good for them, that I am too white. So I help. Ivan tries to help too sometimes but all the aunties think that is weird and he is shooed back to where he belongs.

They all adore Devi, of course. When I am there I don't have to look after Devi at all. It is one of the good things about being in Durban: they cuddle and play and bathe and take her on walks, buy Easter eggs and hide them and find them for her, and she chuckles in amazement and loves every minute. It jars sometimes that my way of being a woman seems less caring, less loving, than theirs. I don't have a solution for that.

Wherever I am, in Durban or Johannesburg, I never stop feeling that I am white. White privilege is in the shops, at the bus station, the government buildings, the taxi ranks. Both black and white people will consistently, almost without exception, treat the madam better than the maid. A lot better. When we call a garden service for our yard in Yeoville, the boss makes his black workers do all the gardening while he stinks up our toilet. He goes there repeatedly, staying in there for at least half an hour at a time. I don't mind that he has a stomach bug – at least I hope that this is not his usual pattern – but it remains bizarre that he forbids his workers from using the same toilet, while I'd rather have all twelve of them using it than the massive rotting corpse-stench he produces. The weird thing is that even the workers, who walk by and must smell it as well, seem to think that stinking up somebody's place is simply part of white privilege, too.

Even after our move away from Yeo Gardens, I still see Sunday regularly, often visiting as I pass by, walking with Devi in the pram between our house and Bart's flat. She sometimes asks me to make phone calls for her: to the radio store because they failed to repair her CD player properly; to Mandla's Yeoville Primary school where he should be admitted because he lives here, but isn't; to the pharmacy because they won't give her the discount Sunday has seen white customers getting (she is using her aunt's medical aid card but they don't *know* that); and to the sheriff of the maintenance court, where she finally is trying her luck again, in response to my endless urging. It doesn't always help, though. The sheriff hangs up the phone in the middle of my carefully rehearsed white madam rant. 'We'll have to go there,' says Sunday. And so starts a new chapter in my South African life as a helper madam.

Nightmare circus

I have learned by now that quite a few white madams assist their domestic workers. We are usually the only white people they know well enough, the first station where you ask for help. Of course many white women are and have been woke enough to see the structural injustice and have tried to do more than help an individual maid; from the Black Sash[112] to the Helen Josephs and the Ruth Firsts,[113] the rape counsellors, the voluntary staff of shelters, the NGO workers mediating access to the institutions. But even the ordinary non-activist white women in the system, even if they voted National Party, supported white patriarchy and spent too much of their time making baked puddings and tomato jam, even if they only help on the personal level, they too have taken 'Dora' and 'Elsie' to the hospital when it mattered in the middle of the night, and got their children into school.

Yes, they are – we are – paternalistic, patronising and overbearing; we confuse charity with understanding and aren't very good at building relationships of equality. 'Still white', as Sunday calls it. But, simply because we are white and have the privilege of being listened to by the powerful as long as they are also white, we are useful too. Which is why I proudly wear the title allocated to me by Sunday: screwdriver, she calls me. You use a screwdriver to open doors that have been stuck shut for you. It is how Sunday uses me, very deftly, and with my full consent.

My considerable madam presence and attitude, not taking no for an answer, employing my call-the-manager voice I am perfecting with practice, get us into the maintenance court, and give us access to the various powers that be there. A couple of old white male magistrates smile at us, benevolently and questioningly, as we barge from office to office, asking where a woman with two children and a defaulting husband can get some help. Then they gently direct us to a room where we find a group of NGO workers – mostly white women – already in a meeting about the exact same question.

So we are not the only ones.

We happily join the group, thinking that the new South Africa is already getting somewhere, only to find months later what we should have seen from the start, that we are nowhere near getting anywhere at all. Because, as far as transformation is concerned, allocating space to concerned women to have meetings is all that the maintenance court does. Outside room 409, the system continues as it always has: women queue and fill in forms, clerks then file and lose the forms, women come back to ask about their file and are told it is misplaced ('Not lost', chief clerk Almond Nogcinisa, with whom we develop a relationship of fierce mutual hatred will keep telling us: 'We don't lose files here. They get misplaced.') Clerks, say the women, also extort sexual favours in return for finding their files again.

For a long time, our group's efforts to raise issues within the court remain fruitless. Nogcinisa, instructed to meet with us by his seniors, always sports a sour face, tells us that what we want is impossible, and doesn't follow up on anything. There is nothing we can do about it. His bosses simply refer us back to him when we raise issues with them. Even NEHAWU, the union to which the clerks belong, is as uninterested in the quality of the court's service as it is in any social justice issue for penniless women and their children. ('Yes, we also don't like Nogcinisa,' says a union man in the court building called Malatji, whom I approach for help and I feel hope for a few minutes, until I discover that Malatji's beef with Nogcinisa is only about how senior clerks treat junior clerks and about little else.) Even Zwelinzima Vavi, head of the umbrella union COSATU, doesn't respond when we write to him to ask for a discussion about how workers could be encouraged to pay for their children's upkeep. We write to Vavi four times, but no reply ever comes.

'We have to change the system,' says Ivan when I complain, not only about Almond Nogcinisa, the bosses and the unions, but also about the ridiculous procedures and chaotic filing. 'Bosses as well as clerks will likely behave differently if they start being held accountable for customer service.'

Besides his usual reading, which he still does prodigiously – Maya Angelou and *Essential Physics* now – Ivan has recently been buying and reading one management book after the other, often quoting entire pages, explaining how adopting some or other process could be useful for the transformation of what is still the apartheid state, and contribute to building a state that can serve all.

I read his books to some extent too, but only come away in despair, thinking that this is going to be extremely difficult. Especially if you are not just talking about one maintenance court, but about the entire state machinery. It'll have to be changed in motion, like repairing a car when it is moving. And who among us actually knows anything about management in the first place?

The more we become acquainted with the maintenance court, the more we feel like we are in a Kafkaesque science fiction movie. Nothing here works, paper floating from room to room doesn't mean anything at all, the bureaucrats dance in a circle, victimising the women at every turn, answering questions the way Josef K. had his queries dealt with. The women just don't understand. They must wait. They will be told. No, nobody knows when. Or about what. Questioning the system itself is met with almost astonished indignation, as if you are the one who is mad. The maintenance court is the underworld to which many black mothers are doomed, the caves of hell underlying separate development, the horror above which the SABC broadcasts its messages of peace and happiness.

Fighting Ndivhuho

Sunday gets her money, finally, in a different way. A very large woman named Ndivhuho Sekoba helps women, for a fee, to fill in forms and gives advice to them in the maintenance court. She accompanies Sunday to the Pick n Pay supermarket in Victory Park, where ex-partner Abel[114] works, and berates him in front of his boss. Immediately after that, Abel keeps the court appointment, agrees to a garnishee order, and a deduction is now made from his salary on a monthly basis.

In an unforeseen plot twist, however, the same Ndivhuho Sekoba becomes our enemy shortly after we establish our Maintenance Forum

Desk at the court. Funded by a charitable donation that pays for an advisor and a coordinator (me), our service means that the women don't need to pay Ndivhuho Sekoba anymore. Which makes her so angry that she drags me by my sleeve into the court administrations office and starts shouting at them to fire me as well as advisor Portia. We have invaded here, she thunders, in the terrifying manner that she usually reserves for deadbeat fathers. 'This one must go back to Holland!' she screams. 'Why did she come here and kick me out to take my job? Go back to *Holland*!'

I learn from the experience that in dysfunctional institutions, where state officials are paid a salary to do nothing, you will get others like Sekoba to do the work in their own way for a fee. Sometimes the same state officials double in the Sekoba role, cashing in their salaries as well as the extra fee or payment in kind before helping anyone. But are we any different from her? I later wonder whether we did the right thing by displacing Ndivhuho Sekoba, taking her job from her and servicing maintenance court clients in her place. Wouldn't it have been better if we had organised the donor money to pay her instead? 'It depends on whether whoever was paid would eventually make themselves superfluous,' notes Ivan. 'Surely, if your goal was to make the court system more efficient, and you succeeded in improving it, then you would not be needed anymore after a while. But that lady, Sekoba, would probably not want to work herself out of a job.'

The question is, do *we*? Many donor-aided structures in African countries supplement government structures, enabling state bureaucracies to continue their useless and exasperating merry-go-rounds. Such benefactors rarely ever do themselves out of jobs, either. It is a joke one hears often in donor circles: God forbid that the situation ever improves, then we won't have jobs anymore! The joke is heard from Somalia to Ghana and from Angola to Malawi, but it is also true.

After more than a year, we finally achieve a small victory. A law is passed that makes it possible to deduct maintenance money from a fathers' salary, albeit after a still lengthy procedure.

When our funding runs out, we call it quits and remove ourselves from the Maintenance Court.

Late 1994

Ivan's mother Dhanam Naicker, now 79 and dying of cancer, comes to stay with us in Muller Street for a while. Thin as a rake and in pain, but sharp as ever, she tells me she has voted, and is happy about it, and also happy that we bring up a family in a nice way, with nice jobs and freedom. She loves to gaze at Devi as she sits on the floor and plays with and sucks on a mango pip she has given her. 'It's messy but it doesn't matter, they are happy for a long while, then you wash them' she says, and it's true. I never knew you could keep a toddler happy with something so simple. 'Gundu,' she calls Devi, Round Face in Tamil. Then she tells me to bring a chair and a notebook and a pen. 'Now write.' I am excited, anticipating her life story, until she starts talking. 'Take half a cup of lentils and a pinch of jeera seeds, ginger and garlic.' It's a recipe.

I write, disappointed at first, but more animatedly as she goes on to number four and five. Lamb chop chutney, special roast chicken, dhal with brinjal and herbs. These recipes are wonderful, I realise as I consider them, and I ask for more and more, and she gives them to me, the clear soup you give the baby when she is sick, the herbs that add spice without irritating the stomach for Ivan, the vegetables that you use to make the curry thick even if you don't have meat. We spend an afternoon and an evening and my hand cramps when she is finally tired and I am allowed to stop writing. I have written fifteen recipes or so, and they are gold.

She grows weaker and is in more pain after that, and we don't have another session. Neither will she tell me her life story. But I realise afterwards when I look at the recipes that these are in a way her life story. It's what she has done for more than sixty years and what she is most proud of: her expertise, her art, her legacy. When she returns to Durban, driven there by relatives, Ivan soon follows. She won't live long now. 'It's better if you and Devi stay here,' he says. 'There is so much going on with family and ceremonies and arrangements. I need a clear head to deal with it all.'

One evening, a few days later as I am putting Devi to bed, there is a red butterfly on her pillow. It sits quietly and doesn't seem scared, doesn't fly off, even when I wave my hand next to it. It takes its time before it calmly and slowly flies up and disappears through the window. That is the exact moment that Ivan phones to tell me mum Dhanam has died.

The damage of children
1995

Getting to know Zanele, Pamela's younger sister, is to learn to appreciate the wholesomeness of loving families again, or, conversely, the horror of lost children growing up with cold, hunger and neglect. Pamela told me how they used to live before she had a salary. She was a teenager, trying to keep the little ones warm by huddling together under plastic on cold nights in their shack, where winds raged through the gaps in the walls and roof of corrugated iron. There was only food sometimes.

I never meet the other children Pamela cared for, now all teenagers, but Zanele, who fills in for her elder sister while Pamela is on maternity leave, is clearly very damaged. Her mind seems absent as she fills ever more bowls with sugar, forgetting that we have a designated one; as she allows Devi just to put everything she finds in the yard and street in her mouth; then suddenly decides she wants to take a bath herself and then doesn't look after the two-year-old at all. Once she tries extremely hard to be a good cleaner, throwing away all the papers she can find in the lounge and kitchen drawers, mum Dhanam's recipes among them, and cries when I can't hide my distress at that. 'I'll make it up to you,' she insists. 'I'll buy you a house. And a car. Or actually I should kill myself. I tried that once, I drank bleach, but it just hurt and I didn't die.'

I consider psychologists, therapy, perhaps some care can be found in the neighbourhood clinic, but she insists she is fine now, and I don't push it. Pamela will decide what to do.

In the meantime, I leave Devi with Sunday when I have to go out.

* * *

'It's the boys in the townships,' the old man outside Vereeniging[115] says. 'We don't do such things. It's them.' My colleague Ellen Elmendorp and I are in the area, 70 kilometres south of Johannesburg, to interview workers on farms where several white farmers have recently been robbed and murdered, sometimes after being tortured. Conservative newspapers have claimed that there are political motives, that the ANC, now in government, has been inciting black farm workers to murder whites.

We investigate this in a series of visits arranged by Philip Masia and his Vereeniging-based farm worker union friends. ('For us it's easy, we just say we are with the church,' he told me. 'The baas doesn't mind that.') Photographer Ellen Elmendorp is also part of AABN circles and lives in Johannesburg too. We meet individual workers in outlying parts of each farm, with one of the unionists with us to translate.

They won't talk much about the ANC, politics still being dicey, but they don't hate whites. We are talking to an old man, a few young women with children, and one man in his thirties. They also deny that they have anything to do with what has happened: these robberies and murders are carried out by criminals and gangsters from the big towns. They would never get involved.

It's only when the conversation proceeds and we keep coming back to their lives and feelings that they hesitantly start telling the stories of shouting and beating, of tying workers up and whipping them, threatening to kill them, evicting them from their huts in winter, and underpayment. In the end, ''n skof', a scoundrel, is the epithet a worker assigns to one of the murdered amabhunu.

It sounds genuine, though, when they explain why they do not retaliate in spite of it all. They need the baas for their jobs, what would they do if the farm closed down? It is then that the old man talks of the boys in the townships, sighing. 'Some of them are our grandsons and cousins. They have joined gangs. When they decide where to go to steal, they say that this particular farmer has been cruel to their grandmothers, and then they decide to rob this place, and sometimes kill the people. But they don't ask us for permission – they just do what they want.'

When Ellen and I work on our report, we still think that the nascent democracy will take care of the workers, rein in the cruelty, support well-meaning farmers and bring in more and more black farmers, too. That it will all be implemented until both slavery and rage have disappeared. But the ANC government will remain invisible in the areas where the farms and the boys in the townships are, and farm workers will continue to be tormented and farmers killed.

Years later, Chris Louw, who has moved to a farm near Hartbeespoort, will tell me that his neighbouring white farmers walk around the farm paths with their rifles to check for criminals. The farmers wear balaclavas because they don't want to be recognised and targeted. 'But,' he laughs, 'all the farm workers know these guys so well, they have worked for them for ages. So when they meet them with their masks on they still greet them by their names: 'Môre baas Prinsloo! Môre baas Kobus! Môre baas

Fanie!' It is a sunny Sunday afternoon, with the farm in full bloom, and we laugh.

The memory of our joking and laughter is why the news of his suicide in 2009 will hit me so hard. Did his tale of continued racial tension, though it was comical, hide the reality of his despair? He had hoped so desperately for better human relations in a better South Africa. Was he now convinced that nothing would change? That it was in vain, that the country was still as tormented as it always had been, that people still saw the other as the enemy? That they would still rob you, kill you, because of continued divisions and continued hatred?

He is gatvol now, he writes in a suicide note. There is no more muddling through. I read that he has in conversations mentioned suffering from anxiety, depression, PTSD.

In 1995, Ellen and I have no clue that in 2018 a boy will be shot and killed by a farmer on suspicion of stealing sunflowers. Or that right wing whites will still be going all over the world pretending to be the victims and talking of a white genocide. How long does a democratic government have to be in power before something actually changes? Chris Louw is dead now, as is Matlhomola Mosweu, the little sunflower boy.

Helping Pamela

It's a Monday when Pamela rings my bell and stumbles in, hair dishevelled, baby Laura on her back, crying and asking for help. Her boyfriend Enver has attempted to murder her. He has tied her to a chair, poured paraffin all over her and threatened to set her alight. This was, I understand, in order to get her to tell him the truth about a sexual encounter which he thinks she had with his brother Andy. 'But I didn't,' she sobs. Andy tried to do it, but she fought back and it didn't happen.

And if Andy did rape her, how would that have been her fault? Why didn't Enver threaten Andy if he had to threaten someone, I think, but say nothing because surely Pamela knows this and she is crying so hard. 'He started looking for matches, he couldn't find the matches, that is why I am alive,' she explains, still sobbing. 'I was so scared that I would die, and then what would happen to my baby?'

We have long suspected that Enver is abusive. Pamela has often come to work with bruises and explanations that make no sense. One morning, when she was black and blue and hardly able to stand, she had said there had been a train accident, but Ivan pointed out that the news hadn't mentioned it. On another occasion we went to a party Pamela and Enver were hosting in Tladi, but when we arrived there was no party. Enver was drinking in silence and Pamela was clearing up a mess of broken plates and overturned furniture.

We considered speaking to Pamela about it but abandoned that plan when she got pregnant and was so excited and happy. Afterwards when baby Laura was born and Pamela brought her to work and cared for both Devi and Laura, all seemed good. But now she can't go back home, she says. She wants Enver arrested and in jail. She is worried, more for Laura than for herself, and that makes her determined.

I go into full helper madam overdrive. I phone NGOs for counselling, offer her shelter in our house, and offer to help to get the police to act. When she says, 'Please, yes, the police are not listening to me. Can you phone them and ask them to take Enver away?' I do precisely that and I phone for days until I finally reach the officer who went to the house after Pamela first laid her complaint. Thubudi is his name.

Thubudi tells me that he told Enver that that was wrong and that he shouldn't do it again. I then give him the shrill voice treatment. Is he insane? Should I talk to his superior? Does he not know that attempted murder is a crime? That 'but we talked to the guy' is in no way, *in no way*, a satisfactory police response? That we are thinking of reporting him to IPID, the new Independent Police Complaints Directorate? The new minister of police even, perhaps? Does he know that Enver is again threatening Pamela and now also threatening me, because he thinks that Ivan and I are keeping Pamela and her baby prisoner in our house? That he has threatened to come here and break our windows?

After this, Thubudi finally goes and arrests Enver. And then Maisy phones. She is not happy.

It's only then, weirdly, that I remember that Enver is Maisy's brother. I should have considered that it isn't a good thing, historically and socially, when the police kick your door open, apartheid style, and arrest your brother. 'You think you are clever,' Maisy hisses in the low, cold voice that I have only heard once before, when she had threatened an offensive drunk woman in a Tladi shebeen with a broken bottle. 'You think you can do this to me and my family. Without even asking me. We were going to sort this out.'

'But he threatened to kill her, he almost did kill her,' I respond, nervously, feeling guilty because I should have thought of Maisy, even if Enver deserves a long time in jail. I should have phoned her. What does it say about me that I never considered her at all? 'I thought you *had* phoned her,' says Ivan in surprise when I tell him. 'How could you not have done that? She is your friend.' It is true, and yet I had totally forgotten about her. It forces me to face unpleasant questions. Would I have forgotten to phone my friend of many years if the friend had been white?

I am still white, Sunday says. She says it often, especially when I whitesplain things that she already knows, or isn't interested in. 'Why do you always use so many words,' she once asks, 'why can't you just say what you want, like everybody else?'

I phone Maisy back, explaining that it was not I who wanted Enver arrested, it honestly was Pamela herself. I explain what Enver actually did. Maisy did not know this in detail, no one had told her the whole story. It helps, a little. We say goodbye without hostility, but also not warmly.

After a while Pamela moves back to her old home with Laura. She still goes for counselling to the Yeoville NGO though, and seems aware that – as happens to many women in abusive relationships – she may be inclined to forgive Enver, hoping he will change, and move back in with him. But she says she absolutely wants to avoid that. 'They must help me change my mind back if that happens,' she says and, though I don't know for sure, I think she has stuck to her decision. She comes to work again regularly, and doesn't look bruised anymore.

But then, months later, she does stay away again for days without explanation and I am stuck with toddler Devi and can't write, and I miss deadlines. Since there are no cell phones I can't phone her, and frustration and anger builds up until I explode in rage when she finally comes back, not waiting for an explanation. I just shout at her until she says, 'OK madam, I shall quit now,' and walks away.

Truth, humaneness, passion. It had seemed so simple when Mac said that we should try to just live by these things, that night with the bottle of brandy in Hillbrow. And now I am an unhappy madam who has spoiled things with Maisy and with Pamela.

Overcoming

Luckily for us, Sunday wants to become Devi's caregiver. Devi misses Pamela and little Laura, but is elated to have Thandi back in our house.

Mandla is at Yeoville Primary School now, and she goes everywhere again with Sunday's family. It is the best outcome under the circumstances. My toddler was lonely with just me, often looking out of the window at the neighbours' kids playing in the yards across the street, pointing at them and saying 'Fwiends' longingly. But Sunday makes friends, for herself and the children, wherever she goes. After Sunday comes, Devi does not only have Thandi to play with: Sunday also gets other friends to come and play, and organises invitations for the girls elsewhere too.

She also takes both Devi and Thandi to their respective crèches and nursery schools every day, walking with the pram, saying 'Woof to you too!' when passing the dogs that bark through the fences, and the girls both shriek and laugh and enjoy the game. Once, a black man berates her in the street for carrying the white – or whitish – baby in the pram and have the little black girl scurry on next to her. It makes Sunday angry. She fumes when she gets home: 'It's the oldest who walks and the youngest who gets carried. Devi is the baby!' It wounds her to be patronised by her own kind, as if she is too dumb or oppressed to know what she is doing. Sunday always knows what she does, and why.

* * *

Then, one morning, to my surprise, it's Pamela at the door again, a new, straight, wide-eyed Pamela with beads in her hair. 'I just wanted to tell you,' she says, beaming, when we sit and have tea, 'that I have become a sangoma.[116] It's what I really need to do in my life. The ancestors told me so.' She says she woke up one morning to find the ritual beads next to her on her pillow. 'It was a sign.' Apparently, after having been helped by the Yeoville NGO's counsellors, she now wants to assist other people – women, she says – who need to overcome their own pain. 'I know I am not a doctor,' she says. 'When someone comes with a broken arm I'll send them to hospital. But with other pains I can help.'

When we leave Yeoville, because Ivan is getting tired of commuting to Pretoria and wants to move closer to his NIA job, Maisy buys our house. 'I hear you want R 140 000,' she says over the phone, and I say that is correct. She comes and we have tea, almost all nice as ever, and sign the papers and the deal is done.

Years later when I happen to drive by, for the first time ever since we moved away, it occurs to me that I could visit just to see if she is there.

Probably she won't be because, after battling on in the ANC for a while, she is a member of Parliament now and is often in Cape Town. But I stop and knock anyway and out comes Enver, who embraces me as if we are old friends and then we have a brief but friendly chat, in which we talk – not of Pamela, of course not – but of his mum and Maisy and the olden days.

South Africa is so weird.

The state of Pretoria

House-hunting in Pretoria, the estate agent introduces us as 'Dr and Mrs Pillay,' until we make her stop. Ivan is not a doctor, where did she get that idea? 'Oh,' the lady says, with a puzzled look as if she is asking herself how she should introduce us then. Thankfully for her we soon relieve her of the burden since we cannot afford the prices in Lynnwood, Faerie Glen or even Groenkloof anyway. We find a small townhouse in Arcadia, not far from the Union Buildings.

So now we are in what was once the heart of apartheid administration. Without any grand signal, noise or gesture, just in a little townhouse with our three-year-old and Barney the Dinosaur on TV. 'I thought we would be marching to Pretoria,' Ivan said once, when he had just arrived back in the country, taking a bus from Durban to Johannesburg, then, after meeting with me, taking a derelict Metro train to sort out his paperwork in the capital. The remark made us chuckle together as we slowly rattled past cows in patches of countryside and stations where you could still see the faded Whites Only signs. Marching to Pretoria indeed.

Sunday and her family have moved with us. They now occupy a flat close by in Schoeman Street, which has been acquired with the help of a Reconstruction and Development Plan subsidy.[117] We accessed it in true screwdriver partnership style, first by wading through papers and fighting with sullen officials in a number of languages, then by keeping Mr Kotze, the seller of the flat at bay while he keeps threatening to annul the sale because the subsidy money is delayed for months.

Of course, we call him racist. It helps.

I am starting to learn how to do things around here. Not only have we braved estate agents, house owners and government officials, Sunday and I have also done all the travelling between Johannesburg and Pretoria in minibus taxis, often to the great mirth of other passengers, and with a lot of conversation to learn from too. Once in a rusty private taxi with two smelly and rough-looking men who have offered to drive us for R60, Sunday steadfastly holds on to both our handbags while making loud conversation about imaginary friends in the police. It is one of Sunday's streetwise strategies: they will think twice about kidnapping and robbing ladies who have good friends in the police.

The runaround to find a new school for Mandla has been less fun. This is seemingly beyond the capacity and the will of practically all schools around here in Arcadia, Pretoria, and against the policy of the Gauteng Education Department too. Time and again we are told the school we visit is full, which is often true. Sometimes, however, it becomes suddenly full when they realise that the prospective learner isn't white.

The education department does nothing to help. We keep phoning them to ask for guidance, until a director called Mr Tinto phones back, initially to our great delight because Mr Tinto is black and hopefully Mandla will get some help now. But instead he tells us angrily that we must stop going around threatening people. Apparently one of the principals in a school nearby has complained about us, and said he felt intimidated. To Mr Tinto that is the problem, rather than the lack of a school for Mandla. Asked where we must find a school for the boy then, he only offers that 'the township schools have enough place' and slams down the phone when asked why he thinks that is so. Why does he think the black children all want to go to school in town? Why has his department still not equipped even two or three schools in the black areas with learning materials and better teachers?

When we eventually find one, it is Laerskool Ooseind, an Afrikaans school. Mandla can't speak Afrikaans but there is no other way. The principal can't find an argument to refuse us anymore, and her annoyance at having to accept Mandla is obvious. It is not difficult to read her attitude: 'Yet another black kid that probably won't do well.' This is a self-fulfilling prophecy if ever there was one. Mandla *won't* do well. It is hardly surprising after having to stand right there, eight years old, listening as school principal after desk clerk after education official tersely informs his mother just how unwanted, how much of a problem, he is. Once, when sleep walking, as he does, he stumbles into his mother and mumbles, 'Sorry for living.'

I work on a first book, which I have tentatively called *Wonderland*, because even if the new South Africa isn't exactly all we have dreamed of, it is still full of strange and wondrous things. Among them, featuring very prominently, is my life with Maisy, Pamela and Sunday. I know more about their lives now than I know about Ivan's activities and whereabouts, these now being officially secret. All he lets on about his work is that there is a lot of faffing about, as he calls it. The NIA rolls from incident to incident, from one person who has an idea to another who has a suspicion.

Sometimes the suspicions are imaginary. I'll later hear of a wild goose chase, forced on Ivan and colleagues by former Mbokodo officials, to find a conspiracy headed by former apartheid ministers Pik Botha and Magnus Malan. They are said, amongst others, to have smuggled out stacks of gold bars to finance a white right-wing coup, allegedly by a group called the VAG, Verligte Aksie Groep. Since I am also investigating Pik Botha and Magnus Malan for my arms trade research, I would very much like that story to have been true. Alas, there is no trace of any substantiation.

'They wanted us to come up with The Big White Conspiracy,' he remarks later, when it is not secret anymore. 'But there was nothing. All the tracks led back to one source, one former Afrikaner policeman in Bethlehem who turned out to be a fantasist. It imploded there.' One would call it fake news nowadays, he adds. 'But the ANC just wanted to believe it. A very evil white enemy who is still out there, whom we need to focus on. A story of Us versus Them. As long as we do that we don't have to deal with our own chaos.' Spy boss Joe Nhlanhla dismissed the report concluding that the allegations were not supported by evidence. He angrily threw it into the bin.

A slight lack of coordination

When taking Devi to her new nursery school in Vos Street, Sunnyside, a sweet young teacher hands me a plastic packet filled with blue fabric. 'It is a bird suit,' she explains. 'For our birdie dance at the concert later in the year. Of course, it still needs to be sewn.' I stand there, silent and confused. I can't sew a bird suit. I have never sewn anything in my life.

My memory is hazy from there on. I must have stammered something; friendly women in the room must have seen my confusion, maybe understood that I was foreign. Someone must have helped. I distinctly remember not sewing a bird suit.

I also remember that Devi wore a little blue bird suit with a yellow beak at the birdie dance. We still have the pictures, showing little Devi as she hops around the wrong way, against the line made by the other children. Devi is not exactly athletic, or well coordinated. She can't catch a ball, which is mostly my fault, because teacher after teacher has admonished me to practice ball catching with her, but I just don't get around to it.

The child's slight lack of coordination, however, is compensated – or aggravated, depending on how you look at it – by her *joie de vivre*. She continues to take part energetically and eagerly in just about anything that is going on at any given time, often running forward with shiny eyes, arms open in anticipation. Whether it is to participate in a birdie dance, jump into a glistening swimming pool (we quickly learn to be ready to grab her from inviting bodies of water at all times, and of course we get her swimming lessons as soon as possible) or to bounce on her father's shoulders to music, or trying to reach the sky. That goes wrong one day though. As she tries to lean out to see or grab something, she falls backwards from Ivan's shoulders. He manages to catch her before she hits the floor, but puts out his back badly.

It later occurs to me that what this child does, excitedly moving forward, but badly coordinated, is a good metaphor for the new South Africa.

* * *

We will spend most of the remainder of the Mandela years, like so many, trying to work out what our place in this new country is. Or even what this new country is. We don't see much of our network now. Maisy is in Parliament. Totsie is working long hours at her bank. Archie is off to the north, hoping to get a government position or some contracts. Philip is struggling to link up with people who can help him find new work because the farm workers union doesn't have money to pay him anymore. Civil organisations have been dwindling ever since the disbandment of the UDF.

Blood in the water

The justice system doesn't seem to know what to do, how to act, when Elvis Govender is killed by a racist white man. Is it because the transformation process is paralysed or because Elvis is Indian? It doesn't create much noise in the media. Neither does his employer, the department of foreign affairs, show much reaction. Elvis Govender, the Merebank comrade, who had decorated a ceiling in Swaziland with his dagga foil pipes; who was part of a brave underground unit in the police state; who wanted an RPG to demolish the stinking, polluting oil refinery in his neighbourhood; who had great dreams of a future outside confined and crowded Merebank; who succeeded in getting a trainee foreign affairs position and was so happy about that; Elvis has been murdered. An evil white man with an axe killed him, simply for sitting on his boat.

It happened during an outing for the Foreign Affairs crowd at the Vaal River. Interns like Elvis, a few mentors and other employees had been relaxing, swimming, listening to music and drinking. Elvis and a pal, a young fellow trainee woman – I see her on the news, shivering, sobbing – wandered off to explore the yachts in the nearby harbour and had boarded one of them. Maybe they had indeed heard a radio and had wanted to switch it off, as the girl tells the story. Or maybe they just wanted to get onto a luxury yacht for the heck of it. Whatever they were doing there, it was interpreted by an insanely aggressive man, Allan Stokes, as invading his personal property.

Stokes had come in a motorboat with his axe, confronted the couple, refused to listen to explanations – 'Shut up, you brown horse,' he had shouted – and attacked Elvis. Had continued to attack him even after he had fallen or jumped into the water and was desperately trying to swim away. Stokes hacked at him with his axe in the water, the girl said, until Elvis was dead.

Foreign Affairs makes no statement besides saying that it looks forward to the judicial process. When the judicial process is finalised, axe-murderer Allan Stokes is punished with a R3000 fine. Foreign Affairs says nothing after that.

'I want to change what happens inside the police stations,' says Jessie Duarte. 'I get so sick of them only changing the names on the plaques outside.' It's true: new ANC ministers and provincial leaders seem very fond of changing names. There is more changing of street names than anything else. I start to wonder if the new leaders are even aware that they are in charge. They often still behave as if they are

The imagining

activists, complaining about bad state service from the outside. At one press conference, Police Minister Steve Tshwete vehemently accuses the police of being racist and Third Force. Ivan shakes his head, hands in the air, exasperated: 'Dear Minister, you are the *minister*. Please tell us, what will you *do* about it?'

Jessie says all this, too, now that she has become police MEC in Gauteng, in effect the provincial minister of police. She says she is genuinely working to get police stations to deal correctly with complaints, respect complainants and schedule actions according to priority, not according to the colour or status of complainants. We see much of our old UDF friend Jessie now, also because she has been helping me with my investigation into French arms dealers. She had met a man linked to the French military industrial complex who had visited Mandela's office last year.

* * *

Somewhere around this time, I have a miscarriage. Devi's two-year younger sibling is not to be then. What feels like litres of blood coming out of me in our bathtub leaves little hope of that. But I am in not too bad a state. It is still very early in the pregnancy. After all the bleeding, I am still mobile and not in pain. Ivan drives me, packed up with pads and cotton wool, to a nearby hospital. As we arrive at reception, I tell him to go. He has a work commitment and, honestly, I am fine, the nurses are here and I'll phone him. By now mobile phones have been invented.

After he drives away, of course I start to bleed again, standing there at reception, just as the admin nurse puts the forms in front of me. I fill them in as fast as I can because I am about to leak puddles on the white shiny floor. 'You must still fill in your husband's profession,' she says, slowly studying them after I hand them back, clearly not aware of the impending disaster in front of her desk. As I stare at the form and the blank space on it where it says 'Main member profession', for the life of me I don't know what Ivan's profession is.

I panic, feeling the blood running down my legs and all I can do is yell that he is a spy, for god's sakes, and can I get some help already? Then another nurse, who has come from the side to see what the noise is about, smiles, tells the desk nurse to fill in 'intelligence officer', and takes me along to a room with a bed and a shower.

Chapter Three
Rogue One

Verwoerdburg
1997

From the ultrasound it looks like Devi will really have a little sister now, so we need a bigger place than the town house in Arcadia. Most places in Pretoria continue to be out of our reach, but we explore Centurion, formerly Verwoerdburg. It is in the south, almost halfway to Johannesburg.

Guided by a need to find a school not too far away that will be good for all the kids – Mandla, Thandi, Devi and the new one – preferably non-racial, or at least with a trajectory towards it, we end up in a suburb called idyllic in local neighbourhood papers, with lots of little arty enclaves and events. There are cottage industries all around us too: throughout the whole area live ladies, sometimes round and granny-like but also often wiry, with red hair and flowery gowns, who make and sell pottery and jams and jewellery. Ever since the bird suit shock I am suspicious of all such activities, but our new place is nice and shady and the house big enough for all of us, with the new baby and Sunday's family, too. Sunday has agreed to come and work for us as a full-time babysitter, day mother and housekeeper.

Getting involved in the community as Ivan keeps saying we must, remains problematic. Not only is his 'we' still often in practice 'I', but 'community' as such remains a difficult thing to handle too. Our neighbours on the right already present a challenge. They have a coloured grandchild living with them, which at first fills us with expectations in terms of possible friends for our kids, but we find the family not exactly welcoming. Little Suzie's colour is not talked about. She passes off as white although she is very clearly brown, with afro hair. The domestic worker tells Sunday that Suzie is not allowed to play with our children.

The neighbours on the other side own a monstrous dog that continuously jumps and claws at the fence, trying to attack mostly the browner members of the household. I ask its owner one day if he cannot control his dog; he responds that 'it never attacks people'. But it has tried to attack *us*, I say. It has already scared Sunday and some of our friends. Upon which he looks at me as if I have just accused his dog of having a tail and eating dog food. 'Well yeah,' he says and walks away.

The local ANC does not provide much of a community atmosphere either. The chairman, Eddie, is a former municipal council messenger. His executive are a flock of domestic workers who look to Eddie for favours: free food at events, allowances for volunteering. Their meetings are about elections, lists, municipal positions, and rarely about the needs of the community. After attending a few, Ivan phones comrades in the area – there are about five or six he knows – to get them to come too, but they all say they tried to no avail and are tired of it now. One of them tells us that he once asked Chairman Eddie about invitations for veterans, but was told that they operate with a list from the ANC headquarters at Luthuli House and he wasn't on it.

Sunday stays active in the branch a bit longer since she is eager to find support for a plan she has for an after-hours literacy project in a nearby school, 'because so many of us can't read and we always have to fill in forms'. Eddie is only lukewarm about it, but Sunday continues to try to get him to start talks with the school for a while. Then she is accused by one of the exco members of trying to seduce Eddie, after which she also calls it quits.

But we have a new baby now and a pretty good one, too. Vani, full of winning smiles and spunk, is the delight of our own now seven-member community in our house in Willow Street.[118] Sunday's family occupy the garden cottage plus a separate bedroom and bathroom. They are in a part of the house that is in true South African tradition smaller than ours, but adequate. Besides, Sunday has a nest egg from the sale of the Arcadia flat now, and school for the children nearby, plus transport, as our children will now all be attending Protea Primary School.[119]

In the wider scheme of things, the government is not narrowing the gap between dispossessed black and privileged white much at all. The Reconstruction and Development Plan (RDP) has delivered little besides patches of housing shells scattered over the country, with waiting lists full of penniless people who will likely not be able to pay for electricity or upkeep of their new abodes, even if they were to get one. By 1997, the money for the RDP has been spent with not much progress made.

'I worry because we always seem to think governing is easy,' laments Bee Bulunga, an old comrade of Ivan's from struggle days, who has surfaced as a manager at the Gillette company. 'It's like some of us think that if you sit behind a desk and pronounce what you want to do, it will magically happen.' In 2019, twenty-two years later, the RDP period will be described on the SAhistory website as hampered by both the 'poor fiscal and economic legacy after fifty years of Apartheid' and 'a distressful inability of the new government to build the necessary state capacity'. It adds that 'the government (has) suffered from lack of sufficiently skilled managers, while policy co-ordination and implementation methods used were not proven successful' and that it also 'ignored the gathering of new taxes'.[120]

Just after Vani is born and the RDP has come and gone, in the first months of 1998, Pravin Gordhan joins the South African tax agency, SARS, as deputy commissioner. He supports its plans to increase the tax base and equip the government with sufficient income to do what it needs to do, he says on TV, and Ivan sits upright. Here is a chance to get things going, he says. Money, tax money, can provide the needed houses, schools, clinics, roads and water services for all citizens. With enough money, ministries will have less of an excuse for non-delivery.

It's not going to be easy, of course. The tax base is pathetically small. Little tax comes from the large informal economy: being mostly black, the sector is historically and understandably not enthusiastic about paying for what was always an apartheid state. The well-off strata, mainly white, have never been exactly excited about it either. There is simply no culture of tax compliance in South Africa. A large proportion of revenue comes from salaried people, who have no choice in the matter.

Old demons and new hope

Having had an operation to fuse vertebrae in his spine, Ivan spends three compulsory months flat on his back in bed. Visitors come to see him; some I know from the struggle days, some are new. Among the latter are two white men Ivan has met in the course of his intelligence work. One, Johann van Loggerenberg, is tall and handsome; the other, Steve Burnett, is rather scrawny and wild-eyed but also friendly and sociable. It will be a while before I know their background: They don't talk much about themselves.

As they keep coming, spending more time, staying for supper, I learn with a mixture of disbelief, shock and fascination, that Steve is a former British soldier who worked for the security police in the latter half of the eighties. He is the very Steve Burnett I read about when researching assassinations of ANC members outside South Africa's borders; he had attacked ANC operative Ronnie Watson in Botswana in 1987.[121] The mission had not ended well for Steve, since Watson, a bear-sized former rugby player, simply grabbed him and delivered him to the local police. Steve spent time in jail in Botswana and has only recently been released. I understand that he has repented of his past and now works for the police organised crime unit. It is where he got to know Johann, who started working there in 1993. Steve had met Ivan during a specific project, had then introduced Ivan and Johann.

Ivan's bedside visitors talk a lot about organised crime, especially with regard to the challenge it poses to the state. During the apartheid years, the state – especially the military and the police, but also the departments of minerals and energy, and foreign affairs – were thoroughly infiltrated by rhino poaching, ivory, oil and diamond smuggling, arms trade and drug syndicates.[122] When the apartheid regime disintegrated politically, under the pressure of boycotts, struggle and worldwide outrage, many high officials – even ministers – with access to resources developed links with such syndicates.

I recognise much of what they talk about. Research by investigative journalists, including myself, has in recent years revealed that several Western arms, oil and diamond traders had close ties with apartheid's military intelligence and that even Minister Pik Botha – he is still a minister, and of minerals and energy at that – was involved with some of them. I came across such links when investigating the still unexplained professional assassination of ANC representative Dulcie September in

Paris in 1988, as well as that of SWAPO activist Anton Lubowski, who was murdered in Windhoek a year later. I found similar patterns in these two cases, indications that both murders were linked to illicit dealings with the apartheid regime.[123]

As a democracy, South Africa can now do business openly and transparently. It no longer needs to depend on international mafia elements to buy and sell strategic resources. But criminals are still out there, and criminalised structures of the state will probably not automatically purge themselves of profiteers. Governing elites in many African countries still transfer public money, including proceeds from the sale of natural commodities, into the pockets of local and international business partners and themselves. The question is if the comrades who are now in power will stand firm and fight off such temptations.

Activists[124] have already protested against the intended purchase of corvettes by the defence ministry under Joe Modise as part of a larger military equipment deal that appears to be in the pipeline. The country is to spend two billion rand on the corvettes alone. There might be a need for upkeep of the army, but are warships such a priority, especially since South Africa is not under any threat of attack by anyone? Besides, arms deals are notoriously corrupt.

'You can't automatically equate arms companies with criminal syndicates,' says Johann van Loggerenberg during one supper when I raise this. 'But there is certainly a need in such contracts to monitor the adherence to legal processes. They'll often try to tweak the rules to fit in shady contract partners at increased cost to the country. It's not only arms companies that do this, it is a far wider scourge.' He says he is planning to leave the organised crime unit and hopes to join SARS precisely to help beef up its investigative capacity in this regard.

Johann is very different from Steve, who appears confused and a tad paranoid, sometimes mentioning that he suspects people he works with of having ulterior motives and untoward connections. Over time I start to understand that his work may be partly to blame for this. Some of the NIA's pet projects, running after alleged conspiracies by enemies out there, might have had an effect on him. Besides gold smuggling by the mythical Verligte Aksie Groep, there have also been a number of Mandela assassination plots and the now legendary fake story that right-wing Afrikaners in rural areas would have nuclear missiles stored in grain silos, ready to wage war on the ANC government.[125]

I am aware that digging into such allegations can make one paranoid to some extent. During my research into the Dulcie September murder, I came across a former French secret service informer who was severely affected in this way and for a few months, I found myself frantically looking under my bed and over my shoulder too.

Johann seems armed with a healthy dose of scepticism. He will look at allegations, but discards them as soon as he finds that their sources, often fake news peddlers trying to make a few bucks, are 'dodgy as hell'. Steve, however, besides being more inclined to lend credence to alleged plots, has a few conspiracy theories of his own. Feeling that he has been lied to and manipulated to carry out atrocious acts like the attack on Ronnie Watson, he compulsively looks for signs that new superiors and colleagues might use him in such malicious ways again. He calls himself self-mockingly the Manchurian candidate, that Hollywood interpretation of a zombie soldier controlled by evil forces. Steve's good nature mostly keeps the upper hand, and he really wants to fight criminals, but it is clear that he teeters on the brink of disintegration.

Johann is also battling depression, but is much more optimistic than Steve about the possibilities of a great new South Africa. He was always hopeful, I will find when he allows me an interview: eager to be good, do good, and a bit starry-eyed too. In a picture taken around 1988 that he shows me stands an eighteen-year-old in police uniform with wide open eyes and an eager, pleasant smile. He had done his national service in the police in KwaZulu, he tells me, 'as a way to avoid conscription into the apartheid army'. He had thought that the police at least wouldn't be so bad. 'I was ready to "protect and serve" citizens, as the police motto said.'

A series of upsetting experiences had made him understand that in the apartheid state the police wasn't really doing this. 'It was often more about fighting the opposition, or supporting Inkatha. We would hear of an impending massacre, for instance, where an Inkatha impi was preparing to attack a village that was sympathetic to the ANC. We would call for backup to get enough force together to keep the peace. No vehicle would come. But afterwards, when there were dead bodies lying around all over, we would find out that one of our vehicles had been nearby, monitoring but not intervening.' Questioning superiors didn't help: you'd get punishment drill or kitchen duty. On several occasions his superiors made him remove dead bodies – including a child on one occasion – from the killing fields in a trailer behind a police car.

The depression and stress disorder started then, he thinks. He got out in 1990, as soon as he could. After doing odd jobs – bar tending, a carpet cleaning business – he found work at the Goldstone Commission into the Third Force, where he helped investigate assassinations carried out by, and secret government money flows to, Inkatha. In 1993, when the Transitional Executive Authority came into being, he joined the organised crime intelligence unit in the South African Police Force, soon to be renamed the South African Police Service. 'I was now infiltrating syndicates of diamond smugglers and ivory poachers. But after a while I realised that once again those of us who were honest were put in danger by corrupt colleagues and superiors. I noticed that diamonds were disappearing from evidence rooms and confiscated ivory was going in all the wrong directions too.'

He recalls how he once drove 'all over Durban' with a huge elephant tusk, trying to get it safely labelled and stored to be used in court. 'But not one of our commanding officers agreed to have that tusk stored in their evidence rooms. They wanted nothing to do with it.'

Operating as a deep cover agent in crime syndicates would take its toll, especially as he was arrested, beaten up and tortured by policemen he was not allowed to tell he was a colleague. Not even his own family was in the know with regard to the true nature of his work; he had had to keep up the façade of a no-good son with bad friends for years.[126] Altogether, combined with the above-mentioned fake plots and scams he would regularly come across, he had accumulated a fervent desire to get away from anything related to secret intelligence work. He has had his hopes fixed on the new SARS for a while now, and his excitement is palpable as he talks about how tax officials could bring to book the Al Capones of this country and continent.

Higher purpose

Talking with Johann significantly helps my arms trade research. I have a bit more time now to dedicate to this, and hope eventually to write a book about the connections between assassinations of southern African freedom fighters and the international arms trade. Sunday and I leave Vani on Ivan's tummy for most of the day and go about our business, while he tries to read the newspaper, simultaneously keeping her quiet with funny faces and little conversations. He has an ability to calm children; they always feel comfortable around him.

After Johann starts at SARS at the end of 1998, Ivan follows a few months later. He has become convinced that that is where he wants to be too: using his skills in getting money from the rich in order to build services for the poor, a bit like Robin Hood, and stop the siphoning off of public money by criminal syndicates and the corrupt. Ivan's skills – scanning an environment, planning how to engage with it, designing solutions, implementing action – will turn out useful. After he starts at SARS, he will acquire the habit of asking me to note down the number plates of Ferraris and Lamborghinis we pass on the road.

In the year or two to come, other comrades from the old struggle days start coming in to SARS: Bee Bulunga, Shirish Soni, Dipuo Mvelase, Vuso Shabalala, whose brother Mbuso was one of the Vula comrades murdered by the security police. Pravin Gordhan, of course, is there already. It is perhaps weird that so much passion is converging in a stuffy old tax agency, but it seems as if SARS is becoming a vanguard institution now. It is about the same thing that the struggle was: creating a more just and better-led South Africa.

*　*　*

They work with a lot of people from the old order. Almost all employees above the level of cleaner and lunch room attendant are white; some seniors can rightfully be called former apartheid state operatives. I ask Ivan how this interaction pans out, but he says he doesn't encounter trouble, confident that even the grey bureaucrats can be shown that it is better on our side – lighter, more exhilarating, more satisfying. Come and work with us, the new SARS must communicate. Be part of a network of good people, working for the good.

I will see the process of former white state officials joining 'us' unfolding in years to come, as fatigued bureaucrats at SARS, who had always seen their job as just a job, start to get a spring in their step and a glint in their eye. I will see Johann happy to be somewhere where he feels good and useful, and right, and righteous, perhaps for the first time since his twenties. Le Hae La Sars, he will say when he talks about his new work place, proudly pronouncing the Sotho words that mean 'Home of

SARS'. Higher purpose is the term they develop for what drives the new SARS.

Sunday, meanwhile, helps create a better street. She networks with all the neighbours and often serves as a communication channel between the white neighbours – at least those who will listen – to the black domestic workers who often need support, living as many of them do in rooms as small as broom cupboards. Sunday is the one who notices, one morning, that the left side of Betty's face – Betty next door, who works for the family with the coloured grandchild – is drooping, and she rings alarm bells and gets Betty to hospital.

Sunday also warns the older, more gullible, domestic workers to stay away from the many, many con men who approach them. Alas, this often fails and the Doras and the Joyces – not their real names but the names the employers call them by – keep giving part of their savings and wages away to men with pyramid schemes and fake disease cures and dollar signs in their eyes. Sunday shakes her head at the Doras and the Joyces but also knows that the women keep falling for scams, desperate for promises of a better life, just like the Soweto happy clappy women I met, because they need hope: it is all they can have.

She also deals with the tsotsis who come to do their research in the street, planning to rob the white houses, asking domestic workers if they can help them in exchange for a mobile phone. 'I just tell them this is my house,' she says. 'Like, "Can't you see from this face brick place that I don't even have money to paint?" Then they laugh and say okay sister, we'll leave you alone.' I don't know if I am happy with the way she describes our rustic house, but we never experience a burglary in Willow Street.

Sinterklaas
November 1999

Kapoentje, Philip – Uncle Philip – calls Vani when he visits. He has taken to this toddler with the naughty eyes and the penchant for singing along loudly and unintelligibly with the Dutch songs we sing at this time of year, which are to welcome Sinterklaas, the Dutch version of Santa Claus, to Centurion. The simplest and most often sung among these is 'Sinterklaas Kapoentje,' with the second word in this title most enthusiastically belted out by Vani. The word is surrounded by mystery:

nobody knows exactly what it means, only that it rhymes with the phrase 'gooi wat in mijn schoentje', which begs Sinterklaas to fill the eager child's shoe with sweets.

Our Sinterklaas is unmarred by Philip's fight with a Father Christmas long ago in a department store in Eloff Street. Otherwise, the two are similar: both powerful white magical men who want you to be on your best behaviour and also to sing for them and place water and snacks out. The Dutch version is a bit more demanding, though. You have to start singing next to your open shoe, and presenting water and carrots for Sinterklaas's horse every evening in front of the window for weeks before the big Sinterklaas Day on 5 December. And on the 5th itself, you give each other not just gifts, but also cheeky little poems where you make fun of one another anonymously, as all poems are purported to come from Sinterklaas.

The practice catches on with old and young, and Sunday's family enjoys it too. Especially the cheeky poems, which give Sunday a chance to tell 'makhulubaas', big boss, as she calls Ivan jokingly, a few household truths while I, in turn, find the courage to write about how Sunday herself is a way better community activist, storyteller and caregiver than she is a domestic cleaner. Twelve-year-old Mandla is too big to buy into the story, but Thandi and Devi, who are eight and six respectively, still believe wholeheartedly. They try their best not to attract Sinterklaas's gently scolding written references to untidy rooms, and sing loudly every evening. Once, when I tell Devi that things will happen for her 'if she is good', she looks at me defiantly and states, matter-of-factly: 'But I am good.'

Less cutely, the Sinterklaas story also embodies all that is racist and neoliberal in the world. The holy white man's subordinate Black Pete is a black servant, poor and uneducated, while Sinterklaas himself is rich and powerful. Traditionally, Sinterklaas does not care about the social injustice in that arrangement; all that one can hope for from him is charity, crumbs from his rich table, trickle down in capitalist speak. It fits seamlessly with the neoliberalism that has, meanwhile, arrived in South Africa on a somewhat larger scale. With the RDP abandoned, President Thabo Mbeki and Finance Minister Trevor Manuel are firmly decided to grow the economy by incentivising the business sector. Mbeki, in many an opinion piece, continues to insist that the RDP is not dead and that his and Manuel's new Growth, Employment and Redistribution policy, or GEAR, is intended to generate the money to pay for it. Many on the left, however, argue that the wealth gap between rich and poor will widen even further.

There is a lot of growth happening though, one has to give Mbeki and Manuel credit for that. So far it's not translating into less poverty, more services and more equality, but that may have more to do with the lack of state capacity than with GEAR itself. Nevertheless, in our house in Willow Street, the concept of a rich white boss who comes to dish out charity, helped by a presumably underpaid black servant, is simply accepted as a reality. It is so real to Sunday that at first she does not even understand that Sinterklaas does not exist.

It was my fault: I omitted the fact of his fictitiousness when I first told her the story of the upcoming visit by Sinterklaas and Black Pete, and had remained unaware for some time that the whole arrangement had sounded eminently normal to her. She had only started to ask questions when I raised the need to sing Sinterklaas songs in the evening next to our shoes. How can this man hear anything two weeks before he arrives, she asked.

We start discussing the issue of racism surrounding Sinterklaas as our children grow bigger and have many an animated discussion about this: should Pete rebel and overthrow his master? Strike for better pay? Should there be training and empowerment so that Sinterklaas will retire peacefully and Pete can take his place? I will argue for such an empowerment trajectory in a Dutch newspaper, in 2010 or thereabouts, during a raging Sinterklaas-equals-racism debate in the Netherlands. Sadly, not many readers catch on: most Dutch people like the tradition as it is, racism and all, and the anti-racism activists simply want to do away with Black Pete altogether.

'But if Black Pete goes, where must he go?' asks Sunday. 'Why must only the white man remain?'

I haven't heard an answer to that question yet.

Still, as Sinterklaas's wealth trickles down to our household, ours trickles down to Sunday's, and what they have too much of trickles down to the squatters in Olievenhoutbosch, where Sunday often goes to deliver clothes and food and voter education.

Only Vani has no one to trickle down to, nor does she want this to be so. Now two years old, she is in a way the neoliberal ideal of the little person who makes it on her own. She is an unstoppable force for her own benefit, no match for her soft and sweet elder sister, who never knew it was even possible, let alone allowed, for someone to be like that and who watches her in a mixture of amazement, admiration and fear. As Vani learns to walk she will soon occupy the premises in their entirety, dribbling between front yard and back yard as if she alone owns the entire place, true to her name, which I believe means 'Mistress of the Universe'.

She appropriates everything. One cannot leave chocolate anywhere: Vani will find it and hide it under a table or in a cupboard until it's finished and her face smeared black like black-face Pete himself.[127] She delights in getting dirty and once empties an entire jar of Vaseline on her head and in her hair. She climbs on the coffee table and cheers victoriously for herself. When cross with disciplining elders on one end of the house, she will waddle through the yard, muddy or not, to loudly complain at the other end. And usually, as so often with the baby of the family, Kapoentje gets her way.

Of course – and this is where neoliberalism has it wrong – Vani is not *really* making it on her own. She is born with the privilege of our middle-class, albeit multiracial, family. She is not starting from scratch, but standing on the shoulders of generations' worth of social capital, built up by communities both in Durban and Amsterdam, including social struggle by these communities. My domestic worker grandmother, medical doctor father, and feminist mother; Ivan's indentured sugarcane labourer ancestors, his homemaker mother and insurance salesman father, plus his furniture salesmen brothers and family caregiver Sister, all together, made Vani's, as well as her sister Devi's, life possible.

What is remarkable, however, is that Vani turns Sunday's family in the back yard into an asset, too, absorbing the tools and weapons of a universe where one has to fight for everything and anything. Where Devi will be fine with Thandi using her books and pencils – 'sharing is caring,' we have taught her – Vani will indignantly claim back any item of hers she discovers on the other side of the house. She brings back forks and spoons of ours that are being used by Sunday, and one day even takes sheets and dishcloths Sunday has taken out into the yard for washing, because 'they are my mum's'. She sits in Mandla's room, listens to hip-hop and rap music with him, and raps along. Of course he adores her too.

Trolling Mr Evans

It is this kind of community, where backgrounds merge and one benefits from another's experiences and strengths, that we envisage for our children's schools. Here, in the former Model C Protea Primary school, the intent of becoming involved in the community – this is now definitely leaning towards *me* doing that rather than a *we* – gets me into the school runs and the parent teacher association (PTA).

I don't intend to upset what I know to be a traditional Christian community. So what if Devi, after a few months, comes home singing 'Fishing for Jesus', casting an imaginary fishing line; then, confusing God and Sinterklaas, decides at some point that God is on the roof and we must sing to him to get presents? She doesn't seem to suffer so we let all that be. But the climate is probably right to start contributing in some way to a new, diverse community of learners and teachers in the school. And for a while I think I can do that without causing too much trouble.

'No, but we make boerewors rolls,' a white mother tells me, frowning, after I have made several suggestions for the next fundraising campaign. Mr Evans,[128] the principal, has just told our PTA meeting in the small boardroom next to his office that we are to raise funds for floodlights on the hockey field. It is a ludicrous idea. Who even thinks that flood lights for nearby wealthy white children to play even more hockey are a priority at this school, that now caters for a sizeable population of horrendously disadvantaged children from Tembisa and Olievenhoutbosch?

I propose that funds should be raised for a school bus for the scores of families who are in deep transport trouble, or for assistance with homework for those whose often single and overworked parents can't help them, or are too exhausted to try, or for aftercare for those who can only be picked up after working hours. Most white kids have taxi mothers who have nothing to do besides ferrying their little treasures between school and scouts and handcraft and birthdays. A number of the black Tembisa and Olievenhoutbosch kids will fall behind and drop out. Surely we don't want that? But my suggestions fall on a stunned silence, with only the boerewors roll mother correcting my clearly erroneous understanding of what we are here for.

What follows are seven years of continuous trolling on my part of Mr Evans and his governing body. 'Trolling' being a word that doesn't exist, or at least I don't know of its existence, at the time. But trolling it is, I will understand from the children, years later, when we reminisce about our experience at the school: 'You were so trolling Mr Evans!' Thandi and Devi will cry out, laughing.

Sadly, I am the least successful troll ever. Mr Evans always knocks down whatever I say with one of two arguments: either what I want is a 'logistical nightmare', or it is undesirable 'because we are already bending over backwards for them'. Ah, *them*. We always come back to talking about *them*. Everything would be peace and happiness in Mr Evans's kingdom if it wasn't for *them*.

It will remain 'them', even if over the years the component of black children grows from a quarter, to a third, to over half, to a large majority. In seven years, very few white parents, and one or two black ones or the odd coloured and Indian parents make any effort to talk to the school leadership about any changes from the old. We mutter, share anecdotes and plot, but largely to no avail. To every issue we raise, Mr Evans and his coterie steadfastly counter that they treat every child the same. They don't even see colour. They are not racist; we are.

Somehow it never occurs to me to ask: If he doesn't see colour, who does he mean when he talks about *them*?

Our increasingly desperate argument, that they must see colour, because the demographic they serve has changed fundamentally, that their colour blindness really is a form of blindness, continually goes down like so many lead balloons. The conversation always changes back to the position that the school already does so much, and the overstressed leadership can't possibly do even more. It is the parents who should do better: these wayward parents in the communities who are clearly irresponsible, sending their kids in questionable minibuses and not talking English, not helping with the homework, never sewing a nice ribbon on any project and not attending PTA meetings. Often they invite sage grey reverends and blonde psychologist ladies to help with the poor parenting they observe. Then they complain that so few parents attend these talks. All the while, the number of frustrated, black children ferried up and down in rusty taxis keeps growing.

Still, Mr Evans and his cluck-clucking body of teachers are not bad people. They work very hard. They really would like all the kids to have good marks and be happy. They spend hours after school trying to bring the underprivileged ones up to scratch. It's just that they end up shouting because the children never seem to understand them; they seem sullen and stubborn. Even sharing their own sandwiches with the kids, which many teachers often do, doesn't change anything.

Maybe it is precisely that they don't know what to do with *them* that terrifies them so. That all simple stop-gap measures and remedies – a smile, a bite of bread, an extra lesson, a hug, even – will fail. Maybe the scariest prospect is that they will be forced to listen one day, and abandon certainties that have always stood as tall as houses. Are they scared that if the paradigm fails, the foundations of their existence will crack too? That then floodgates of angry black people will open and all of us whites will die? Is our small progressive group unrealistic and romantic in their eyes because we don't share that fear?

I start to think that behind the patronising smiles there is sheer panic.

Shouting at Mandla

I probably should sympathise more with the despairing teachers, though, because I can't teach Mandla very well either. After four years in Laerskool Ooseind he is absorbing little anymore; his marks keep going down and since Sunday can't handle the Grade 6 and 7 material, although I am not much better, I do try to help him with homework. And like the teachers I complain about, I also don't succeed. I can't see what he finds difficult and he looks at me with glazed eyes, as if my words don't mean anything. In the end, I too end up shouting as if at a deaf person, and he starts hiding his books, telling us he doesn't have any homework that day. Sunday doesn't believe him and searches his room, finds the red comments and the low marks, and smacks him because he has lied.

While Thandi gets by, as girls do, even if they give her a name badge with 'Tendy' on the first day and never learn her proper name, and while Devi, as she grows, enters a state of continuous wonder at the strange things these people seem to believe – how does a teacher think that two loaves and fishes can feed hundreds of people? She tries to demonstrate mathematically to the teacher that it is simply not possible, that that Bible is wrong: You can make the pieces smaller, but the food does not become more; but it is to no avail, as all our conversations are to no avail. Mandla lags further and further behind.

Yet, he is quick on the uptake generally. His response, for instance, to chaotic announcements of new plans by the government that we discuss at home is apt: 'It's because everybody wants to have an idea of their own,' which is exactly what it is. But when it comes to abstract communication there is a gap between him and the school, and also between him and me. On both sides we are alienated from the world of the other; it really is as if we live in different universes. As whites we have mostly lived in security, affirmation and comfort; in Mandla's existence nothing has ever been reliable or consistent. He has been a toddler with quarrelling parents in a violent Soweto. Aged three he was almost thrown out of a bus window by his mother, just before the effort of an impi to board was narrowly averted through a screeching start by the bus driver. Mandla never went to crèche, had to juggle three languages, and was seen as a potential problem from the first day he ever went to school.

'I want to go back to Soweto,' he writes one day, when we ask him to write down his own thoughts about the problem. There are so many black boys like Mandla in the former Model C schools, with white women berating them. What do they even want here? Our world belongs to little Esmée whose father is that fun guy with the racing bike who drinks Red Bull and whose mother bakes a cake on the principal's birthday.

We try to tell Mr Evans and his governing body that the kids need role models they can relate to. Inviting black doctors and business owners to future career days might help, not only the black kids but also the frustrated teaching body. But Mr Evans again puts the ball back in the court of the black community. Where are those black parents who are role models, then? Don't I know that he would dearly love to see them coming to school evenings and governing body elections, just like us?

The amorphous mass of *them*. Mr Evans is still not talking about anybody he knows; hasn't even tried to get to know any of *them*. He doesn't know Ntswaki,[129] little quicksilver Ntswaki with the broad smile, Vani's friend in Grade 1, whose parents work so very hard in their internet café in Tembisa; doesn't know of all the efforts made by Ntswaki's father to get a Black Economic Empowerment, BEE, subsidy – all unsuccessful, making him think, as he tells me, that BEE to him is 'like a bee that flies around and you can never catch' – doesn't know how hard it is for her parents to take time off to come to Protea Primary for Mr Evans's meetings.

When we suggest that the parents who reside outside white Centurion could be surveyed and asked what times and meeting places are convenient for them, and that we could do this even in Sotho or Tswana, since English may be a problem in some households, the response from the principal and the governing body is a vehement no:

'We are an English-language school.'

And so, year after year, overworked mothers and fathers without transport will continue to be blamed in all-white assemblies for being bad. Black kids will lag behind, be difficult and drop out while we get invited to yet another evening of inspiration with yet another white therapist or dominee. Mandla will pass Grade 7 with the bare minimum.

Some God

'As long as black parents don't get involved – the actual community, not just one or two individuals – there is little hope,' says Ivan. 'We can't be liberals who do nice things for them. They must do it for themselves, too. We need a movement, not charity.' I propose that we make one last effort. I know he is still struggling with back pain, but I tell him it would be good if he would come too. There is to be another parents' assembly and I am curious to see what will happen, since during a recent talk with Mr Evans I was stunned to find out that after a wave of thefts at the school, he had come to believe that stealing is part of black culture.

'It's their way to just take things, especially from white people,' he told me, impressing on me as usual that he was dealing with huge problems, and that I was only adding to his burden. 'Their families teach them to steal. How can I punish them if that is what they learn at home? They simply don't believe that it is wrong, like we do.' Horrified, I said that was nonsense. What would Sunday say if she heard this? I told him that every culture in the world has something like the Ten Commandments: no murdering, no stealing, no lying and so on. He nodded, and looked at me as if he was thinking for the very first time about something I'd said.

Ivan comes with me to the parents' assembly that follows this exchange. And indeed Mr Evans talks of the Ten Commandments and how we must all abide by them. Then adds that he follows God and that he understands that 'you people' have a God, too, so 'you people' must also do what that your God says.

Oh sweet Jesus no, this is how he has digested our conversation. His God is *The* God, but others also have, like, *some* God. I look in bewilderment as I see Ivan get up, with his back pain and all and see him walk up to the front. He climbs up the stage, and calmly takes Mr Evans's microphone away from him and says three sentences: 'We are not "you people", we are *people*. As long as you continue to divide us between 'your people' and 'you people', you will have problems in this school. It is our school and it belongs to all of us.'

I wish I could say that that changed everything and all was well in Protea after that, but that would not be the truth. One day, in the midst of the AIDS epidemic, I talk to the school counsellor, a thin stiff woman with a red bob called Mrs Grobler,[130] about the need to reach out to families and children who might be dealing with sick and dying relatives, especially in the poorer areas with fragmented, traumatised communities and the histories of forced removals and migrant labour. She listens carefully to me, with big eyes that I mistake for concern, until she asks me in a shaky voice for a list of all the children who've got AIDS, and I understand that fear of 'them' also consumes Mrs Grobler. So many kids who are already different, unruly, needy and demanding. And now these same kids bring AIDS.

The fear extends to demons here too. We noticed in the nursery school that fed into Protea Primary, that some parents believed in these things. Vani's friend Libby's[131] mother was convinced that the TV cartoon Pokémon was of the devil (which was remarkable, because Libby's father worked for entities I would consider way more hellish: the state weapons trader, Armscor, and military intelligence). Libby couldn't play at our house because her mum was scared that I would allow them to watch the programme.

Come Halloween, several white families around the school always cordon off their houses to keep out the bands of older kids who dress up as witches and try to trick or treat. The witch-repelling crowd then do their own thing, marching together, holding lanterns and chanting feverishly, 'For the light of Jesus.' At the height of a community-wide terror wave about demons and related matters, the school's newsletter promises to 'look into the Harry Potter issue'.

* * *

After a while I start noticing that it is not just the coterie around Mr Evans anymore that is wary of our auto-denominated rainbow parents group. A number of new middle-class black parents, much better off than the Tembisa and Olieven crowd, start avoiding us on the school grounds, too. First, a black mother called Bomi, who lives in a massively expensive walled city nearby and makes sandwiches at hockey matches with the white mothers, stops greeting me. I think I may have offended her until Sunday tells me the woman doesn't say hello to her anymore either. 'She has just become *snooby*, that one. Always looks right past me now. But you must see her smiling at Mr Evans!' An Indian mother who volunteers at the PTA stops talking to me, too. Then a black businessman who owns property around the train station and who has recently, with our support, become the first black person to be elected to the governing body, becomes distant. I hear he has taken up golfing with Mr Evans at the Centurion Country Club.

Mr Evans now passes Sunday and me in the corridors of the school with a triumphant glint in his eye. The members of our rainbow parents group – a nice man who works for Telkom, a taxi driver, a resolute Afrikaans woman, descendant of a farming family who just wants to get on with the new South Africa, and of course Sunday – are disgusted, but there is nothing we can do. We have been out-transformed.

Freddy from the department

The question that is left is where the ANC government was in all this. In all those years, we haven't seen it once. Besides teachers complaining about yet another curriculum, plan or framework, issued like mantras, from Outcomes Based Learning to Strategic Vision to Action Plan and back – yet another set of forms they had to fill in, every time, yet more bureaucracy and less time to spend on the children – we have never seen the education department engaging with the school. In all these years, battling with fear of communism and AIDS and demons and white supremacy, between helpless smiles and helpless shouting, our education leaders simply are not here.

Perhaps they assume all is well, because the kids who come to this school from Tembisa and Olieven are considered fortunate. However, we have not seen any efforts to create decent schools in the black ghettos either. Nor have we noticed an awareness that the skills and resources in former white schools could be used to assist the disadvantaged ones.

After all is said and done, Mr Evans is a passable manager. Time-keeping, teacher discipline, books and other supplies are always in order at his school. A steering team including him working with black principal colleagues, guided by well thought-out priorities, could, with help from the education department, do a lot to improve the situation on both sides of the race divide.

But all that happens is Freddy.

Freddy is an official who comes from the department one day, after we have made many, many calls for help. He attends a parents' meeting and sits among us in the audience, facing the school leadership, just like us. He asks a few questions as if he is an activist parent. He uses the word 'racism'. That is it.

'Many of us still don't seem to know that we are in government,' says Ivan.

One day in Doringkloof, chairman Eddie brings a white lady, who was with the National Party last year but is now apparently our ANC candidate, to the small public area in front of a corner café nearby. 'We will bring workshops and education to your area,' she enthuses at the small crowd of passers-by and café customers, mostly domestic workers and gardeners. 'We'll teach you how to fry vetkoek!' She means for sales, probably, but Sunday is not impressed. 'Who doesn't know how to fry vetkoek? It's gwinyas. We've been frying gwinyas since before your Jan van Riebeeck,' she mutters.

When the lady has finished, Sunday asks where she can register to help. 'But I already have a helper,' says the lady.

'We used to have the UDF and the mass democratic movement at least,' muses Ivan. 'But these structures are gone.' Jessie Duarte, in whose house this conversation takes place, nods. 'We used to even run sewing projects and crèches. Then the ANC came back and told us we are not needed anymore. Next thing we know, all the activists are in Parliament and working for the state and there is nobody and nothing left on the streets.' With a sigh she adds, 'Thabo did that.'

The racist and the fury
Centurion, 1999

Medicines are increasingly scarce in the clinic where Betty, who works for one of our neighbours, goes for check-ups. Whenever she sees any lying around, she waits until the nurse turns her back, then slips a handful into her apron. She doesn't know what they are for but there is always a shortage of pills, and what with the new epidemic, people are talking about needing pills, so she simply grabs what she can. Thabo

Mbeki, heralded as 'Mr Delivery' when he became president in May this year, has so far not lived up to the promise.

I began to feel something was wrong with Mbeki in a really unhealthy way since he made that awful joke during his victory speech. 'I don't want to step in your shoes because you always wear ugly shoes,' he said, addressing Nelson Mandela. Analysts said this meant that Mbeki intended to be his own man and would not try to be like his predecessor. Fine. But the joke was not at all funny. Why say 'ugly shoes' instead of a gracious 'too big'?

It has only got worse after that. First, he surrounds himself with sycophants, those most fawning and complimentary; then comes the distrust of comrades and others who criticise or simply tell the truth. A former good friend, progressive politician Van Zyl Slabbert, is never spoken to again after he tells Mbeki that, if he was president, he would welcome advisors 'who tell me how stupid I am'.[132] In less than a year, full-on palace intrigue will have reached the SABC, where critical programmes are under fire 'for attacking black people in powerful positions', a praise singing choir[133] is formed, and editor-in-chief Barney Mthombothi is heard muttering that 'the dark days of the old SABC' may be back.[134]

This is unexpected, to say the least. Thabo, the crown prince from exile, O.R. Tambo's trusted heir, was supposed to be the pipe-smoking, Surrey-educated, urbane one. South Africa's anxious white minority pinned its hopes on him, the neoliberal, the British African, and saw him as the antithesis of Robert Mugabe. Now they see, in shock and horror, President Mbeki adopting the attitudes of so many African strong men: vilifying whites generally, he soon blames the West for inventing the AIDS epidemic as a hoax to insult black people. It simply cannot be true, the president says, that black people are dying in their thousands because of a sexually transmitted disease, since this would mean that they are 'amoral, promiscuous, sexually depraved, animalistic, savage and rapist'. Obviously, only racists would paint such a picture.

That the West would be seen with suspicion by an African, president or not, especially with regard to AIDS is not that crazy in itself. In an interview,[135] Zackie Achmat, the AIDS activist and leader of the Treatment Action Campaign, admits, 'I had (Thabo Mbeki's) position before... it is probably what led me to become infected. I couldn't believe that you could have a convenient disease which kills fags, prostitutes and blacks... I thought it was a CIA conspiracy, you know, or propaganda.'

I will later meet quite a few journalist colleagues in other African countries who express similar views. Centuries of colonialism, the slave trade, oppression, apartheid and all-pervasive anti-black racial stereotyping throughout world history abundantly warrant such suspicion.

What strikes me, however, is that Thabo Mbeki also increasingly fulminates against comrades and allies on this matter, calling them 'agents of the West' when they take the threat of AIDS seriously. This president doesn't listen to ANC comrades who are doctors. He doesn't seem to see, as Zackie Achmat will do really soon, that many people are dying of what must, in fact, be a very real disease. Andrew Feinstein, a former ANC MP and now arms trade researcher, will later write in his book *After the Party*[136] that many parliamentarians are secretly on antiretrovirals, but do not dare to challenge the president's denialism, which becomes the official line.

For a long time I struggle to understand how the new president can be so unwilling to consider any rational argument. How does this very well-educated, avidly reading, ANC leader not know that all through history, sexually transmitted diseases have flourished in places ravaged by violence, displacement and dispossession? Syphilis was all over Europe at the time of the Napoleonic wars.

'I'll tell you how we get AIDS,' says Sunday one day, after hearing Mbeki on the radio. 'You have no food in the fridge, not even mealie meal in the cupboard, no husband who brings money. Your kids are hungry. So mother goes out into the streets. To look for food. To ask a guy if he can help her. That is how we get AIDS.'

It is only when I read – sadly I cannot remember where exactly – Mbeki quoting, with much approval, one particular white American AIDS denialist who has reported visiting a village in KwaZulu-Natal and seeing only 'decent church-going women' instead of 'a bunch of promiscuous savages', that I start to understand that this president may in many ways not see reality at all, just like that white American. Neither of the two seem to understand that the 'church-going women' the man saw live in a region where warlords and impis have caused bloodshed and dislocation for decades.

Even without civil war, does Mbeki really not know that in rural areas like KwaZulu-Natal, formally employed men are absent for most of the year, relegated to urban worker hostels where relief comes in the form of alcohol and town girls? Does he have no idea of how women who live in poverty in the city or in the rural areas might get money to feed themselves and their children?

Mark Gevisser's biography of Thabo Mbeki, *The Dream Deferred*, indicates that the president from exile may indeed have no idea of such realities; from the UK he may even have adopted a stereotypical noble primitive bias when gazing at Africa. The book quotes Mbeki's friend Joel Netshitenzhe as saying that Mbeki may imagine the 'ideal' of the 'child barefooted in the beautiful rural area' without seeing the 'real people'.[137] It also mentions how Mbeki talks of the 'real Africa' when alluding to images of rebellious Nigerian musician Fela Kuti 'trotting around with a saxophone, clad only in loincloth', in groovy freedom. Thabo Mbeki's Africa, as represented in *The Dream Deferred*, 'is a tropical holiday, a dream/nightmare where you find yourself wearing only underwear and a saxophone... a tropical phantasm taking hold of its dreamer...'.[138]

It dawns on me that this president might imagine himself to be in Wakanda, that fictional, prosperous African country in the Marvel universe ruled by a superhero called the Black Panther.

It would explain a lot. It would explain, for example, Mbeki's mistaking a motley array of dysfunctional offices in Lusaka for a 'government in waiting', as he has called it,[139] ready for the ruler to bring it home. It would explain his insistence that everyone should defer and make space, and his expectation that comrades will now be his loyal palace guard. It would most of all explain his vision of a noble, grateful and happy people, serenely singing in churches in an African Kingdom of Peace and Happiness and who no longer need to worry or protest in the streets, for the Black Panther is now back.

Maybe it explains the arms deal, too.

Many had been puzzled by Mbeki's insistence that a massive R60 billion should be spent on military jets, warships and weaponry, when there was so much else that needed to be done in the country. His reason for spending over half that amount on British jets – a type that the South African Air Force did not even want[140] – was a mystery. For someone who was always fulminating against Western imperialists, Mbeki seemed very intent on emulating all that was British. He had his new elite corruption-fighting unit, the Scorpions, trained by the UK-based security threat consultancy Kroll. He had contracted the British Military Advisory Training Team to oversee the final merger of the South

African military forces. And now he wanted British weapons.

Was this, perhaps, part of his dream of an ideal Africa, a kind of powerful and great black Britain? Was the beckoning arms arsenal Thabo's version of vibranium, the magical natural wealth of Wakanda?

Driving around Centurion, we pass a field that is barren and ravaged, and I wonder what was growing there before. 'It's teacher Susan's farm,' says Sunday, who has started assisting at a nearby nursery school. 'It was garlic. She has no harvest left.' Garlic is one of the three natural AIDS cures – the others are beetroot and olive oil – promoted by Thabo Mbeki's government, most vehemently so by his loyal Minister of Health, Manto Tshabalala-Msimang.

Purging Totsie
2000

Does one who cannot see his own people's reality also not see the real enemies of his people? As dismissive as the president is of the AIDS virus, he pays equally little attention to the still-dilapidated schools in black urban and rural areas, the failing RDP, the growing wealth gap, or the upcoming scourge of the Wa Benzi – 'they who drive Mercedes Benzs'. These are members of the ANC elite with its burgeoning numbers of 'tenderpreneurs', who siphon off money from the state via the tender system in exchange for goods or services that are sometimes non-existent or not delivered. In contrast, anyone who tickles the president's suspicions against comrades who might be against him, or racist, or racist because they are against him, will receive immediate gratification.

This is how Totsie Memela is made to resign from the Land Bank.

Turmoil started in that institution last year with an accusation of racism against CEO Helena Dolny. Under Dolny, a white ANC comrade, the bank, which was traditionally a lender to white farmers, took up the challenge of developing black farming in the inherited apartheid landscape. Helena Dolny was the widow of ANC and MK stalwart Joe Slovo, who had died of bone marrow cancer in 1995. Thabo Mbeki disliked Joe Slovo with a passion, the way he usually disliked – particularly white – comrades who openly disagreed with him.[141] Maybe that had something to do with it.

Over the past few years, Totsie, who was brought into the Land Bank by Helena, has been telling us enthusiastically about the challenge of renewed black farming in a country where her own ancestors had been violently driven off the land into homelessness and dispossession. She told us that the Land Bank had up to 1994 never given a black farmer a loan, but that that was about to change. 'It's so nice to be somewhere where you can make a difference,' she said, beaming, and we felt that this woman who had once been a girl in the underground and who was now a banker was exactly where she was meant to be in the new country.

But Bonile Jack, the Land Bank board chairman accused Helena Dolny of giving 'too few loans' to black people and of refusing to appoint recommended black management candidates. A long letter with purported examples of Dolny's racism was sent by Jack to Thabo Mbeki.[142] Presumably because the president reacts furiously whenever he perceives or hears of any racism, her fate was sealed. 'The problem was also that Helena and I were appointed by a previous agriculture minister,' Totsie will tell me later. 'Thabo Mbeki had that idea that one should not be careerist, and that a new minister must bring in his own people.' It certainly doesn't help that that previous minister was Derek Hanekom, another white leftie comrade.

A commission of enquiry is appointed to investigate the charge of racism against Dolny. It calls on Totsie, who asserts that Dolny is definitely not racist. After that, an accusation of racism is raised against Totsie herself: the fact that she has a management coach from the Finnish Land Bank is proof. To make matters worse, the board accuses her of 'unilaterally renovating the board room without consultation'. After attempting for months to weather the storm, Totsie leaves, too.

In the following years, the Land Bank will give loans to many politically connected individuals, and more such individuals will be given managerial jobs in the institution, too. In a few years' time, the amount of money given out in this way will come to over R1 billion, including an R800-million loan – 40 per cent of the banks' reserves – to a shady ANC-linked food company called Pamodzi. Loans also fund a series of golfing estates and empowerment companies.[143]

Meanwhile, at the once-again compliant SABC, where Chris Louw is editor of the Afrikaans channel Radio Sonder Grense, he and his colleagues are told that white middle management is the problem and that many like him are expected to leave soon.[144]

He takes up farming.

***

This year – 2000 – is not good for any of our old friends, it seems. Philip Masia is not well. For a while I think he too may have been attacked by the ubiquitous virus: like most activists of the time, he was always quite proud of his reputation as a ladies' man. But Phil also smokes very heavily and his wiry body is wracked by coughing. 'The doctor says I must stop, but I just can't,' he says when he visits one day. It turns out that he had a mild heart attack a few years earlier and that doctors in New Delhi – he is now deployed at the South African embassy in India – have suggested a bypass operation. He is back in South Africa to get a second opinion.

He will die of cardiac arrest a year from now, in India.

Then suddenly Devi is sick too. Continuously feeling pain in her stomach, weak and fatigued, our girl sits and lies about trying to find a comfortable position, sometimes crying, because she doesn't know what is wrong with her and neither does anyone else. She is put on a diet of little more than pasta – lunchboxes full of bland pasta, day after day – but the pain does not go away. At some point we start to think it may be psychological, what with all the tension in school and in the country, maybe she is just sensitive to that. A doctor prescribes a mild antidepressant, and I try warm, hopefully soothing, baths, but that doesn't help either. 'I am not depressed,' she maintains. 'My head is fine. Just my tummy hurts.'

After four months I start to realise what it feels like to see your child in pain, and there is nothing you can do. And even if I have medical aid and a hospital nearby, and doctors say it is probably not a deathly disease although they don't really know what it is, little Devi is in relentless pain, my skinny, dreamy girl, who was so happy before. I cry at night and Ivan phones every doctor and medical person he knows, but we are powerless.

I become so desperate that one morning I decide to listen to a rather esoteric friend who recommends a foot reflexologist. I tend to scoff at all things homeopathic, naturopathic, muti, magic and otherwise quack, but this is a demon I don't know how to fight otherwise and in the end I go with my Devi to Benoni, where the reflexologist lives.

Of course all that happens is that Devi giggles a little when the woman feels and pinches her feet and I am grateful at least for hearing her giggle again. But, also of course, the woman doesn't deliver the cure we need.

She pinpoints a problem in the tummy; yes, we knew that, that is why we are here, we told you that the tummy is sore. But then it suddenly occurs to me that with all the tests and possible diagnoses, appendicitis wasn't one of them. What if it is appendicitis, I hear myself say aloud. Upon which the woman nods vehemently. 'I was just going to say that.' She then emphatically recommends a diet of yoghurt and grated apple, which is better than surgery because 'these doctors' will just want to cut it out.

I don't stay to listen to why it shouldn't be just cut out, because it most definitely must be. I take my child and drive very fast to a hospital, and luckily one of the doctors is available. He presses on a few spots and then looks at me. 'Her appendix is located a bit towards the back, that is why we missed it.' A small procedure later it has been removed, and Devi is fine. Ivan and I have never been so happy in our entire lives. 'I told you my head is not the problem,' says Devi indignantly, as I reflect on the hundreds of thousands of families who have children and parents and sisters and brothers in pain and who are left with tales of yoghurt and grated apple, beetroot and garlic.

Gangsters and old cases

2001

At least SARS is doing well. It has recently made waves by targeting a number of businesses that have evaded tax for some time: MetCash, Hyundai, Profurn. The enforcement division has also done a large Mandrax bust, and gangsters have been arrested. They are presumed to be pretty upset with Ivan, Johann and others in SARS, and security guards now take shifts in a little Wendy house in our yard.

On my side, I try to interest the powers that be in the criminals I have come across in my own research: individuals in the apartheid government and international arms and other mafias who appear to be connected to the murders of Dulcie September and Anton Lubowski.[145] Last year, I had already attempted to explain my suspicions to former Goldstone Commission advocate Torie Pretorius, who is now a prominent member of the Scorpions. Pretorius had actually called me, then, inviting me to a discussion about one of the mafia men I had focused on: a French diamonds and arms merchant named Alain Guenon, the same French arms trader who had managed to work his way into Winnie Mandela's and even the Presidency's circles. Strangely, however, Pretorius seemed to have lost all interest in Guenon when we met. After arriving over an hour late to the appointment, he first made idle conversation. Then after I asked him when we were going to talk about Guenon, he said he only had a general interest in such businessmen, and it wasn't really important.

I had spent the previous hour while waiting for Pretorius with another Scorpion named Neels de Lange, who dismissed everything I put to him, complaining that these old apartheid cases should be over and done with now, because they got in the way of his real work. 'Next I will find a file on the Piet Retief killings on my desk,' he grumbled. 'It has to be over.' I didn't tell him that one of the victims at Piet Retief was Prani's boyfriend.

As if two unsolved murders weren't enough, I have come to suspect that Chris Hani's killing too might have been carried out by military intelligence in cahoots with arms traders. Only in Hani's case the arms traders were probably not French, but English. 'MK had to be sold out to the arms industry,' two comrades in the ANC's former army have told me. 'British Aerospace was predominant. Chris stood in the way.' Their views, and other inconsistencies I have found, fly in the face of the official narrative that two right wingers, the assassin Janusz Waluś and an older co-conspirator Clive Derby-Lewis, killed Hani and that that was all there was to it.

I manage to wrangle an appointment with Pretorius's colleague Gerrie Nel, who prosecuted Waluś and Derby-Lewis in the Hani case, and he promises to get back to me. But once again my efforts end in silence.

Rudolf Mastenbroek, a friend who is now head of SARS's criminal investigations but has worked for the Scorpions, tries to help. He takes the first draft of my manuscript straight to Scorpions head Bulelani Ngcuka, but also finds lack of interest. 'It's disappointing,' he says. 'There isn't any higher up we can go.' I still find a higher way to go after that, though: through a comrade who sees President Mbeki personally every now and then. But even that goes nowhere. 'Honestly, I gave it to him in his hands,' the go-between will later tell us, hands elevated.

I start to think that our Africanist president, busy as he is fighting perceived racists and other enemies around him, may not be able to see real criminals even if you offer them to him on a platter. Amid increasing questions around promoters and middlemen in the money-guzzling arms deal, the presidency insists that all is in order, and no one must fabricate stories of corruption. 'Who do you think you are, questioning the integrity of the government, the ministers and the president?' shouts Essop Pahad, Mbeki's close friend and minister in the presidency, at members of the parliamentary Public Accounts Committee when they question the deal.[146]

Jessie Duarte, who told me about French arms dealers' attempts to approach Mandela's office when she was working there, listens to my frustrated accounts but there is nothing she can do. She has been redeployed and is now the high commissioner to Mozambique. 'It's fine with me,' she says resignedly when we visit her in Maputo with Ivan, Devi, Vani, Thandi and Mandla.[147]

We have a good time in Maputo, but I do worry about Jessie sometimes as I catch half-spoken memories of a troubled youth and childhood, and needs of reassurance and validation. She often seems to think that people are against her and want to hurt her. Driving along Mozambique's coastline, we sing along with old Dean Martin's tear jerkers, that without exception oscillate between conflicting messages such as 'Don't leave me', 'I'll die without you' and 'Set me free'. 'My father used to sing those songs, when he had had a few,' says Jessie.

Congress consultants
Still 2000

'And I have names here,' shouts Patricia de Lille, a Pan African Congress parliamentarian, as she speaks into a microphone and waves a stack of papers around. 'All these individuals have corruptly benefitted from the arms deal!' My memory fails me with regard to the occasion; all I can remember is being fascinated at the thickness of the file she waves.

Alas, I will find out later that De Lille's dossier is no more than a tsunami of largely unsubstantiated accusations against everybody and anybody in the ANC, often related to the arms deal but also sometimes not. The source turns out to be none other than Bheki Jacobs, the same Bheki Jacobs Ivan had once intervened to free from the Quatro detention camp in Angola.

Apparently, Jacobs now markets himself as a secret agent in South Africa's political circles, using several names: his original one Hassan

Solomon, his ANC struggle name Bheki Jacobs, and yet another one, Vladimir Uranin. People who have met him say he proudly possesses three passports, too. He is said to provide intelligence services to the presidency through a firm called Congress Consultants and apparently feels a 'deep loyalty to Thabo Mbeki'.[148]

In the memoir he will publish in 2018, then ex-secret services head Vusi Mavimbela recalls how Mbeki's close confidante Essop Pahad brought Jacobs, whom he describes as an 'intelligent gnome with the deceitful face of a baby',[149] to his office in 1994, telling him to 'talk to that man'. Bheki Jacobs then presented Mavimbela, the latter writes, with a thick A4 folder full of 'harebrained conspiracy theories about ANC succession battles, gold smuggling, and money laundering'. In his book *After the Party*, Andrew Feinstein will later describe emerging 'punch drunk and exhausted by (the) verbal onslaught' from the same 'compulsively verbose' Jacobs. 'After a few hours listening, 'it gradually occurred to me that... almost the only people in the ANC Bheki hadn't maligned were [fellow MP and sympathiser of Feinstein's efforts to investigate the arms deal] Barbara Hogan and myself,' Feinstein writes. 'My instinct was that there were kernels of truth embedded amidst flamboyant hyperbole and some outright fabrication.'[150]

'Well, what do you know,' says Ivan when he hears about it. 'So he is still doing what he did then.'

A grand conspiracy
April 2001

For the moment, at least outwardly, Thabo Mbeki seems unconcerned by Jacobs's allegations: in his discourse, the arms deal still remains entirely above board. What the president is suddenly concerned about, however, is the murder of Chris Hani. Only it is not the murder itself, but the weird notion that some people may be accusing *him*, Thabo Mbeki, of being behind it. On national TV news on the evening of 23 April, Minister of Police Steve Tshwete accuses three ANC leaders – Cyril Ramaphosa, Tokyo Sexwale and Mathews Phosa – of spreading the story that Thabo Mbeki was personally involved in killing Hani. 'To say that the president of the ANC was behind (this) assassination is actually to set him up for physical assault,' Tshwete says.[151]

There is little doubt that Tshwete's decision to publicly announce this grand conspiracy has been made at least with the approval, and more likely even at the behest, of our president, whom news reports increasingly describe as succumbing to paranoia.

Could it be a guilty conscience, I wonder? Not that I believe that Mbeki really had anything to do with Chris Hani's assassination. But, for all his anti-white talk, our president was and is close to the old white establishment and its secret services. He rarely shows any displeasure with whites who agree with him, and many clever old whites know very well how to sycophant. My discovery of secret service and arms dealer contacts in Janusz Waluś's address book, and of evidence that South Africa's secret services had agents occupying houses in the street where Hani lived led me to believe that members of apartheid intelligence circles were involved.[152] I asserted that in the manuscript that was handed to the president.

Mbeki was also friendly with British intelligence, which I suspected of having played a role as well.[153] MI6 would already have been marketing British Aerospace Hawk jets in 1992, when Hani was still alive, with good reason to fear that Hani might frustrate the deal. In his memoirs,[154] Robin Renwick, who was the UK's ambassador in South Africa from 1987 to 1991, would later describe Hani as a dangerous obstacle to peaceful negotiations during that period.[155]

Still, even if it was a matter of realpolitik to let Hani's murder lie unresolved, it is still baffling that 'a whole president', as Sunday puts it, would entertain – never mind hysterically put his police minister on TV as if a coup attempt has been foiled – gossip about some politicians who might be saying that he might know more about the case. Especially when it turns out that the source of that information is ANC Youth leader James Nkambule, a known confabulator from Mpumalanga.

The accusation has an effect, though. Even if Tshwete will formally apologise in December 2001, after, he says, an 'investigation has cleared (the three)', nothing has been heard from any one of the accused politicians for the past eight months. 'People have natural ambitions,' I recall Mbeki saying on TV about the matter. 'Some people want to be president of South Africa. That's fine, but the matter that's arising is the manner in which people pursue their ambitions.'[156]

Vula Boys
November 2001

And then the arms deal is back. It turns out that there has been corruption after all. Only it is not in the big contracts, apparently nothing to do with British Aerospace, the British, Joe Modise or Thabo Mbeki. Instead, it appears to be about Vula.

In the same week that the Scorpions arrest Shabir Shaik – a wheeler-dealing businessman and a half-brother of Moe Shaik – for corruption with regard to a smallish French slice in the arms deal, an article appears in a little-read political gossip newsletter. It links the arms deal to what it calls the 'Vula Boys', '(an ANC faction) anxious to maintain their grip on power and their cut of the arms deal profits.' It links Shabir Shaik's interest in a company called African Defence Systems, which has a partnership with French arms company Thomson CSF, to Moe Shaik; then names Moe as an operative of Operation Vula and continues: 'It is said that, in the course of their arms-deal inquiry, the Scorpions have taken an interest in the relationship between Maharaj, Gordhan, Zuma and the Shaiks.'

The Scorpions' target, in reality, may not be Shabir Shaik, or his brothers, or even Mac Maharaj or Pravin Gordhan. I suspect that the ultimate goal of this investigation is to deal a blow to Jacob Zuma, the deputy president. Jacob Zuma is a known beneficiary of Shabir Shaik's various businesses,[157] which include a sub-contract with Thomson CSF. An arms deal investigation against him will help Mbeki to get rid of his bothersome deputy. Zuma is indeed a pain: he outwardly professes loyalty to his boss,[158] but actively campaigns at grassroots level to pull the ANC rug from under Mbeki. Shabir Shaik's arrest by the Scorpions for soliciting a bribe from Thomson CSF has very obviously taken place with a nod from the president.

All that is understandable. What we don't understand, however, is how this has anything to do with Vula. Jacob Zuma wasn't in Vula, and nor was Shabir Shaik. His only link is that he is related to Moe Shaik, who assisted Vula, running, inter alia, a high level informant inside the security police.[159] The Shaik family has a struggle background in Durban, and therefore the Shaiks know Mac, and Ivan, and Pravin. It is also true that the transport ministry, where Mac is a minister, has allocated a tender to Shabir Shaik with regard to a contract for a driver licensing system.¹⁶⁰ But it is rather a jump to then connect all three, as well as others in Vula, to the arms deal.

Mac is as bewildered about it as we are. 'What do I have to do with the arms deal?' he asks, shaking his head. As we sit puzzled, having tea that will soon be replaced by whisky, all we can think of is that Thabo Mbeki now feels that – after Ramaphosa, Sexwale, Mathews Phosa and his deputy, Jacob Zuma – 'the Vula Boys' are threatening him too.

The article quotes a number of rumours about plots in the ANC, lending credence to such a suspicion as it goes beyond the arms deal narrative into ANC rivalries in general. 'It was alleged that (Vula operative) Siphiwe Nyanda was plotting with ANC radicals against the government,' it claims somewhere in the middle, and adds that 'there could have been something to the story – only the plot is more likely to have been against Mbeki than Mandela...' Then there is Mac again: 'Maharaj's name was floated by ANC sources in connection with ... plot allegations.'

Pravin Gordhan and Mac Maharaj are indeed regarded as lefties in the ANC. This is hardly equal to plotting by 'radicals', but if such stories are now circulating, they will have most certainly reached Thabo Mbeki himself. And we know by now how Mbeki responds to 'people pursuing their ambitions', real or perceived, in the wrong manner.

The author of the Vula Boys piece, Sam Sole – an otherwise reputable journalist whom I vaguely know – does seem to have sources in the Scorpions who confirm that they are investigating Vula operatives for arms deal corruption. Sources besides Bheki Jacobs, that is. We are by now fairly sure that Bheki Jacobs has told Sam Sole most of what he wrote.¹⁶¹

You got Bheki out of that cell in Quatro, I remind Ivan. 'Yes,' he responds. 'Should I have left him there?'

2003

Now they are after Mac. It makes him the only high-profile politician besides Jacob Zuma to be investigated by the Scorpions for the arms deal.¹⁶² Remarkably, the investigators still don't seem to be interested in the arms deal as a whole; instead they keep focusing on the fact that Mac and his wife Zarina have received gifts and money from Shabir Shaik. Among the gifts they are investigating are a trip to Disney World in the US, a marble table, computers, and several payments into Zarina's bank account over a period of time, amounting to close to R2 million altogether.

The Scorpions' argument is that Maharaj and his wife could have known that their wealthy friend Shabir Shaik would want political favours in return for his gifts. This would make Mac guilty of receiving money given 'with corrupt intent' even if he does not, in exchange, do anything corrupt himself. What the Scorpions' apartheid-era prosecutors Torie Pretorius, Gerrie Nel and Andrew Leask overlook, however, subconsciously or knowingly, is that many returning ANC combatants, exiles and prisoners have been given money and assets by businessmen friends. Not having built up savings, careers or pensions, they came back with nothing, though they were older and had families. Eager to become friends with the country's new leaders, business people assisted the returnees. Mark Gevisser's *The Dream Deferred* notes that Anglo American helped Thabo Mbeki stay at the Carlton Hotel for months.[163]

The Scorpion investigators appear to be in their comfort zone with all this. They target the enemies of the day, just as the justice system did in the apartheid years. Barry Gilder, a member of the ANC and retired secret service head, will record much later in his book *Songs and Secrets*[164] that Gerrie Nel once reminded him of his former power in that regard. Trying to bully Gilder into making an incriminating statement against another Scorpions target, Police Commissioner Jackie Selebi, Nel will tell Gilder: 'Remember Barry, that is what we used to do to your comrades in the old days – your comrades who refused to testify against their comrades. They used to sit in jail until they eventually agreed to testify.'

Shabir Shaik will eventually be convicted of soliciting a bribe for Jacob Zuma from the French arms company Thomson CSF, in exchange for 'protection' of the company by Zuma in the arms deal investigation. It is not clear if Zuma actually collected that bribe, an estimated R500,000, but if he did, and if you then add a series of other payments by Shaik to Zuma, and then also Shaik's payments to Mac and Zarina Maharaj, it would at most add up to R3 to R4 million. A very conservative estimate of corrupt arms deal payments to ANC-connected figures by British Aerospace alone amounts to a billion rand.[165]

As the Scorpions' hunt for Jacob Zuma proceeds, more and more of Mbeki's rivals and political enemies are labelled corrupt. Being targeted for investigation is becoming a curse in itself.

'That happens in our country all the time,' comments a new

acquaintance of mine, investigative editor Chief Bisong Etahoben from Cameroon, whom I get to know in the course of my arms trade research (the same arms companies that supply South Africa deal with other African countries, too, after all). 'The corrupt are being prosecuted, but only the corrupt that our president does not like.'[166]

Electricity for Ivory Park

One day in Willow Street, a friendly neighbour calls out to me: 'Hey, Evelyn, you know what, you should put electricity in Ivory Park!' After my initial misunderstanding and panic – what, they need electricity in Ivory Park, is it an emergency, is that something I should look into, do I know an electricity NGO? – I realise that my friendly neighbour Mandy,[167] separated wife of an economic empowerment chief in one of the provinces, is offering me a tender. Sweet, slightly dim-witted Mandy, has got wind of all this free money people can get, and, since she likes me, she wants me to have some, too.

SARS cannot do much about the tenderpreneurs, since it has no say in the ways the government spends its money. It can check, however, on those who do business with the state and at the very least ensure that they pay their taxes. But to do that, it needs to be an efficient, incorruptible machine itself. Under Pravin Gordhan's leadership the institution is building systems based on a wide array of good governance models, rules and practices of the kind Ivan has been so voraciously reading about.

'It's important to systematically build values into the system,' he will explain, at times reading excerpts from his books aloud to me in the evenings. 'The challenge is to get people to want to do what is right and to take pride in doing their jobs well. If the system doesn't have values, it encourages self-interest, which results in more and more individuals behaving corruptly. In the end, a thoroughly corrupt environment will even push out the few remaining good people, who will by then be regarded as a foreign virus.'

You can't fight such breakdowns by going after corrupt individuals alone, he adds. 'Besides there being little point, because the system will continue to encourage corruption, you will also have to choose who you target first. Then political and other rivalries come in, and the whole thing gets skewed. The basic question is: what needs to happen to make all – well most – of us do the right thing?'

In his office, which Johann van Loggerenberg will later describe in his book *Death and Taxes*,[168] Ivan has prominently displayed a diagram in the shape of a rugby ball. The wider outline reflects the values of SARS: the higher purpose of getting everyone to contribute to a better South Africa. The inner outline shows individual human personality traits, like the desire to work for the greater good. The more alignment there is between work place values and those of the employees, he often says, the more effective the institution will be.

On another wall of his office hangs the framed photograph he has kept all his life and carried with him from Swaziland to Zambia back home and now to Pretoria: the portrait of his murdered best friend, Krishna Rabilal.

* * *

Meanwhile, linking up with other investigative journalists on the continent, I realise that while stories about individually corrupt people tend to get boring ('Person X took money, X is bad'), stories about African systems of corruption are fascinating. How come so many relatively poor countries, often without any foreign enemies and with many pressing needs, eagerly pay out the little they have on shiny new weapons, technology and other instruments of prestige? Those who rule through systems of patronage simply seem to love grand projects and expensive contracts. The bigger the better, and the more their chains of beneficiaries can come in for a share of the luscious and abundant pie through consultancy and other sub-contracts.

Ivan tells the story of how SARS at one stage, when developing customs system software for itself, offered all neighbouring countries the same system free of charge. Use of the same system would reduce friction in cross border movement of goods and people. It would be as 'smooth as silk', he says. However, no country responded, except one which said it wasn't interested. A little later that same country applied for World Bank assistance to purchase the same system. They preferred the expensive software rather than to get it free. 'As a gift, it wouldn't have come with any benefit for anyone,' he chuckles. 'So they did not even bother.'

Frantz Fanon's famous observations of post-independence elites resonate practically everywhere that my newly found colleagues and I look. We exchange stories about Robert Mugabe, Uganda's Museveni, Sudan's Al-Bashir, Angola's Dos Santos family and others 'who brazenly tout nationalist and anti-colonialist propaganda', while they 'fill (their) pockets as rapidly as possible (...) and transfer into native hands the unfair advantages which are a legacy of the colonial period'.[169] We note that while languages, cultures and personalities vastly differ, the systems in which African elites operate dictate their behaviour. Patronage is hardwired, only the patrons have changed: first the colonialists were the wealth extractors; then the new elites joined them and started doing the same, all the while continuing to blame their predecessors in the West for all ills.

* * *

Of course corruption is not the sole privilege of Africa. You only have to look at the practices of US multinational Halliburton in Nigeria, the Israeli diamond companies in the DRC, or the Angolagate scandal, in which French politicians and businessmen reverse-funded themselves from arms contracts to know that. In South Africa, as it was busting sanctions and waging war, the apartheid regime got deeper and deeper into bed with organised crime, too.[170] But the difference is that the (former and neo-) colonisers made sure that at least their own home bases functioned. Buses, roads and water delivery might be imperfect, but they work, in France, Portugal, Spain, the UK and the Netherlands. In contrast, former colonial systems were never meant to service people. No one cares about Africa's citizens.

Our old comrade, Bee Bulunga, makes a joke that illustrates the difference between taking some money off the top, as powerful companies and individuals in the West might do, and systemic looting that destroys a country. The joke has a Mozambican minister of transport visiting his Portuguese counterpart and being given a bird's-eye view of Portugal as the two take a helicopter ride together. The Portuguese minister, pointing at bridges, roads, dams and flyovers, grins and pats his back pocket every time, saying: '10 per cent.' The year after, the Portuguese minister visits Mozambique and there is once again a helicopter ride. Only this time, there is no bridge, road, dam or flyover to be seen. As they land, the fast-learning Mozambican pats his back pocket, laughing heartily: '100 per cent!' The joke has morphed into different countries in Africa, I am told, but the essence of it stays the same.

Rocket science

Key words and phrases in daily conversations in the new SARS and elsewhere in government are incentivising, transparency, priorities, checks and balances, value for money, key performance indicators. The challenge remains how to translate all that theory into a caring, effective country. All around us, the AIDS epidemic still kills and child-headed households multiply in sandy villages and squatter camps.

'Books and models help,' Ivan says. 'But that is only the start of the work. I have known from the underground days that we will have to build up this country practically from scratch and that it will need an almost superhuman effort. But sadly, we are not superhuman.'

There are many brave and dedicated people in South Africa, but will their passion be enough? In an opinion piece, which I hope to get published in the progressive weekly *Mail & Guardian*,[171] I write how it is probably unrealistic for us, activists and struggle sympathisers, to think that a bunch of former guerrilla soldiers, university graduates, a couple of aspiring poets, hundreds of angry street kids and the odd lawyer can take over the management of the apartheid state machinery and not only make it work, but also make it ten times bigger and better, and fully democratic too, just like that.

I also write that we journalists will not help if we just stand on the sidelines and nag new leaders about failing, or about being corrupt. I stipulate that even corruption, at times, might be explained by sheer powerlessness at the magnitude of the task ahead. Perhaps it is not that surprising that many individuals, now suddenly in charge and feeling out of their depth, contract out more and more tasks to consultants. Maybe my neighbour Mandy really believes that I can put electricity in Ivory Park.

They don't publish it. 'You make it sound like it's rocket science,' says Sam Sole, who now works at *Mail & Guardian*. 'They must simply do their jobs and not steal. Why are you making excuses?'

I have got to know Sam Sole a little since I went to shout at him in his office about that dumb 'Vula Boys' article. My memory of that afternoon in Durban's Independent Newspapers' office – where Sole worked at the time – is hazy. Did I really go there just to shout at Sam Sole? Or did we meet generally about the arms deal investigation? We will start to interact more closely at *Mail & Guardian* as more revelations, particularly about British Aerospace, come to light. But I remember standing there in his Durban office and yelling at him that Pravin and Mac – and all the other Vula operatives as far as I know them – are persons of integrity.

He hasn't been writing about Vula Boys anymore though; only about Mac Maharaj and the money from Shabir Shaik, about which I will still fight with him again and again. Sam Sole will eventually agree that Thabo Mbeki has been using the Scorpions as 'primarily a means to secure and protect political dominance',[172] but he continues to differ with me on the issue I raise in my article about good governance, and the ANC's lack of capability.

It is ironic, I think, that he and the inept politicians he lambasts seem to agree that governing is not that hard; not rocket science at all.

* * *

Maybe Sam Sole would have seen my point if I had asked Mandla, Sunday's now sixteen-year-old son, to explain it to him. Because Mandla one day captures the sheer unpreparedness that must be felt by many of those who are new in government. When doing a holiday job at SARS, he comments: 'I did not know people worked so hard.' At first the remark puzzles me, because of course Mandla has seen people working hard. The domestic workers, patrol cop Buthelezi, his own mum scrubbing staircases, the pavement construction workers down the road, they all work very hard and long hours.

The penny drops when I realise that he has probably never seen white people work so hard.

It must be one of the main truths of South Africa in 2003 that sizeable numbers of black people have not seen white people work at all. They have only seen them boss blacks around. The foreman standing with his arms crossed as you dig the soil with a pick axe. Pieter-Dirk Uys's character Nowelle Fine, the proverbial madam who does nothing but lunching and beautifying herself, says she often gets asked the question what she does to keep her hands so shiny and milky and soft. Her answer: 'Why, nothing!' Maybe that is why many have entered the new administration thinking it's going to be easy, as Bee Bulunga puts it.

'Of course we don't know how to do those things,' says Sunday when we discuss what I am writing. 'We were supposed only to clean and polish that government machine. So we need time to get to know it. But the problem is men. Our guys cannot admit that they don't know things, they like to pretend to know.' She tells me how her grandfather, who was a headman of Cala in the Eastern Cape, used to be different. 'He was wise. He castigated you when you had a big mouth about something, saying no, you don't know. You only think you know.' He taught me that if I wanted to learn something I should stop thinking that I knew everything already.'[173]

Admitting that you don't know is difficult for anybody, especially if you have suffered, I would imagine, through centuries of powerful oppressors telling you how stupid you are. You are not going to admit that. Not to *them*. Not as long as mostly white reporters in the still mainly white-owned media, seem to be challenging you, taunting you, to admit precisely that. You get your back up and rage at them: racist white media. I still talk to Sam Sole about this as *Mail & Guardian* does more and more corruption stories. Of course when someone steals a lot of money they need to be exposed, but, I argue, we could also try to locate good civil servants and support them. Write, for a change, about what is working well. When most things are dysfunctional, isn't it newsworthy to pinpoint something that does work and ask what makes the difference? But Sam remains convinced that our officials could do their jobs if they only tried. I don't know if that makes me more racist than him or the other way around.

Meanwhile, SARS seems to have found a way to work with the established white and the incoming black staff. Pravin Gordhan is making white bureaucrats and financial experts acquaint the newcomers with know-how while also introducing new struggle values, a non-racial vision and ideals, constitutional equality and rights, new people, new policies, new skills, and programmes for extending and transforming systems. Siyakha, or 'building', is the motto of the SARS transformation drive. 'Doing the right thing' becomes a buzzword next to 'higher purpose'; the kitty for a well-resourced and capable state is growing. 'Even I am happier about paying tax now than I have ever been before, and I have worked here twenty years,' says one beaming middle-aged administrative functionary I meet.

An African king
Institute for the Advancement of Journalism, 2003

As South African colleagues continue to run with stories about how Shabir Shaik paid money to Mac and Zarina Maharaj, and call Mac corrupt, I defend him and they look away and smile. I am his friend, they know that, and I suspect some think of me as romantic and naïve.

At least with regard to other African countries, I can still call myself unbiased. In an exhilarating new development in African investigative journalism, colleagues from inter alia Mozambique, Namibia, Kenya and Ghana are meeting a couple of South Africans, and me, at the Institute for the Advancement of Journalism (IAJ) in Johannesburg to discuss setting up a new continental network. The idea is that such a network will serve to encourage one another, as well as to share stories that are of more than local interest. Investigations into the plundering of gold and other resources, criminal syndicates and arms companies often cross borders, after all. IAJ director Gwen Ansell – formerly part of ANC structures in Botswana – who is excited about the idea, hosts us here.

I have worked with Ansell to make this happen, producing a report on the challenges faced by journalists in several African countries. The report, for which I have travelled around a bit and interviewed colleagues, is called 'Patriots or puppets', a title given by Ansell because of the finding that ruling parties, local power players and even NGOs and opposition parties, while invoking patriotism and other lofty values, still often treat journalists as puppets. Almost without exception, these entities pay journalists to produce the desired content. There is virtually no income to be had in the field of real investigative journalism that exposes wrongs and digs for truth, in the media sector in most African countries.

As we grapple with the idea of becoming an organisation, one of the South Africans, a newcomer and a rather big man, nods and gravely says that he supports the plan. 'I always wanted to run something like that,' he says.

There are two things that I remember thinking then.

The first one is: huh, you are the boss now?

The other one is: but where did he get that name?

The name Mzilikazi wa Afrika is probably a pseudonym. Which is not extraordinary in itself: many writers use those. It's just that this one is so weird. Mzilikazi is the name of a legendary king in Matabeland, in what was then Southern Rhodesia. The surname simply means 'of Africa'. Translated to a Western context, the equivalent would be something like 'Napoleon of Europe'.

I guess that answers the first question, too.

The African king becomes a member of the new network, but instead of getting to run it he will be expelled the following year after he is also fired by his employer, the *Sunday Times*, when it emerges that he has facilitated a hotel deal in Mozambique in partnership with a South African business owner whom he knows from the Travelgate corruption scandal. Travelgate refers to South African members of parliament who misused travel vouchers to fund luxury holidays with families and friends with the assistance of unscrupulous travel agents. Wa Afrika has written about it while simultaneously doing business with one of the implicated travel agents.

He will assert later that it was all a misunderstanding, and will be rehired by the *Sunday Times* in 2010, after a few reports elsewhere enable him, as a *Mail & Guardian* report puts it, to 'claw his way back into the mainstream'.[174]

I can't remember Mzilikazi wa Afrika saying anything of substance during the two days we meet at the IAJ. But others contribute a lot and we establish our shared principles of journalism, our mission 'to dig deeper and unearth more truths', and a mailing list. We decide on a name: the Forum for African Investigative Reporters, FAIR.

I have a faint memory every now and then of one of the other two South Africans present referring to the Zuma and the Maharaj arms deal corruption allegations, glancing at me intermittently.

True communists

Journalists should not write about someone they know, especially not if the person is mired in some or other controversy. If you do, it must be very clear that you have personal connections and you must declare your bias.[175] But I would argue that a problem also arises from not knowing the person you write about. One should at least establish a profile based on record, reputation and patterns of behaviour. I too have reported allegations against people who, when looked at more closely, didn't deserve that at all. Even if you do allow them the opportunity to present their own side – which you, of course, should always do – some of the dirt will still linger.

In addition, hurtful allegations often come from grievances, and accusations of corruption are regularly made by parties who are not that clean themselves. All of us in the network struggle to assess tip-offs from individuals with bones to pick; who try to use journalists to fight their own personal or political battles. A corruption accusation is a weapon. All over the world, politicians and businesspeople accuse one another, their nemeses, their rivals. Don't look at me, they go: Write about that *other* one.

'Why do you guys never look at job performance?' grumbles Ivan. 'Do you want to know what Mac is doing with his budget as transport minister? Then check that! But all you do is run around repeating allegations.'

It so happens that if you know Mac's profile – what he has done in life, the patterns of his behaviour, does he chase material gain, is he doing a good job as a minister – then you'll hesitate to link him to corruption. Because, as boisterous and self-righteous and vain and mistaken and frankly annoying as Mac can be, he likes to make a good job of what he is doing and he won't do bad things in exchange for money. 'It is no coincidence that Mac came to head Operation Vula,' says Ivan. 'It's mainly the true communists who volunteer for such dangerous missions.'

True communists. It's funny how we still use that epithet. Neither of us believe in the practice of communism or socialism anymore, at least not in terms of an economic system. We have seen how socialist economies simply do not generate enough money for people and countries to prosper, and seen that it doesn't stop a new elite from living the good life at the expense of the masses who continue to live in hardship. But we still use the word. Communist, khomanisi. It is a feeling, a personal value more than it is an ideology now. We still believe in truth, humaneness and passion, combined with good old fighting spirit, though no longer in the notion of a social class as the enemy.

We have learned that things like flags and sloganeering and fist waving should be regarded with the utmost caution. In fact, as Fanon would say of the post-colonial situation, Africa's new elite politicians who shout 'slogans of independence' while being 'completely ignorant about the economy of their own country', and the new proprietors of nationalised wealth who 'use two or three slogans' to 'demand an enormous amount of work from agricultural labourers'[176] should be profoundly mistrusted.

New populist politician Julius Malema fits Fanon's description to a hilt. Malema, a demagogue of considerable skill, talks about 'taking back the land' and 'nationalisation', even of 'killing the boers', which seems to be his favourite song – when it was sung in the struggle it referred to the apartheid army – yet remains unable to answer the question what the state, which he wants to lead, should do with the land once it owns it. He is a bit like a dog chasing a car in that way.

'The state,' says Ivan, 'owns a lot of land already. What is it doing with it?' I think back to what happened at the Land Bank.[177]

In the case of the corruption accusations against Mac Maharaj and the fabrications surrounding Vula operatives, I worry that they may go for Ivan next, then dismiss that fear. Ivan is not a threat to anyone. He is certainly not crossing Thabo Mbeki.

Boy going wrong

Meanwhile we battle with Mandla. Not that he is not sweet and clever and perceptive and funny and caring. 'Bhuti' is still one of the rocks of little Vani's existence. He knows all the modern music and TV programmes and we wouldn't know who *The Boondocks* character Uncle Ruckus was if it wasn't for him.

In a better society, where black and male would not be such massive markers for 'little chance to make it', Mandla might have been a children's caregiver or psychologist. He has long been Vani's babysitter, genuinely enjoying her tricks and games, with her delighting in them, too. Even at a year old, she was so taken with 'Manda' that all black people, for a while, then, were pointed and smiled at amid happy cries of 'Mandaas! Mandaas!'

But where is this better society? We are of the worst when it comes to obstructing the paths of black children. Mandla is now a sixteen-year-old black boy in Lyttelton Manor, a former Model C high school in Verwoerdburg, where once again all the teachers are white.

He understands the teachers as much as they understand him, which is not at all. His marks stay low and as he is growing to be a man I imagine he has no idea what sort of a man he is going to be. What paths are open to him? How does he find a way to be useful in the world, not to mention being appreciated or respected? His sister, who just started high school, still gets by, continuously adapting, as girls do.

But save for a minority that does well and somehow stays on the straight and narrow – often helped along, I note, by a background of good parents and cohesive families – the black boys of Lyttelton Manor seek and find comfort with one another. They rebel together, make fun of teachers together, hang out together, and try whatever is there to smoke or experiment with. Sunday finds foil and pipes in Mandla's room, and of course he denies it, saying he is keeping it for a friend. Of course, we don't believe him.

I fleetingly think of what Mac told me about his youth, when he lost his eye in a knife fight between gangs, one of which he was part of. It was primitive rebellion, he told me during my interview with him over a bottle of brandy, and then he soon moved on to actual rebellion in the freedom struggle. But there is no freedom struggle now. How is Mandla going to make his mark in his country, his community, the world? He goes with his mum sometimes to deliver clothes and food to Olievenhoutbosch and helps with catering for the church, but that's all in the category of being a nice boy who helps his mum, and hardly enough. If there was only a bit more going on, something important and young and brave that aimed to make a difference, but there is nothing.

There isn't even an ANC branch. Chairman Eddie still hangs around with his madam councillor, and we don't see the domestic workers attending Eddie's meetings in front of the corner café anymore.

When Mandla starts taking my car, I am pretty angry. Somehow, as soon as we are out, or not looking, he finds the keys, no matter where I hide them and then drives to wherever his friends and the parties are. He tries to be back before we notice it is gone, but regularly fails to do so, and then Sunday beats him with whatever broomstick and belt she can find, and of course that doesn't help. In the afternoons, when told to do his homework, he will sit in his room for a while, staring at school books, strange letters and symbols in front of his eyes, and then go haywire again.

At times he gets into other petty criminal trouble with his group of wayward friends – never violence though – and when Sunday gets wind of that she asks me to take her and him to the police station in Lyttelton, and insists that the police there talk to him, scare him, teach him a lesson.

Slowly, very slowly, and as he gets older, it gets a bit better. What may have helped is a psychologist friend Ivan asks to meet with Mandla, a contact he met in SARS's liaison with the Scorpions. Besides being a psychological adviser in law enforcement cases, Charl Fourie is also a charitable community activist, and perhaps the first male ever to introduce the boy to a few other men, often black, who work to do some good, for example, a cricketer and a fundraiser for good causes.

Charl also talks to me to help me process my anger with Mandla. I am entitled to be angry, he says, and he doesn't mean that we mustn't discipline him, but I must also please understand that the boy's character is still the same. Charl says he hasn't turned into a bad human being all of a sudden. He is not violent, and he will never hurt anyone; he merely wants to belong. Well, I reply, he hurts me when he takes my car without asking. 'But that is because he trusts you, which is good,' the psychologist responds. 'He would not steal a car from a stranger in the street. He thinks he can just borrow yours and get away with it, because you are family.' He repeats it: 'Mandla trusts you.'

Well, that is grand, I think. I wouldn't mind if he trusted me a little less.

I don't know what eventually does the trick: whether it is the police intervention or the psychologist, or our extended family simply not leaving him alone, and sitting on his case unrelentingly, or just getting older, or all combined. Maybe Vani's adoration has helped. Later, Mandla will be just as kind a babysitter for his sister Thandi's daughter, Khanyi, while he also manages to hold day jobs.

Apartheid spy tales
January 2004

Things with Mac and the arms deal have gone from bad to worse. Now he and Moe Shaik have made Thabo Mbeki very angry indeed by counter-accusing Mac's accuser, Scorpions boss Bulelani Ngcuka – whose people are also still chasing after Jacob Zuma – of having been an apartheid spy. This is frightening, because Ngcuka is very close to the president. Wrath from up high is thus to be feared.

But 'Mac and Moe', as newspapers will soon routinely headline the two, also have a point. The way Ngcuka has selected his arms deal corruption priorities – Shabir Shaik, Mac, Zuma – appears so clearly biased that they might feel a need to hit back. Some speculate that forces of the old regime really do still have a hold on the head of prosecutions. Or Ngcuka does all this because Moe Shaik and Mac Maharaj once investigated him? Whatever the case may be, Moe has, through a friendly journalist, leaked a report he drew up about Bulelani Ngcuka in the eighties, when the ANC indeed suspected him of being an apartheid spy.

They thought it was an open and shut case then. Ngcuka got passports even after the security police had arrested him for terrorism. Strangely, he got off lightly on a terrorism charge and was not sent to Robben Island, when everybody else who was suspected of ANC terrorism was. So now the headline 'Mac and Moe say Ngcuka is a spy' is all over the front pages.

It is indeed probably not wise for the two men, already out of favour in Wakanda, to produce such an accusation against someone in Thabo Mbeki's inner circle. The president promptly establishes a commission to formally investigate the accusations against Ngcuka, but in reality to smash the credibility of Moe Shaik and Mac Maharaj.[178] The terms of reference of the commission, under Judge Hefer, are tailored, undergoing multiple changes, to predetermine such an outcome. Ngcuka's accusers are now requested to prove something which they cannot prove because the information they once had is now held by the state, and therefore only legally accessible – for public use – to the head of state, who is Thabo Mbeki. The question why it is now locked away as a state secret, away from even access by the ANC itself, will remain unanswered.

Several ANC comrades try to stop the president from going ahead with this plan. Why have a public commission at taxpayers' expense to establish something that cannot really be established? This will likely only cause unnecessary rifts in the ANC, society and the state, they warn. If it is so important, as Judge Hefer will later write in his report,[179] that the perception of 'unquestionable proficiency and integrity' of the head of prosecutions is 'intact and unassailed by rumour', the president can request the information himself; he can then decide what, if anything, to do about it. He can slam the rumours. He can make any statement he sees fit.

Then secret services head Vusi Mavimbela[180] describes how Walter Sisulu's daughter Lindiwe Sisulu, who is minister of intelligence at the time, is left exhausted, half-crying, 'like a jilted lover', after one occasion where she has tried to see Mbeki in an effort to convince him not to go through with it. Mbeki has not even allowed her into his official residence to supplicate. Mavimbela also writes that Police Commissioner Jackie Selebi has repeatedly and forcefully contacted the president in an effort to get him to abandon the idea as well. But Mbeki goes ahead nevertheless.

In the weeks to come, we stare in horror at the TV screen as we see Mac and Moe's testimony torn to shreds. Is it the actual dossier on Ngcuka that you have here? No, sir, it was the eighties and we were in the bush, so this is reconstructed ... Ha, reconstructed, what does that even mean? You mean to say you made most of it up just this year? But he was RS 452, that was his agent number in the apartheid records. No, it actually wasn't. Because – this is the interrogating lawyer now, who, remarkably, seems to be getting a lot of state information from outside the state – here is this woman in the UK, Vanessa Brereton, who says that not Ngcuka, but she was the spy who was around in student movement circles at the time; she was RS 452![181]

When that happens, our two comrades are finished. Ngcuka was not RS 452, ergo he was not the spy, ergo he was not *a* spy. There is an outpouring of hatred towards Mac and Moe everywhere now: how dared they smear Ngcuka, the intrepid corruption fighter? They lied, they concocted information, only to take revenge on him because he is investigating Mac for corruption. Corrupt Mac defamed a man whose whole life was about achieving justice.

I have doubts, though, about the very public confession of RS 452 Vanessa Brereton, who has agreed to have her name, city of residence and even her picture published in the papers. Why would this woman, who has by all accounts been living a comfortable anonymous life in London, surrounded with new friends and colleagues, most of whom probably did not know she had once served the vile apartheid regime, all of a sudden feel the need to stand up and confess that she had been that disgusting creature, an apartheid police agent? Isn't it odd that she would do that, just to help out a black man who was unjustly accused in South Africa? Has she been feeling so guilty about her past as an apartheid spy that she just had to unburden herself now and come to the comrade's rescue? That was mighty good and fair of her, then.

* * *

The question is whether there is really a point to these spy stories in the current climate. Apartheid spies are all among us, after all, as are apartheid killers and torturers. The National Prosecuting Authority has so far started cases against exactly one of these, the now jailed security police death squad commander Eugene de Kock. No efforts have been made to investigate or prosecute anyone else. Perhaps as a consequence, former spies have become currency in political games rather than objects of truth-seeking and prosecution. Aziz Pahad, still a Mbeki confidante and now deputy minister of foreign affairs, asked me a few years back if I knew of any spies, if I could help him with a list. Zuma will later make political currency out of having the names of spies too.

Many politicians like to have kompromat on enemies, rivals or underlings. If someone has a dark past and you know about it, you want them working for you. They'll be your slaves.

Perhaps it is better to ask who is a good person *now*. Chances are that good people now would have been good people then, too. And when it comes to people who are bad now, I don't really care what they were in the past.

Ivan is annoyed by the whole spectacle. 'We never discuss what we should be discussing. What is the core business of the Scorpions? How do they process priorities? Is there a fair case selection system? How do we know if they are serious about combating crime or merely targeting political opponents?' Of course he thinks it is the latter. Bulelani Ngcuka has clearly become personally invested in chasing Zuma and Mac too, and holds press conferences and meetings about both.

Ivan doubts the usefulness of the Scorpions as a special unit in the first place. He always has. 'We had a first meeting when they discussed the establishment of what would become the Directorate of Special Operations (the Scorpions' official title) in 1999. I asked then what I always ask: Why *must* there be a new structure? Every time I hear them going on, all enthusiastically, that they are going to build this and that, it usually means trouble. It takes up your time, it costs money, and you are not solving anything. If the police was not doing its job, the solution would be to improve the police.' He doesn't know if there were any subsequent meetings, he says. 'But if there were, I was not invited.'

He is most irked about the way ANC fights are now being fought at the state's expense. 'In the past we could still get away with fumbling and stumbling. We didn't have resources, the environment was hostile. But now we are the governing party. Our fissures impact on the state. We cannot afford to mess about anymore.'

A Scorpions problem
Centurion, 2004

The Scorpions are now pressurising Ivan to help them find more charges against Thabo Mbeki's hated rival, Deputy President Jacob Zuma. They want to add tax crimes to Zuma's charge sheet, in addition to the large number of charges (783 to be exact) already amassed, which all relate to bribery efforts by Shabir Shaik and the French arms company Thomson CSF. Ivan is not inclined to help. 'You should generally be careful with criminal charges on tax matters,' he says. 'There is an escalating toolbox of remedies. It is only when all else fails that one considers that route.'

He is not at all happy with the way the Scorpions try to tie Zuma, and by extension now SARS, too, to the arms deal quagmire. 'Zuma had very little to do with that. He was not even in government at the time. Why should we come in to bail them out on what is essentially their faulty arms deal investigation? If it is about the person of Zuma and they have 783 charges, then why don't they just go ahead?' Even more annoyingly, the same Scorpions spend little time on the tax evasion cases that SARS does present to them for prosecution. 'And these cases are ready!' he fulminates one evening. 'They are big, too. But we hit a wall all the time!'

He sees Zuma, visits him a number of times, explaining to the man that he must put his tax affairs in order and pay his dues. He tells him that SARS must not be dragged into his case.

Meanwhile, however, unbeknown to us, SARS's criminal tax investigations head Rudolf Mastenbroek is fuming. Mastenbroek is still close to Bulelani Ngcuka and eager to help the Scorpions with the Zuma case. But SARS simply won't play ball and it's all Ivan's fault, he believes. 'Pillay was an open supporter of the closing down of the Scorpions. I, on the other hand, had recently come from the National Prosecuting Authority, where, among other things, I was part of the process of defending Bulelani Ngcuka (director of public prosecutions) from the false allegations that he was an apartheid spy,' Mastenbroek will write later in an article about what he perceived to be their falling out.[182]

At the time, Ivan does not know about Rudolf Mastenbroek's strong feelings since Rudolf does not speak to him personally about any of this, but Rudolf's enthusiasm for the Scorpions' Zuma hunt, or for hunting corrupt individuals in general, is not a secret. At some point Mastenbroek wants to charge twenty-seven ANC municipal councillors in Gauteng who are all defaulting on their taxes in exactly the same way. The common factor seems to be that they have all been advised to do something wrong by the same tax advisor. Ivan refuses. He wants to take the advisor to task, rather than create twenty-seven criminal cases – and possibly more, because the man might be doing the same with other clients as well. 'Firstly, we only go for criminal prosecutions when all other options are exhausted. Secondly, to add twenty-seven, likely more, cases to the backlog of 7000 cases we already had waiting for the Scorpions was futile,' he says, later. 'It was more effective and efficient to prosecute only the key facilitator, the crooked tax advisor.'

SARS penalised the councillors financially. A SARS team led by Ivan also engaged the mayor of Johannesburg, explained the problems and arranged for taxpayer education interventions to take place to ensure that there would not be a repeat. This was, he says, 'true to the compliance model which combined education of the taxpayer with a process that made it easy to comply, with enforcement reserved for the really unwilling or malicious'.

'Ivan makes SARS cases disappear,' Mastenbroek will later tell a journalist. 'He has withdrawn cases against ANC councillors in order to protect them.' Adding a few other examples, he tries to get the journalist – she happens to be Pearlie Joubert,[183] who is also an old friend of Rudolf's – to write about the wrongs he perceives. Joubert shrugs his accusations off. She knows some SARS investigators and believes they are doing a fine job.

We were friends with Rudolf, though not for as long as Pearlie had been, or not as close as he once was with Pravin Gordhan and his wife, Vani. Rudolf has been to our house. He helped me get my manuscript to Bulelani Ngcuka. But, even if Rudolf's final departure from SARS and his accusations will only materialise years later, relations are getting frosty already. Ivan continues to complain about SARS going it alone in criminal cases worth billions, while the Scorpions get ever more intense about Zuma.

The main problem with SARS giving the Scorpions Zuma's tax information, I understand from Ivan, is that it is illegal. Tax information is not easily shared with other arms of law enforcement because SARS has wide-ranging powers that place the burden of proof on the taxpayer. SARS can only use those wide powers to conduct its own tax investigations; it cannot transfer them to the police, since in the criminal justice system the burden of proof lies – and must lie – with the prosecution. Passing the information under the table would be wrong. Johann van Loggerenberg will later note in his book *Death and Taxes* that one Scorpions investigator plainly told him that 'we don't want the man to be president, even if it means we must bend the law a little'.

Mid next year, in 2005, the conviction of Zuma's generous donor Shabir Shaik will allow Thabo Mbeki to do what he wanted to do all along: Get rid of Zuma. Shaik's money was given to Zuma with 'corrupt intent', reads the verdict in Shaik's case. You clearly can't have a deputy president with such a big a cloud over his head.

The new deputy president is Bulelani Ngcuka's wife, Phumzile.

Bulelani Ngcuka himself will have resigned by then, after failing to charge Zuma himself in spite of there being 'prima facie evidence' of corruption, as he has put it in a briefing to a group of media editors. 'I was 'waiting for my president,' Bulelani Ngcuka will admit later.[184]

Ngcuka's decision not to charge Zuma, however, means that the Scorpions leave Ivan alone for a bit.

Or seem to.

Getting Jackie
February 2005

At first it seems silly and unimportant: a cartoon of Ivan as a plucked turkey on the lap of Brett Kebble, a mining billionaire, tax evader and ANC donor with a dodgy reputation. The accompanying story insinuates that, like some other ANC people who have been accused in media reports, Ivan has been corrupted by this Kebble. We shrug it off, since it's that same gossip magazine again; its editor has had his sights on Ivan ever since Bheki Jacobs came out with his story about the 'Vula Boys'. Now, two anonymous SARS officials are given ample space to complain that their boss, Ivan, is protecting Kebble. Why Ivan would do that is not clear, since Ivan does not know Brett Kebble, but that is not in the story. He has not been asked to comment.

As it turns out, the two SARS officials who are the source of the story have a bone to pick with Ivan. The two investigated Brett Kebble's affairs, or purported to, but Ivan had taken them off the case. It is this act of Ivan's that is reported as corrupt: why else would an investigation be stopped, if not to protect corrupt interests?

The question could have formed the basis for an interesting story if SARS's Kebble investigation was indeed stopped, but this is not the case. The investigation is simply carried out by others in SARS. 'Kebble had varied interests in many parts of the country. This means that you have to work from the centre, pull everything, look at the connections. It made sense to put a high-powered team in charge and drive the cases from head office,' Ivan explains.

There are questions in Parliament about the affair and Pravin Gordhan, speaking for SARS, answers these by submitting a diary that shows that the case is in fact ongoing, noting daily activity in terms of warrants, threats of arrest and negotiations with lawyers. The man has not paid up yet, but it is not unusual for such cases to take years. Men like Kebble use every procedure in the book and lawyer after lawyer to keep delaying. SARS is soon to institute criminal proceedings against Brett Kebble for tax evasion and fraud in May this year. The claim amounts to over R183 million.

All the same, we are dealing with a very concerned Sister and her daughter Jenny in Chatsworth, and an emotional Coastal, who phones from Merebank to ask nobody in particular how can they do this. To Ivan? Don't they know that Ivan is good? 'A tttturkey,' he splutters indignantly. 'Can't something be done about these people? It should not be allowed!'

'I wish we can keep the media posted so that they know when Kebble pays up,' says Ivan. 'But we are not allowed to give information about taxpayers.' Though not enraged like Coastal, he finds it a bit annoying that this accusation is out there, the first ever stain on his public record.

He laughs when Sam Sole and his colleague Stefaans Brümmer try to convince him to keep them updated about the Kebble investigation. 'We get that you can't talk about taxpayers,' they say.[185] 'But the thing is that Kebble has not paid tax and is therefore not a taxpayer. So you can talk about him.' The clever effort does not work, as they have probably foreseen, and the conversation ends there.

And then Brett Kebble does not pay. Because suddenly, on 27 September 2005, he is murdered by three beefy underworld figures in a hit on his car. Those involved will maintain that this happened with Kebble's own approval and participation, claiming it to have been an 'assisted suicide'.[186] A shady dealmaker and fraudster called Glenn Agliotti is the suspected mastermind of the assassination.

***

A few months later, sources in the know tell Ivan that he is now under investigation by the Scorpions in connection with the case. The Scorpions think he is linked to Agliotti, which is strange, because, he says, SARS enforcement has just spent months trying to convince the Scorpions to help them to investigate and prosecute Agliotti. He shakes his head. 'God knows what they are up to now.'

As it turns out, the Scorpions want to use an allegation about Ivan having had a meeting with Agliotti not so much in the Brett Kebble murder case, but as ammunition in another case they are now pursuing: a corruption matter involving Police Commissioner Jackie Selebi. The charge against Selebi is that the commissioner would have been given money and gifts by Agliotti. The Scorpions also seek to prove that Selebi had done fixer Agliott a favour by organising such a meeting between him and Ivan. Agliotti would dearly love such an introduction: the man was always looking for connections to mint in his trade-offs with others, making himself look influential. 'Perhaps they wanted us to testify to that,' Ivan says. 'But we could not say that because we didn't know for a fact that that is what happened.'

The alleged encounter was in fact a meeting between Ivan and Johann van Loggerenberg for SARS and some white businessmen. The occasion had indeed come about through an intervention by Police Commissioner Selebi. 'Selebi had called me to say he could provide information about a businessman called Gary Porritt, whom we were investigating for fraud, racketeering, tax evasion and a number of other things,' Ivan says.[187] 'He, Selebi, invited me to a meeting. I checked with Commissioner Gordhan if that was OK. Pravin said yes, but don't go alone.' He had gone with Johann.

The house at the address given by Selebi was very big. 'Palatial. There was a main lounge with a large table full of food and a number of smaller lounges. There were several persons standing around. Selebi was there. We sat down in one of the smaller lounges and were offered food and drink. We refused, taking only water; we had by then instituted a zero-gift rule at SARS. Then the two businessmen, whom we did not know at the time – but who the Scorpions later said were connected to Agliotti – came to tell us certain things about Porritt. We listened and made arrangements to pick up documents which would, they said, substantiate what they said. We drank the water and left.'

SARS was not pleased with this Scorpions démarche. 'We were supposed to be working together for law enforcement. If they thought Johann and I had been involved in anything unseemly, they should have talked to our boss, Pravin Gordhan. Pravin was very annoyed with them for not speaking to him. When they sent written requests for us to be interviewed at the NPA, Pravin engaged them, asking, 'Why are you writing letters to us now? Why not just talk to us?'

It is vintage Scorpions, whose entire focus is on Jackie Selebi. They ignore SARS's concerns with regard to Agliotti or even Porritt, who may or may not have been in Agliotti's, or any of his associates', bad books at the time. They simply very badly want to prosecute and convict the police commissioner, who is their main rival in law enforcement, and who has opposed their very formation as a separate directorate independent of the South African Police Services. They want that so much that not only have they threatened Barry Gilder, a former head of various sections in the secret services, to get him to cooperate with the case (as noted above) but they have also offered indemnity to the hitmen who shot Kebble. The purpose of this is to get the hitmen to pressurise Agliotti, who then in turn will testify that he has corrupted Selebi.

Agliotti will later state that a Scorpions team offered to let him walk free on a charge of murder, if he gave them Selebi. Mandy Wiener, in her book *Killing Kebble*, will later repeatedly ask why underworld killers and their alleged mastermind were allowed to go free [188] merely to convict the police commissioner under a 'weight of feathers', a somewhat incoherent mass of small pieces of evidence which might still have been insufficient to convict Selebi if he had not eventually admitted in the witness box to having received money.

In 2010, Selebi will be convicted to fifteen years in jail for having accepted R166 000 from Glenn Agliotti. After being released on parole when he falls ill in 2012, he will die three years later, aged sixty-four.

Back in the days of the Goldstone Commission, more than a decade before, prosecutor Torie Pretorius had told me he and his colleagues would never work with criminals at all. He had been appalled when I had asked why they did not offer some Third Force train shooters who had been arrested amnesty in return for the names of their bosses. 'We can't do that,' he had said. 'This is a regstaat, a state of law.' But the regstaat seems to have morphed into something else, because they do precisely that now, only the other way around: Instead of working with the lower-level criminal to catch the mafia boss, they work with assassins and a mafia boss to catch a police commissioner who did not deny that he received some money, a Louis Vuitton bag and a suit.

It is, of course, also true that a country cannot have a compromised police commissioner. 'Even if Jackie Selebi saw Agliotti as no more than a friendly informant,' Ivan asks, 'what business does a police commissioner have engaging personally with such a person?' He feels that the relevant minister should at least have moved Selebi sideways, or suspended him much earlier, and wonders why that hasn't happened.

President Thabo Mbeki will remain inactive in the matter, allowing two law enforcement institutions to fight with one another for close to two years. Many interpret this as protection by Mbeki of his friend Selebi, but I wonder if that is all there is to it. Selebi, a former ANC Youth League head and an Mbeki appointee, might have been close to the president once, but after vehemently opposing both the establishment of the Scorpions and the Hefer Commission, it is unlikely that he is still in his boss's good books now. People have fallen out of favour with Thabo for much, much less.

Perhaps a more likely explanation is that the troubled president has entered a state of paralysis, torn between his Scorpions, old loyalties and concerned comrades who warned that what was happening in the Selebi case wasn't right. It will be only after the Scorpions apply for an arrest warrant for Selebi, two years into the investigation, that Mbeki acts. He opposes the warrant for Selebi and instead places him on leave, while also suspending new Scorpions head Vusi Pikoli. This is 'in the interests of national security', he will be reported as saying, adding that 'the police are very angry'.

So he sees that now.

Mbeki will then appoint yet another commission to help him find a way out of the matter. 'There we go again,' says Ivan. 'Another scandal and another commission.'[189]

Remnants of the old

Few of my colleagues worry about the possibility that the Scorpions might have an agenda of its own. The Scorpions' cherry-picking of cases against certain individuals is routinely mentioned in the media, but only as a strategy 'to ensure a high conviction rate'. What seems to be a complete absence of rational assessment of priorities goes unnoticed. 'So what if they pick one case and not another,' a colleague counters when I raise my problems with their apparent bias and targeting. 'A case is a case.'

Still, the NPA hasn't started any of the prosecutions they were expected to carry out against known apartheid torturers and killers, apart from the one already jailed death-squad commander, Eugene de Kock. Prosecuting apartheid criminals who have not come forward to request amnesty in the Truth and Reconciliation process was announced as a priority for the justice department at the time. At its closure, the Truth and Reconciliation Commission recommended a list of more than 300 cases to the National Prosecuting Authority for investigation and since then, thirty dockets were prepared pertaining to serious cases of murder, torture and disappearance. But apart from the case of Eugene de Kock, none of the other dockets have been taken forward.

Remarkably, the Scorpions seem concerned that such killers and torturers might be 'targeted'. A 2003 memo by then Scorpions director Geoffrey Ledwaba notes that an internal task team that was 'stacked with intelligence officers... seemed more concerned about why the cases were targeted rather than taking them forward.'[190] A strange concern, that is. The Scorpions are all about targeting individuals; they themselves admit to that. So why not target the monsters of the old regime, the death squad members, the water boarders, the killers of Pat and Jabu Msomi and Shadrack Maphumulo, the men who ran electric shocks through Coastal's body? What power does the old regime hold over justice in the new South Africa?

It appears from journalists' investigations into the matter, and from a later affidavit by Scorpions head at the time, Vusi Pikoli, that the power of the old is real. Pikoli's affidavit states that politicians – notably in the department of justice, the SAPS and certain 'individuals in the top echelons of NIA' – have 'blocked' the NPA from investigating the apartheid crimes. Pikoli writes that this was the result of 'a fear by the ANC that should prosecutions begin, then the ANC too could face investigations for some of its actions in the struggle against apartheid'.

Which raises the question of who is being terrified by whom. Many ANC comrades who fought in the struggle have duly applied for and been granted amnesty through the TRC process. So who in the ANC might still be prosecuted and who is scaring them so? Why did a task team of intelligence officials, presumably of the old regime, have the power, in 2003 – in Bulelani Ngcuka's time – to enforce a moratorium? Has kompromat been at work? Who has dossiers on whom?

So much of the old is still creeping into the new. Former apartheid minister Pik Botha, now a representative of arms company Paramount, is bullying Jacana Media with regard to their intended publication of my book on assassinations and arms trade. The former minister, friend of weapons and diamond smugglers, and somehow always there when an obstacle to shady business deals needs to be removed, shouts, threatens, and tells publisher Maggie Davey that 'the world is a dangerous place, you know'.

The ANC remains immersed in faction fights. A new black elite enriches itself. People keep dying of AIDS and other diseases and Thabo Mbeki becomes ever more frantic. He is openly fighting even with anti-apartheid legends and struggle icons, Nelson Mandela and Desmond Tutu, now. After allowing hecklers to tell Mandela to 'sit down, old man'[191] at a National Executive Committee meeting last year in 2004 – after Mandela argued that as funeral companies were springing up like mushrooms all over the country, medicines should now really be given to the people – Mbeki is reportedly not taking his calls anymore. He has penned a diatribe of over three thousand words, attacking Tutu's concerns about new black elite self-enrichment as 'gratuitous insults', 'false messages', and 'serving agendas'. Mbeki's now almost hysterical self-righteousness is fuelling intense opposition to him. And as it grows, Jacob Zuma is right in the middle of it.

Compared to Mbeki, Zuma is starting to look almost acceptable.

* * *

The Kebble story, meanwhile, does not go away. In October, eight months after the story in the gossip newsletter, I discover that even a close colleague whom I regarded as a friend still believes that Ivan is corrupt. The colleague backtracks when I tell him about SARS's Kebble investigation diary that was presented in Parliament, but still doesn't sound very convinced.

It is a new and unsettling experience. I have only ever met people who adored Ivan. In our former Vula circles, the anti-apartheid movement in the Netherlands, the extended family and community in Chatsworth and Merebank, as well as at SARS, everyone I meet always tells me how great he is. I have learned to nod resignedly, and confirm that yes, he is very nice, I like him too.

Then the gossip newsletter's editor is invited to the investigative journalism conference our network has organised in partnership with the University of the Witwatersrand, or Wits.

As the recently appointed coordinator of the Forum for African Investigative Reporters, I had worked hard for this. I may be only a smurf, as I call myself – enabling and connecting and fundraising, without doing any actual stories – but I am a good smurf. I got colleagues to come to the conference. They have crucial stories to present and debate, among which Mozambican plunder of their national bank, related assassinations, and a resurgence of child marriage in Malawi as a consequence of poverty. There is a hard-hitting exposé on killings of disabled children in Benin, carried out because a largely nomadic people, deprived of state services, simply cannot cope with children who are not mobile. We are discovering that destructive habits and traditions, even tribal hatred, have everything to do with failing governments in these countries, as in Kenya, where different ethnic groups are fighting for scarce resources, and Cameroon, where political party officials from different regions kill one another for access to state coffers.

The stories have been published all over the continent. Colleagues have learned from reports from other countries that similar things happen in theirs too. We have outlined the parallels, made the stories more prominent, and now we have organised an investigative journalism summit at Wits. We hope to learn from experiences on the rest of the continent, as colleagues in Kenya and Benin may learn from the South African struggle, from its anti-tribalism and its belief in human dignity for all. I have raised funds so that the invited journalists can come here and meet and share.

And then suddenly, in one of the rooms next door, there is this man who talks about Ivan as an example of corruption and there is nothing I can do about it.

I propose that a special committee in FAIR should look into the relationship between Ivan and Kebble. You don't want your coordinator tainted by allegations of corruption, I tell them, and offer to step down while they investigate. But the response is negative. The newly elected board says that what my husband does has nothing to do with me, which means that there is no problem.

I find that a weird answer, at least from those among them who accused Mac Maharaj of corruption when money was paid to his wife. The FAIR network benefits from the fact that Ivan supports me financially. What if that financial support has partly come from the late Brett Kebble? But they still refuse to look into the matter, and things continue as they were.

In May 2006, seven months after his death, SARS will recover R50 million of its total claim against Brett Kebble's estate. Criminal proceedings instituted in 2002 by SARS against Brett's father Roger Kebble[192] will result in the recovery of moneys by SARS as well, in spite of the NPA dropping the case in 2007.

Meanwhile, Pik Botha wins. At a grave meeting, attended by the entire Jacana board, publishing director Mike Martin tells me that they are dropping the plan to publish my book. The risk of being bankrupted by Botha's lawyers is simply too great. There have been other threats, too. The secret service agent who lived opposite Chris Hani and was first to arrive on the murder scene has threatened Jacana with a visit by the Scorpions.

I still try to get the book published elsewhere, and find some interest, but am told after a while that 'someone in government' has advised this new publisher against even looking at it.

The monster
December 2005

'But they are all like that,' I argue with Gwen Ansell. Ansell, director of the IAJ and our pan-African network's godmother, and I now regularly have coffee in the Rosebank mall in Johannesburg. As it turns out, we don't only share an interest in investigative journalism but also know many of the same people in the ANC, coming from her time in Botswana. This time our discussion is more fired up than usual. Fezeka Kuzwayo, Judson Kuzwayo's daughter, has laid charges of rape against Jacob Zuma and Gwen is angry; she blasts invective at Zuma and his attitude towards women, calling him a predator.

Zuma may well be a serial harasser of women, even a rapist, I say, but I wonder if he is so different from a lot of other men in positions of power. My thoughts spiral off to the dozens of abuse, harassment and rape cases I have come across in my life: personal as well as friends' experiences, interviews I have done, and rumours about men I know, including some I once revered as freedom fighters.

My thoughts jump from Archie's story about an ANC official with his Scrabble board to the aide in Mbeki's delegation who was seen on TV carrying a pair of women's shoes; from the comrades who would call one racist for not wanting to sleep with them; to the high-ranking SARS official who touches women's breasts wherever he can; and the senior foreign correspondent who insisted that a meeting in his hotel room should be what he calls romantic.

Yes, that behaviour is horrific. It's one of the reasons why we have feminism. And indeed Zuma's forcing himself on Fezeka in his house is unacceptable. But that behaviour is not exceptional, I say to Gwen: not in the traditional patriarchal context in which many, especially powerful, men operate.

I don't know much about the person of Jacob Zuma, other than what I've been told by Ivan: that he is an ambitious and traditional Zulu patriarch who always builds his own power base and surreptitiously undermines the current leadership. This is, of course, precisely why he has emerged as the one man in the ANC who is able, and clearly very willing, to take on Thabo Mbeki. But I don't understand Gwen's very specific blasting of Jacob Zuma on the issue of his attitude to women. As if there aren't hundreds, thousands like him, also in the ANC.

'You are wrong,' she says. 'Yes, many men feel entitled to women's bodies. But Zuma is an extreme version. He *will* rape you. He is a monster.'

Of course we support Fezeka. Ivan has been in touch with her, he has been ever since he began working with Judson and Beauty Kuzwayo sometime in 1977. Fez-Fez grew up into a school girl in front of Ivan, he had been 'malume' – uncle – to her. When Judson died in a car accident in Zimbabwe in 1985, when she was ten, Ivan had been one of the uncles and aunts trying to see to the well-being of Beauty and the child. The underground conditions and the world of exile were harsh, and Beauty and her daughter continued to suffer hardship and poverty as well as abuse from comrades who were not worthy of that name. After the trauma of her father's death, Fezeka was hurt by such things again and again. Somehow, however, she had remained trusting and naïve, often indiscriminately turning to people for help, any people. She asked her other uncle, Ronnie Kasrils, and Ivan several times for support for her studies. In this last case, she had asked Zuma. The reports say that she visited Malume Jacob some time last November, for help with some or other study plan overseas.

'I don't understand that Beauty allowed it,' Ivan said, shaking his head in disbelief. 'We all know that the old man will pounce on any woman who is nearby.' But does Ivan realise, I asked, that Fezeka is now thirty years old? Though she still lives with her mother, it is hardly likely that Beauty could have stopped her even if she wanted to. Besides, Fezeka should be able to spend the night in the house of a family friend safely. It is unlikely that she thought she would be alone with Zuma. His daughter was there, too.

That is the theory and the morality of it, and the stance to take. Nevertheless, Ivan is also right. Fezeka should have known – Beauty would have known – to stay far away from a man like Zuma, especially at night in his house, no matter who else is also there. The old man will inevitably try something he shouldn't. But every time I think that, I realise that Fezeka was not savvy in that way. Sunny she was, and happy-go-lucky with everything and everybody. She would have trusted Jacob, maybe not as much as she would trust Uncle Ronnie and Malume Ivan, but trust she would nevertheless. Jacob had been an 'uncle', too.

'Uncle!' spits out Sue Rabkin, an old comrade from Maputo days, when we meet for dinner. 'Uncle he was! That was Judson's little girl! The man has absolutely no shame.' During the subsequent court case, Jacob Zuma will deny that he raped her, will say that he thought the sex was consensual. Fezeka will admit that she did not say no, that she just froze. Uncle Jacob will be acquitted of rape. But to Sue, and us, and many others, it doesn't make much of a difference. To enter the room unannounced of the daughter of a comrade you once shared a cell with and lie down on her is beyond horrific.

As Sue talks that evening, I notice she expresses the same outrage that Gwen Ansell did. Perhaps Gwen was right. There is something about Jacob Zuma that surpasses traditional patriarchal attitudes, something beyond the generally awful male thinking that you can just try something with any and all women. Something cold, shameless, devoid of any moral values or human kindness. Something fitting his middle name Gedleyihlekisa: he who laughs as he drives the knife into your back.

Something monstrous.

In the months that follow, Zuma's followers will be angrily dancing and picketing outside the court as the rape case is heard. They will set fire to pictures of Fezeka and sing 'burn the bitch'. The Friends of Jacob Zuma Trust will issue a rather lame disclaimer, saying 'these are not our real supporters, they are only masquerading as such', but the whistling of the dogs' master is clear. As Zuma talks of 'plots to bring him down', he signals to his masses that he endorses their rage, encouraging them to act without actually instructing them to do so.

If there is anything this old man can do exceptionally well, it is playing the victim. He exudes hurt, turning what he did to Fezeka into yet another attack on him by his enemies. It was a honey trap, his supporters say, though there is no evidence at all that such a plan ever existed. And even if it did, who in their right mind would have sex with Jacob Zuma and then go through the ordeal of a rape case in court, only because some politicians wanted her to? Even a calculating, shrewd person would only agree to do such a thing if she could count on a substantial reward. But there was no evidence of any such reward having been offered to Fezeka, who is anything but calculating.

Fezeka and her mother have only suffered after laying the rape charge. Their house has been attacked and set on fire; elders in the Zulu community, including some aunts and other relatives, have been incited against the two. Their lives are in very real danger.

Malignance

Jacob Zuma's exploitation of victimhood is helped along greatly by the Scorpions. A new intelligence report, titled 'Browse Mole', smears 'JZ' in such bizarre ways[193] that one almost feels sympathy for the predator again. By all that is holy, when are Mbeki and his prosecutorial goons going to stop being ridiculous? Don't they realise that they continuously play right into Zuma's innocently raised, simple peasant hands?

The Browse Mole report backfires spectacularly, discrediting the Scorpions rather than Zuma. After the murky Selebi and Kebble cases, with their deals with criminals and political targeting, the corruption-fighting unit is by now well on its way to becoming a snake pit of personal vendettas, faction fighting and smear-versus-smear. When Ivan is in Hong Kong to represent SARS at a law enforcement conference, deputy Scorpions head Leonard McCarthy invites him to join him and a company of some young women at a table with drinks. McCarthy then takes a photograph of the group, after which he turns to Ivan, grinning, and says, 'Now I've got you.' It is a joke, of course. But it will later become a matter of public record that a sex tape of at least one deputy head at the National Prosecuting Authority has been circulated, exposing the person to the risk of blackmail by those who have access to the tape. A similar rumour exists about another former high-profile prosecutions head.

These days, the question of what Mbeki's victims will do once he is gone becomes relevant. Will the walking wounded strike back? Jacob Zuma will come to power two years from now and answer that question very clearly. When the looting, vicious monster, grown to its full terrifying size under Mbeki, starts to manipulate the National Prosecuting Authority to serve him and only him, he will do what he learned from his former master.

October 2006

Devi is sick again. She had a pain in her foot when we were in Italy in July, and sometimes had to sit down because she could not walk anymore. I initially didn't think much of it. We were walking a lot, and my feet were also sore. When she was back at school in September, and a lump appeared at the bottom of that same foot, the doctor had thought it was a sprained and swollen muscle, plantar fasciitis, and a physiotherapist treated it with massage and ultrasound. But it still didn't go down and we were finally referred to an orthopaedic surgeon who had looked worried and examined the lymph nodes in her armpits and groin. I knew what that meant; at thirteen, I hoped Devi didn't.

I asked the doctor as soon as he finished the examination to have her wait outside so that he and I could talk, but he responded that we should 'tell truth' to the child. He proceeded to tell us that he suspected synovial sarcoma, a soft tissue cancer with a very low survival rate. I was torn between rage with him and panic. How could he tell 'truth' to the child when he didn't yet know the truth? Why should she be terrified to death just because of a suspicion? Who even knew that foot cancer existed?

After two weeks of tests – X-rays, MRI scans and a biopsy – and then another ten days of waiting for the final verdict, it turns out it is a haemangioma, no more dangerous than the thorn in Pumpkin Patch's Timothy Traddle's foot that had made her cry so bitterly when she was only three. Like her appendix years ago, this, too, can be safely cut out. According to a Google search, haemangiomas are often misdiagnosed.

It is not the haemangioma itself, but the experience of being told that she would be in hospital, have agonising treatments and then die, only to exist a little beyond thirteen, that has affected Devi's life and ours since then. It is hard to get over the weird bible therapist we apparently had to have – there was no discussion about this, she was just there – to sit next to Devi's bed to prepare her for the end, and the solemn but bizarrely excited specialist who was convinced he was dealing with a dying child, and told us he'd make her comfortable and that we should hang in there for as long as possible. Which, we were given to understand repeatedly, wouldn't be very long.

Strangely, many tests showed that it might not be cancer. Devi's lymph nodes were actually fine; she had not lost any weight; her lungs were clear; even the ultrasound man had said he'd be really surprised if it wasn't benign. But the therapist and the specialist would insist on assuring us that that didn't actually mean good news. We should not have false hope, and be prepared for the worst: not only the death of our little girl, but to be precise, her spending the rest of all time tortured in hell. A dominee visits Devi one night uninvited, as she lies strangely accessible in a dark room and alone in a Pretoria hospital, and tells her to repent and convert to Christianity now because 'eternity is a long time to burn'.

We are, naturally, infinitely grateful that it isn't cancer; we are still so very fortunate compared to those who have actually lost a child. But the three weeks until a biopsy comprehensively shows that all this preparation was unnecessary will have the effect of sinking Devi in a deep post-traumatic depression that she is battling to overcome to this day. She would probably have dealt better with the physical issues of this tumour in her foot – which, though benign, will need two operations with two periods of six months in crutches each – if it wasn't for the hopelessness she was bashed with, every day, for those three weeks.

Cancer is such an overused word. Alcohol and drug abuse, loose morals, ethnic tensions, corruption, have all been described as 'cancers' of community and society. White right-wingers, thinking themselves witty, describe the ANC as 'cANCer'. Just as dramatic as that specialist was with his morbid eagerness to find synovial sarcoma in a young girl, they also think that all hope is lost, that the entire country is about to die and rot, a nightmare to run away from; they also want all of us to feel that.

'Actually, I had that too,' says Ivan, as we have a rest in the hospital canteen while our daughter gets dressed to go home. 'I forgot. I had a lump in my foot when I was in my late teens. The Chatsworth hospital just cut it out and sent me home.'

'Ah,' I say. 'Now you tell me.' How ironic that the basic health care Ivan had would turn out to be less traumatic in the long term than all the highly specialised, expensive tests our thirteen-year-old had had to go through, administered on the basis of all-consuming fear.

'I forgot,' he repeats.

There is real grief in his eyes now, grief that I hadn't seen before these weeks of panic, when he remained calm as always, quiet and calm.

Money from whites

Meanwhile, FAIR has been doing really well. 'I write what I like' is a concept that, with apologies to the memory of Steve Biko, has been taking many colleagues by storm as they free themselves from the shackles of state media and press conference reporting. Investigating why children are getting sick after drinking water in northern Zambia, reporter Zarina Geloo has found that neglected pipes carry chemicals from copper mining that have seeped through into tap water. In the Ivory Coast, a country blessed with myriad cocoa plantations and expert farmers, the fact that it can't get one chocolate factory to work turns out to be connected to those in charge losing interest after getting the state subsidy from their relatives in government.

Several of the colleagues I now interact with were born during independence struggles. Anas Aremeyaw Anas's dad was a soldier who once fought Ghana's colonists, fired with idealism; Anas now risks his life making undercover films about sloppy government offices, dangerous pesticides dropped on the black market, exploitative churches and abusive orphanage schemes with links to the politically powerful. Sage Gayala's [194] dad was an intellectual and revolutionary, one of a wave of academics working for progress and freedom in Zaire during and after the rule of Mobutu Sese Seko. Today Congo's political leaders hold many academics and journalists on a leash, reduced to pitiful propagandists singing for their supper, but Sage refuses to be one of those and exposes the fake AIDS-cure rackets that involve many an elected official.

South Africa is still fortunate to have its struggle legacy and traditions of mass democratic activism. The UDF may have closed down but many civic organisations are reviving and new ones are being established. From the Ahmed Kathrada Foundation[195] to the health activists of the Treatment Action Campaign, to the questioning media – never mind their love of the Scorpions – we have the power in society to keep our rulers in check. Thabo Mbeki's rule may be dictatorial, paranoid and close to genocidal in the case of the AIDS epidemic, but this country can also count its blessings.

South Africa is especially fortunate that it doesn't depend on donors. The more FAIR looks at donor dependency in the countries to the north of us, the more we realise that the post-colonial kleptocracies are kept going by dollar infusions mostly from Western countries and institutions that call themselves development partners. There are ever new projects, from Kribi harbour in Cameroon to the Ajaokuta Steel Mill in Nigeria, to water pipes in Kinshasa and several consecutive Rift Valley dams in Kenya. All demand big budgets and many linked contracts for the politically connected, all start with glitzy launches, green papers and bombastic speeches, then all go invariably wrong. Those in power, after digesting one pie, move on to the next crumbly railway, creaky power plant, top-heavy dam or unnecessary bridge, in Fanon's words 'sending out frenzied appeals for help to the former mother country'.[196]

Donor aid is also, of course, a way for neocolonial powers to continue exploiting Africa's resources. Handouts to ruling elites will ensure the continued shipping away of timber, diamonds, cocoa, coffee, coal and oil at the cheapest of rates, with no benefit to the citizens from whose hands and under whose feet these riches are taken.

We have tapped into the donor environment because FAIR needs funds too. It has, however, not been easy to find international media development organisations willing to fund investigations. 'We can do activities in Nigeria, but we don't want to anger the Nigerian government,' a German representative has told us. 'Because then we can't work there anymore.' We have received the same message from UK donor officials in Uganda and French ones in the Ivory Coast.

We have recently tried, therefore, to add investigative components to projects that do tend to get funding, such as training of journalists, or advocacy campaigns for press freedom which are often rather toothless, so as not to offend. It is in the context of the latter that I met last June with the NGO *Journaliste en Danger* (JED) in Kinshasa, DRC.

Journalists often operate in poor and risky conditions in this country; they are regularly attacked, and sometimes murdered. JED, we were told, was there for them. With colleagues Sage Gayala and Dutch compatriot Bram Posthumus, I was asked by the Netherlands Institute for Southern Africa (NIZA) to investigate such a murder.[197]

Journalist Franck Ngyke, assassinated in Kinshasa last year November, in 2005, became in the past year the poster victim for journalists under threat in the DRC. Donors including NIZA raised tens of thousands of dollars to fund protests against this murder, and for an awareness campaign around journalists' safety generally. The money has been paid to JED, which is conducting the campaign.

Remarkably, Posthumus, Gayala and I found that the assassinated Franck Ngyke was not a real journalist at all. 'He was a bit of a blackmailer, indeed, *hehehehe*,' JED director Donat M'Baya Msimanga, a large man in a blue flowing traditional *boubou* dress, giggled. Even during our first conversation M'Baya Msimanga had no problem admitting that Ngyke was paid by politicians either to write PR pieces for them or alternatively to smear their enemies. He explained that Ngyke also made money by 'finding out something bad about you and then asking for a little incentive not to publish'.

Asked why the assassination of Ngyke, probably by a double-crossed paymaster – among whom, we understand, is the Agence Nationale des Renseignements (ANR), President Joseph Kabila's secret service – was used by JED in a campaign for 'safety for journalists,' M'Baya shrugged his broad shoulders. '*Beaucoup de journalistes travaillent au service des individus,* many journalists work for individuals.'

JED remained similarly unperturbed when 'individuals' briefly kidnapped Bram Posthumus. M'Baya and his much smaller and quieter deputy, Tshivhis Tshivuadi, showed no signs of shock when, on the second day of our stay, we came to tell them that Bram was forced into a black Mercedes, driven to a deserted corner, shaken down and left without a laptop. They affirmed that it was quite possibly the ANR, as if it was business as usual. When I lost my notebook, also on the second day in Kinshasa, it reappeared two days later on Tshivhis Tshivuadi's desk. He laughed when I asked him how that got there, responding with a chuckle, 'No one can read your handwriting anyway.'

'You must forgive us. We are under great stress. We are working in such terrible conditions. We are receiving so many death threats ourselves,' Donat M'Baya intervened then, and showed me a text message on his phone. I could not read it since it was in Lingala, but according to M'Baya it said that the sender was coming to kill him and his entire family.

'We both receive such messages all the time,' Tshivhuadi added gravely.

I had asked why they didn't go underground for a while, like colleagues in Nigeria and Uganda did when they got wind of unsavoury types asking around about them. They spent months, sometimes, staying in friends' houses in other towns, or cheap hotels, before the heat was off. 'No,' M'Baya had said. 'We are safest in our office.' This was hiding in plain sight: *Journaliste en Danger* was written on the outside wall of the office in big letters.

As I write this, I picture the two men at their desks on the day we leave, both energetically texting on their phones. Is this what Western development aid, purportedly charity from those richer and more powerful, does to a country? Does it turn proud independents into donation addicts, propping up corrupt elites and poisoning journalism itself?

'Some of us want to leave the DRC because we don't want to play such games,' said Sage Gayala, who would end up finding a new place to live and work in Canada.

November 2006

'They make themselves foeitog,' says Sunday, using an Afrikaans word that loosely translates as 'you poor thing'. 'Of course, we are poor. And, of course, we suffer. But to use it to get things, that is making yourself foeitog. Like the guys who beg at the robots. They are poor, but they tell you they are hungry, with those very sad faces, instead of just asking normally.' Having told Sunday about JED, she has – even if a persecution story is not a starvation story – seamlessly linked it to the behaviour of a cleaning lady called Maria, who works at the crèche run by a neighbour, Mrs Oosthuyse, in our street.[198]

Apparently, Maria has just acquired a new jersey from her employer. 'She showed up at work in a T-shirt, shivering. So Mrs Oosthuyse exclaimed, "But no, Maria, don't you have a jersey?" And Maria of course shook her head. Then madam immediately took her to go buy a jersey.' I venture that Maria probably *does* have a jersey or two at home and Sunday has nodded. 'Of course. Who doesn't have a jersey? That is what I mean when I say we make ourselves foeitog.'

Ivan has had quite a few such experiences. At SARS, when faced with job applicants who believe that it is simply their turn to have a high-level management job, having always been disadvantaged, he will ask, 'Tell me what is so good about you?'

It is one thing to say that you need some compensation for suffering caused by apartheid – a land subsidy, business assistance, health care, a bursary, counselling – but quite another to say you must have this or that position. 'We need to build a developmental state. That needs competence. We would prefer a black person, preferably female, of course, but there must be evidence that they can do what they are supposed to.'

He admits that it is difficult to keep strictly to that, when apartheid wrongs are still so visibly and painfully present. At SARS, like elsewhere, most tea ladies, cleaners and security personnel are still black. Passionate and promising black employees rightly need recognition, which is why many previously disadvantaged SARS staff are promoted whenever possible. And, even if mistakes are made – fast tracking the career of one Jonas Makwakwa, about whom more later, might not have been their very best choice – many of them will shine. Others, however, get annoyed at the perceived continued lack of opportunities.

'Dad, don't pop my balloon,' I remember a remark made by Vani out of the blue, when she was four years old. Had she had a dream about her father doing that? It is precisely what Ivan does. He does it to me when I announce grand plans for books and spectacular investigations. Ivan will almost always say something dry, to the effect of 'I'll see that when I see that', popping your balloon.

A major balloon that gets popped at SARS is guaranteed bonuses: when the new leadership introduces bonuses for good performance only, resentful whites who long for the good old days of their own kingdom of peace and happiness are suddenly very much in agreement with equally outraged black colleagues and the union NEHAWU.

Nevertheless, many others in the institution remain heartbreakingly dedicated to non-racial and non-sexist ideals, the new Constitution and the new SARS. They work overtime, donate part of their salaries to worthy causes, read the books Ivan gives them. Even if their community and families have never inculcated social justice values in them, they have embraced them now, sometimes with an enthusiasm I can only liken to Devi's toddler years when she ran, arms outstretched, eyes wide, head over heels into everything new.

Charl Fourie is one of them, the human resources psychologist who in his free time coaches Mandla and other boys who risk getting lost; as is another burly white man, part of a team that protects SARS investigators when they have to investigate suspicious warehouses. He advises Sunday and me to take shooting lessons so we can protect ourselves when we are home alone, and shows us how we can conceal a weapon just above our socks. A third nice man patiently helps me retrieve alarm sensors that I threw into our household rubbish because I had thought they were the old alarm sensors, and puts them all back too. I will later learn that the burly security man is Andries 'Skollie' Janse van Rensburg. The kind alarm systems man is Helgaard Lombard.

We also still meet Steven Burnett, former apartheid mercenary and now SARS contract investigator. He continues to feel tormented by notions that evil powers, both from the present and the past, battle to control him. He talks, sometimes unintelligibly, of dark interests held by shady groups that pollute every single project around us. I invite him to a party once, to be held at what used to be a military veterans resort but is now open to everybody, but he suspects nefarious motives behind the invitation, and doesn't come. He will succumb to fears, imagining conspiracies of illuminati and alien reptiles, and commit suicide in 2007 not long after this.

A fragile alliance

Many of the sources who help us expose kleptocratic rulers in countries on this continent are state officials: whistle blowers who work, or who have worked, within corrupted state and public service systems. They help substantiate our investigations, often at great risk to themselves. In Mozambique, it's not only journalist Carlos Cardoso who has been murdered for exposing large-scale looting of the central bank. The bank's auditor Antonio Siba-Siba Macuacua, who had worked with law enforcement to straighten out the mess, was assassinated too. Sources from within the Nigerian state oil company, the Zambian department of mining, Cameroonian agriculture authorities and Ghanaian police and social welfare departments also risk their jobs and livelihood by talking to our colleagues.

'It's just that people want to do their jobs,' says Ghanaian colleague Anas Aremeyaw Anas, when I ask him how he got into an office issuing fraudulent drivers' licenses, and close to the tables where the corrupt count their money. 'Even a post office worker wants to be proud of what he does. They see that their own grannies need that mail, or that attention in the hospital. You get good policemen, too. They will confide in me about the pressure they are under to join in the corruption. They resist because they have ethics, and those are our sources.'

It is as if an incipient alliance is growing, thin and fragile, between journalists wanting to be real journalists and state officials wanting to serve their countries.

Early 2007

Journalism is blossoming in South Africa too. Investigative journalism awards still mostly go to esteemed colleagues in the traditionally white media, but this is not surprising. First, these publications have always been better resourced. Maybe, even more importantly, among those who wanted to question authority, it was mainly the white journalists who were ever able to come close to interrogating white power. They could, if they tried, find the corrupt contracts, the sources in the departments, sometimes force through interviews, while black journalists risked arrest and disappearance at every turn; what they did was more akin to war correspondence from the trenches.

It was always a harmful divide, of course. For what is investigative journalism, that exposes injustice, without being able to report fully on the experiences of the victims? Rural reporting would have been academic without the experiences of prisoners killed on the potato fields in the Orange Free State; economic journalism irrelevant without reports from the mines and factories; law and order writing perverse without the stories describing the heartbreak and cruelty of forced removals. All such stories were written by black journalists, often at great risk. Apartheid may have kept them away from Pretoria's circles of power, but it kept their white colleagues away from the reality of black life under its monstrous regime.

But exhilaratingly, the two strands are coming together. In a story about infant deaths in Mount Frere hospital,[199] Ntando Makhubu, Chandré Prince and Brett Horner jointly record the neglect that has led to dozens of infant victims. Together they put names and faces to those responsible, and get the health ministry to investigate too.

The story rightly wins a major award. Such stories are the answer

– must be the answer – to the dishonest politicians who siphon off funds from state coffers, funds that otherwise could have been used for functioning health care for the babies who are now dead. These stories are the answer to the argument, increasingly made by dishonest politicians, that whites simply don't want black people to have money. Julius Malema, at this point in time still a leader of the ANC Youth League as well as a diehard Zuma fan, uses that argument a lot, especially when questioned about the money with which he buys his Gucci suits and Rolex watches. In two years SARS will be investigating Julius Malema, and a number of other wealthy politicians, precisely because the money they take[200] is meant for other things: better hospital care, running water for poor households, electricity.

I am almost feeling optimistic about this new South Africa again. Especially now that Thabo Mbeki and his awful Scorpions definitely seem on the way out.

When Polokwane comes in December, I see hundreds of ANC delegates make the hand movements that wave Thabo away, roll him over to make place for Jacob Zuma.

Days later, on the 28th, the Scorpions charge Zuma, but it is too little, too late. In a few months, devastatingly, the political interference by Thabo Mbeki loyalists in the case will be proven when recordings of phone calls, discussing the timing of charges against Jacob Zuma, and Mbeki's wishes in this regard are leaked to the media.[201] Zuma's side, thanks to his intelligence friends who have leaked the tapes, temporarily wins the day. The decision to charge Zuma is reversed.[202]

The underbelly

2008

I don't follow much of the first half of the interregnum, that year when there were two centres of power in the ANC, when Mbeki is recalled and quiet, place holder Kgalema Motlanthe becomes interim president, and a judge rules that Zuma's prosecution is irreparably tainted and charges against him must fall. I am too consumed with Devi being sick again, doctors having to operate again, having to deal with her pain and panic again after the new doctor says we should test for cancer again, just to be safe. She hobbles beside me for another three months on crutches that cause her back and shoulder muscles to contort in cramps, her face cramped too, as school friends innocently – thinking it is a game, having fun, not seeing how scared she is of falling – play with her in her wheelchair, rolling her up and down passages, while she desperately pleads with them to stop.

I don't notice that the country may be similarly crying out in fear for what lies ahead, until we march against xenophobia. It is May now, the onset of winter, and foreigners have been killed and shops set alight in outpourings of aggression against Somalis, Mozambicans and Zimbabweans, seen as taking away jobs, business opportunities and places on RDP house waiting lists. Devi, just able to walk again, joins Thandi and me and a bunch of like-minded activists in a march through Johannesburg with our home-painted placards that say 'Stop the hatred'.

Disconcertingly, most of us seem to belong to the more privileged progressive classes: white intellectuals, Indian and coloured activists, middle-class African students from the world of civic organisations and NGOs. Barbara Harmel is here, a veteran former ANC underground operative, exile and communist; and Lucia, the Dutch Vula operative I met in Lusaka, who now lives in Johannesburg and works for the Nelson Mandela Foundation; the South African History Archive crowd from Wits University; and Yunis Shaik, Moe's and Shabir's brother, who carries his own placard too.

Marching through the city we pass locals in front of dilapidated buildings, hawkers who sell their tomatoes and oranges on the street for a few rand. They look at us sometimes with curiosity, often indifferently, going about their business. But the mood changes when we enter Hillbrow, over the Twist Street railway bridge past Joubert Park, and we suddenly see a crowd of men standing next to the taxis, staring at us hard, with anger and disgust glowing behind their eyes. We feel what they think of us, hippies and lefties. We live in nice places, not in areas with scarce resources where you fight one another to survive. The anger is so palpable that I am certain that, if this was a deserted planet with no laws, authorities, consequences or other parties with guns, they would rip all of us to shreds.

I lived here once, but it now seems to be another universe.

'Zulus,' a black student next to us mutters under his breath, and I wonder how he knows. Is it because most taxi drivers here are Zulus? Does he pass by here often, taking taxis? Or is it simply that the men look like they could form a Zulu impi at any moment?

Of course it is still all the government's fault. The waiting lists for

RDP houses are notoriously corrupted. Undocumented foreigners, who often operate small shops and carry cash because they don't have bank accounts, can bargain with corrupt officials for places on such waiting lists and other favours. Often they are shaken down by corrupt policemen: I hear that they even call illegals 'ATMs' for this reason. The inner cities and other black areas count rapidly increasing numbers of such illegals, courtesy mainly of the devastation in Zimbabwe and the fact that the borders are porous. It is not difficult to understand why deprived and dispossessed locals will take out their frustrations on the foreigners. They are easy targets, accessible and unarmed.

And even if some of the violence is nightmarishly cruel, for example when a Mozambican man is set on fire, many in the ANC will express understanding for the mobs who vent their anger. 'Our communities must not be blamed,' a comrade writes on Facebook. 'Certainly not by people who have never experienced hardship.'

Thabo Mbeki was hailed as Mr Delivery, but actual delivery of services to the places where the black majority lives is still very limited. Real grievances there are plenty. The question is why the ANC with all its non-racial, non-tribalist, moral high ground seems to be allowing, understanding, maybe even encouraging, the violence by the deprived against those whose lives are even more precarious.

Zuma's power is based on Zulu ethnicity, I recall Ivan saying as I cower before the taxi drivers.

Maybe all is not going to be well.

At one stage during the upcoming Zuma years, I will accompany Ntando Makhubu as she reports on the raiding, looting and burning of foreigners' property in Mamelodi township near Pretoria. 'The ANC and the police do nothing to stop this,' she says. 'They are actually part of it.' She shows photographs of looters in uniform, and violent pamphlets signed by unknowns, whom she has investigated and identified as ANC members. She will also point out areas where even South African blacks from other regions and ethnic communities have been attacked in the street.

After the march we encounter Yunis Shaik again. He tells us that, together with Moe, he has taken up the cudgel of supporting Jacob Zuma as a responsible leader since the man by all accounts will be the country's next president and the only alternative to Mbeki. But Yunis shakes his head as he tells us how all that dusting off and making presentable is going. 'We are dealing with so much shit,' he says. 'Spading through truckloads of it.'

'We can only hope he will listen to advice,' Ivan says that evening. 'At least, unlike Thabo, he does not think he knows everything.'

In response to the feverish media and public opinion, with the still mainly white opposition campaigning on a 'stop Zuma' ticket in the upcoming elections, and Zuma's take-over wave consuming the country, increasingly the question is asked who we are with. Are we with them or with us?

Suddenly, I have no idea who is us.

Chapter Four
Swimming with the crocodiles

May 2009

At a press conference held by the newly elected president, I ask Jacob Zuma if he will reopen the arms deal investigation. He looks surprised, then amused. 'We must see about that,' he says, and giggles.

It doesn't augur well, but we still have hope: not that Zuma might turn out to be a passable president after all, but that newcomers in government might make a difference. Collins Chabane, a comrade of much integrity, has been appointed minister in the presidency for performance monitoring and administration. Kgalema Motlanthe, not the most effective politician but a decent human being, is deputy president. Trevor Manuel stays on as minister of planning, while Pravin Gordhan takes over the finance portfolio. The fiercely honest and efficient Barbara Hogan is minister of state enterprises.

Mac Maharaj is back, too. He has been appointed as Zuma's special envoy in North Africa and the Middle East and also represents him on the G20 infrastructure working group. He is also, we are told, advising Zuma on political strategy.

There are few better than Mac when it comes to political strategy. He may help the country to get the best cabinet, bring relevant skills into the departments, address housing and education backlogs, and don't forget health. Zuma – that at least inspires hope, too – has no denial issues and is indeed rolling out antiretrovirals to combat HIV/AIDS. We only need the hospitals to function now.

Even so, South Africa has become a troubled place. It is not right for Devi now: too harsh, too insecure and unsafe and the girl, now sixteen, is still troubled by depression and anxiety. Though she is doing fine at school, if not in sports then at least in the thinking arena – she is an avid debater, particularly on anti-racism and anti-sexism topics – the stress disorder makes her get panicky in crowds. She once loses consciousness in a queue for an ATM machine, and once in a train. How is she going to cope next year, among masses of students on campuses in Johannesburg or Cape Town?

It feels like a defeat, a betrayal of principle, but nevertheless I start to think Devi must go to the Netherlands. Damn it, she is Dutch, like me. I start inquiring about universities in my home country.

We'll need money for that, of course. Ivan thinks he can qualify for an early pension pay-out, since he will soon be over fifty-five. 'It means that we'll get less money later,' he warns, but we both agree that this needs to happen.

Six months later, the favourable answer comes. We hug each other, happy that our plans have worked out, but also sad because it means separation.

Devi can't go alone. My family there won't have time to provide the safety net she needs, what with everybody, all the aunts and uncles and cousins, working long hours. We don't have people like Sister anymore in Amsterdam, no mother or aunt you can come home to, no one with a warm room and comfort and tea and so on. One is on one's own in modern Western society and even if our atomised family can cope with these things – my mother, at seventy-one, lives contentedly alone in a mountain village in the French Alps – I don't think it's good for Devi. So I decide to tag along. With Vani too, of course, because how can we leave the twelve-year-old behind? The two sisters are so close.

Ivan is not happy at the prospect of being all alone, but also feels it is for the best. 'And it's only for two years,' I tell Vani, who keeps frowning at the idea, no matter how much I try to tempt her with tales of exciting new schools and friends and finally getting to know her Dutch family a bit more. Devi's studies will be for three years but after two she will probably cope and we, Vani and I, can come back. She looks at me and asks: 'What about Thandi and Mandla and Mawe?' I tell her Sunday's family is moving out anyway since Sunday has started working fulltime as a nursery school teacher nearby. We are leaving our house in Centurion and are hunting for two apartments, one for Ivan and one for Sunday and her children.

As Vani bursts into tears, I realise that we are breaking up her family.

***

Chris Louw commits suicide on 1 December 2009. According to newspaper reports, he shot himself with an AK47 that morning, at a special spot on his farm where he had planted flowers. Shocked at the disaster befallen Johanita and the children, Ivan and I start to feel eerily like we live in a kind of 'ten little soldiers' nursery rhyme. We had once started our new lives full of expectation and energy in this new country, with close friends and comrades around us. Now Philip and Chris are dead, Elvis was murdered, and we haven't heard from Maisy at all. Mac is still there but is fully occupied as Zuma's envoy and we don't hear much from him either.

Cutting loose
2010

Ivan is now deputy to the new SARS commissioner, Oupa Magashula. Previously one of three deputies to Pravin Gordhan, Ivan is now the only one, since Magashula was a deputy before, and the third, Edward Kieswetter, has left. For the first time in my life I get invited to dinners as a wife, sitting at the table in front, having to mind my manners, not chew chicken bones, not speak too loudly, and deal with the occasional person calling me 'Madam Deputy Commissioner'. Some of those who approach us with servile smiles have clearly not caught on to the whole higher purpose thing.

Our conversations with Jessie Duarte – often together with ex-spouse, but still friendly, John Duarte – are also becoming more fraught with difficulty than they used to be. Now that she is in the top layers of ANC power – one of the so-called top six in the NEC – we don't talk much of old ideals anymore. Jessie increasingly talks in terms of 'us' and 'them', with 'them' mostly being the white media, while she rages at these white media that are anti-ANC for no other reason, presumably, than that they are. I sometimes try to remind her that I am a journalist too, not to mention white, and ask her what the 'white media' said that was actually wrong. Did any journalist tell a lie about the ANC and if so, what then was the truth? Where can we see anything good that the ANC is doing in the rural areas, in hospitals, in schools?

She never responds when I ask such things. She talks of factional battles without explaining what is so great about the group she supports, or what is so bad about the other. I once ask her if right and wrong even still come into it at all. She says no, of course not.

Preparing to leave for the Netherlands, the relief that at least I'll escape from this difficult new environment does not weigh up against all that we will be leaving behind. Devi and Vani have been relishing World Cup time, partying with school friends near the stadium in Centurion, South African flags painted on their faces and Shakira blasting. At home we still let our hair down together with friends: Johann, Sri the Indian consultant from India, Johann's office manager Patricia Langa, Yolisa Pikie. Often Adrian Lackay, joins in too, an old comrade and now the SARS spokesperson, which makes for good fun when he and Yolisa reminisce about the days when they were on the run from the police. They often re-enact past highlights with a mixture of Marxist-Leninist language and South African proverbs, and gravely speak about 'not swimming in the river with the crocodiles, comrade, when the class enemy is encroaching on our leadership'.

* * *

Of all the organising that needs to be done for the move, cutting myself loose from the FAIR network is the most complicated. I cannot simply leave because by now I do too much. 'Smurf' was the job description I allocated to myself in jest, but how do you interview any successors for that? Initially we hoped that a board member called Jimmy,[203] who had recently returned from a scholarship in the USA, could help us professionalise as an organisation. Upon his return to South Africa, Jimmy had shown great interest in FAIR. He had assured us that we could do story projects of 'international standard', which would impress 'big funders'.

This would be nice, of course. Even if we got some support now, we were still working for pittances, both in the office and in the field, where journalists often did months of risky work on a $500 story grant. 'You are going to get so much money,' Jimmy stated with a delighted expression on his face, perhaps knowing something we didn't.

But it had soon turned out that Jimmy's plans for professionalisation included getting rid of some of our bravest members. He called a Kenyan colleague who had reported on botched backstreet abortions in that country a 'token' and felt we needed more members who had hard computer skills. Such 'high standard' professionals should, he felt, then work under 'international', preferably American, editors to raise the quality of our output. In practice, going this route would mean booting out a good number of colleagues who lived and worked in places where there was seldom electricity or internet access. Many of these colleagues could not even aspire to develop high-tech hard skills any time soon, troubled as they were by malaria and warlords and violent police.

Dealing with Jimmy, I had started to hear echoes of the upcoming careerists in SARS and Jessie's 'right and wrong don't come into it', but for months had kept hoping I was wrong. Jimmy had been a social justice warrior like us, once; surely his US fellowship couldn't have changed him that much? But when I asked him what stories we would do as a collective of relatively privileged, fully computerised, American-editor-guided professionals, his answer was disconcerting. 'Let the form come first, the content will follow,' he had said. 'And to get the big money, you must be guided by what stories the funders want to support anyway.'

I was not the only one to be particularly horrified by that last bit. International developmental media funders already too often regarded African journalists as students to be trained, instead of as reporters with stories to tell. Countless workshops given by those who Jimmy wanted to enlist as our new editors routinely set story subjects and themes for their African 'pupils' to work with. FAIR had always resisted this, impressing on the trainers that they should *listen* for a change.

When I and a core of fellow veteran members oppose Jimmy's ideas, he changes tack and starts arguing that my management has been dismal, the office a mess. He insists that now that I am leaving, I should be replaced by an experienced media manager. In the meantime, though he acknowledges that we don't actually have the budget to attract the kind of person he has in mind, he will personally ensure professionalisation of our operations.

I was not able to argue much against that. I ran the office very basically, with two columns for finance: one for money in, one for money out. Our bookkeeper, who also worked for other NGOs, had never raised any issues with that, but perhaps we did need more sophisticated processes.

2011, long distance

Back in a Holland that is still cold and grey as we are approaching June, I battle with now two depressed daughters – Vani wears black and grunts more than she talks – and a fully-fledged takeover campaign waged by Jimmy at the FAIR office. A new office manager, a well-meaning young media professional called Rajiv,[204] who operates under my long-distance mentorship for the time being, has already started buckling under the pressure of Jimmy's increasingly complex management demands.

Supported by some on the board who are impressed by Jimmy's use of professional terms and jargon, we are told that our two-and-a-half-person office should adhere to the highest company management standards. This means drawing up protocols for every single activity, preparing concomitant non-disclosure agreements for all members, maintaining an asset registry for our three desks with computers, conducting a weekly staff audit, handling our funds in multi-sourced Excel budget sheets and a host of other things none of us are trained to do, on top of our story project and publishing work.

Rajiv had not expected such pressure. Soon after his appointment he cheerfully announced on Facebook that he was now a ***director*** and printed business cards that said so, and expanded the office with a director's room of his own. But under fire from Jimmy, and increasingly aware that he has been handed a poisoned chalice, Rajiv's behaviour becomes first stressed, than erratic. At one point, in a fit of rage, he threatens to fire a cleaner who works for the landlord and not for us. Then, in the middle of introducing our new financial accountancy systems, he fires the bookkeeper, too.

In July, Jimmy accuses me of corruption. It is his 'fiduciary duty as a board member', he says, to no longer keep silent on the mismanagement that has occurred under my administration. The lid must be lifted off my corrupt reign, as Gwen Ansell will later jokingly call it. I defend myself. Yes, I have sometimes signed off on payments without formally requesting the treasurer's authority and also sometimes authorised salary advances when there was a need. But no moneys were ever misspent or went missing. I submit detailed expenditure showing that.

However, under Jimmy's indignant avalanches, in which words like wasteful and fruitless and unauthorised and irregular abound, some funders withdraw and FAIR becomes a shadow of its former self. Little work goes on anymore as members all over Africa are asking what is going on with the corrupt leadership of their organisation. During one of our Skype talks between continents, I wail to Ivan about Jimmy. What is this guy doing, I ask indignantly. We are not corrupt and Jimmy knows it! 'I thought you knew how this works' is his response. 'This is what they do when they want to get rid of you.'

It has taken me a while to talk to Ivan in detail about all this, and as our conversation proceeds it starts to dawn on me that I haven't handled the situation well at all. 'Virtually all consultants and project marketeers tell you that you have problems, then sell you their solution,' Ivan says. 'They are like hammers looking for nails. But you have to be a few steps ahead of them. Are you a nail? How do you see your strengths and weaknesses? How are you improving? What solutions do you need? Didn't you ask yourselves all that before this guy came along?'

Know your strengths and weaknesses. Be in control. If flies come into your house, it is no use blaming the flies; you should have put up fly screens. I have heard Ivan say such things for the past twenty years, yet have not applied it to our situation at FAIR. I was blissfully running with stories, neglecting organisational development. When Jimmy came from the US with his jargon and his standards, I did not understand what was happening until it was too late.

The king's return
Late 2012

If the office was ever a shambles, it was never as great a shambles as it is now. As in the case of so many newly risen directors in this country, the cocktail of daunting challenges, attacks, demands, conflicts, accusations, lack of experience and a desperate drive to remain in charge, has resulted in Rajiv not listening to anyone anymore, deleting from the FAIR website anything that came before him and imagining threats from all and sundry.

Even though Jimmy has called it a day by now, Rajiv continues to shoot down all efforts to improve the situation. Most of his emails imply that he is being undermined. Most of the time he locks himself in his office.

Finally, in November 2012, I write him a letter. In what I think is a non-threatening, perhaps even motherly, tone, I advise him to seek urgent management assistance. I receive a letter back to say that, in addition to other perceived failures of mine, I am patronising Rajiv in an absolutely reprehensible tone and that I must stop interfering with FAIR.

It is signed by Mzilikazi wa Afrika.

The FAIR annual general meeting in October, which I attended – timing a brief stay in South Africa to coincide with the event, a last chance to ward off the downfall – had elected the African king as its new chairman. It was felt that the disarray of the organisation called for a South African to supervise the staff and office, and he, Mzilikazi, was the only South African in the running. Mzilikazi had also just won the main prize at our awards ceremony for a series of articles called the Cato Manor story.

According to the *Mail & Guardian*, Mzilikazi had really 'clawed his way back into the mainstream' after the Travelgate debacle then. For the Cato Manor story, he and colleague Stephan Hofstatter seemed to have successfully investigated some unexplained killings in taxi driver and criminal circles in Cato Manor in Durban. I wasn't quite sure that the story deserved such high accolades, though. Reading it, I briefly wondered how different the Cato Manor police were from other police in South Africa in that regard. Shootings by police in gangster-ridden areas were and are regular occurrences in this country; I thought that only to expose one police unit, and to brand its head, a General Johan Booysen, as the main villain, was a tad devoid of context.

In years to come, the story will turn out to have been a hatchet job inspired by President Jacob Zuma's information peddlers in police crime intelligence. It will be revealed that Zuma had it in for Booysen because of the latter's investigation into a business associate of the president.[205] But I don't have an inkling of that as yet, in 2012. The only thing I do consider, when I read the Cato Manor series at the time, is that Mzilikazi and Hofstatter might be relying too much on shady sources from crime intelligence. Crime intelligence commissioner Richard Mdluli was officially suspended because of a murder charge, but reportedly remained very influential behind the scenes. He is known for carrying out agendas that advance both his clique in crime intelligence and President Zuma, to whom he is close.[206]

Mdluli has also been accused of planting stories in the *Sunday Times*. Six months before, a colonel in the new police unit the Hawks – which has taken over from the now disbanded Scorpions[207] – stated that the same Mzilikazi wa Afrika and Stephan Hofstatter were paid by Mdluli from a secret crime intelligence fund to do a negative story on Hawks boss Anwa Dramat and another senior Hawks officer.[208] There was no evidence of that, though, and the then *Sunday Times* editor, Ray Hartley, vehemently denied it.[209]

But for the moment, at the FAIR AGM and awards ceremony in October 2012, there are more urgent problems to address. I hope to have a word with Mzilikazi about my belief that Rajiv needs bookkeeping and management assistance and also that FAIR might look to SARS for such support. The tax agency recently successfully helped Home Affairs implement more efficient systems; it also was assisting the Eastern Cape health department to fight tender fraud. Ivan said that SARS might support NGOs in that way too. SARS saw its higher purpose also in terms of being useful to citizens and society at large. Assisting an investigative journalism organisation to run itself efficiently was definitely in the public interest, and they would do it for free too.

It is difficult to speak to Mzilikazi wa Afrika about this during the ceremony and the dinner, surrounded as he is with well-wishers, but I finally find an opportunity when taking a lift down to the parking area. He looks nonplussed, however, as if talking about SARS assistance for FAIR does not make sense at all. I ask if he knows of SARS. 'Of course I do,' he says. And after a pause: 'There is something fishy there.'

I have no idea what he means. Ivan, who accompanied me to the awards dinner after the AGM, is standing near me waiting for the lift. Has Mzilikazi not noticed him? I introduce Ivan to our new chairman. He shakes Ivan's hand and says thanks for the offered help, that he will consider it.

I receive Mzilikazi's letter banning me from any further interference with FAIR a month later.

Fishy things
November 2012

I still don't know what it was that Mzilikazi thought was fishy at SARS. We reached the parking level before I could ask him that. But it continues to puzzle me. As far as I know, only good things have been reported about the institution of which Ivan is a deputy commissioner. An academic at Princeton University has used the staggering improvements in tax collection in South Africa as a case study,[210] and Pravin Gordhan has twice occupied the chairmanship of the World Customs Organisation in recognition of these efforts. Collections are up, the informal economy is brought into the mainstream, risk assessment with regard to defaulting entities is professionalised and SARS's enforcement is making inroads into the tobacco, electronics and mining sectors. At the time of our conversation in the lift, SARS investigators have just billed Fana Hlongwane, the arms deal middleman, and Robert Huang, a business partner of President Zuma's nephew, Khulubuse.

Maybe even more importantly, SARS is working to convince Treasury that it should have a system to regulate state procurement. Having noted firstly that the state often pays far too much for items like bread, water bottles, desks and other regular purchases,[211] SARS has realised that there is at present no coherent system that fixes acceptable price ranges. Procurement processes are fragmented, with different pieces in different places, and very much open to abuse. SARS advocates that a procurement office be set up at the National Treasury to own the procurement system and be accountable for its efficiency and effectiveness. This office must 'reduce leakages including corruption in procurement of goods and services', Ivan notes in a document he is working on in the evenings, and that will form the basis for next year's SARS strategic plan. The strategy will aim to ensure that 'SARS is corruption free and (will also assist) in anti-corruption measures across Government, particularly in procurement processes'.

I ask what is so different about this project. Every department, state enterprise and ministry has been announcing plans to stop corruption, after all. 'Ah, but it is not just a pronouncement,' he explains. 'The state is haemorrhaging money. We need to block those leakages. We have been working with Treasury, the Financial Intelligence Centre and other institutions on how to do this for months.'

SARS's strategic plan for 2013 will state that 'Unfavourable public perception of poor state service delivery and corruption poses the largest compliance risk to SARS. Research and empirical evidence show that taxpayers' attitude towards compliance, and their willingness to comply, is influenced by how they perceive public funds to be utilised... Recent surveys show that corruption has replaced crime as the number one issue concerning South African citizens. Perception about the quality of service delivery is equally a serious concern. Recent protests about poor service delivery bear testimony to this. The media has published articles questioning the need for citizens to fulfil their tax obligations, when parts of the State are allegedly corrupt or incompetent. These factors affect SARS's ability to achieve compliance.'[212]

The document that SARS puts out is carefully phrased, but unmistakeably says: we are done with collecting money for you to squander and steal.

Nothing fishy about that.

Snowmen and arrows

On the other hand, maybe there actually are some fishy things going on at SARS. I haven't been paying much attention to the rumour campaigns and anonymous memos that have been circulating for the past ten years now, but they can certainly be called somewhat fishy. At least since 2002, gossipy allegations have been launched, at intervals, mainly against Pravin Gordhan, Ivan and Johann, and sometimes also against tax and customs enforcement manager Gene Ravele. Ivan is supposed to have had love children with at least two colleagues. Johann has been accused of being an apartheid agent, or alternatively – and perhaps surprisingly – part of an Indian cabal. Populist loudmouth Julius Malema, who has alleged before that SARS targets supporters of Jacob Zuma, has – after his expulsion earlier this year from the ANC for sowing division and undermining the leadership – inverted his allegation. Now he says that SARS has been actually attacking Zuma's opponents.

Since SARS has been investigating Malema's tender deals in his home province of Limpopo for a while now,[213] both are true, since in both cases Malema probably means himself.

When Ivan meets either of his alleged mistresses, he occasionally asks them how the kids are, and they chuckle. One of the women has never had children at all.

SARS has responded to more serious charges, for instance when a thick dossier called 'Project Snowman' surfaced, which alleged that SARS was plotting to overthrow President Zuma. The main source of the allegations was Mike Peega, a former employee who was fired by the SARS investigative unit because he was found to be involved in rhino poaching. Even though his stories were devoid of fact, SARS still took the time to meticulously refute every one of them.[214] Zuma is turning out to be just as conspiracy-minded as his predecessor, if not more so.

'So we try to pre-empt such things,' says Ivan. 'We work very hard to collect and present the evidence to disprove the smears.'

I will learn later that SARS spokesman Adrian Lackay visited *Sunday Times* editor, Phylicia Oppelt – who happens to be married to our friend, Rudolf Mastenbroek – to show her stacks of documents disproving what Peega says.

SARS doesn't know this at the time, but the Peega dossier isn't just the work of Mike Peega. By the time he makes his accusations, there is already a network of twenty-one National Intelligence Agency agents active at SARS, working undercover to report finally to Jacob Zuma.[215] And they don't merely report. The murky ponds of the intelligence services, already contaminated by information peddlers with personal interests, who collect dirt on individuals and advance conspiracies by one political faction against the other, grew murkier and murkier under Thabo Mbeki's sycophants; they are now outright cesspools under Zuma. Giving him allegations to use against his real or perceived enemies is just the way to get closer to Number One.

The spy network inside SARS has been in place since at least mid-2004, when Zuma was still deputy president to Thabo Mbeki. It started in that year with the managerial appointment of domestic intelligence agent Mandisa Mokwena, who was also – unbeknown to the rest of SARS at first – a business partner of Zuma's wife Thobeka.

Zuma would plant his agents everywhere. That in itself is no surprise to Ivan. 'It is what Jacob Zuma does. He builds loyal bases wherever he can.' Ivan just wonders when Zuma started seeing SARS as a priority target for such activities.

In 2009, when Julius Malema began circulating the Peega dossier, Mandisa Mokwena was found to have dished out SARS contracts to friends, and left SARS under a cloud. During her trial in 2010 she explained that she had been paid as a secret agent while at SARS, and that she had been 'sanctioned by a higher authority than the minister of intelligence himself'[216] for this work. Since the money in her bank account proved to have come from the SSA (formerly the NIA), the court would eventually acquit her, although it found an associate at SARS guilty, together with the friends who had gotten the contracts.[217]

How deeply concerned Zuma personally is about SARS will remain unclear for the near future. At this stage, however, in late 2012, Ivan merely believes that the man simply 'cannot grasp what exactly it means to head a constitutional state with rule of law,' as he puts it. He recalls how when he was deputy president, Zuma asked for a meeting at Waterkloof Airport, as far back as 2004. He and SARS customs manager Gene Ravele duly went there and had found that Zuma wanted to discuss the case of a businessman who was, Zuma said, 'very useful to the South African government'. The businessman, Hennie Delport, owned a private jet and often travelled on business within Africa. Ivan thought that Delport had probably offered himself to the intelligence community as a good source of information, which would serve as insurance in case he was ever called to account for his financial dealings. He was being investigated for – and would later be criminally charged with – VAT fraud. SARS suspected that Delport was directly stealing tax money by falsifying documents to obtain VAT refunds to which he had no right.[218]

At the meeting, Ivan narrates, he said, 'Sure, if Mr Delport will make full disclosure, and take responsibility for what happened, we can work with him to reach a settlement.' This was policy – if you cooperated, penalties would be lowered. He adds, 'But there can't be a disappearance of debt. I don't think Zuma understood that. I don't think he understands that even now.'

In spite of what he thought was a clear response, a go-between would still come to SARS a few days later to see Ivan again. 'He said that comrade Zuma had told him that I would resolve the Delport matter. I repeated what I told Zuma. Unsurprisingly, that was the end of that initiative.' A few years later, a memorandum from Delport, circulated to politicians, which accused SARS of destroying South African businesses, would be added to the growing stack of dossiers in Ivan's filing cabinet.

From that meeting onward, Ivan decided to be proactive with Zuma, in order to pre-empt requests and situations that would make SARS compromise its principles and the law. 'I kept reminding him that he needed to become tax compliant. But the message did not seem to land.

Either he himself, or his lawyer Michael Hulley, who was always present at our meetings, seemed to believe that we would somehow wave a wand and the tax obligations would disappear. At the end we had to resort to summoning him to court.'

Would Zuma have started to consider a more pleasant, more pliable SARS even then?

The Italian restaurant connection

Among the fishy things that I don't know when I meet Mzilikazi wa Afrika in a lift in Braamfontein in 2012 is that Zuma may indeed have had plans for a SARS commissioner of his very own for some time already.

It was during a holiday around 2007 that Ivan received a phone call from the office to inform him that, according to a certain high level taxpayer, a customs manager at SARS had told him, the taxpayer, that he, the customs manager, was going to be the 'next commissioner of SARS' and that therefore the taxpayer could safely make a deal with him. Ivan had been thoroughly puzzled. 'That man was not even in the correct division to make any arrangements with taxpayers,' he told me, much later, when it had become public news that the manager was one Leonard Radebe and the taxpayer was Dave King, a billionaire who owed SARS vast amounts of money. It was also reported that SARS and King had reached a settlement.

SARS's legal people dealing with Dave King, did not know what to make of the reported statement. Radebe denied he ever said such a thing and SARS put it down to a misunderstanding or misinformation by King. Nevertheless, Ivan informed then commissioner Pravin Gordhan.

Sometime later, however, on 9 August 2008, when SARS general manager of corporate services, Oupa Magashula, visited his favourite Italian restaurant Casalinga in Muldersdrift, he met the restaurant manager, who told him how nice it was to see SARS people again: just the previous evening, he had seen Mr Leonard Radebe here, 'having dinner with Mr Dave King'.

'Again we called Radebe,' Ivan narrates. 'He was off work, saying he had flu, but he came anyway. It was a brief discussion. We told him that there was an allegation that he was in contact with King. He denied it. Since he said that he was not well, we asked him to come the next morning. When he came, after an hour of evasion and diversion, he confessed and we placed him on suspension. Shortly afterwards, he resigned.'

Investigations would later unearth that wheeler-dealer Glenn Agliotti, Jackie Selebi's former friend and nemesis, was involved in the scheme. Agliotti had just delivered Selebi to the Scorpions in 2008. As a result he was still a free man, and he continued to position himself close to powerful people.[219] When such individuals found themselves in tax or legal trouble, Agliotti often offered to 'make things go away' for a fee. Agliotti, now apparently close to Dave King, cultivated SARS manager Leonard Radebe as a handy friend. The fake draft settlement between Dave King and SARS that left King off the hook for a large part of his debt was drawn up with the help of a contact of Agliotti's.

Ivan wondered if soon-to-be President Zuma 'might just have intimated to Radebe that he was the preferred choice'. When, in 2009, in the Broken Arrow project – the disinformation campaign against SARS management and notably Ivan, Johann and Pravin Gordhan –came to light[220] it was found that one Mabheleni Ntuli was one of the plotters. 'We learned later that Ntuli was also a member of Zuma's kitchen cabinet,' he says, adding that 'perhaps Radebe was in discussions with Zuma's trusted associates.'[221]

Shortly after the custom manager's suspension, Ivan went to see Zuma, prepared to once again 'pre-empt the pressure and the lobbying that was sure to come.' At that discussion, Ivan briefed Zuma about Radebe's dodgy dealings and said that SARS was going to act against him. He also asked Zuma if he perhaps knew the man. 'He told me no, but that he knew the Radebe family. He then just said "Ivan, I know you will do the right thing" and asked me about the succession at SARS. He said he had heard that Oupa Magashula had been recommended by Pravin and I said indeed, Oupa was the right person. Then Zuma asked me what was it that I wanted – meaning if there was any position I aspired to – and I told him I was fine where I was.'

Zuma was to ask Ivan 'what he wants' on at least two more occasions. 'I understood that it was his way of making you dependent on his goodwill. My answer always remained the same.'

Ivan recalls how at the meeting Zuma had also praised the work of SARS. 'He confirmed that he expected us to support and assist other state institutions as well. I said we would do that. As always, he gave the impression that he was listening.' One usually came away from meeting Zuma with the feeling that he was willing to listen and take advice, he says. 'He is very calculating in that way: one persona is of the simple man who wants the country to succeed and who values your input; the other one has an uncanny ability to spot, select and affirm faulty individuals who are in need of favours. That is why he asks you what you want. If you then ask him a favour, you'll get it and then you will be beholden to him for life.'

Much later, we will understand how enraged Zuma was when Pravin Gordhan, upon becoming finance minister in 2009, indeed recommended Oupa Magashula to be the next SARS commissioner and the recommendation was agreed to and ratified by cabinet. 'The *president* appoints the commissioner,' Zuma will fulminate in a conversation with Gordhan's successor as finance minister, Nhlanhla Nene, when the latter raises the issue of renewing the process to identify candidates for the vacant position of commissioner in 2014. 'Not the minister of finance!'[222]

According to one media report, a short while after his resignation from SARS, in 2009, Leonard Radebe handed Mike Peega's Snowman dossier in amended form to Jacob Zuma,[223] now the president. The amended version explicitly named all the members of SARS's High Risk Investigative Unit, or HRIU. Since the investigators dealt with organised crime, and several had been assaulted and burgled already, it was now no longer safe to keep them in the unit. They were transferred elsewhere in enforcement; only seven remained in the HRIU.[224]

The small group nevertheless would continue to investigate alleged gangsters like Mark Lifman, Jerome 'Donkie' Booysen, Quinton 'Mr Big' Marinus and their ally, self-confessed cigarette smuggler – and later Julius Malema funder – Adriano Mazzotti, in support of an intrepid SARS team in the Western Cape, led by Keith Hendricks. The investigators would also continue to dent the tobacco smuggling networks, catching three smugglers' trucks in 2010, raiding a smuggler's company in 2011, and exposing syndicate links with the SSA in 2012.[225] During this time SARS also temporarily blocks transport of 'medical equipment for [Zuma's home estate] in Nkandla' in a Russian jet sent by a former KGB agent and nickel-mining tycoon of Zuma's acquaintance[226] because its documentation is not in order. Investigative journalist Jacques Pauw will later record in his book *The President's Keepers* that SARS also found, in addition to the medical equipment, several bundles of cash in the jet. The tax agency had to let it go after secret service boss Siyabonga Cwele ordered it to do so, saying it was a matter of national security, but other actions against shady business and organised crime continued.

Some of the drugs and tobacco busts come out in the media[227] and my father in Holland bursts with pride. He brags everywhere about his son-in-law, who is 'the South African Elliot Ness', chief of the Untouchables, the American law enforcement squad that nailed Al Capone.

Nevertheless, the dossiers keep coming. Edward Zuma himself – Jacob Zuma's son – who is in tobacco, is reportedly now compiling one, too.[228] Adrian Lackay keeps refuting them, but like the mythical seven-headed dragon, as soon as you cut off one head, it grows back seven times over. SARS spy ring head Mandisa Mokwena's accusation, made during her trial, that SARS's investigators have 'sabotaged her career as a black manager', becomes part of the ever-morphing dossiers, too.

All along, SARS has continued desperately to try ward off Zuma's ire. In 2009, he was personally and timeously informed of Mokwena's suspension and the charges. 'We knew by then that she had been in business with his wife, Thobeka, so it was better if he heard from us what happened,' says Ivan. But the spy activities and dossiers continue and when SARS receives credible information that a rogue unit operates in the domestic intelligence service, which reportedly has big money, is heavily armed and said to be reporting directly to JZ, Ivan talks to the president again, mentioning that a certain Thulani Dlomo is reportedly a key member of that unit. 'On that occasion, Zuma responded that he was aware of Dlomo, but that Dlomo did not report to him.' An SSA member will later allege that Dlomo was the head of an entire spy ring stationed at government agencies, working directly for Zuma.[229]

Comrade Jacob is outwardly still very friendly with Ivan. When Ivan visits him to discuss his taxes, they hug and call each other comrade as ANC members do. By now he is well aware that Zuma's middle name Gedleyihlekisa seems well chosen.

Border management

Another fishy thing appeared in Jacob Zuma's State of the Nation address held on 3 June 2009, two months after he was elected president. There was a short sentence hidden somewhere in the speech: 'Amongst other key initiatives, we will start the process of setting up a Border Management Agency.' It sounded innocuous and no one in the media picked it up, but Ivan wondered what it meant. The SARS customs agency was in control of the borders, together with Home Affairs. The cooperation was logical: SARS checked on the transport of goods, Home Affairs on the border crossings of people. At the time of this State of the Nation address, the cooperation was well on its way. Which was an excellent thing, since it didn't happen too often that two different arms of the South African state worked together for the common good.

There was also the fact, usually left unsaid, that SARS was by now well aware that it was making enemies. 'Offering help and positive contributions to other departments was also a defensive strategy,' Ivan will reflect later. 'At the time, we felt acutely that we needed alliances with others that wanted to work for good in the public service.'

Over the next two to three years, SARS was invited to discussions about the pending BMA. All others involved with border security, including the health and transport departments, each of which played smaller roles, were also invited. Ivan initially hoped that the plan might be able to do something about the very leaky borders, but was soon disabused of the notion. It turned out that the aim was to merge all involved into one authority, which was to reside under the ministry of intelligence.

It was already strange as a concept. How could an intelligence department deliver border crossing services to the public?

What made it even stranger was the fact that the wife of this particular minister of intelligence was a drug trafficker, and everyone knew it. The evidence against Sheryl Cwele, in cahoots with a Nigerian drug lord, had been making headlines before the State of the Nation Address mentioned the plan for the BMA.[230] Sheryl Cwele was arrested in 2010 and convicted, together with the Nigerian, in 2011, both receiving twelve-year jail terms.[231]

It was bad form and, therefore, impossible to ask the minister about the issue with his wife. But in the subsequent BMA meetings, SARS asked a lot of questions. Could the minister explain what issue he was trying to solve? What at the border was now not working as well as it should? Alternatively, what was working well and, therefore, should probably be left alone? The Home Affairs delegation had the same questions.

There were more intricate concerns as well. SARS's customs mandate included functions that impacted revenue collection. How would the new authority handle that aspect? SARS was also about to complete its new electronic customs system which could potentially serve the entire southern African region. Would the BMA throw that aside and build its own system? 'Once again they want to build a new thing,' he sighed one evening. 'And this time it is even worse because what already exists is actually starting to work really well.'

Soon, SARS and Home Affairs became minority voices in the meetings. The minister invited more and more officials working for health, transport and other departments, who agreed with him. SARS started to suspect mala fides. Besides controlling the border posts, Ivan thought, the new BMA would obviously also bring about lucrative contracts for consultants, new technology, buildings, motor vehicles and the usual set of connected individuals.

After a few such acrimonious encounters, where SARS refused to back down each time, an unofficial advisor to Cwele invited Ivan to an informal meeting with the minister. Over dinner at a very large house in Midrand, Ivan tried his best to present all SARS's arguments cohesively and clearly. SARS was by now recognised as a world-class institution, he said, and Home Affairs was vastly improved. The cooperation at the border had impacted positively on the performance at the border posts. If you wanted to solve a problem, he repeated, you should rather look at the border fence, over which control was really non-existent.

'But I had the impression that he was not even listening,' Ivan will tell me later. 'He just smiled, in a sort of arrogant way. It was a bit nauseating in fact. He just kept smiling, even when I pointed out that unfortunately there had been very few success stories in terms of big government projects, and that it could be anticipated that this one, too, would not have the desired output. That efficiency would drop very soon after the government started changing everything around. Still, that arrogant smile stayed.'

Ivan was so irritated that he 'gradually started overcoming the inhibitions I had in talking to a minister and a member of a political party that I used to be proud of. When he finally suggested that I was surely reluctant to support the new authority because that would result in a reduction of the SARS budget, I reached boiling point. I told him, "That is not my worry! My worry is that you will fuck up what we have built!" But even after that, he just continued to smile.'

This was not the response of a healthy person. Normally, a senior authority would not respond with a smile to a junior who has just accused you of bad faith. For the first time, the thought crept into Ivan's mind that Jacob Zuma was surrounding himself with people who were not just incompetent, or a bit crooked, or worse – Zuma-linked businessman Robert Huang was a convicted murderer[232] – but close to delusional. Women's League chairwoman Bathabile Dlamini, whom Zuma had just promoted to minister of social development, hardly ever made any sense. New appointee at the SABC Hlaudi Motsoeneng often described himself in terms of superhuman intelligence and power.

It was an unsettling realisation.

The defiance by SARS on the issue of the Border Management Authority did have one positive result. 'The minister later did change tack at least a bit, agreeing that the BMA would not report to the Ministry of Intelligence but to the Department of Home Affairs. But there was also a negative consequence. 'With our recalcitrance, the tax authority had defined itself, once more, as an obstacle to what the powers that be wanted. We were not with them but against them. We were a problem that had to be overcome.'

***

2011

In the meantime, Moe Shaik has helped to get Fezeka and Beauty Kuzwayo back to South Africa. They have been living in exile since 2007, first in Amsterdam where Ivan visited them twice, later in Tanzania. They asked Ivan if he could find out if it would be safe for them again in KwaZulu-Natal. They really wanted to come home. Upon receiving the request, Ivan asked Moe to ask Zuma about their safety. Moe returned a message to Ivan, presumably from Zuma, informing him that Fez and her mother could return and that nothing would happen to them. ('Such power! And such blindness to its reach!' Fezeka's biographer Redi Tlhabi will later write.) Indeed, the mob that threatened them was switched off. After some detours, the two have come back to their home in KwaMashu, Durban.

Moe is under pressure himself in his new position as head of the foreign branch of the State Security Agency (SSA). Intelligence Minister Siyabonga Cwele, the same Cwele who wants to control the borders, has told him to abandon a planned investigation into President Zuma's close business friends, the increasingly powerful Guptas. The three brothers from India, who once started out as shoe salesmen and then sold computers out of the boots of their cars, are now wielding quite a bit of influence over Zuma and his government. Information is floating around that the president eats at their Saxonwold residence almost every week, and that government affairs are discussed there. The Gupta brothers are said to be behind the appointments of certain individuals now heading ministries, departments and state enterprises, who then invariably give them very lucrative business contracts. They are also said to have their eye on a uranium mine and, perhaps, a future nuclear project to which to sell the resource.

Moe Shaik and two fellow SSA executives have decided to turn it into a formal investigation. In the next year, all three will resign from the agency separately.[233]

7 May 2012

As fishy things go, the sudden belligerence of ANC parliamentarian Des van Rooyen against SARS might have been the most recent alarm bell in the period just before I meet Mzilikazi wa Afrika in a lift in Braamfontein. When SARS presents its strategic plan for the coming year to the Standing Committee on Finance in Parliament, the little-known MP is hostile throughout, especially with regard to SARS's stated concerns regarding public perceptions of corruption and their impact on the willingness of the public to pay tax. Van Rooyen is not impressed. What corruption is SARS referring to? Later, he focuses on the presence of whites and Indians in the SARS delegation. 'We don't wish to see the same faces in the SARS Exco in future,' he admonishes.

The delegation comes away puzzled. Previously there was nothing remarkable about Des van Rooyen's behaviour in the meetings at Parliament, which took place about twice a year. Why is he now flexing his muscles? Does he know something SARS doesn't? For that matter, does Mzilikazi wa Afrika?

Jokes and banter
July 2013

SARS Commissioner Oupa Magashula has to resign after offering a job to a young woman accountant named Nosipho Mba. This should not in itself be a problem, since SARS needs and wants more African women accountants, but the way it happened was not appropriate: on the phone in an 'unprofessional and over intimate' conversation full of 'jokes and banter'.[234] When the conversation turns out to have been recorded and is published, a subsequent SARS investigation finds that this was 'an attempt to blackmail the commissioner', but nevertheless recommends the suspension of Magashula as well as a disciplinary inquiry.[235]

As it turns out, Magashula was enticed into the phone conversation by a crime intelligence official named Timmy Marimuthu, who was once convicted on a drug charge. In a crime intelligence environment riddled with information peddling and extortion, the recording is then used by dodgy individuals to pressurise SARS, and then leaked to the media. The *Sunday Times* headlines the allegation that 'a convicted drug lord' has Magashula 'in his pocket'.[236]

Magashula's departure paves the way for the appointment, little more than a year later, of Tom Moyane, a former prisons boss and Zuma favourite. When a student in Mozambique, decades ago, Moyane was a babysitter for Zuma's oldest children, among whom the twins Duduzane and Duduzile, both now employed by their father's wheeler-dealing friends, the Gupta brothers from Uttar Pradesh.[237]

From what I know of SARS, Oupa Magashula has been a good commissioner. However, the phone call to Nosipho Mba[238] takes place in the context of an increasingly unsavoury culture in some quarters of the tax agency. Earlier glimpses of jostling for promotion, ostentation and cars, and jokes about sex for career advancement, have recently been supplemented by harrowing tales of a sex pest who tried to enter a female colleague's hotel room during an official trip. He seems to enjoy the protection of some of his superiors.

As the phone call scandal plays out, I note the tension between Ivan and Oupa Magashula around this issue. Later, with the arrival of Tom Moyane at SARS in 2014, Ivan hears through the grapevine that Moyane and his trusted associates, among whom are several SSA-aligned individuals at SARS, are now trying to convince Magashula that it was

SARS's investigators, notably Ivan, who had trapped him by recording the phone call with Mba. This false accusation is also added to the content of the dossiers that continue to circulate in full force.

Later on still, relations between Ivan and Oupa will improve again, but these are hectic and unpleasant times.

As he is thrown into the position of acting commissioner, it is Ivan's unenviable task to explain Magashula's resignation at a meeting of SARS headquarter employees on 12 July 2013. He tries to do so by talking of a 'culture where we need expensive whisky, shiny cars and female favours to impress one another' and emphasises that one should rather aspire to higher purpose and live simple lives. The attempt at promoting moral values backfires, however, when a newspaper report on his speech summarises it as accusing mainly black male employees of drinking and adultery. Ivan's racism is thrown into the dossier mix even more fervently afterwards.

The sex pest at SARS against whom complaints buzz around is white, by the way.

***

Prominent among the careerists and self-promoters at SARS is one Luther Lebelo, head of employee relations in SARS's human resources department, and a former chair of the Midrand branch of the ANC. One day Lebelo approaches Ivan to offer himself as an adviser, adding that he will exercise this duty with the utmost loyalty. Unimpressed, Ivan, who suspects him of leveraging his ANC and trade union connections to advance his personal agenda, tells him that Luther's direct boss, the head of human resources, is a member of SARS's exco. 'If there is anything you'd like to raise,' he suggests, 'why not address it through your own direct channel?'

Luther Lebelo, known to be very critical of Zuma at the time, will later somersault and become both a Moyane and a Zuma loyalist.

Mandela stuff
November 2013

To say that Vani has not liked it in the Netherlands, living alone in an apartment with her mother, is an understatement. Devi, who lives on campus, only comes weekends, if at all. Vani misses her happy South African nest and finds our individualised lives in Holland alien, cold and strange: a kind of purgatory when compared to the seven-member family that always surrounded her with a buzz, sunshine, comfort and hugs, where she used to be the adorable and adored centre of attention.

Vani's Dutch is not sufficient to follow lessons in a regular school, and the international English high school is full of other uprooted kids. They are mostly diplomats' children. I see them as spoiled brats who only seem to have designer handbags, clothing, makeup and parties on their minds, until Vani tells me that many of them have moved around countries constantly since early childhood, most of them with divorced parents, floating aimlessly, never rooted in any stable family life. 'They are all depressed and alone, Mum,' she said. I did not understand then that she was talking about herself, too.

I agree that she must go home. Besides the fact that the extended family is there, Pretoria Girls High, where Devi went, is also much better than this. It may be led by middle-aged white biddies with racial issues,[239] but, the fact that well-trained black high school teachers are still a scarce commodity is not their fault, and the school is nevertheless a well-managed part of the South African social experiment. Its teachers, even if some have outdated views, all feel strongly about teaching Important Stuff to Tomorrow's Citizens. No one here has time to feel alienated. One is forced to grapple with this society and its rainbow ideals, however fuzzy and unrealistic these may be. The curriculum is about respecting all cultures and ethnicities and the challenge of living and sharing together.

Mandela stuff.

It's what South Africa is all about and it is, beside family and structure for her life, what Vani misses so much.

Fake leaders

Mandela dies on 5 December 2013, the day of Sinterklaas and Black Pete. A few days later, I join Yolisa Pikie, Ivan's co-worker and our friend, for a visit to the old man's former Houghton home, where people have gathered in the streets to bring songs, thoughts and flowers. To go there is part of a pilgrimage for him, Yolisa said. He has already been back home to his Eastern Cape village, having gone there immediately after hearing the news, to link up with family and comrades from his youth, reminiscing and drinking.

'Asimbonanga', they sing in front of Mandela's house. It literally means 'we have not seen you'. And it is true: South Africa, including Yolisa, has not seen him, not really, not even after he emerged from the darkness of jail. Yes they witnessed his presidency, his vibe, his jive, his speeches, but these, like the Mandela curriculum in schools, were mostly hopes, the imagination of a nation that desperately wanted to be one, but wasn't. The forlorn individuals in the crowds, all colours, all families, sometimes sing along with the performers, but mostly just walk about sadly, dazed, after leaving their flowers and cards. Mandela's absence is his presence again, like the picture of a parent held in the hand of an abandoned child.

Yolisa can't access the depths of his own past, not yet. 'If I tried to talk to my mother about our history, she would disintegrate,' he says as we stand in the pouring rain in some side street. Yolisa is 'special', as he says, ironically. He is the son of a businessman from the former Ciskei homeland and a poor rural woman whom class would separate physically as he was growing up. He lived with his father: part of an 'elite who drove expensive cars and sent their children to good schools'. His father committed suicide when the homeland structure was abolished, in 1994.

Like South Africa itself, you can't see the trauma when you first meet. Yolisa's conversation is usually peppered with healthy self-deprecating jokes about how articulate and intellectual he is. It is the kind of compliment he receives every now and then from whites, who tell him he is not like other blacks. It is not funny when that happens, though. 'Then I just don't know where to look. It can come as a bolt out of the blue.'

Yolisa's mother was like the other blacks. She came from a family of farm workers in the Karoo. They had had land and cattle, but that was taken from them, bit by bit. One day, their property would be declared a nature reserve, later it suddenly became a white area. An uncle of Yolisa's mother had resisted the expropriation of his land and cattle and had been shot dead by the new owners. 'Uncle Kiki's photo hung in everyone's living room. But I never knew about the history until much later. We – my father's family – visited my mother's family, but never spent time in their houses. We would stay in a bed & breakfast. My mother's family was given our old clothes.'

Yolisa was twelve and at boarding school when he started to understand his father's background and the reason for his elite existence. 'Friends at school showed me books that were banned, about our history, about Mandela. I understood that my father and the homeland rulers who were his friends were crooks. They were in cahoots with the same government that had impoverished and disenfranchised my mother's family.'

As an ANC activist of nineteen, he discovered that a street sweeper in the village where they lived was his great-uncle Abie, a brother of Uncle Kiki. 'I asked my aunt why they had never introduced me to him, and she got angry, as if that was a bad question.' But when this uncle started going on day-long trips, Yolisa asked him where he was going all the time. He replied that we was looking for his cattle in the mountains. 'I understood then that something was wrong with his mind, because he had not had cattle for many years. I later learnt that he had given up his land and cattle to the whites without fighting like Uncle Kiki had. So, in addition to losing his land and cattle, he had also been called a coward by the family.'

Yolisa also learned that Uncle Abie, though entitled to a state pension as a street sweeper, had never received this. 'A cousin who was also an activist, and myself, decided to take him to the pension office in the nearby white town. The whites were not going to get away with this. After everything they had done to him, they were now not going to take his pension, too.' Together they took Uncle Abie to town. 'But when we got to the office he did not want to move. He clung to a tree and absolutely refused to go in. My cousin and I fought with him, trying to loosen his grip from the tree.'

The skirmish attracted the attention of a white lady in the pension office, who recognised the street-sweeper. 'We were shocked to see this madam come out and meet us, with my uncle's pension money counted out in an envelope. She wanted to give it to him. She said: "Abie, why did you never come for your pension? Do take it, it's yours." The two were even more shaken to see their uncle break down, then. 'He went on his knees and started apologising. "Sorry madam, sorry, I did not want to bother you … it's them, they made me bother you."' Yolisa and his cousin had been prepared for anger and a fight, but not for this. 'He was defeated. So defeated. It was terrible. After it was over, my cousin and I sat on a bench and cried.'

We discuss the present state of the leadership, among whom, he says, so many are fake. 'Those who make speeches and drive expensive cars but don't worry for a moment about doing their jobs. Leadership!' He points at a man with clenched fist standing in front of the muddy floral tribute at the Mandela house, singing ANC songs, filmed by German TV. With angry eyes: 'He doesn't even know the words.' Let him be, I suggest, maybe he just wants some attention, too, but Yolisa shakes his head. 'It would not annoy me so much if such people weren't in government.' I ask what he thinks is the cause of such behaviour. Laziness? Lack of moral values? 'Fear of failure. An inferiority complex. They are defeated. Like Uncle Abie. There are differences – they feel entitled to money, he didn't – but the defeated part is the same.'

Roughly a year later, on 10 December 2014, Yolisa Pikie will leave SARS. He will have been branded a member of a rogue unit, and a servant of what is now called 'white monopoly capital'. He will be accused of destroying SARS property, and found guilty by a disciplinary hearing held in his absence after he resigned. *Sunday Times* articles by Mzilikazi wa Afrika, Stephan Hofstatter and now also a colleague named Piet Rampedi will regularly carry a picture of him, taken at an unguarded moment, with him sticking out his tongue. A stupid picture.

A perfect storm
2014

The SARS people know that they are dealing with a hornet's nest by now, but what can one do other than one's job? When, just before the April 2014 elections, SARS stops a consignment of ANC T-shirts with Zuma's face on it, brought in from China without the payment of import duties, Ivan receives several phone calls pressurising him to let it go. The T-shirts are meant for Zuma's campaign, so it is urgent. But import duties are the law. They need to be paid. '(Ivan) refuses to be bullied,' a source will tell a newspaper later.

Ivan told his team of investigators in February that 'a storm is brewing' and that 'they' are coming for SARS. Remarkably, no one at the meeting asked who 'they' are. Fraudsters, tobacco smugglers, criminal politicians, ambitious megalomaniacs, common gangsters, disgruntled and corrupt SARS officials, rogue secret agents connected to Zuma's kitchen cabinet and intelligence network in the SSA, and information peddlers have joined forces and everyone knows it. And many in these categories are linked to the highest office in the land.

'I saw JZ in his office again,' says Ivan one day as we eat dinner. 'I asked him about the dossiers and told him that some of his close associates, including his personal legal advisor Bonisiwe Makhene,[240] seem to be involved in the smear campaigns. That, for years now, these people have been going around asking for any dirt on the heads of SARS.' Zuma jumped, he continues. 'He was very emotional. He got up from the couch and walked around agitatedly. He shouted, "Not me, comrade Ivan! I did not do that, I don't know of these things!"'

There is a pause at our dinner table. Then: 'Zuma always reminds me of a child caught with chocolate all over its face, insisting that it didn't have any chocolate.'

Is there still a scenario in which things will return to normal in the end, I ask. 'I doubt it,' he says. 'We are in the eye of a perfect storm.'

A few months later journalist Pearlie Joubert phones Johann van Loggerenberg and one or two other acquaintances at SARS. She is frantic, telling them that Western Cape politician and parliamentarian, formerly a premier of the province and her old friend Lynne Brown, has just informed her that 'they are going to remove the top guys at SARS, smear them, compromise them, so that they will never get work again'. Joubert hasn't been able to find out from Brown how she knows this or who said this; she only knows that Brown has become close to presidential circles recently.

Brown appeared to be very anxious. 'She was tearful and said she was scared,' Joubert will recall later. 'I advised her to write a statement. Even if she didn't go public now, she should have it documented somewhere, perhaps in a lawyers' office.' Joubert doesn't know if Brown ever did that. 'We lost contact.'

In the elections in April this year, Zuma wins his second term.

His new cabinet is a nightmare. Trevor Manuel, Kgalema Motlanthe and Barbara Hogan are gone. The secret services portfolio is now handled by David Mahlobo from Mpumalanga, a province well known for its criminalised politics.[241] A crucial player in Zuma's kitchen cabinet and personal intelligence networks, Nathi Nhleko, is minister of police. Malusi Gigaba, who has appointed several of Zuma's associates to head state enterprises, from where they have proceeded to dish out contracts to Zuma-friendly businessmen, notably the Gupta brothers,[242] now heads the home affairs department.

A number of notoriously underperforming, but Zuma-adoring, sycophant women are ministers now too: Nomvula Mokonyane, most known for screeching at rallies, is appointed to head of water affairs, as if it is not bad enough that pipes in many poor areas have already broken down and municipal councillors are selling water to communities expensively from their own tanks. South Africa's poor are once again served with Women's League head and Zuma praise singer Bathabile Dlamini – who is in four years' time to be called 'reckless and grossly negligent' by the Constitutional Court[243] – in the portfolio of social development. Faith Muthambi, a regional politician reputed for allocating vehicles and state money to herself and relatives,[244] gets communications, the portfolio that oversees the SABC.

That particular appointment doesn't augur well for the public broadcaster, already battling to survive under megalomaniac chief of operations Hlaudi Motsoeneng, with his North Korea-like emphasis on 'positive news' and his breakfast show for the Gupta-owned newspaper *The New Age*. A few months into her portfolio, Faith Muthambi will purge the SABC board of all members who are concerned about Motsoeneng. According to an inside source, Muthambi will say in an informal conversation that 'her job is to ensure that Hlaudi is safe'.

Some individuals with better reputations remain ministers: Ngoako Ramathlodi gets minerals, Pravin Gordhan is moved to the local government ministry and his former deputy Nhlanhla Nene now heads the finance department, but will they form a counterweight? Jeff Radebe is the minister in the presidency, of course. I guess there is always Jeff Radebe.

Lynne Brown is appointed as minister of state enterprises.

Ivan is concerned. 'The old man is promoting more and more faulty individuals. As if the president *wants* people who are incompetent. Or delusional.'

Minister Maite Nkoana-Mashabane has returned in the portfolio of international relations. Last year, she said nothing after President Zuma's Gupta friends used the Waterkloof air force base to land two hundred of their family members to attend a wedding at Sun City. She subsequently rewarded the key culprit in the scandal, chief of state protocol Bruce Koloane, with an ambassadorship to the Netherlands. Years later she will gain dubious international fame when she proudly claims in an interview with Al Jazeera that she has a hole in her head.[245]

Rogue unit
10 August 2014

Two very different stories appear in two different Sunday newspapers.

'A City Press investigation has revealed the existence of a State Security Agency Special Operations Unit (SOU) where rogue agents use state resources to conduct dirty tricks campaigns, smuggle cigarettes and disgrace top civil servants,' the report headlines. It says that the SOU has, inter alia, been working to 'replace the level from acting commissioner Ivan Pillay to Johann van Loggerenberg' at SARS. The reason why the SSA Special Operations people would do that is that SARS was 'investigating tobacco smugglers with close links to the unit'.[246] It will later turn out that the tobacco smugglers and their spy associates have links to Zuma's son Edward.[247]

The article, written by Jacques Pauw, calls the SOU a rogue unit. The SSA has a rogue unit that conducts dirty tricks campaigns, smuggles cigarettes, and disgraces top civil servants. I remember thinking that that is a catchy term, rogue unit.

I first met Jacques Pauw ages ago, in London in 1989. We had both reported on the so-called death squad hearings under South African judge Louis Harms. The judge had come all the way from Pretoria to London to hear revelations by former Vlakplaas death squad captain Dirk Coetzee about the torture and murders he and his people had committed in the service of apartheid. The hearings could not be held in South Africa itself – it was still an apartheid state then – but the white regime had not been able to avoid an inquiry into the testimony. So they had sent a judge to London.

Harms largely presided over a whitewash, consistently siding with state lawyers who argued that if policemen had done anything bad, like roasting people alive and keeping young women naked and starving in cold cells for weeks before killing them – and that was a big if – then that surely wasn't because their superiors had instructed them to. Nevertheless, the Harms Commission was Jacques Pauw's achievement. As a young crime reporter, he had discovered Dirk Coetzee and got him to talk. He had followed up all the leads, spoke to other Vlakplaas policemen, unearthed the entire story of South Africa's death squads.

The last time I had met Jacques Pauw was twenty years before, just before the first democratic elections in 1994. We had run into one another in Newtown, around the Market Theatre, a place then buzzing with politics and hope. Jacques Pauw had talked about meeting Jacob Zuma, back in 1989. As head of the ANC's intelligence structures, he had organised death squad captain Dirk Coetzee's temporary relocation in exile. Zuma had said he was grateful. He had promised Pauw that as soon as he was in government, he would appoint him as ambassador to the Maldives. We had all laughed.

And now Pauw has exposed Zuma's secret service's plans to get rid of some good civil servants.

The other story appears in the *Sunday Times* and it is about SARS, too. I look at it with trepidation, suspecting it will have been written by Mzilikazi wa Afrika. But no, it is by a reporter named Malcom Rees. Then I remember: Mzilikazi might not have time for this. I have heard that he is busy publishing a memoir of what he terms his 'fights against corruption' and the book will come out any day now. I don't expect much of it but, at least, I hope, it will keep him too busy to write about fishy things going on at SARS.

The *Sunday Times* story by Malcom Rees is a nasty piece anyway. Headlined 'Love Affair Rocks SARS'[248] it calls Johann a 'former apartheid undercover agent' and gives a lot of unsavoury detail about his break-up with lady friend Belinda Walter, someone I had heard about but never met. I only know that the relationship was serious. Johann had introduced Belinda to his mother.

Why Johann's break-up is in the *Sunday Times* becomes clear as I read the article. Belinda Walter, it turns out, is a lawyer who works for an institute called the Fair Trade Independent Tobacco Association that consists of 'tobacco firms that have frequently had skirmishes with the tax authorities'. Belinda Walter has also separately represented Carnilinx, a tobacco firm associated with Glenn Agliotti, self-confessed cigarette-smuggler Mazzotti, and soon also with populist demagogue Julius Malema's new crowd. (Malema, who fell out with President Zuma the year before, started the Economic Freedom Fighters (EFF), a political party which will receive much funding from Carnilinx in years to come.)

If I get the gist of the article correctly, Belinda Walter is a State Security Agency agent as well. And now like others in spy networks before, she has shared phone recordings from SARS with the *Sunday Times* people. WhatsApp messages between herself and Johann show, she says, that Johann committed the crime of sharing taxpayers' information with her.

Walter is mentioned in Jacques Pauw's story in *City Press* too, but his article names her as one of the 'rogue elements' in the SSA who are 'working to replace' SARS's top management, as well as other civil servants. Pauw writes that she is a member of a group of 'former full-time SSA agents, police officers, military intelligence agents and former members of the Civil Cooperation Bureau, the defence force's death squad during apartheid', who work with the current SOU. The SOU, the article says, specifically targets Ivan Pillay and Johann van Loggerenberg to protect 'tobacco smuggling networks within the SSA'.

Johann doesn't think that it was all pretence from her throughout the affair, though. 'I think we were genuinely in love at first. She must have sought some stability and protection with me. She had been dealing with abuse and exploitation in the dodgy networks around her. I thought I was rescuing a damsel in distress. I understand she is back now with the men she wished to be protected from.'[249]

Belinda Walter will later retract her earlier statement against Johann. But, later still, when she is back with her SSA handler Chris Burger, she will retract her retraction.

A while later I see Belinda Walter performing in the TV programme *Carte Blanche*. In the sympathetic company of rhino poacher and dossier-producer Mike Peega and a new lover, crime intelligence Lieutenant Colonel Hennie Niemann, she waxes on in detail about how badly she was treated by Johann. 'Do you think you have been naïve?' the wide-eyed interviewer gushes. 'Yes,' says Belinda, now wide-eyed as well. 'That is what it is. I have been so naïve.'

But naïve is not a term I would use to describe her now, especially as in recent years lawyer Belinda has been advising tax dodgers on how to resist SARS. The narrative that SARS – not the SSA – has a rogue unit headed by Ivan and Johann is a godsend, since they can claim to have been unfairly targeted by rogues. The so-called 'rogue unit defence'[250] is used in court cases by companies like Carnilinx, their associate Martin Wingate-Pearse, strip club boss Mark Lifman and alleged fraudster Hennie Delport – the same Delport whom Ivan was asked by Zuma to help out. It is now one of Belinda Walter's special products.[251]

'n Naai soos ons
September 2014

Around the time that Tom Moyane is appointed as the new commissioner of SARS by Jacob Zuma, all hugs and affable comradeship, Ivan's niece Kogie visits us. She is worried about a brain drain from the university in Durban where she works as a medical lecturer. 'People who just try to do their jobs get criticised, disciplined, fired and ultimately replaced,' she reports indignantly, 'often by a new person who has no idea what the job is about.'

Ivan feels that the ANC is failing to give guidance to its people who come to work in structures from which they were previously excluded. 'They want to work, have a role, so that they can help their families. But the ANC doesn't help them get to grips with what is happening, doesn't explain that it is about learning, and about receiving the right assistance and tools. The ANC should also explain that a state job is not your family business, to do with as you please. We are failing in our messages around all that.'

'But what about the outright criminals?' Kogie asks then, showing anger that must have been bottled up for a while. 'Some of the new bosses are connected with friends high up in government. They are using university funds and contracts for themselves. I sometimes feel that we are being ruled by gangsters.'

I argue that it might not be that bad yet. Yes, perhaps Jacob Zuma, the former peasant, actually believes that a president is like a king and that he and his vassals are entitled to a share of every deal: Ivan has told me that at one of his meetings with Zuma, the president had asked Ivan why he had to account to Parliament. 'Putin doesn't account to Parliament,' he had said, almost indignantly. 'Why must I?' If Thabo Mbeki had a Wakanda-type vision of his reign, Jacob Zuma appears to fancy himself in some kind of dreamed-up Zulu pastoral kingdom. But we are not subject to gangster rule yet: I remind Kogie that Nhlanhla Nene and Pravin Gordhan are still in the cabinet.

I look at Ivan to see if he has anything to add, but it's 7 pm and he has switched on the news on TV.

***

When Kogie visits us, I do not know yet that Zuma has held meetings with gangsters. But, at least in one case, Ivan has recently become aware of it. The president has held discussions with criminals-turned-politicians Gayton McKenzie and Kenny Kunene at his Nkandla residence already three years before, in 2011. Having found out about it, Ivan has raised it with Zuma. The president diverted the question and made it sound innocent, he will tell me later. 'He used some truth to confuse the issue, mentioning that a Griqua[252] leader was present at the meeting, who complained that his people were being ignored by the ANC. Zuma added that McKenzie and Kunene now wanted to create a political organisation that would not oppose the ANC but instead absorb opposition votes like the Griqua's. They were there to promise that after the elections they would throw their lot in with the ANC.'[253]

Ivan did not believe that this was all there was to the Nkandla meeting, but didn't press the issue, he says. All he had wanted was 'to demonstrate to the old man that other people including SARS were aware of his manoeuvres. In hindsight, my raising this with him, combined with the other issues I had discussed with him, plus the barrage of the so-called dossiers, would have convinced the president that we were monitoring him.'

The investigative news outlet Amabhungane will later write that Zuma had also met with gangsters in Cape Town, also in 2011. That meeting had been attended by the Americans gang leader Igshaan Davids and Quinton 'Mr Big' Marinus – the same Marinus SARS was investigating, together with his friends Lifman and Donkie Booysen. The Amabhungane article quotes a conversation at the meeting between Marinus and President Zuma as follows: 'Sir, we're having big problems with SARS (the South African Revenue Service).' Zuma listened. He said: 'We will look into that.' The article points out that SARS had by then seized assets belonging to Marinus, including his home in the upmarket Cape suburb of Plattekloof, to recover his tax debt.[254]

The article also reports that the go-between who organised the meeting, a gangster named Lloyd Hill who is a longstanding acquaintance of the Zuma family, introduced the parties by saying about Zuma, 'Die ou is 'n naai soos ons' or the old man is a fuck like us. 'The sources said it seemed he knew the president well enough to address him in this way. They said it also broke the ice: everybody laughed.'

Rogue and counter-rogue
10 October 2014

After the publication of Mzilikazi's book *Nothing Left to Steal*, which deals with certain corrupt politicians of his own choosing,[255] he is back on the front pages of the *Sunday Times*.

Wa Afrika is skyrocketing now. The extensive praise his book has received, often from white reviewers ('fearless corruption buster', 'unambiguous folk hero', 'figure of crusading righteousness', 'as fearless and determined as he is modest', with extra accolades because he was arrested once),[256] makes me think that many white people have never imagined that a black person could be so much against corruption. The reviews do note that Mzilikazi promotes himself 'without the slightest whiff of modesty' and is 'perhaps a touch bombastic' in his sound bites about 'willing to die for the truth' and so on, but he still, they say, is really, truly a hero.

I smile, thinking that many on the African continent who bravely fight corruption end up in jail, hurt or in mortal danger and never get any press, and that Mzilikazi usually only exposes those 'corrupt' individuals about whom he received dossiers from his intelligence sources. On the other hand, there are some passable stories in the book so perhaps he is not so bad after all.

Then I read what he and his colleagues wrote on today's *Sunday Times* front page. Attacking SARS, they splash out all the contents of the previous spy dossiers and more, and attach the label 'rogue unit' – originally applied to the SSA's Special Operations by Jacques Pauw – to the SARS investigators. The inside spread, adorned with a film noirish drawing of a shady man in raincoat, denounces a 'rogue spy unit' at the tax agency that would have 'bugged (then deputy) President Zuma, targeted politicians, intercepted phone calls, faked identities, broke into houses', and possibly even murdered people, like former SARS executive Leonard Radebe, 'whose phone was tapped and meeting with Zuma bugged'. Radebe 'later died in a mysterious car accident', the story notes ominously, leaving the impression that there may well be more to that car crash than one might think.[257]

How can the *Sunday Times*' editors allow such a paragraph? Phylicia Oppelt had already seen most of this at least four years earlier, when Adrian Lackay had showed her records, minutes, to prove that the Peega allegations were untrue. Yet, she allows all this to be published now, and with a sensational murder allegation thrown in, too. Two murder allegations, actually: the article also insinuates that there was foul play in the case of another SARS manager, George Nkadimeng, who also died in a car accident.

I briefly consider if the Radebe car crash could in theory have been associated with his dalliance with Dave King, or his presumed frustrated ambitions to become the new SARS commissioner, or his later alleged handing of the Peega dossier to the president. But even if any of this had prompted anyone at all to engineer a car crash, they waited a long time to take such action: The crash occurred in 2012, four years after Radebe had left SARS. It had also not actually killed him; he died of an illness a little later.

I had never heard of the other car crash victim mentioned in the *Sunday Times* article, SARS official George Nkadimeng, but hear that he was regarded as a very nice man.

Being accused of playing undercover detective is one thing. But murder accusations are very different. Such writing lingers. Where there is smoke, there is fire, they say. Still in 2019, public protector Busisiwe Mkhwebane who is strongly aligned with the Zuma faction will resuscitate the rogue unit investigation and say, 'I believe people have died.'

I want to talk to Ivan, but I am in Holland with Devi and he has just gone back to South Africa with Vani. Today, of all days; they have just landed back home.

He does not talk on the phone. Not about things like this.

Brothels and ice cream
South Africa, later in the year

'Why must they publish my picture,' Ivan says angrily, and I can't help laughing. The *Sunday Times* has been headlining rogue unit stories about him and his fellow enforcement people for weeks now, but what gets him even more than the content is that they display his face every time. I am reminded once again of how this man hates the spotlight.

On one occasion, the continuous exposure yields some benefit, though. Driving at night through Burnett Street in Hatfield, there is a police road block for license disks, or alcohol, or both, and we are called over. Though we haven't had anything to drink and the license is in order, we are nevertheless prepared for the police's increasingly common scare tactics and fishing for bribes. The policeman who stops us shines his torch in Ivan's face and seems ready to demand things, but then his expression changes. He reflects a bit, then waves us on. Has he seen the pictures, does he fear that this must be a person with connections? For the first time that day Ivan smiles. 'Yes, that's *Mr* Rogue to you.'

These are weird days, when friends and relatives commiserate about all the bad stuff in the papers, but sometimes still with doubt in their voices, because what if some of it is in fact true? You must be in very real trouble, the message often shines through. I continuously reassure them that we are fine, really. So what if they spied on organised criminals, is that not what one *should* do?

One of the published allegations is that the SARS rogue unit ran a brothel. It's an excellent concept, of course. Catching tax dodgers with the help of a contingent of sex workers (equipped, also of course, with professional skills, preparation and training, health care and good wages) seems like a great way to bridge the revenue gap. I'd love to run an outfit like that, to use Mzilikazi wa Afrika's words, and dream away about dressing the part. The funniest bit is the thought of Ivan as a brothel boss, with his extremely well ironed shirts and squeaky-clean behaviour, a man who still hesitates a bit before pronouncing the word 'sex'.

'They *should* have done all that,' says Gwen Ansell, who has entertained similar images. 'Why *didn't* they?' We reminisce about Elliot Ness and the Untouchables and so many other stories about unconventional law enforcers. We doubt that any of them ever ran a brothel, but feel that it should certainly be an option. Our coffee talks are back to being peaceful and non-argumentative. I have sent her an email to say 'Boy, were you right about Zuma.'

'I told Gwen I would run an operation like that any time,' I tell Ivan as we meet back at home. 'You're not the only one', is the answer. 'Some women from work asked me why I didn't inform them of such career opportunities.'

When a clearly upset Johann van Loggerenberg tells me that certain people in the investigative unit have experienced marital problems because of the brothel story, I can't help arguing. Even if it were true, running a brothel project surely doesn't mean cheating on any wives or partners? Most commercial brothel owners (I did know a few in

Amsterdam, back in the day) would not even tolerate such dalliances.

Johann shrugs. 'It's just that traditionally prostitution and brothels are such triggers in most people's minds. I guess that is why they made one up to slander us. You could also say that we ran an ice cream parlour, but it doesn't have the same ring to it, does it?'

The brothel accusation will be exploited by Tom Moyane, when he takes over SARS and disbands the executive: He doesn't want to hear any more brothel stories, he says. Remarkably, people don't seem to think that the accusation of murder in the story about mysterious car crashes comes even close to it.

Death squad captain Dirk Coetzee once used sex work as an example of evil, too. I met him in London, in 1989, during the Harms hearings that were triggered by Jacques Pauw's revelations. Coetzee had testified there. Interviewing the captain in a nearby pizza restaurant, I remember that I could not eat much, but Coetzee was chewing away with abandon. I also remember, very starkly, that Coetzee described one of the worst murderers and torturers in his circles as 'worse than a prostitute'.

In the quagmire

No one in the network of investigative journalists in Africa has heard much from the FAIR office in Johannesburg or the chairman, Mzilikazi wa Afrika, recently. A new African Investigative Publishing Collective, formed on the side by core FAIR members, takes up the cudgel of simply doing stories.

It is going quite well, actually. It is in many ways a relief not to have an office and salaries and institutional assets and all these protocols. I realised, way too late perhaps, that the comment once made by Bee Bulunga about governance and management ('Why do we think it is easy?') applied to us, too. Unlike politicians, who sign up for such things, we concluded that we should not even try to be what we were not. Thanks to my old friend Bart, the magazine he now edits, ZAM,[258] has come on board to do our admin and finances for us as well as publish our stories. Downsized, with our hands and heads free to focus on journalism, we get on with the job.

Gangsters networking with politicians is an increasingly recurrent theme. A Mozambican colleague who has investigated extrajudicial killings of suspected rhino poachers – sometimes just migrants – in the Kruger Park is reporting how the gangs who control the poaching game are closely connected to the ruling party in Mozambique; one such gang is funding the Frelimo office in Gaza province. Gold smugglers in Cameroon get protection from government departments and police too, as do Nigerian human traffickers and abusive, charity-expropriating Ghanaian orphanage owners.

What we see and report increasingly gives rise to an uncanny awareness that it is becoming difficult to distinguish right from wrong in many African countries. Between corrupt governments and criminalised police, ordinary thieves and political looters, random fraudsters, sex work traffickers, violent terrorists, militias and even opposition parties that behave exactly as the previous rulers did on assuming power, who is good and who bad? Who are to be held accountable for what and by whom?

In Nigeria, the state does not even pretend to be about public service anymore: It is simply a system of access to state coffers and favouritism. 'Your first concern on the job, even if you were a good candidate, is to repay favour', as the head of Nigeria's science academy, Oyewale Tomori, puts it in one of the articles we write for ZAM.[259] It is all about turf, about your own family and patronage network. Never about the interests of citizens.

Frantz Fanon echoes more and more loudly in my mind as Zuma's praise singers and cronies start sloganeering about what they call Radical Economic Transformation (RET). The RET choir – as Thabo Mbeki had once done, but much louder – focuses on the West as the enemy. It portrays its hero, Zuma, as the great scourge of white monopoly capital, as well as its foremost victim. Remarkably, several protagonists in this crowd see no problem dealing with white – or at best olive-skinned – criminals, like the Gupta brothers, strip club mogul Mark Lifman, conman Glenn Agliotti and self-confessed tobacco smuggler Mazzotti. Their ire is mostly directed at established companies, which is all the more remarkable because most of these have not been exactly white for some time now. State pension funds are major shareholders in most stock exchange-listed entities.

Might the problem be that some in the RET crowd have missed the boat during the past empowerment rounds? Cyril Ramaphosa, Tokyo Sexwale and Mathews Phosa are well ensconced, Zuma's new vassals not so much.

This flocking towards rogue businessmen while attacking regular companies is eerily reminiscent of something a colleague from the DRC reported two years back. In 2012 in that country, an Australian mine, First Quantum, was ejected for insisting on paying tax and regular salaries. The DRC government much preferred a shady Israeli wheeler-dealer named Dan Gertler, who operated on a profit-sharing basis with the officials who gave him opportunities.[260]

South Africa may very well escape this fate. Compared with other African countries, it is still mind-blowingly lucky to have, with all its shortcomings, a free and aware civil society and media, inspired by old ANC values of justice and equality for all, and an independent judiciary. Jacob Zuma may dismiss 'clever blacks',[261] just like the mines in Transkei once did, causing Lizo Semane to play dumber than he was, but many black journalists, civil servants, artists, businesspeople, analysts and critics have adopted the epithet with pride.

Nevertheless, the looting is on. The entire board of South African Airways already resigned two years ago to allow for an environment more conducive to patronage, under new board chair Dudu Myeni, who also chairs the Zuma Foundation. It will later transpire that Myeni writes fake whistle blower reports about people she wants out of the enterprise, feigns shock when she comes to hear about the reports, then removes the accused.[262]

Zuma- and Gupta-allies are also being appointed to the board of the electricity utility Eskom.[263] Transnet, the rail, port and pipeline enterprise, has likewise landed in the hands of 'a group of people (...) with a common purpose to advance interests of those pursuing quick accumulation of wealth for themselves', as Popo Molefe (the board chairman appointed in 2018 to salvage the bankrupt entity) will later state to the Zondo Commission of Enquiry into Allegations of State Capture.[264] At state arms manufacturer Denel, former MK comrade Riaz Saloojee receives invitation after invitation from wheeler-dealer Salim Essa, known as the 'fourth Gupta brother', to meet with Guptas; he is assured that 'this comes from the very top'.[265] Denel will later report having lost R30 billion in contracts because of kickback demands made by the Guptas that business partners refused to entertain.[266]

Imagine, I think: there were arms companies that were too decent for the Guptas.

The choir cheers all this on. Former *Sunday Independent* editor

Moshoeshoe Monare will later talk about the 'red-eyed fanatics and loyalists' at his newspaper, who earlier in 2014 kicked him and other independent minds out. Such colleagues, he will narrate,[267] felt excited about talk of black excellence, 'but what they perceived as empowerment was in fact sycophancy and undermined the practice of journalism'. The description applies to many of those now dominating the Gupta media: their *New Age* newspaper, ANN7 TV and the SABC. Together with Independent Newspapers, they circulate and rehash disinformation and bring in analysts no one has ever heard of to explain how white ploys undermine the Radical Economic Transformation project.

It will later transpire that government communications (GCIS) head Themba Maseko's departure from that agency in 2010, a small operation at the time, had come about as a result of his refusal to facilitate the flow of R600 million from GCIS to the *New Age*.[268] His colleague Phumla Williams will state before the Zondo Commission in 2018 that, post-Maseko, she felt as much under pressure in that office as she had under apartheid. She was once Ivan's comrade, Flo, in Swaziland, was arrested in Soweto, spent weeks in detention in 1988 and now works at government communications. 'I relived the torture in the police cells,' she will say about Zuma Minister Faith Muthambi's subsequent reign at GCIS. 'I was no longer sleeping, I had nightmares. My facial twitches were back. I had panic attacks. I saw torture going through my body again.'

Phumla's former boss Themba Maseko's replacement, and Muthambi favourite, was the RET choir's smooth-voiced leading member Jimmy Mzwanele Manyi, whose contribution to the struggle seems to have been limited to dropping the Western name Jimmy a few years before and insisting on being called Mzwanele. From his Twitter account it does appear as if he feels really strongly about that.

There are more collapses of water supply, mainly in the townships. There are also more potholes on roads, buses break down more often, and patients sleep on floors in state hospitals. The chief procurement office in the finance ministry, championed by SARS, is fledgling.

In the service of individuals

The *Sunday Times* is such an interesting case. On the one hand it will write about 'Zuma corruption' – indeed, many headlines are about that – but in the same edition it will help get rid of good civil servants. It keeps attacking Hawks' head Anwa Dramat with accusations that he sent 'Zimbabwean suspects home to die',[269] a campaign that will eventually see Dramat replaced by Berning Ntlemeza, a crude and vulgar ex-Transkei homeland policeman who rose through the ranks from 1981, at the height of jailings and torture of activists.[270] Similarly, the paper demolished the career of KwaZulu-Natal Hawks head Johan Booysen, who had investigated corruption cases against Zuma family associates: Booysen and his Gauteng colleague Shadrack Sibiya were not only removed from the Hawks but also criminally charged. The *Sunday Times* is still busy with SARS's 'rogue unit', too.

Mzilikazi wa Afrika is usually the main author of such stories. It is by now widely suspected that he gets his leads and anonymous sources from within President Zuma's secret service empire, and many surmise that his pen is used, as poor murdered scribe Franck Ngyke's once was in Kinshasa, 'at the service of individuals'. Later testimony before the Zondo Commission will once again refer to bribes.[271] Zuma minister Dina Pule and new Zuma appointee Matshela Koko at Eskom will publicly complain about being blackmailed by Wa Afrika. The allegations fit the picture of a Ngyke: a journalist who, without any real conviction of his own, simply writes for or against his targets, depending on whom he writes for.

Mzilikazi wa Afrika will always furiously deny allegations that he has ever received bribes, or any untoward funds at all, and it must be noted that Dina Pule will later retract and apologise.[272]

But there is just such a Kinshasa feel about all this. Having private meetings with powerful individuals to discuss negative stories; having friends in businesses dealing with the same ministers you write about; it all has very little to do with the pursuit of truth and social justice.

But maybe it's the ones who *don't* operate like this who are out of step with the spirit of the time by now. How do you maintain ethics when right and wrong don't seem to be in the universe anymore?

Unlike literally every other media house in South Africa, the *Sunday Times* never writes about any of the scandals surrounding crime intelligence head Richard Mdluli.[273] It stays mum on reports that Mdluli informed President Zuma which individuals should be acted against because they were plotting against him; doesn't write about the corrupt slush fund that paid not only to plant stories but for cars and trips for individuals; doesn't even report on Mdluli's own murder case.[274]

'I was always puzzled about us not covering the Mdluli stories,' Pearlie Joubert, in 2014 still a member of the *Sunday Times*' investigative unit, will tell us later. 'At one meeting I suggested that we should follow up on one case where he, Mdluli, played a role. Then Mzilikazi got up and left the room.' Pearlie Joubert will eventually resign because of the rogue unit stories by her colleagues. But more about that later.

The suspended buddies club
December 2014

What's with 5 December? Is Sinterklaas cross because of all the racism accusations, shouted louder and louder in Holland, against the stereotype of his Black Pete? Last year, we buried Mandela, now Ivan has been suspended. He is not alone: Pete Richer is next, then Yolisa Pikie. Moyane is now in practice the undisputed boss of SARS, faithfully served by Luther Lebelo, the same Luther Lebelo who had once pledged his undying loyalty to Ivan. Moyane has morphed Johann van Loggerenberg's special leave, dating back to the Belinda Walter affair, to suspension.

The atmosphere in the house is subdued, with men – Yolisa, Ivan, Johann, Sri the Indian consultant, who will not last much longer than the others – sitting around the table, scratching their heads and looking through *Sunday Times* stories and their own papers, preparing for Labour Court litigation. It's only at this court that they can plead their side; otherwise they can't comment or defend themselves since suspension comes with strict muzzling rules.

We talk about Belinda and I ask Johann, jokingly, to 'find a more normal woman' next time. Sri, who has become a good friend of ours, grins at that. I know he has expressed amazement at Johann's previous partnership choice. Others have, too. Belinda may be pretty but that she is messed up in the head should have been obvious from the start, they feel.

Johann nods ruefully, he knows that he has not been the best judge of character, or very adept at human relationships. He will describe in his later book *Rogue* how after a life of undercover operations among organised criminals he battled for a long time to have any human relationships at all, and drowned himself in work. The working week was such a blur, he writes, that it often felt like it was just all one and the same day.

He is still on anti-depressants and makes regular emergency disappearances to the platteland where he puts his head back in order in silence. On the good side, however, he has just started a new life with Nicole, who will in a few years be the mother of their daughter. She jokes that she deserves a medal for rescuing him from Belinda, the torment of the rogue unit accusations, and the demons of his past. He often says, and has written, that beautiful, independent, solid, stable, funny and warm Nicole has been his salvation. It's a great happy ending, I reflect, for someone who always thought he was there to rescue and protect others.

The suspended buddies club, Vani calls the gatherings around our dining table. She brings drinks, helps to photocopy, avails her phone sometimes, when the men, who are accused of illicit eavesdropping, have reason to fear that someone is eavesdropping on them. Vani is concerned, of course, but in a way also in her element. She likes to run around and help out, a community organiser if ever there was one.

The dinner table gatherings remind me once again of that 'queer-looking party that assembled on the bank' in *Alice in Wonderland*. Besides Johann the troubled law-and-order man and Yolisa the Ciskei comrade, there's also Pete Richer, the barley-juice-swigging yoga practitioner with the ANC intelligence background, and Adrian, who often lightens the atmosphere by performing, with Yolisa, their comrades jargon skits. Talking of what South Africa has become, or may be becoming, Sri the engineering whiz from India will contribute stories of families back in his country who, when burgled, robbed or victimised by violence, have to avoid getting the police involved at all costs 'because they will rob and hurt you all over again'. Sri had been employed at SARS as a specialist, hoping to implement his dream of better public service here, only to find that he was now seen as part of a rogue unit.

Each member of this motley crew had projected their own hopes on SARS. They had thought they were helping to create something good, that would help lift dispossessed millions out of poverty and bring the marginalised into the formal economy, too. Charge them tax, yes, but from each according to capability, for all according to need. Schools, hospitals, roads, safety. They had built SARS to fill tax coffers so that all these things could happen. They had hoped to fund and help enable the building of a developmental state.

Being the enemy

'I just don't understand why they still have to fight with us,' Ivan says repeatedly, during those evenings around the dinner table. 'We are gone. Why must they destroy us as if we are the enemy?' They were going to be removed and smeared so that they would never work again, Lynne Brown had said, but why?

The rogue unit stories continue. Moyane is probably involved in leaking them. 'It could just be Luther Lebelo all by himself,' Ivan says, but he doubts it. 'Moyane would do something about it if he did not approve.' We have no clue, at the time, what Moyane's plans are. We only know that, from the time he was appointed, he has not shown any interest in hearing from Ivan, not even in a hand-over from him as previous acting commissioner. 'I would have expected an interest in the goings on, who does what and where, where are we with the tax season. But there has been nothing,' he said at the time, puzzled.

Someone at SARS was most certainly involved in the recent *Sunday Times* headline about Ivan's pension payout, three years before. 'Pravin's pal scores on early retirement,' it said. Mzilikazi wa Afrika and his colleagues could only have got that from SARS sources. Luther Lebelo was in the human resources department that processed the pension.

When the story came out, last October, I asked Ivan if there really had not been anything irregular about the early pension pay out that had helped fund Devi's study in the Netherlands. 'No,' he said, bewildered. 'I requested it and I went through all the channels. The answer came back that it was fine. I am told that thousands of people in the public service have been allowed such arrangements.'

The problem with the early pension payout is not so much the re-employment as such, but the fact that Ivan did not pay any penalty for taking it, calculated as a sum of approximately R 1.2 million to be subtracted from the payout. In the mind of Mzilikazi wa Afrika and friends, Ivan's 'pal' Pravin Gordhan, then minister of finance, agreed to waive the penalties in Ivan's case out of nepotism, forcing SARS to make up the difference by compensating the pension fund.

But it wasn't Pravin Gordhan who had proposed that. The arrangement had been recommended by then SARS Commissioner Oupa Magashula, who wanted to retain Ivan's services as a contract employee and did not want a penalty to stand in the way of doing that. 'We understood Ivan's request. He had done a lot for SARS and for this country and we wanted him to continue to contribute. In such a situation, you really don't want to penalise him,' Magashula will reflect later.

'Applying a penalty was definitely going to be a bad deal,' SARS lawyer Vlok Symington will also confirm later. Symington had advised that the waiving of the penalty was both legal and acceptable in Ivan's case. 'You can do that if you don't care much for the employee, but in the case of Ivan, you want that man to give his all to SARS until he is 115 years old.' Symington had also warned at the time that 'if penalties were to be applied, it would be better for Ivan not to take early retirement at all'. Having received Magashula's recommendation, Gordhan had asked views from a range of legal and public service experts. His approval of the arrangement was considered over more than six months and only processed after widely obtained go-aheads.

Vlok Symington, whom we had not known very well before, has become a friend after the *Sunday Times* hullabaloo since he could not accept that the arrangement he had supported was presented as corrupt.

Later, in 2016, Symington will become famous for refusing to let go of a set of documents that contain a similar opinion to his own from law firm Mashiane Moodley Monana (MMM), whom Commissioner Tom Moyane, doggedly staying on Ivan's 'pension scandal', consults on the issue. In October that year a sensational hostage incident at SARS takes place when Symington refuses to return a printed email in this respect from MMM to Moyane. The email was handed to Symington – presumably by accident – as part of a set of documents sent to SARS by the National Prosecuting Authority because charges have been laid in connection with Ivan's early retirement and it wants to confirm Symington's earlier advice.[275]

At the time when security men barge into his office demanding it back, Symington does not know that the email print-out in his possession is evidence that Moyane is trying to suppress a legal opinion in the case. Vlok simply resists the attitude of Moyane's VIP protector and accompanying Hawks detectives, who are there to take his statement, but refuse to explain why they want these papers back so badly. He photographs the documents before he lets go of them, which is how they find their way into the public domain. Vlok Symington, as it turns out, is kind of a stubborn person.[276]

The *Sunday Times* stays on it through it all, continuously making it sound like Ivan siphoned off corrupt moneys. They have also headlined bad things about Yolisa, who they allege has lied about his qualifications and has destroyed SARS property, meaning two SIM cards used by Ivan's team.

Pete Richer is pictured like Ivan: a dangerous spy. 'My daughters find it interesting,' Pete jokes. 'They always said I was boring. Now that they hear that I ran a brothel as well as a spy ring, they say: "Hey, Dad is cool."'

Sikhakhane
Still December 2014

As the *Sunday Times* campaign gains steam, people start avoiding us at the Brooklyn Mall. The mall is so close to the SARS office that it is jokingly called 'Block M', as a continuation of the various blocks at the headquarters. Having moved into that Pretoria area in 2010 so that Ivan could be close to work, we had regularly met Ivan's colleagues there. Even when living in Amsterdam, I had often spent time in South Africa. But now they seem to have mysteriously vanished from the shopping complex, at least when we are there. Once or twice we see some pass by, but they are engaged in conversation, looking at shop windows.

SARS colleagues who remain friends start visiting at night. They leave their cars at the mall and walk, sometimes with caps on, apologetically explaining that they'll be in trouble if the new leadership finds out that they still have anything to do with Ivan.

Ivan could not believe his eyes at first when the Sikhakhane report came out at the end of November. Advocate Muzi Sikhakhane and his team had initially been brought in by Ivan, then still acting commissioner, to investigate issues around Johann van Loggerenberg's relationship with Belinda Walter. But the panel's terms of reference had changed after Tom Moyane's arrival at SARS. The Sikhakhane report stated that this change happened following escalating media reports that a rogue unit existed at SARS. It also stated that Belinda Walter had complained of a covert unit at SARS which was, as far as Ivan knew, not true. More puzzlingly, the report said that the existence of an investigative unit 'was not volunteered to the panel (by SARS's senior management) until it was revealed in the media'. This was contradicted by the report itself, which, on pages 17 and 18, quoted from Ivan's own statement to the panel that 'a unit (...) known by different names, including (...) the NRG and later the High Risk Investigations Unit, (was created) to conduct surveillance, investigate and monitor those involved in the illicit economy' at SARS. The report also said that 'Mr Pillay provided the panel with (...) a submission which deals with issues related to the (unit), its resources and funding.' According to the report, Ivan's first statement to Sikhakhane about the investigative unit was made on 14 September 2014, a month before the first 'rogue unit' story appeared in the *Sunday Times*.

The Sikhakhane panel concluded that the establishment of the High Risk Investigations Unit 'without the requisite statutory authority was indeed unlawful'.[277]

It was enough for Moyane to quickly expedite the suspensions.

The day that Muzi Sikhakhane started work, he asked for a confidential meeting with Ivan and confided in him that 'this matter will be a political hot potato'. It should have rung more alarm bells than it did. Ivan thought Sikhakhane would be able to 'manage the political pressures', as he put it. That was clearly a mistaken assumption.

He wonders what could have happened to Muzi. In his conversations with the panel, it had not posed a single question on a rogue unit. If the question had been put, Ivan says, he would have gone into more detail about the investigative unit's legal basis.[278]

But perhaps to do that would have been useless too. The Sikhakhane report in the end did not reflect anything Ivan presented. 'They did not take my submission into account at all,' he tells me, still in disbelief. 'They just ignored it.' The report was almost immediately leaked to the *Sunday Times*.

Tentative talk about a meeting with Sikhakhane later – initiated by Sikhakhane himself – does not result in it ever taking place. Ivan delays answering until he has resigned from SARS and thereafter responds via a common acquaintance, but there is silence after that. Ivan and Yolisa Pikie will at some point hear, through the grapevine that Sikhakhane seems convinced that they – the 'rogue unit', presumably – are threatening him. 'I think Zuma and Tom have been messing with his head,' says Ivan. Advocate Muzi Sikhakhane will later surface as Jacob Zuma's lawyer in the latter's corruption trial.

Clearly, Tom Moyane was very happy with the opinion he received. So happy that he refused to read Ivan's response to it, however much Ivan and Yolisa had spent days and evenings before their suspension meticulously refuting each and every accusation. 'No, I haven't read it,'

Moyane told him curtly, when he came to discuss it on 4 December, a day before his suspension. He also told Ivan not to circulate his response among the chief officers at SARS. 'At this stage I do not consider it appropriate that you share your views (with the chief officers) as this could be construed as an attempt to influence or impose your own views on them.'[279]

The final version of the Sikakhane report, to be released publicly in a few months' time, will not reflect any elements of Ivan's response. Nor will the *Sunday Times*. On 21 December, the Labour Court rules that Ivan's and Pete Richer's suspensions by Tom Moyane are unlawful and they must be reinstated, but it is to no avail: the two are told by SARS that they will just be suspended again.

The atmosphere is fast becoming despondent. They can try the courts again but that costs money and SARS won't assist with legal fees. SARS's insurers AIG have, presumably at the behest of Tom Moyane, written up a separate rule specifically excluding cover for legal costs of Ivan Pillay, Johann van Loggerenberg and a few others.[280] The suspended men have also learned that Moyane has contracted KPMG to investigate the 'rogue unit' yet again.

Three days later, on 24 December, the head of the Hawks, former MK comrade Anwa Dramat, is suspended to make place for Berning Ntlemeza, who is soon to lead police action against the SARS investigators.

City Press meanwhile reports that the education department is now practically ruled by officials of SADTU, an ANC-supporting teachers union, which allocates principals' jobs to one another, regardless of capability.[281] As in the case of the maintenance court, more and more unions, once principled defenders of human rights, of the social contract and the national interest, seem to have lost their concern for the well-being of the institutions for they work. At SARS, the same NEHAWU union I once encountered in the maintenance court supports Moyane.

Rolling back seven years of work to implement a robust performance reward system based on productivity and ethical behaviour, Moyane's reinstatement of automatic bonuses and easy promotion for favourites was all that took.

Murder for water
Christmas 2014

We are slowly getting used to things deteriorating when, suddenly, there is a murder at department of water affairs. 'Mark-Anthony Williams has been killed,' Bart says over the phone. 'Shot five times by intruders, just a few days ago on the 23rd. He was a deputy director at the department. Friends of his say that he was exposing corruption and have asked ZAM to alert the South African media '

When I contact these friends – former anti-apartheid activists in the Netherlands, who met Mark-Anthony in the days of the struggle – they confirm that they don't believe that he was killed by burglars, as the police would have it. His wife Emelia says he was concerned about corruption at the department. This is corroborated by a former close co-worker I meet at a restaurant in Pretoria. 'Contracts were given to companies that did not have any water expertise at all, but were run by friends of highly placed people,' the co-worker says. 'He used to fight with those who wanted such deals. It came to an explosive confrontation at a meeting in Centurion. One week after that meeting he was dead.'

'Here they are,' Mark-Anthony Williams had said to Emelia that night, just before Christmas, when burglars broke the front door down. Emelia, friends and colleagues all say that he had been aware that someone was after him.

When I visit the water affairs department in Pretoria and talk with colleagues, I find that he was working in a window-free meeting room prior to his death. 'Here they can't shoot me,' he told the colleague who asked. After the murder, the colleagues had the impression that Mark-Anthony's documents had something to do with what had happened. His office was sealed by security guards during Christmas; his secretary Riana was not allowed to enter even after the holiday. 'The head of security said nobody was allowed to get at the papers,' she says when I visit the department.

She has no idea what papers were so sensitive. The three colleagues Riana introduces me to and with whom I speak – always with the doors closed, in their small offices on this grey, poorly lit passage in a grey government building in Pretoria – don't know either. At least not exactly. 'There are five contracts going on for dam projects throughout the country. They all go to companies that are favoured by our political bosses. So not necessarily the companies that are best at building dams,' says one of the colleagues, an engineer. 'Mark-Anthony could have had fights about any one of these projects. But it could also have been about the project in Lepelle.'

He explains that Lepelle is a R3-billion, water-and-sewage project in northern Limpopo province. The contract was concluded with a small, relatively unknown engineering company, LTE, in 2014. 'The CEO of LTE, Thulani Majola, is a good friend of Nomvula Mokonyane, the minister of water affairs. The company was recently in the news because the chairman of the board resigned. He said he did not want anything to do with irregular contracts.' The engineer hands me a copy of a newspaper cutting on the affair. It says that the chairman of the board of LTE, an Asogan Pillay (no relation to Ivan), had not even asked for water contracts. His company got the deal irregularly, apparently via CEO Majola; the board chairman wanted nothing to do with it.[282]

A few days after Asogan Pillay had publicly asked questions about the suspicious contracts, armed intruders broke into his house. There were no casualties but, a few days later, Pillay resigned as chairman of LTE. All this had happened in the first half of December 2014; not even two weeks before the murder of Mark-Anthony Williams.[283]

For better and worse
Early 2015

How good we've had it in recent years. I had enough time to edit the story projects in our new African Investigative Publishing Collective, the AIPC, only interrupted by Vani's school run. Now, both Vani and I have to help: printing, finding information on the internet, borrowing her phone to circumvent any tapping, running errands. Ivan has been denied access to his office where all the work-related information still is, so he needs to find the documentary information needed to refute from scratch the present and probable future accusations and investigations against him, Johann, Pete and all the others. As for her part, Vani can't find her little bits of jewellery – family pieces given to her as birthday presents and kept for safekeeping at the office – though we can't be sure where or how exactly that happened, since doors were left open when the cardboard boxes of personal items were delivered.

It is a difficult change from having had not only an office, but also administrative and secretarial support. 'I hate that you don't have a secretary now,' I tell Ivan, only half joking.

Only a few years back, I was stressed because I thought Ivan was one of those in the running for Oupa Magashula's replacement. He had the highest rating among managers, the best record. He did not want to be the commissioner, had not applied but I – clearly mistakenly – was worried that Zuma just might appoint him. I even fought with Sunday, who was eager to see 'makhulubaas' become something really big. If we were moving up, she felt, that would by implication move her up too. 'You don't think I am still going to babysit for you if you do that,' she had almost furiously thrown down the gauntlet once, when Ivan had considered buying a smaller car. 'I can't work for people who drive an Uno.'

She was not actually working for us anymore when the SARS vacancy came up, but still felt strongly about such things. She had assumed that, as a wife, I would be eager for Ivan to achieve such a promotion too. But I was by then thoroughly fed up with being Madam Deputy Commissioner. I also thought that Ivan should be working less, not more. 'It's not going to happen!' I almost screamed at Sunday when she jabbered on about it.

Only Ivan's work subscription to the Sunday newspapers is still intact, paid for the year, and so almost mockingly, the *Sunday Times* lands in our yard every week. Almost every time, it comes with yet more headlines about Ivan and his 'rogue unit'. The stories, eventually totalling thirty-six, seem never-ending. 'We can't even cancel our subscription,' says Ivan. 'Only SARS can do that. I have asked them a few times already.'

Making Celia cry

Most of what we hear through the few colleagues who still dare speak to us remains depressing. There is a hunt at SARS for anyone seen as close to the previous management. If you're considered a friend of Ivan's, you are toast. No one argues with Tom Moyane or the favourites he has picked from the old and disgruntled – Jonas Makwakwa, Luther Lebelo – or the new, often dubious, appointments he is bringing in, like an IT manager who doesn't seem to know anything about computers.[284] You invite disciplinary action and suspension if you do.

We hear how several former colleagues who are still there, presumably anxious about their jobs and career prospects, also try to get on the new man's good side. One, noting that Ivan's former secretary Celia continues to process mails that are addressed to Ivan, tells Tom Moyane. Informing him that Celia 'is doing work for the previous commissioner' predictably enrages Moyane. He strolls over and shouts at Celia, who cries.

Another manager whose birthday party we once attended – and who then waxed lyrical about his admiration for Ivan – is overheard muttering that 'Ivan and his unit' were really 'doing bad things'. Yet another one publicly gushes that Tom Moyane is the best commissioner SARS ever had. A fourth, a friend we thought of as a comrade, has even started talking about there being too many Indians at the office. There was one Indian, precisely, in SARS top management. There are only a few others in middle management.

'The man is mad,' says our old friend Jessie Duarte about Tom Moyane, when we meet her in a last-ditch effort to raise what now amounts to a risk of serious damage to SARS. Adrian Lackay, who still works at SARS at this point in time, has come along to meet Jessie to confirm that experienced people are on their way out; that Tom doesn't show any knowledge of, or even any interest in, the core business of SARS; that those who oppose Tom's purges may soon be purged themselves; that incapable people, Tom's friends, are appointed into powerful positions instead. Jessie adds: 'I hear that from others, too.'

The response is encouraging; we hope that Jessie, being in the top six of the ANC, may do something to help. Ivan impresses on her that SARS is the goose that lays the golden eggs: the institution that funds housing, health, water, grants and services for the poor. He explains that it is not about he or Pete Richer or anyone wanting their jobs back; his concern is that SARS may be damaged by what Moyane is doing. She says she is also worried about that and promises to raise it with the top six and the president, to whom she is close.

'I don't know if it will do any good,' says Ivan. 'But we can always hope.' He will later tell me that he had little expectation that our meeting will help much, because a few weeks after Moyane's appointment, he had already seen Jessie's former husband John Duarte and their son at a SARS event, as special guests of the new SARS commissioner. 'Still,' he shrugs. 'It is worth a try.'

Forced removals
March 2015

Robert McBride and the institution he heads, the Independent Police Complaints Directorate (IPID), are accused of protecting suspended Hawks head Anwa Dramat. Urged in a variety of ways to find against Dramat and refusing to do so, the institution is now in trouble itself. The *Sunday Times* has been reporting on an accusation that IPID has falsified a report to protect Dramat.[285] McBride is suspended on 12 March, while others at IPID are soon to follow.

The Zondo Commission will later hear, to the sound of audience jaws dropping, how new Hawks head, former apartheid policeman Berning Ntlemeza, pressurised an IPID official to find Dramat guilty, since it would be necessary for him, Ntlemeza, to permanently take over control of the Hawks. 'Otherwise, he – Ntlemeza – implied ... my life would be threatened,' testifies the official.[286] When the bullying at IPID doesn't have the desired effect, police minister Nhleko obtains legal opinion to justify accusing McBride of falsifying his own report about Dramat, and then suspends McBride. His replacement at IPID proceeds to ignore and put aside all cases the organisation has on Zuma associates in the police force.[287]

The pattern is repeated again and again. Two months after Robert McBride's suspension, it is the turn of new NPA head Mxolisi Nxasana, an attorney with twenty years of experience and a former head of the Durban branch of the Black Lawyers' Association. Nxasana is forced out after Mzilikazi wa Afrika and friends reveal in the *Sunday Times* that the man was once charged for murder when he was 18 years old. Though the young Nxasana was found innocent, the point of the article is that Nxasana must still go because he should have disclosed the fact.

Nxasana fights back for a bit, commenting that he suspects the campaign is political because, he says, there are 'rumours that I want to reinstate charges against President Jacob Zuma, (and) that I want to reinstate charges in (another case involving ANC politicians)'.[288] But when he is made to understand that there is no way he will be allowed to stay on, he accepts a golden handshake. He will be replaced[289] by the inexperienced and pliable Shaun Abrahams, soon to be nicknamed Shaun the Sheep. Helped by his own deputy, Zuma-aligned Nomgcobo Jiba and also by Berning Ntlemeza, Abrahams will soon start criminal prosecutions against practically all who have been smeared in the *Sunday Times* campaigns: Oupa Magashula, Pravin Gordhan, Ivan, Johan Booysen, Anwa Dramat, Shadrack Sibiya and Robert McBride, among others.[290]

In September, Denel head Riaz Saloojee is suspended on trumped-up charges to make way for a new board and CEO, who are both eager to conduct business deals with Zuma's friends, the Guptas. He will be made to resign two months later.[291]

Project Phoenix

As urgent tax cases against Mark Lifman, Robert Huang and others go nowhere, SARS is paying millions to Bain & Company, a consultancy firm brought in by Moyane to restructure the tax agency in expensive, unnecessary, dislodging and damaging ways, as the Nugent Commission of Inquiry[292] will later show. The reason for the entire exercise is unclear since SARS's systems have received praise both locally and internationally. 'By the time we were suspended, SARS had already been weaned away from consultants,' says Ivan. 'We had developed an internal capability of analysts, designers, engineers and operational policy makers. We provided consultancy and support services to the department of home affairs, the Government Employees Pension Fund, the Eastern Cape health department, the financial cluster multi-agency working group on procurement, and the office of the public protector. If there was still a need for consultants, it would only be for very specific projects with a limited scope.'

In four years' time, the Nugent Commission will reveal that Bain and Moyane had met at least a year before the latter's appointment to discuss the mammoth restructuring project. According to an affidavit made to the commission by Bain South Africa head Vittorio Massone, that meeting was also attended by Sipho Maseko, a close Zuma associate, and CEO of Telkom, the parastatal phone company. He had previously contracted Bain for Telkom and had also introduced the consultants to President Zuma.[293] Another close associate of Zuma's, Duma ka Ndlovu, had also attended. According to Massone, more such meetings had ensued.

Duma ka Ndlovu is a playwright who has written SABC dramas, a background which may give rise to the question what would equip him to engage with SARS. However, his reputation as a member of the president's so-called kitchen cabinet[294] may explain his role as an 'external consultant' for Bain, as Massone calls him in his affidavit. We talk to two independent sources who surmise that Duma ka Ndlovu is not only associated with the massive restructuring exercise at SARS, but also involved in the appointments of key Zuma allies to other state institutions. The sources, who have separate knowledge of at least two such incidents, talk of a Project Phoenix as the apex plan, authored by Bain together with Zuma's inner circle, to establish and consolidate the Zuma network's hold on the state.

Vittorio Massone, in his evidence before Judge Nugent, also talks of Project Phoenix. According to him, the project was simply about Bain 'getting business in all of South Africa's public institutions'. But at least in the case of SARS, Phoenix also included 'identifying individuals to neutralize'.[295]

They had Ivan and the others targeted long before Moyane even got to SARS.

Meanwhile, we hear from former colleagues that the new commissioner snaps at anyone who doesn't extol his virtues, on one occasion reprimanding a manager for 'not saying anything to support' him at a meeting. At visits Moyane makes to SARS offices all over the country, 'a red carpet must be laid out for him; people must sing and dance, and bring him presents', an official involved in organising these events tells us. Those who contradict or disagree with him are rewarded with investigations into their conduct and if fault is found – which is often – suspension.

The KPMG team, hired by Moyane to investigate everything the previous management did from 2003 onward, digs up documents and interrogates anyone who ever worked with Ivan, Johann or Pete Richer, except those perceived to be friendly to them. 'No, don't speak to that one,' a friend tells us a KPMG investigator was told in his presence, when the man attempted to interview him. Johann offers KPMG all his tax investigation documents, but there is no interest.[296]

When, during another SARS meeting, the new commissioner impresses on those present just how scary the previous leadership was – clearly relishing a phrase about a 'climate of fear' caused by the 'rogue unit' in the Sikhakhane report – a legal manager, outspoken Makungu Mthebule will tell him he must be mistaken. 'Everyone is actually scared of *you*,' she says, referring to the by-now countless Moyane-inspired investigations into people he finds disagreeable.

The story, as it is later related to us, then continues with Moyane getting so upset with Mthebule that he storms out of the meeting, locks himself in his office and refuses to come out, causing his loyal sycophant and now exco member Jonas Makwakwa to turn to Mthebule angrily, saying, 'You have upset the chief!' From that day on Moyane will refuse to speak to Mthebule in their shared Shangaan language, preferring to deal with her in English.

Head of the informal business division, Sobantu Ndlangalavu, will later also mention pervasive fear under Moyane in a statement before the Nugent enquiry. Ndlangalavu will also reveal, more bizarrely, that Moyane himself seemed very scared too: he had trees in the parking area cut because 'these might present a security risk'. Moyane also seemed to believe that others, even his own victims, mysteriously exercise power over him. A fired official tells us that Moyane gave him his walking orders with tears in his eyes, saying, 'Look now what you made me do.'

Maybe this answers Ivan's question why Zuma and friends would not let the old SARS leadership go in peace. The increasing number of faulty people at the top of the South African state, including the bizarre Tom Moyane, perhaps partly explains that.

Il faut lancer des fausses pistes, a French secret service agent told me long ago. Toujours, des fausses pistes. False tracks. Bamboozle. Fake news, we would call it nowadays. How better to protect your own moves than to draw attention to others whom you are replacing? You call them rogues, firstly, to destroy their credibility should they speak out against what has happened. Secondly, and perhaps even more importantly, show them to be bad. Not just bad because of an incident or two, but totally, completely bad. So bad that reputations are destroyed, so bad that, in Lynne Brown's words, they will never work again.

Because only then those who do wrong can make it appear as if they are crusaders against corrupt others. The good civil servants are the enemy. It's not an exaggeration, a misconception, a mistake, or even paranoia; they actually are. 'A foreign virus,' Ivan once called those who try to do a good job in a corrupt environment.

And so history is rewritten.

The narratives in the *Sunday Times* and also now on Facebook and Twitter, start to spiral: from SARS spying on Zuma, to being a cabal, then anti-ANC, then pro-white. The rogue unit still exists, but now it does so outside SARS. At this stage the facts don't matter at all anymore: the rogues are still conspiring, still serving white monopoly capital, now underground but still very powerful. It wants to bring white rule back. It is anti-black and therefore the enemy. The RET choir on social media increasingly describes other sidelined comrades and purged civil servants as being on the side of the rogues, and at the service of apartheid agendas and white monopoly capital.

In 2019, five years after the suspensions and removals of all SARS senior management and the subsequent exit of close to two thousand employees, Mzilikazi wa Afrika and his red-eyed fanatic Zuma-aligned colleague Piet Rampedi post Twitter photographs of what they say are SARS 'rogue unit' vehicles following them in the street. I have flashbacks to Kinshasa again: particularly my last glimpse of the *Journaliste en Danger* office with two officials frantically texting on their phones, leaving me with the distinct impression that they were sending death threats to themselves.

Factually, tax criminals Huang and Lifman, whose investigations have been stopped by Tom Moyane, are not black at all. The president's nephew, Khulubuse Zuma, and his mine, acquired to service the Guptas,[297] have reduced thousands of very black miners and their families to starvation. The businessmen in Jacob Zuma's web are generally worse employers – and pay less tax, if at all – than many established companies, which have long been behaving better than they used to precisely because of struggle by combative unions.

But never mind all that. We must be on the wrong side, so that they can be right. If *we* are pro-white and pro-apartheid, then Zuma's people are the rightful inheritors of the ANC and the struggle.

The ticking clock
7 April 2015

Mac is retiring. 'I am turning 80,' he says when we meet at the airport to catch up quickly during one of his many travels. 'I really should slow down. So I told Zuma that I am retiring on my birthday, on the 22nd.' We used to joke that 22 April was Lenin's birthday, too.

We are deep into Zuma's second term now, and frequent cabinet reshuffles have gotten rid of virtually all ministers who were any good at all. Collins Chabane, who by all accounts had tried to run a tight, procedural ship in the ministry of public services, is dead: his car crashed on the freeway last March as a result of a truck driver making a dangerous U-turn.[298]

Treasury under Finance Minister Nhlanhla Nene is reportedly under much pressure to keep dishing out money for questionable projects. 'I don't know why Nhlanhla Nene doesn't stand up,' says Ivan. 'He is also not doing anything about SARS.'

'When do you get out?' Pravin Gordhan will ask me rhetorically, in an interview years later, when I ask why he stuck it out with Zuma for so long. 'When do you know enough? When is it enough?' He must have been asked that question hundreds of times, he says. 'The nuclear deal was a big warning light, of course.' You could say that again. A recent nuclear agreement with Russia, in which Putin took a direct interest, confirmed an intention by the South African government to purchase a set of new nuclear power stations from Russian company Rosatom for R1 trillion. Exposed by Amabhungane months before, in February 2015,[299] it is the arms deal on steroids.

'Still, even then you think that if you keep defending the procurement rules and regulations, keep refusing to sign off on irregular paperwork, you will have an effect. But I noticed that then they'll get the deal done anyway, bypassing you,' Gordhan remarks. 'It is like a clock. You think the minutes are passing slowly as it is ticking. Then you look again and suddenly it's a year later and there's disaster all around.'

Even now, nobody in the ANC or government talks openly. All these are ANC matters, and such issues are pussyfooted around in-house, as has become the ANC way. The media do expose and attack corruption, including the suspicion of it in the nuclear deal, but the only really big public scandal, ongoing since 2009, is Nkandla, Zuma's palace, with its security upgrades that house chickens, and its swimming pool described as a fire emergency feature. It even makes international news, for example, in an article in the *Guardian* titled 'Zuma accused of corruption on a grand scale'.[300]

The public is rightly angry that so much money has been spent on the president's house. But the outrage about the Nkandla issue overshadows everything else and the focus on his house allows Zuma to play the victim once again. He did not even ask for the improvements, he says, and what is wrong with having a swimming pool? Can't a president have one? Can only white leaders of state have nice houses?

Ivan, incidentally, warned the president about tax consequences that might emanate from the Nkandla matter. After Public Protector Thuli Madonsela had found in early April 2014, that Zuma might have benefited unduly, Ivan met him to discuss it. In response to questions asked in Parliament, Ivan stated that SARS would deal with Zuma's Nkandla tax issue 'in the normal course of (its) duties and functions'.[301]

It can't have helped endear him to the president.

As Ivan is negotiating his permanent exit from SARS, helped by Jessie Duarte who has managed to involve the ANC to ensure a minimally fair deal, we talk to Mac about his birthday and his retirement after years of working close to Zuma. The job is obviously marked by the daily strain of having to defend the indefensible. But Mac simply will not talk about that. When I try, I only get speeches about armchair critics and taking responsibility in the structures: where was I at the last branch meeting? We leave the conversation at his turning eighty, even if we both know there is a lot more to his retiring than that.

Later

There is a new blow when the SARS board, just established by Nhlanhla Nene, endorses the Sikhakhane report. Though many legal experts agree that Sikhakhane's opinion, as Ivan has put it, 'errs in fact and in law', the board, headed by an Eastern Cape judge named Frank Kroon, echoes Sikhakhane's opinion that SARS must not 'gather intelligence'.

Maybe we should have expected this. The Kroon board is loaded with representatives from Tom Moyane's new exco, including Jonas Makwakwa, who has become Moyane's Mini-Me. It is still a shock that a judge is in agreement, though. It will later transpire that the board did not even consider or interrogate Sikhakhane's opinion; it just rubber stamped it. Later still, testifying at the Nugent Commission of Inquiry into Tax Administration and Governance, Kroon will withdraw his judgment and apologise for it.[302] But that will only happen three years from now. For the time being, the *Sunday Times* keeps writing that 'now two investigations' have vindicated the stories written by Mzilikazi and friends.

Even today you still find references from certain quarters to the Sikhakhane report. If it was all false, the argument will go, why was this report never set aside? The answer to that is that you can't set aside an opinion. It has no standing. You can agree with the lawyers and follow their opinions, or not.

I will later learn that our old friend Rudolf Mastenbroek, who is on the Kroon board, drafted the statement that endorsed Sikhakhane.

Kgosi Mampuru
7 May 2015

Ivan resigns from SARS together with Pete Richer, after a lengthy process about a settlement, during which Moyane once requested to meet with Ivan at Kgosi Mampuru prison in Pretoria. Was it an attempt to show Ivan where he was going, if Moyane, the former Correctional Services boss, had his way? 'I just smiled,' Ivan says. 'I told him I knew the place.' It was where he had often met the prisons colonel with whom he had worked in the Transnational Executive Authority before the 1994 elections.

In the end, Ivan and Pete Richer receive a payout of part of their remaining contracts. After the efforts of Deputy President Cyril Ramaphosa's office, roped in by Jessie, have gone nowhere, the settlement eventually came through, ironically after a rather unplanned intervention by President Zuma himself. A concerned Moe Shaik ran into Zuma at a conference, and asked the president why Ivan and Pete were still being victimised. Zuma responded defensively that he was not behind it, and that he had asked the deputy minister of finance, Mcebisi Jonas, to sort it out.

Jonas was surprised to hear that bit of news when contacted by Ivan, and agreed to help. At a subsequent meeting with both Jessie and Jonas, Zuma's mandate was tabled, with the settlement as a result.

Officially unemployed now, Ivan starts looking for any state enterprise or private firm that will have him, Yolisa, Pete, Johann and similarly purged others. 'I worry about them. I still have my pension,' he says as we sit on the couch, going through our accounts. 'But others are still raising families.' Ivan checks with a number of accountancy firms and sends out feelers here and there about starting a consultancy, but no one will have anyone related to the 'rogue unit'. The country has become one giant Block M and everyone turns away.

On the bright side, most media remain professional. With the exception of the *Sunday Times*, they have all reported on Tom Moyane's purges.[303] Less brightly, the media make little difference on the practical side of things. On 16 May 2015, a few days after Tom Moyane and Ivan sign the agreement that states that his resignation will be the end of the matter and no further action will be taken against him, Moyane lays charges for a whole list of alleged illicit activities – early retirement and 'rogue unit' all combined – at the Brooklyn police station in Pretoria.[304] In subsequent investigations and prosecutions, different charges and different suspects will be picked from this document as the case keeps morphing.[305]

When SARS spokesman Adrian Lackay sends a letter with a full account of the damage wrought by Moyane at SARS to Parliament's Finance Committee,[306] it is ignored. Never mind that the committee is headed by Yunus Carrim, an old ANC comrade: nobody in Zuma's Parliament, or in the ANC, is brave enough to make noises about any purged struggle veterans. The only result of the letter for now is that Adrian Lackay is sued by Tom Moyane too, forcing him, as in our case, to incur high legal expenses.

All Tom Moyane's cases are funded by the taxpayer.

Blessers in fine silk

'Everything is going to pieces, sir,' says Nomsa,[307] an administrative manager who visits us sometimes, always at night, walking from Brooklyn Mall where she leaves her car to avoid it being seen outside our house. 'We are not collecting tax as we did. Instead we are getting instructions about things that have nothing to do with anything.' She recounts that all the women now have to wear stockings and heels, because the male management around Moyane says that they 'need something to look at', and that there are now silly events like Walks for Tax 'where we just march around promoting SARS'.

Nomsa describes an event in which all employees had to gather in the parking lot at head office to listen to Moyane speak. 'And then, sir, there is nothing important that he said. Just some pep talk about how great SARS is, especially he – Tom.' She adds that a fellow exco member 'was dancing around him as he was introducing him to us, talking about the commissioner's shirt that is of the finest silk and his suit that is such good quality, and how this man is the greatest blesser'. A blesser is a sugar daddy, understood in common parlance as a man who pays young girls for sex. Nomsa pauses when she sees my incredulous face. 'For real, you know! We are getting used to that nonsense. But that is what is going on!'

She continues, 'No one takes any decisions any more. Nobody knows if this way to collect tax is correct, or you should go somewhere else. If you go the wrong way and touch something that you must not touch, you are going to be investigated. So people are scared to do anything. They don't follow up, they refer, they postpone.'

The final report of the Nugent Commission of Inquiry[308] will describe, in 2018, how Tom Moyane 'arrived at SARS without integrity and then dismantled the elements of governance one by one'. It lists in great detail, quoting dozens of exasperated, often traumatised former and present employees, how enforcement capacity has been destroyed. The High Court Litigation Unit that processed cases of unwilling payers has, in the words of one witness, splintered to a 'shadow of its former self' so that now, due to fragmentation of units in the restructuring exercise, no one part of SARS has a complete view of one single case. Keith Hendricks, Western Cape head of SARS's organised crime project will tell the commission he could not believe his eyes when he 'looked at the new model and saw that (the organised crime project) was not there... That is how we were informed that it was disbanded.'

Similarly, the capacity to take action against companies suspected of trying to conceal assets from SARS was damaged, another witness states. 'Such an order (to act against such a company) used to require four to six signatures (from relevant superiors); now it is eight to even twelve. Hundreds of millions were lost (because of the delays).' Yet another witness reports how a gap of over nine billion rand had occurred in textile imports in 2015 alone after the customs compliance section was ripped apart too.

Smearing with the enemy
December 2015

Complaints against the *Sunday Times* 'rogue unit' stories, lodged by Pravin Gordhan, Ivan and Johann with the Press Council, are successful. The Press Ombudsman's verdict[309] that the paper must retract key allegations and apologise comes on 5 December, and welcome it is too; it's about time we had a nice gift from Sinterklaas again.

But for the time being, nothing tangible happens, and the reality that we still live in Zuma's South Africa is once again hammered home when a few days later, on the 10th, Minister of Finance Nhlanhla Nene is fired and replaced by Zuma-ite MP Des van Rooyen: the same Des van Rooyen who, in Parliament in 2012, told a SARS delegation that he didn't understand why they were going on about corruption and that he wanted to see 'a different exco' next time. The replacement is widely seen as placing South Africa's national treasury at risk and, for four days in December, the country will teeter on the brink of a meltdown. However, massive protests from the private sector, civil society and international investors, force President Zuma to remove Van Rooyen again. Lasting only these four days, from Thursday when he is sworn in to the end of the weekend, Van Rooyen will be immortalised under the name Weekend Special, a somewhat ill-fitting reference to a hit song by South African icon Brenda Fassie about a woman who is only paid attention by her lover on weekends.

Zuma doesn't put former Finance Minister Nene back, though. It will turn out later that he is irreparably out of favour because of his refusal to sign off on the Russian nuclear contract.[310]

The nuclear pressure was a step too far for Nene then, even if he had done little to help the embattled SARS management. We were thoroughly puzzled when Nene appointed the terrible Kroon committee to investigate the turmoil at SARS, because it was so loaded with Tom Moyane's supporters. We had thought that he was either uncaring, or scared of Zuma, or both; we now consider that Nene must have been rather too preoccupied with the pressure he was under regarding the nuclear deal to spend much time on SARS.

What remains a mystery to me, however, is the role played by our old friend Rudolf Mastenbroek who had drawn up Kroon's endorsement of Muzi Sikhakhane's 'rogue unit' report. For months I will keep trying to work out how Mastenbroek, that staunch anti-Zuma man, could sit beside Moyane's henchmen and do the very thing that sealed the downfall of SARS.

It is just so bizarre. Rudolf was critical of Ivan because he had seen him as too patient with Zuma and the ANC. Coming from the Scorpions, he had always remained close to prosecutors like Pretorius, Leask and Nel, who wanted to nail any and all ANC officials and office bearers for any whiff of corruption.

From time to time in the early 2000s, Rudolf had differed with Ivan in this regard, wanting a more radical approach. However, when he left SARS in 2013, we were not aware how extreme his negative feelings about Ivan had become. We were surprised when Pearlie Joubert who had been friends with Mastenbroek, told us – in the course of the complaint against the *Sunday Times* before the Press Ombudsman to which she had contributed an affidavit – that Rudolf had tried for two years after he had left SARS to get her to write negative stories about Ivan and Pravin Gordhan. According to Pearlie, Rudolf had called Ivan a 'bagman', who would do 'the dirty' for Gordhan in 'making certain cases go away'. Pearlie had ignored him, not thinking his allegations worth much.

When her colleagues at the *Sunday Times* started the 'rogue unit' stories, she was concerned that the Mastenbroek allegations might be fed into that mix. Mastenbroek, at the time, was married to *Sunday Times* editor-in-chief, Phylicia Oppelt. This was perhaps the reason she was very supportive of the stories that lambasted the then SARS management. Pearlie had tried to speak with Oppelt about it, but her interventions were rejected and she was eventually sidelined.

It was a shock for us to read in Pearlie's affidavit for the Press Ombudsman how much vitriol had come from Rudolf,[311] especially since he had always remained outwardly friendly with the Gordhans. And how could he possibly have joined forces with Zuma's new vassals at SARS? 'The enemy of my enemy becomes my friend,' Ivan smiles, despondently. 'Lots of people are like that.'

What Mastenbroek tried over a period of time to tell Pearlie Joubert leaves space for almost no other conclusion. His accusations against Ivan and Pravin Gordhan paint a worrying picture of a man apparently so consumed with anger that he has gone full circle, to the point of lapping up all the allegations in the dossiers in Zuma's web. Featured next to his own grievances were also the Mike Peega smears, labelling Johann van Loggerenberg a former apartheid spy, and the fabricated story that the SARS investigative unit had engineered the departure of Oupa Magashule by recording his ill-fated phone call to a female accountant.

Nevertheless, now that Weekend Special Des van Rooyen has left the finance building, hope glimmers again. On the Sunday evening of that weekend, a rumour does the rounds that Pravin Gordhan will be reappointed minister of finance and, as it turns out, that is true. Gordhan comes out with guns blazing on Monday morning, warning that state enterprises will no longer be used as 'personal toys' and that sound fiscal management will be the motto from now on.[312]

We feel like partying, but don't. The battle is far from over.

Through the Looking Glass
February 2016

There is a distorted feeling in the atmosphere as most South Africans begin to understand what is going on, but things continue in ways that have now become normal. Two months after the Press Ombudsman finds for Pravin Gordhan, Johann van Loggerenberg and Ivan, and the *Sunday Times* is ordered to retract key rogue unit allegations, their authors Mzilikazi wa Afrika, and his colleagues Piet Rampedi and Stephan Hofstatter, are still in their jobs in the *Sunday Times'* investigative unit. The only unit member forced out so far is Pearlie Joubert, who resigned last year because of her colleagues' 'unethical and immoral' practices', as she had said in her affidavit. Since then, while the 'rogue unit' fabricators still receive their salaries, she has to freelance, fending for herself and her children alone.

Ivan goes to see her once, when in Cape Town. 'It was a good conversation. But she sure swears a lot,' he says upon his return, a bit intimidated. I laugh out loud. Maybe I should have warned him. Pearlie is always 'fok' this and 'fok' that.

She is absolutely right, of course. There is just so much about which to say fok.

For instance, the fact that Pravin Gordhan is now being hunted by the police again, too. A list of twenty-seven questions about the rogue unit and Gordhan's suspected involvement has been sent to the new minister on 19 February, not even two months after his reappointment. It is mere days before he is supposed to deliver a crucial budget speech.

Gordhan blows his top when we meet. 'I am busy!' he shouts. 'They just put me here to make some sense of this country's dismal finances and now this!' When he calms down we look at one another and it is silent. 'Well,' he continues then, softly. 'It is probably precisely what they want me not to do.'

Gordhan is also obstructed at every turn by Tom Moyane at SARS. The tax commissioner openly defies the minister, refusing Gordhan's request to suspend Bain Consultancy's bizarre restructuring project, and Gordhan hits a wall on practically all other queries, too. 'The man keeps reminding me that he has the protection of Zuma,' Gordhan grunts. 'I get emails saying that 'he'll go to the president' to authorise this or that. It's either that, or he says that he happens to be very sick at the moment and cannot possibly respond.' At a press conference, Gordhan throws the gauntlet down publicly, saying that 'it is absolutely unacceptable for the head of a government entity to be defiant of the executive authority that is responsible for that entity. And if there is such defiance, one must ask the question what is there to hide.'

The president says nothing about the matter, but the dog whistling among his supporters against Gordhan and others who battle to save the economy continues. A new dossier, pointedly called 'Spiderweb', surfaced about a month ago, linking Gordhan, his predecessor Trevor Manuel and the Treasury to white businessmen. The dossier gives the individuals it mentions fancy code names, like King of Leaves and The Hustler and so on, but, intriguingly – as with much in the SARS 'rogue unit' narrative – it doesn't explain what misdemeanours all these individuals might actually have committed. The gist of it is that they are white and they are 'influencing'.[313]

The press ombudsman's verdict that the rogue unit stories were mostly wrong has not made any difference then. It has also not helped that Jessie Duarte, in a sweet, but awkward gesture of comradeship, invited Ivan, Robert McBride and Anwa Dramat to be her guests at the State of the Nation Address in Parliament earlier this month.

They did go, but Jessie did not consult them about their experiences or views, I understand when Ivan returns. Which is understandable. How do you raise the issue that one of Weekend Special's advisers, with whom the man had walked into the finance ministry, telling flabbergasted staff to take their instructions from these gentlemen is Ian Whitley, Jessie Duarte's own son-in-law? How do you even begin to ask her about the fact that the other adviser, Mo Bobat, works for Gupta-linked empowerment company Trillian that will later be found to have siphoned off millions from state coffers?

They sat in Parliament's gallery and listened to Zuma's speech. Between themselves, the men had joked about theirs having been a 'rogue's gallery'.

In January, *Business Day* editor Songezo Zibi is the second journalist forced to resign because of his resistance to the smear campaign in the *Sunday Times*, *Business Day*'s sister newspaper. He had his own team look at some of the allegations and concluded that there was little that was rogue about the SARS investigative unit. The purpose of what the *Sunday Times* had called a 'rogue unit' was tax investigations in risky, sometimes criminal, environments. Which is precisely why it was called the High Risk Investigative Unit. His team wrote about that, refuting the *Sunday Times* stories.

'I won't pass moral judgement on my colleagues at the *Sunday Times* but I also know that we did not struggle all that much to find information (about the SARS investigative unit) that they could not find, for some reason,' Zibi will write later.[314] 'One simply had to read the same documents they were reading in some instances. It made no sense.'

Like Nhlanhla Nene's exit from the ministry of finance, Zibi's departure from *Business Day* is shrouded in silence, but rumours abound of overall managerial interference in the Times Media enterprise, of which both the *Sunday Times* and *Business Day* are part.

2 March 2016

I can imagine *Sunday Times* editor Phylicia Oppelt already penning her next editorial 'Now even *Ministers* say we were right', when secret service minister David Mahlobo and police minister Nathi Nhleko appear together one autumn afternoon on prime time TV to affirm to the nation that the SARS rogue unit narrative is real. It is yet another bizarre experience. When have government ministers ever come out on TV to broadcast sensational allegations involving state officials, and so loudly too?

Nathi Nhleko, goat skin bracelet on his wrist as always, is sweating again, as he did last year when he called the swimming pool at Zuma's Nkandla residence a 'fire pool', i.e. a reservoir of water to protect the president's home from any fire that might break out. David Mahlobo is cool as a cucumber though as he pulls from under the podium something that looks like a cross between a table fan and a bread machine. 'This is a grabber,' he says proudly. 'It can overhear conversations on your mobile phone. They had that. The rogue unit had that.'

Grabber devices are powerful and very expensive.[315] They will later be mentioned in connection with South Africa's spy agencies, sometimes the international underworld, and ultimately with the South African police. No such device, however, has ever featured among any SARS equipment. There are accounts of what has been purchased, either by investigators or other SARS departments, and nobody has ever seen even a listing of it.

Shrugging is by now something Ivan does daily, but I can't help thinking back to *Alice in Wonderland* every time I realise that the country is now ruled by individuals who often seem stark raving mad.

Ozymandias

But then, in a press statement two weeks after Mahlobo and Nhleko appear on TV, on 16 March, Deputy Finance Minister Mcebisi Jonas reveals that the Gupta brothers offered him the position of minister of finance six months before, in October 2015. It is an indication that plans were already afoot then to remove Nhlanhla Nene. Jonas says the offer was made in the presence of Jacob Zuma's son Duduzane at the Gupta's place in Saxonwold, Johannesburg. He will add later that he was offered R600 million as a bonus for accepting the post. If he had done so he would have been compromised, and would have had no power to refuse to sign off on the nuclear deal, as his predecessor Nene had done. But he refused to be bought.

It is then for the first time that the ANC publicly acknowledges that there may be an issue with the brothers from Uttar Pradesh. ANC Secretary-General Gwede Mantashe issues an invitation to all who have something to say about the Guptas to come forward and tell the ANC about it. When he receives a response of exactly one person – former government communications head Themba Maseko who was fired in 2010 because he refused to allocate a R600-million advertising budget to the Guptas' *New Age* newspaper – the ANC still downplays the seriousness of the issue. If there is only one complaint, how bad can it be?

The attitude annoys Ivan. 'How do you issue a general invitation to people to come and just talk about the pressures they experience, to the very ANC that is regarded as a source of the pressure? How can you simply sit and wait and be surprised when they don't come? Gwede is only going through the motions here. It reminds me of Mr Evans in our primary school, shouting at black parents to come to his meetings.'[316] But nevertheless, something has changed. A lid has been lifted and, a little later, ANC veteran Mavuso Msimang blows the whistle as well.

Firstly, Msimang, formerly the director-general of home affairs, criticises the ANC's inquiry as an 'anaemic call'. In an op-ed in *City Press*, he lists what the ANC should act on: Mcebisi Jonas's statement about being offered the finance minister's post; the Gupta's use of strategic Waterkloof airport; Nhlanhla Nene's firing; and the removal of the heads of the intelligence services when they wanted to investigate the Guptas. Then, for the first time by a prominent ANC member and state official, Mavuso Msimang openly calls out Zuma. Ozzy, he calls him, after Ozymandias in Shelley's poem about a mighty pharaoh, Rameses II, on whose statue are inscribed these words: 'My name is Ozymandias, king of kings; Look on my works, ye Mighty, and despair!' At the end of the poem nothing is left of the statue, except for two huge stone legs and, half sunk in the sand, a shattered face with a 'frown, and wrinkled lip, and sneer of cold command.' No 'works', mighty or not, remain to look on either, except for a whole lot of desert.[317]

A few days later still, on 31 March, Ahmed Kathrada calls on Zuma to resign. He is Nelson Mandela's comrade in arms, former Defiance Campaigner, Treason Trialist and Robben Island prisoner, as well as the husband of Barbara Hogan. 'Dear Comrade President, don't you think your continued stay as president will only serve to deepen the crisis of confidence in the government of the country?' he writes in an open letter.[318] 'Are you aware that your outstanding contribution to the liberation struggle stands to be severely tarnished if the remainder of your term as president continues to be dogged by crises and a growing public loss of confidence in the ANC and government as a whole?... To paraphrase the famous MK slogan of the time, "There comes a time in the life of every nation when it must choose to submit or fight." Today, I appeal to our president to submit to the will of the people and resign.'

Zuma says nothing; the ANC leadership again says nothing, too. 'They are like a child that sits with a blanket over its head and thinks it can't be seen,' says Ivan.

The country is still far from open rebellion, however. Most state officials and others with families who depend on Ozymandias's reign won't talk yet, especially not if their bosses and municipal authorities are vassals of the new administration, which is often the case. Pravin Gordhan, when testifying at the Zondo Commission in 2018, will explain the deafening silence after the ANC's 'anaemic call' for statements, by saying that 'many were scared for their lives'.

Indeed, political murders in South Africa are on the increase. At the end of 2014, the Institute for Security Studies listed fifty-six hits in recent years in KwaZulu-Natal, Jacob Zuma's home province alone, mostly 'for positions of power in the ANC and structures of government'. It also reported that an assassination industry had arisen in that province and that there was 'a direct risk to South Africa's democratic institutions'.[319] Since then, assassinations of political competitors, whistle blowers and others perceived as obstacles have only increased further. A study done at the University of Cape Town in 2017 will put the tally at 291.[320]

Finally, on the third of April 2016 – presumably after much managerial interference and counter-interference – a new *Sunday Times* editor carries out the press ombudsman's instruction to publish an apology. Bongani Siqoko, who has replaced the sideways-promoted Phylicia Oppelt, has admitted the paper got 'certain things wrong' in its 'rogue unit' stories.[321] Among the 'certain things' Siqoko apologises for is the fact that a letter once written by Johann van Loggerenberg to Tom Moyane, which the newspaper described as a confession, 'was, in fact, a denial'.

The edition also carries an article written by Johann himself, titled 'Rogue Unit never broke the law and was very effective', and one by Ivan, which predicts almost literally what the Nugent Commission will later find: 'In time, the full measure of the damage caused to the South African Revenue Service arising from false news coverage will manifest itself in a tarnished reputation, questionable independence and lower levels of compliance with tax and customs law.'

The newspaper's about-turn will soon see fanatical Zuma-ite Piet Rampedi resign very angrily, while Mzilikazi wa Afrika and Stephan Hofstatter stay on, as cynics do, to write a few articles about Zuma government corruption.[322] I wait a bit for the new editors to call Pearlie Joubert back, but they don't.

The apology is a full page, with Ivan's picture on it. I have it framed.

The good civil servants
May 2016

'It is time to get together as civil servants,' says Ivan, and Anwa Dramat and Robert McBride feel the same.

Talking to the current ANC leadership clearly doesn't serve any purpose anymore. An attempt to galvanise the organisation into action on the single issue of comrades hounded out of state institutions proved to be a waste of time. In a meeting last April at Luthuli House, the three and other ANC veterans in similar situations asked for assistance and also for an intervention to repair the damage done to their workplaces. But ANC Secretary-General Gwede Mantashe, his deputy Jessie Duarte and Treasurer Zweli Mkhize[323] 'provided no meaningful response,' says Ivan, 'beside the usual waffle.'

According to Ivan, Gwede Mantashe had mainly solicited sympathy for himself. 'He said that indeed he finds it difficult to answer questions from the media and the public nowadays. He said he found himself up to his neck in shit every day. As if we should feel sorry for him. We told him and the others that, since we clearly were not receiving their support, we were going to act to defend ourselves.'

On 17 May 2016, the group of affected officials issue a press statement.

The manner in which officials were removed has followed a similar pattern. Internal documents or allegations from within institutions are leaked to select journalists. Working in tandem with anonymous sources, facts are distorted in the media. It is unclear how the leaks happen, but they do not originate from the accused. After the information is leaked, the institution in question then launches an 'investigation' into the accused officials, using news reports as pretext. The results of these 'investigations' are then leaked to the same journalists again.

During the 'investigations' the affected officials are suspended and prevented from defending themselves publicly. They are never called to answer to any allegations by the investigators. Any representation is usually ignored, distorted or rejected by the institution in question. The investigations are open-ended and the allegations constantly change. When an 'investigation' fails to reach a conclusion, the institutions enter into settlements with the officials. Later, based on the same allegations that preceded the settlement, officials are then criminally charged. It appears from this pattern that the intent is to hound officials out of institutions and destroy their credibility publicly.

Throughout, the affected officials are required to bear all the costs for their legal defence although the charges against them relate directly to the execution of their duties as state officials. The state, on the other hand, can rely on unlimited resources.

In all institutions cited here (the Hawks, IPID, SARS, the SSA,

Denel, Crime Intelligence[324] and the National Prosecuting Authority (NPA)), the effective top leadership was removed and replaced. The replacements then institute far-reaching structural and operational changes in the institutions. Often, the replacements themselves face legal challenges by public interest groups based on either their appointments, or their subsequent actions.'[325]

Invariably, where 'news reports' are mentioned, they mean the *Sunday Times*.

A week before the press statement, on 10 May 2016, an email appears on the old FAIR mailing list. Coming from a neighbour of its former small office in the building in Auckland Park, it reads: 'As to the office, apparently rent has not been paid since last year. The owners of the building have now changed the locks and put FAIR goods into storage.' The neighbour asks if anyone at all is interested in salvaging the situation. No one replies.

The mirth in the suffering
25 August 2016

It is a nippy spring day when a small crowd gathers outside the Hawks's General Piet Joubert building in Visagie Street in Pretoria. Ivan and his suspended friends are here, together with a group of good governance activists and NGOs, plus two supportive celebrities: legendary struggle advocate George Bizos and Judge Johann Kriegler, who presided over the Independent Electoral Commission in 1994. Ivan and Johann have been summoned here to answer to a warning statement issued by the Hawks on 'rogue unit' charges. The interrogator of the two is Nyameka Xaba, Berning Ntlemeza's sidekick.

It takes long. At one point I go in to ask, and a nervous receptionist tries hard to get a message 'from above' about proceedings. Eventually I am told we don't have to worry because 'there is no torture'.

TV crews have also come: ENCA, SABC and even ANN7 want to interview me, Ivan Pillay's wife. They all ask how I am feeling. How has this been for the family? How much are we suffering under all this? I feel irritated. Is this all it is then, a suffering family? Yes sure, Ivan has suffered, and is undoubtedly presently suffering under what must be the excruciatingly uninformed and probably crude interrogation by

Ntlemeza's adjutants. Former SARS investigators and officials, especially those who are now unemployed and have small children, suffer a lot. But their questions are about me. They want something personal from me, about our pain as a family, and I don't know what to say.

Our daughters may be affected a bit, I guess, though they seem the same as usual. Devi is here at the little gathering with some fellow student friends, good governance activists all of them. Vani, now back in Holland – this time of her own free will – to study neuroscience, just gets cross when she reads something in the papers we have not told her about first.

As for me, I don't suffer much at all, actually. As annoying and stressing as it is for Ivan, we generally still have good times together. As a journalist I find all this frightfully interesting; my only regret is that I can't practice any journalism about it, being an interested party. But, surely our feelings are not the point of all this? Isn't it about what is happening to SARS? The destruction in the country? With ancient Communist Youth workshop instructions still somewhere in my mind ('Always give information. Focus on the social justice issue and on the people. It's not about you.') I rattle on about how dealing with nasty cops has always been part of social struggles and we are not fazed at all, since we are here for that struggle, for a developmental state that can provide services to the dispossessed majority, and against looters and liars.

There are many post-revolutionary stories in this vein.

Our recent African Investigative Publishing Collective story on good civil servants showed that ethical officials have been victimised in other countries too. A Ghanaian High Court employee was beaten in the streets and fired on trumped-up allegations for refusing bribes; a Nigerian elections supervisor who had counted votes properly against her bosses' wishes was demoted to a faraway province, then shot at in her car. Compared to many others, we are very fine indeed.

But that is surely not all there is to it, my friend Bart says when I tell him about the interviews. 'You can't get away with some bland gloss-over about how we must be strong revolutionaries. You must have wondered if what happened to Mark-Anthony could not happen to Ivan, too. How did you deal with that?'

I frown, still thinking that we hadn't really been much affected. Ivan and I have been better off than those whose houses and cars were broken into, or homes raided by police; certainly better off than those now unemployed with small children, or than Robert McBride and the others at IPID, who face corrupt men with weapons, even if it means speaking in code over the phone and always changing venues and meeting places, like in the days of the underground. Come to think of it, Ivan did that too, for a while.

Maybe I am just thick, maybe it hasn't sunk in, have I been in denial? 'I know you always laugh a lot when telling me what is happening,' says Bart. 'I guess that's a coping strategy too.'

Well, yes. Of course there is that.

It had been one for my Oma Lenie, who would laugh at the ranting drunkards and cheating shopkeepers, even women who introduced herself as 'your husband's fiancée', in her neighbourhood. She would merrily chuckle, head thrown back, even if she didn't have a 'dime to scratch herself with', as she would have said. Humour had helped my mum and aunties, who had dealt with life's mishaps – problematic husbands, low-paying jobs, bad influences on wayward children – in much the same way. In South Africa, Maisy would see the fun side even of ingrained servitude and lack of privilege; her laughter had resonated from Soweto via Hillbrow to Yeoville, where Archie told his tales of philandering ANC bigwigs and mishaps in the underground. Later, Sunday had had me in stitches with her tales of Centurion's false prophets and weirdly racist neighbours; she could laugh even when narrating how as a child she had been beaten with a broom by a mḻungu who had found her residing illegally in her mother's servant's room. You don't want to make the children cry with such stories. 'You eat your own food and you laugh at your own jokes,' Devi and Thandi had accused us, once, when we had so been so engrossed in her merry anecdotes that we had forgotten about their lunch.

So many things in what happened recently have in fact been hilarious. Like Yolisa and Adrian gravely performing mock political discussions on Radical Economic Transformation in flowery ANC jargon at our dining room table. Or Sri – back for a holiday after relocating to India – asking, genuinely puzzled, if Moyane and his trusted little group of new executives 'now thought it was their job' to still fight the 'rogue unit' even if Ivan and the others had left SARS over a year ago. Or former colleagues at SARS telling us about the little concrete bunker Moyane had ordered to be built for himself inside the SARS garage, just for his own car, an action thought to have sprung from fear of witchcraft.

Hearing this story, Ivan had mischievously suggested that someone should sprinkle some baby powder around the mini-garage. Of course, we hadn't done that but we had laughed about the idea of it for days.

SARS's newsletters have become an endless source of mirth, too. The weekly missives, which had previously contained practical information interspersed with references to 'higher purpose', now carried large portraits of Tom Moyane himself in every issue and detailed reports of his valiant fights against the rogue unit. One newsletter announced that SARS was now embarking on a SARS Trek under Captain Tom, and featured a drawing of Tom Moyane in a little space ship.

There were also the acts that were devoid of any sense of reality, like Moyane's insistence that Ivan should personally pay back over a R100 million that had been spent on SARS's investigative unit. Moyane had obviously not realised that this logically meant that Ivan, as the owner of the unit, would then need to be paid out the many billions from tax dodgers that the unit had brought into SARS. The performance by the two ministers and their grabber on national TV was also a sight to behold, as was the drama surrounding Weekend Special at the finance ministry. 'They are so bad at being bad,' Devi said.

When I relate my conversation with Bart to Ivan, he says he has just seen the draft KPMG report that has been doing the rounds in the media. 'They write such ridiculous things, so I do laugh, too. But it's also sad. They try to make Johann's charity organisation[326] sound crooked by saying that "it may be possible that it has a foreign bank account in Liechtenstein", but they also say that "no evidence confirming this could be found by us". About me they write they cannot really establish that I gave Ronnie Kasrils a reduction on his tax as a favour, but "given all that is going on around Mr Pillay, it may well be so". These are forensic investigators! Which is what makes it so terrible. They just write what those who pay them want to hear.'

Other than marvelling at the outlandishness of it all, he says, he and Johann and Yolisa have been busy. 'From the first few strange occurrences, like the leaks to the *Sunday Times*, you have to run around to find out what is actually going on. Are they really going to slaughter SARS, the goose with the golden eggs? For a long time you think that they can't be that stupid. So you spend time reading, listening, asking around, hearing from others. Then, when you realise that this is really happening, you go to the Labour Court. Then it gets worse: They set KPMG on you, the police, prosecutions. The smears continue. You are then busy defending yourself: trying to get a reasonable settlement from SARS, talking to lawyers, going to the Press Ombudsman.'

Part of the defence, which is a lot of work all by itself, consists of finding out what the attackers are actually doing, he adds. 'The blows are clear enough, but where will the next one land, and to what effect? Who is pulling the strings, and where?' As we speak, word on the street is that the prosecutors are meeting with Tom Moyane, and that Moyane, in turn, is meeting with Zuma's son Duduzane. KPMG seems to be interacting, besides with Moyane, also with Belinda Walter and shady businessman Mark Lifman. A few months from now, in October, Zuma loyalist and secret service head Arthur Fraser will be seen entering KPMG headquarters together with Lifman.[327]

Then, of course, you don't just have to defend yourself, but the state as well. 'As soon as you realise that the same strategies are being used to remove others, you connect with them too. You talk to whistle blowers, uncover what is happening elsewhere. You realise that Zuma is putting people in place whom he can control: people with low self-esteem, people who are full of resentment. You realise that he does that on purpose, because such people, once selected by Number 1 himself, will be eternally grateful and will loyally defend the man to the end. Their other characteristic is that they are not competent, they are warped, but that is precisely why they are so dependent on him.'

Ivan will later write a short draft note (which he is readying for publication) on how the Zupta (a mocking fusion of Zuma and Gupta coined by Julius Malema) takeover of arms of the state, has in its progress come to resemble an intelligence operation. 'The replacement of independent state officials by warped individuals, recruited not in spite of, but precisely because of their weaknesses, is the first sign of this,' it says. 'The handler at the top needs his agents to be flawed, since he uses their faults to ensure compliance.' The president now handles his appointees as if he were an intelligence officer, tasking and managing them where and if necessary. The note continues: 'Government systems, often hindrances to this style of instructions and tasking, are then broken to make this possible. As everything around him crumbles, Number One becomes even more powerful.'

In the end, the new operating system resembles a criminal syndicate, 'in which the lower ranks are allowed to do their small scams, as long as they comply with the scams of the higher-up'. Crucially, the note concludes, obstacles to the plans must be crushed. 'It is how we at SARS became the enemy.'

September 2016

Tom Moyane's chief officer at SARS, Jonas Makwakwa, has been caught depositing a large amount of cash in small bunches into ATMs. The money, totalling R1.2 million, has gone into accounts belonging to him and a girlfriend, Kelly-Ann Elskie, who also works at SARS. Perhaps thinking that by depositing small amounts every time he will avoid detection, Makwakwa is caught numerous times on the cameras that every ATM is equipped with.

The matter was reported to Tom Moyane by the Financial Intelligence Centre in May, the *Sunday Times* reveals, but, contrary to the swiftness with which Moyane acted against Ivan, Johann, Adrian and others, this time he remains passive. The case will only surface again in December 2018, when the Hawks finally hand a report on it to the NPA, where it has stayed.

The newly appointed public protector Busisiwe Mkhwebane, a Zuma acolyte, will later investigate, upon a complaint by Jonas Makwakwa himself, how his actions became public knowledge.

The biggest fish
October 2016

When I come home from the gym one day, I find Ntlemeza's sidekick Nyameka Xaba, the brigadier who interrogated Ivan and Johann, and three other burly policemen in front of our house. They are here to deliver charges. Oupa Magashula and Pravin Gordhan are being served, too. I understand that it is about the matter of the early retirement.[328]

I tell them that I sadly won't invite them for tea because I know what they are coming for; that this is a less than honourable job; and that, if they were operating in the interests of justice, I would certainly be more hospitable. The three other men look away uncomfortably, but Brigadier Nyameka Xaba puts on a jolly act. He smiles and banters: don't be like that, we don't have to be unpleasant, right? I continue, asking him which criminals he thinks he is after here, and why. I can be really brave when it is patently clear I am not in any danger. Our street is in a mainly white neighbourhood after all, and I am still a white madam myself. They won't shoot me, not here, not yet.

'It's because these are big fish,' answers Xaba finally, as he and his group make their way back to the vehicle. 'You are working for the biggest fish,' I shout after them.

The charge doesn't have any chance of succeeding. The case will be dropped within weeks – right after Vlok Symington's evidence and the Hawks' suppression of same comes to light – by the same Shaun Abrahams who recently announced theatrically, repeatedly drawing out the names of 'Mr Pillay, Mr Gordhan and Mr Magashula' like an overacting dramatist at a poetry reading. Abraham's grave statement that now 'the days of disrespecting the National Prosecuting Authority are over' won't age well.

But again, reputational damage is done. Preparations for a small consultancy by Ivan, Yolisa and Sri will fail as a result.

As the policemen drive away after delivering the charges, the double irony of black policemen serving charges in a middle-class, not quite mixed neighbourhood, and the white madam shouting after them, strikes. Brigadier Xaba and his bosses may live in an area like this, but the other three probably don't. If any of the three men were to walk around here individually, they would probably be quickly picked up by our neighbourhood watch WhatsApp group. Pictures would start to appear on our phone screens: 'Who knows who this gentleman is?' 'Loitering – or worse?' 'I have seen him more than once. Maybe lives in the abandoned building that we have complained about.'

Some of the neighbours are really sweet though, like those next door, who have kept my research papers safe and who will never join any 'OMG I've seen a black person' conversations. Or Hildegard opposite, who identifies with everybody who is poor because her family came from poor Afrikaans roots too. I interview them and other neighbours for a new ZAM project on South Africa, called 'Between Bitter Almonds and Good Hope'.[329] This particular project chapter is called 'The Paradise of Coffee and Milk.' It is a quote I got from Hildegard, because she dreams of that: some country beyond poverty, power struggles, racism, crime and hate.

Yeah. It would be nice.

Sunday tells me that the white teachers and parents at the affluent school where she is now teaching – as an assistant, always the assistant, always underpaid – bark at her about Zoooma this and Zooooma that.

She will respond, stubbornly, that she just loves Zuma. What else is she going to say?

Still October

Fezeka Kuzwayo has just died on the 8th of this month, and Ivan is preparing to attend her funeral in Durban on the 15th when, one evening after dark, John Duarte visits us unannounced. This has not happened before. Mostly when we see the Duartes, it is when we visit Jessie's house. They have hardly ever come here, John certainly not alone. Surprised, we welcome him, offer whisky. We sit at the dinner table and wait for John to tell us what this is about.

After a gulp, arms on the table, looking straight at us, he comes to the point. 'We just have to take it, you know. The companies, the land, the banks. We can't go on like this. The white bosses, they still rule us, even today.' More animatedly, hands waving into the air, his eyes fierce. 'So we must just take it! Like they did in Zimbabwe and Mozambique!' Yeah, because that worked so well there, too, I want to say, but I can't get in a word edgewise. Ivan just sits and listens, eyes thoughtful.

Then, sadder, more reflective, John talks of the many times he ran into white walls in his life: from the day he had to explain to his young son in the public swimming pool that the great slide was there for other children and not for him, until the time a white boss explained to him that the advertised salary of R2000 was only for whites and that a coloured bookkeeper could not expect more than R500. 'I had already bought so many things for my family with that R2000 in my mind.' You have trauma, I nod, and immediately realise that I sound patronising. His face tight, he says, 'It's not trauma. It's rage.'

Then: 'I know what you want to say now. We'll run it all into the ground. And why not? Let's go back to the jungle. Then at least we'll be equal.'

We try to convince him that we might still aim for equality in a better way, by getting the state in order instead of destroying it. But he changes topic and talks of the media, how the media are after us, how we must stick together because the media have damaged his family with Weekend Special reports that identified his and Jessie's son-in-law. I ask if he thinks that the media articles at the root of Ivan's removal from SARS can be compared to the media articles about Des van Rooyen and the Duartes, and he says yes: he is adamant that all the media are working together against all of us. That it is all a campaign against 'darkies' taking over the economy. After which he says good night and we watch him driving off in a very sleek shiny car that wouldn't last long in any jungle.

One who is absolutely not confused is now 78-year-old Sister in Chatsworth. Suffering from Parkinson's, as Father once had, and getting increasingly weaker, thinner and smaller, she is still furious. 'They must go to jail,' she says. Then, in a reference to Jacob Zuma's often-shouted *umshini wam'* slogan, with piercing eyes behind her glasses, 'You can bring me my machine gun, too.'

Looking for the Saxonwold shebeen
December 2016

Pockets of resistance are increasing both in size and in number. On 5 December 2016 – yes, it's Sinterklaas again – a group of 160 veterans and stalwarts of the ANC's liberation struggle have delivered a letter to President Zuma and the others in the ANC top six titled 'For the sake of our future'.

'We have observed the ill-begotten wealth among some of our leaders at all levels and the resulting ruinous effects on the organisation's moral and political fabric and on society as a whole,' it says. And we have 'watched as the leadership of the ANC became mired in a cycle of in-fighting occasioned... by personal interest.' The signatories to the letter note that these factors 'have contributed significantly to the increase in political assassinations'.[330] Among the struggle veterans who have signed the document are Ahmed Kathrada, Albertina Luthuli, Dennis Goldberg, Mandla Langa, Siphiwe Nyanda, Barbara Masekela, Stephanie Kemp, Trevor Manuel and Ivan Pillay.

A number of meetings with veterans, mostly in a Johannesburg Anglican church, has preceded the letter and more are to follow as the movement grows. Most memorable among those for me is a subcommittee gathering in the theme park Gold Reef City, of all places, the old gold mine terrain once used by the robber barons of white monopoly capital, now full of rides, noise, hamburgers and gambling machines. Are the comrades now using this as an underground hideout, I wonder at the occasion, used as I am by now to friends having their phones tapped, laptops hacked, houses broken into. 'I don't think so', is Ivan's response. 'It's probably just that one of us has a contact with connections to a venue here.' Still, if an underground hide-out was ever needed, I guess this would be a good one.

On that day I drop Ivan off, then proceed to the nearby Apartheid Museum on the other side of the fun fair – really, South Africa is so weird – to attend a panel discussion on the value of the country's much-fought-for Constitution in these current times of plunder. 'It's a simple principle, but it works,' former Constitutional Court judge Dikgang Moseneke is saying as I enter, in reference to the ground rule that all citizens are equal. 'The commander in chief simply cannot have all the country's goods.' His colleague and co-author of the Constitution, Albie Sachs, adds that the legal framework was precisely designed to ward off dangers that other liberated, newly independent, countries had faced. 'We had to acknowledge that brave fighters can become authoritarian rulers,' says Sachs. 'Just having a revolution clearly didn't mean that we all suddenly become beautiful people.'

Fortunately, the beautiful people of this country still maintain their sense of humour. Weeks before the Gold Reef City events, intrepid public protector Thuli Madonsela's State of Capture report details that former Transnet railway, now electricity boss, Brian Molefe, visited the upmarket suburb of Saxonwold where the Gupta brothers reside on no less than nineteen occasions during four months in 2015. Molefe responds that that didn't necessarily mean he was visiting the Guptas – there is a shebeen in Saxonwold, he maintains, that he visited. South Africa laughs for days. Twitterati post memes of people looking in empty water drains, around corners and under furniture for the Saxonwold shebeen.

March 2017, Umlazi

The effects of kleptocracy are more than visible by now, as schools creak under damage to their structures and the weight of demotivated children, and politically connected gangsters drive their shiny cars amid the shacks. 'Who is going to work hard to become a teacher, with our old cars, when you can drive a Ferrari? Our youth sees thugs running taxis and shopping centres, simply because they are close to the president,' says a teacher at a high school in Umlazi, whom I interview for ZAM's 'Bitter Almonds' project. The teacher knows that the children here need a lot of support, but despairs about all the bad leaders. 'I know what needs to be done in our schools. But to achieve a position of influence you must be a yes man, which means a dummy. They won't appoint someone who asks questions.'

***

Julius 'Juju' Malema, who was once so loyal to Zuma that he declared he would kill for him, is now vehemently opposed to Zuma. He has consequently even adopted Zuma's enemies as his best friends, and Zuma's friends as his worst enemies. It suddenly makes him sound rather nice.

'Gordhan has done nothing wrong,' Malema asserted strongly in a press conference, last October,[331] gazing convincingly into the camera, on the issue of the early retirement charges against Ivan, Oupa Magashula and Pravin Gordhan. 'So what if he gave Pillay a pension, are human resources matters now crimes for the police to investigate? The real reason why Zuma wants to remove Gordhan is that Gordhan is a moral guru,' he continues, adding that 'Zuma wants Gordhan to go away' so that he can once again 'appoint his own puppet'. He mockingly ventriloquises Shaun Abrahams: 'What must I charge Gordhan with, because the rogue unit charge won't stick?' Then Zuma's reply: 'Anything, charge him with anything.' And that, says Malema, is how 'Pillay's' early retirement case got concocted.

At another press conference last January, he attacked the new public protector Busisiwe Mkhwebane, the former SSA employee who succeeded Thuli Madonsela. 'Once a spy, always a spy,' Malema emphasises. 'She is there to protect the Zuptas: Guptas and Zuma. She is their puppet.'[332]

As I listen and laugh at Malema's antics, thinking that the young EFF leader might still grow into a politician of substance, Ivan scoffs. 'That fellow will say and do anything.' I hope he is wrong, but have to admit that, even as his targets change, Malema's tone and methods do not. He has not talked of killing again, but there is still intense incitement to and threats of violence in what he says, shouts and sings. In Nigeria, the word juju means voodoo.

'Don't you think he can calm down? At least he seems to be applying his mind now,' I tell Ivan, but he shakes his head. 'The behaviour won't change. He remains a fascist.'

A dream that lives at a funeral
29 March 2017

Who would have thought that it would be Kgalema Motlanthe – decent, bland, former interim South African president Kgalema Motlanthe – who would issue the public call to arms? His speech gets five thousand mourners at Ahmed Kathrada's funeral to rise to their feet, shout and even tear up, from sage Muslim men in dresses and caps to African youth excitedly waving a South African Communist Party flag to white NGO types to grey anti-apartheid struggle veterans. The trigger is a quote from the Roman poet Horatius,[333] repeated in calm defiance of the current powers that be: 'Tomorrow do thy worst, for I have lived today.'

It is the second time Motlanthe gets the crowd to jump. The first is when he reads aloud the letter to Zuma penned by Kathrada, the struggle veteran, ANC leader and former Robben Island prisoner. As he reads Kathrada's humble admonition to Zuma to resign, the crowd stands, roars and cries. The only stony faces are those of Deputy President Cyril Ramaphosa and some of his fellow ministers and party members. But plenty of ANC members and even ministers, including Health Minister Aaron Motsoaledi and Derek Hanekom, a struggle veteran and chair of the board of the Ahmed Kathrada Foundation, join in the ovation.

We stand for a third time when Neeshan Balton, executive director of the foundation, asks Zuma's nemesis, Minister of Finance Pravin Gordhan, to stand up. And when we cheer like mad and clap for minutes, Gordhan cannot maintain his composure any longer. He looks down, takes out a hanky and wipes away a tear. The pressure under which he has been for years is impossible to imagine.

Meanwhile, social media, mainstream media, posters, tweets and newscasts broadcast something else that made the crowd at Westpark Cemetery happy to be there: that Zuma would not be welcome. Or that he was welcome but should not speak, depending on which formal or informal spokesperson of Kathrada family and foundation you wanted to go with. Whichever it was, the message was clear: No Zuma for Kathrada, as the *Sowetan* succinctly headlined. It set the tone for the event and its aftermath.

As the funeral in Westpark Cemetery proceeds, it dawns on me that this is about much more than politics. It isn't even about corruption. Other politicians have been accused of corruption, but nobody ever cared to call for a special ban on them. The ban is not about this, I think as I watch the diverse, and yet united, crowd. This ban is about all that the ANC once stood for, which is remembered by the veterans and aspired to by the idealistic youngsters: the humanity, the justice, the drive to build a South Africa that belongs to all who live in it. Kathrada, his contemporaries and the ANC of old symbolised it. This president does not – in his use of ethnic and racial invective to maintain a power base; his flippant attitude towards the new South African Constitution for which thousands have died; his denigration of women; his Trump-like reasoning that he can do what he likes because he is the boss – and he is the antithesis of this idealism. He is, simply, a very bad human being.

And it has nothing to do with the fact that Zuma comes from a traditional rural community with a different culture and values. Ahmed Kathrada was born into a brown, oppressed, traditional community, too. He, too, had grown up with parents, uncles and aunts, who would not always have held progressive opinions. Ahmed Kathrada himself – eighty-seven years old when he died – might have had some old-fashioned feelings with regard to gender and sexual orientation; for most of his life he would probably not even have imagined such a thing as a transgender struggle. But speakers at his funeral on Wednesday, one after the other, underline how Uncle Kathy always cared for the rights and dignity of all human beings.

Struggle veteran Sophie Williams-de Bruyn narrates how Kathrada organised 'a plate of food every day' for her in the canteen of a certain company since he knew people like her worked day and night as activists in the coloured community, often without money for food. How he talked to problematic husbands of women who wanted to be in the struggle too; convinced them to trust their spouses and let them be in politics. It wasn't radical feminism but it was supportive and it had meant the world to the girl she was then, a girl passionate about right and wrong, who wanted to play her role.

Listening to her I remember an interview in which Chris Hani had reminisced on what he had been taught by the generation of Mandela, Tambo, Sisulu and Kathrada in the ANC: that you did not need the most modern of opinions, as long as you lived your life with respect for human dignity. Hani had learned, he told historian Luli Callinicos, from O.R. Tambo that one should support gay rights, for example. Not necessarily because one identified with that sexual orientation but maybe even precisely because one did not, because human rights belonged to all humans. He had told Callinicos[334] how Tambo would probably say: 'Well I am not part of that but everyone has the right to believe and practice (what they want) and who are we to impose preferences?'

Later in the interview, Hani also imagined gays as part of larger struggles for social justice, advocating 'the formation of many democratic formations in this country, organs of civil society, like the civics, independent trade unions, students' organisations, teachers' organisations, organisations of housewives, women, gays ... so that we are kept reminded of the needs of the people on the ground.'

Compare that to Zuma's fondness for the tradition whereby women 'lie down to show respect', or laughingly remembering on prime time television how 'when I was growing up, ungqingili ('homosexuals' in Zulu) could not stand in front of me, I would knock (them) out'.[335] With a leader like that, how could one expect the violence-marked soldiers I had once met, who had made peace with opposing armies on the strength of their mutual hatred of gays and women, to learn and overcome their ways?[336]

At Wednesday's funeral, others beside Sophie Williams-De Bruyn who had been youngsters and children who knew Uncle Kathy talk of how he had been an uncle to them, too. Not just a Guevara-type political icon, though he had been brave and inspiring too, but an actual uncle. Someone who would buy your entire school raffle booklet from you, would praise your drawings, help you with homework, take time to find out how you were. He would be that uncle in a society of damaged fathers; he would be that uncle to any child he came across in his life.

So many children, young and old, cry at Ahmed Kathrada's funeral.

Disappointed activists often ask how it happens that great freedom fighters turn into corrupt leaders once they rise to power. The answer is simple: they don't change. At least not a lot, and not often. They can grow or not, learn or not, but – except in cases of severe damage, through imprisonment, grief, violence or torture – they were almost always who they were.

Like Uncle Kathy, Jacob had been called 'uncle' too, once. But a greater difference in humaneness than the one between these two uncles is hard to imagine.

At the funeral, Derek Hanekom says it best, as he presides over a Muslim ceremony together with Jewish, African Christian and Hindu priests, and many, many atheists: 'We have seen today that our dream is not about the unity of a political party, but about the unity of a country; a unity based on the vision of a just, non-racial, non-sexist, democratic society of human rights for all. We are united for that dream.'

Judging by the faces here, the dream lives still. It lives on because a bunch of Muslims, some of whom may hold old-fashioned views – it is why Kathrada's wife, former minister, political prisoner and armed freedom fighter, Barbara Hogan, at this occasion has a shiny scarf draped loosely over her hair – have come together with communists, feminists and a boring but decent ex-president, ready to carry the same vision further. And when we cheer one last time, before the men only[337] bury Ahmed Kathrada in the soil of his Johannesburg, we all know that Jacob Zuma will not be mourned like this.

It is exactly 29 years today, on 29 March 1988, that Dulcie September was shot for her principled stance against the arms trade mafia, I realise as I walk away from the cemetery.

30 March 2017

Pravin Gordhan has been fired. Well, everybody saw that coming. According to Zuma, his decision to fire the finance minister and his deputy Mcebisi Jonas is based on a set of allegations in yet another dossier from his spy network of 'treasonous conduct' by Gordhan and Jonas. But he would have fired them soon no matter what, certainly after the metaphorical punch in the face he received at Ahmed Kathrada's funeral.

Invited to a party for Gordhan's birthday in a Greek church two weeks later, I bring him a gift from a novelty shop. It is a stress ball in the shape of a Zuma head, meant to squeeze as hard as you can. I imagine all the white people in my street will have one already, and maybe it means I am still white, but what the heck – I imagine Gordhan will need to externalise some stress now as well. I note how he finds it difficult to keep a straight face when he unwraps it.

It is one of these funny South African coincidences that Gordhan shares his birthday on 12 April with President Zuma. We are not invited to that party, but we see it later on TV: way louder, fancier, hipper and more musical than Gordhan's quiet wine and talks event. You just can't help dancing in front of the screen in your lounge, even if you know that the expensive artists and fine food catering are once again all paid by taxpayers. Bread and circuses, this is typical Zuma, a party animal like no other.

Then we see Jessie Duarte, who is the MC at the event. Ivan and I smile at one another as our confused old friend says happy birthday to the old man and brings cake. But I can't watch anymore when I see Jessie, on the stage, emotionally addressing Zuma, praising him for being such a good role model, and so wise. As she exclaims 'Teach us, leader!' with arms wide in adoration I switch off the TV.

* * *

That winter, thanks to intrepid and courageous journalists at Amabhungane and *Daily Maverick*, the Gupta leaks explode,[338] a large set of emails underpinning what so many have been saying for a while now. A few months later, *The President's Keepers* by Jacques Pauw is launched, the book that lists in great detail practically all that is unethical, criminal and disastrous carried out by the sycophants, the red-eyed fanatics, the consultants, the hangers on, the beneficiaries and the direct looters in the current South African government. The ensuing panic, the cease-and-desist letters, the threatened lawsuits by SARS and the SSA against Pauw and his publishers, and of course the actual raid on Pauw's house by Berning Ntlemeza's Hawks, will result in the book selling 200,000 copies within a few months.

Meanwhile, the use of the Constitution becomes a weapon. In lawfare against the state's robber barons, civil society, individuals, even judges themselves, go to court to fight the irregular appointments of the faulty and the incompetent. First, Berning Ntlemeza goes, when the High Court finds that his appointment is invalid and that he lacks integrity and honesty. It is the work of the Helen Suzman Foundation together with Freedom Under Law, the organisation headed by the indefatigable Judge Kriegler. We last saw Kriegler picketing at Piet Joubert building as Johann and Ivan were being interrogated by the Hawks; now the efforts of Kriegler and his colleagues have cut off new ugly head Ntlemeza from that unit.

Beside Freedom under Law and the Helen Suzman Foundation, the Black Sash (famous for its litigation under apartheid to protect the rights of the black majority, mainly women), Corruption Watch and others also take to the courts, often together. After Ntlemeza it's the turn of Zuma's sheep, chief prosecutor Shaun Abrahams, who is also found to have irregularly replaced his predecessor. Then follow the Zuma-whisperers behind Abrahams's crumbled throne, Nomgcobo Jiba and Lawrence Mrwebi, despite their tenacious resistance. Crime Intelligence fearmonger and disinformer in chief, Richard Mdluli, is first removed, then convicted of kidnapping and assault. Robert McBride and his IPID team win victory after victory against Police Minister Nathi Nhleko, and McBride becomes head of IPID again. Bathabile Dlamini, the misgoverning nightmare of the poor who depend on welfare grants, is ordered to pay personal costs when the Constitutional Court finds her 'reckless and grossly negligent' in the way she has carried out her duties.

In future, politics will intrude again. Bathabile Dlamini will be given public office once more when she is appointed head of the Social Housing Board in 2019. A new police minister will, on expiry of McBride's contract, not reappoint him. The National Prosecuting Authority will continue to ail despite a new chief prosecutor, seemingly powerless to act against the thieves of billions. But for now we rejoice even if Zuma's minister of justice, Michael Masutha, mutters that 'judges should not be members of civil society organisations'.[339]

As the protests grow, white faces become a minority at the mass meetings in Johannesburg and marches through Pretoria. Tens of thousands of black South Africans move against a thoroughly bad black president. Black hawker women sell boerewors and juice to black activists, black music blares, and banners and placards are full of black humour and anger. How different this is from the Cape Town anti-Zuma marches just a while ago, where privileged whites in shorts and sandals dominated and I had felt like Sunday, almost tempted to say go away, you racists. This is more like it, more like a giant ANC meeting sans perversion of the old ideals, like an extension of Ahmed Kathrada's funeral.

The EFF is here too in their red overalls, dancing and running in coordinated groups, loudly drawing wormholes through the crowds, and people laugh at them good naturedly. Perhaps, I think, they may not be so bad after all.

December 2017, NASREC Expo Centre, Johannesburg

And then finally he goes. With 179 votes between Cyril Ramaphosa and Zuma's candidate, his former wife Nkosazana Dlamini-Zuma, from a total of close to five thousand voting delegates at the 2017 ANC elective conference. It is not much but these 179 votes might just have saved the country. Judging by Zuma's face as he hears the tally he did not expect it, but it happened. Today, at NASREC, the ANC has elected Cyril Ramaphosa to lead the party and country, hopefully away from kleptocracy.

Even Zuma's female empowerment campaigning – anointing his ex-wife Nkosazana to be his successor – has not done the trick. However much Zuma supporters have clamoured for Nkosazana Dlamini-Zuma as a leader in her own right, and insist that it would be sexist to think she is just there as one of Zuma's women, at least 51 per cent of ANC delegates at the December conference have not bought into that. In fact she only received her 49 per cent of votes precisely because she was Jacob Zuma's candidate. In other respects she has always been rather unimpressive. Being the mother of some of his children, she is quite likely beholden to him too, even if she is a politician with an independent career.

It strikes me that to be called sexist in the name of Zuma is a remarkable experience too, in the Fellini movie that South Africa has become.

Valentine's Day
February 2018

It is at midnight on Valentine's Day 2018 that Zuma resigns and humorous broken heart memes abound on Twitter. 'Just when you thought he had forgotten what day it was, he surprises you,' one comment goes. He made an extremely long speech before he finally said he would go. We didn't listen to the rambling interspersed with expressions of self-pity, allusions to conspiracies and spies and victimhood. We couldn't anymore.

There is hope, now, but it is faint. Once bitten, twice shy, as they say. Or in this case twice bitten, third time shy. Cyril Ramaphosa, Zuma's deputy president, has never opened his mouth during the vampiring of Zuma's second term. He is by all accounts a weak leader, with only 51 per cent of support at that, which means that 49 per cent still support the rent-seeking patriarchy that Zuma exemplifies.

Corruption has been discussed, of course; even the term 'state capture' is now used openly in ANC circles, stated as a phenomenon that has to be fought. In some corners at NASREC, individuals may even have expressed their concern about the tribalism, the misogyny, the racism, the extolling of ignorance, that is bon ton again, in a perverse reversal of the values, 'Not just of the Constitution, but of the ANC itself,' as Ivan says. But it is to be feared that the current ANC leadership will do what it has become accustomed to doing: making bland statements about how corruption must be eradicated, then sinking back into inertia again.

'In the opposition against Thabo, there was still a debate. A divide between the lefties, who were then close to Zuma, and the neoliberals around Mbeki. It wasn't in any depth, but it was somewhat of a debate,' says Ivan. 'Now it is just my side against your side. Them and us.' Them and us, strangely tied together, as it turns out, in the new top six, where Gwede Mantashe and Jessie Duarte continue next to Cyril, with newcomer Paul Mashatile, who, it is said, may go one way or the other, wherever his interests lie. Gupta associate and Zuma loyalist Ace Magashule is secretary-general. D.D. Mabuza,[340] premier of Mpumalanga province, is now the deputy president of the ANC.

So far there has not been an open debate around the question why many good people in townships and municipalities have become averse to the ANC. Why in Umlazi, KwaMashu, Merebank and Chatsworth former UDF and ANC activists are now voting for Inkatha and the still-white Democratic Alliance. Why many communities are desperately trying to get rid of 'these guys who drive Range Rovers, wear Gucci and call each other "leadership"', as tweets on Whatsapp groups say. It is perhaps not surprising. How can the ANC face these things when a majority of delegates at NASREC, even among those belonging to the Cyril faction, answer to that description?

A story from Bethal has it that one former tsotsi comrade has replaced a former municipal accounts manager. The former manager had always driven his own car to work; this new one is chauffeur-driven at state's expense. Those who live around the municipal office daily see him get out of the car and wait there, for the chauffeur to get his jacket and briefcase out from the back and bring these to him. The new one does not know a thing about municipal accounting.

There are so many such stories. It is not a crime, politicians criticised for such things routinely say. 'Since when is that a measure of things,' Ivan asks. 'Since when are our norms and standards as low as those set by the criminal justice system?'

Nevertheless, there is that faint hope.

10 April 2018

And then Ivan is charged again.

Can you fokken believe it, I hear Pearlie say in my head, when Ivan, Johann and Andries 'Skollie' Janse van Rensburg are prosecuted together. I guess it is a present for Jacob Zuma for his upcoming birthday, although perhaps less so for Pravin Gordhan, who shares the date.

It is the fightback.

This time, they say, they have found something that the investigative unit, led by Ivan, has done that is *actually* considered wrong. Curiously, I read all that I can lay my hands on about an apparently illegal operation called 'Sunday Evenings' and also ask Ivan and everyone else I know in our rogue circles.

It is alleged that he and his fellow accused have been spying on the NPA. The charge states that Ivan and the rogue unit recorded NPA meetings in 2007, at the time when the NPA was supposed to investigate the arms deal and charge apartheid torturers and murderers, but didn't; when they targeted only Jacob Zuma and other rivals Thabo Mbeki wanted to get rid of.

I don't know up to what point getting secret information is a crime. I have a lot of files marked secret, confidential, top secret and so on. I think most of my colleagues do. But this, then, is the be all and end all of the newest charges against Ivan and the other two.

The depressing part of it is that it forces Ivan to hire lawyers again, and spend evenings and weekends again drafting papers to defend himself. And Johann too, and Andries Janse van Rensburg, whom I had last seen at the funeral of his five-year-old son.[341]

Damn this 49 per cent and their arsenal of captured institutions.

I curse again when I notice that, next to the signature of Zuma-aligned prosecutor Sello Maema on some of the case documents, I see that of the senior priority crimes deputy director, Torie Pretorius. It is his unit that, Maema in the lead, has been prosecuting Johan Booysen, Shadrack Sibiya, Anwa Dramat, Robert McBride, Pravin Gordhan and others.

Nevertheless, there is some progress, too. Against the captured institutions, as a tool to start the thought process of how to rebuild, stand commissions and enquiries: about Eskom, the SABC, the previous faulty appointments at the NPA. The Nugent Commission hearings about SARS, which start in May, bring out everything we know to have happened at SARS under Tom Moyane: the fear, the persecutions, the destruction of the systems.

So many good civil servants were sidelined, smeared, disciplined, made to resign or fired.

There was never a peep about black empowerment in their case.

In another government
Late 2018

In what is now a low-intensity war between plunderers who want to continue and those who resist them and want to rebuild, Julius Malema has come out fully pro-Zuma again. He calls him 'Baba Msholozi', with respect and by clan name. He also suddenly, remarkably, and absolutely hates Pravin Gordhan. Applying miraculously anti-chronological invective, he blames Gordhan – the newly appointed minister of state enterprises – for their continued failure when he is, in fact, desperately trying to rescue them.

Malema also talks a lot of the SARS 'rogue unit' all of a sudden, as if the long gone investigative entity still exists, equating it, as the RET brigade does, with white monopoly capital as well as an Indian cabal.

A role in his new volte-face may be played by the fact that Gordhan is seen as a dedicated minister tasked with cleaning up the mess in the state. There are risks to Malema if that happens: SARS might look at the Limpopo tender fraud case again, and the NPA, trying to find its feet under newly appointed head Shamila Batohi, might start investigating him for the same.[342] Julius has already stated that Batohi, with her Indian name, might have 'some relationship with the Indian cabal'.[343]

The biggest possible motivator for the red-uniformed populist's new fury, however, may be a suspicion that former SARS investigators have had a hand in a recent report on the looting of the VBS bank, also based in Malema's home province of Limpopo.[344] Malema and some of his Economic Freedom Fighters are said to have benefited from the VBS plunder: a report, 'The Great Bank Heist' by advocate Terry Motau in October this year for the Reserve Bank Prudential Authority that supervises commercial banks, details how Malema's colleagues at the top of his EFF are among those who received hefty loans from the now bankrupt bank, including his associate Floyd Shivambu.[345]

VBS is a tragedy. According to Motau's report, it has, for years, generously dished out sizeable loans, with little prospect of being repaid, to the politically connected. The loans were often funded with moneys extorted from municipalities and state institutions instructed to invest in the bank by provincial and national authorities in the Zuma government. Among the beneficiaries of such loans have also been a set of ANC politicians, including former president Jacob Zuma. In 2016, Zuma received a home loan for his Nkandla estate of over R7 million from the Venda bank, based in the region where he, Zuma, had approvingly said 'women still lie down on the ground' to pay their respect to a man.

As a result of the looting, many pensioners – mostly women – who had invested their savings in the bank, lost it all when the bank went down. Images of grannies sitting outside VBS bank, hoping to recover some of their money, have appeared in the media. Some slept there overnight, as if showing their respect for Zuma by lying down once again.

The new ire of Julius against the SARS rogue unit may be connected to the fact that Johann van Loggerenberg, Yolisa Pikie and Ivan have provided consultancy services to law and forensic firms, some of which helped with the Great Bank Heist report. The three former SARS officials did not participate in the VBS investigation as such, but the mere fact of their connection to firms that did may have caused Malema and his loyal fighters to see even more red than they usually do.

Also, in the end, their work did end up touching on VBS to some extent.

As anti-corruption consultants, Ivan and Yolisa investigated widespread malfeasance at PRASA, the passenger rail agency.[346] In the process, they found that the agency's then board chairwoman, a prospective judge named Tintswalo Makhubele, pressurised the agency to deposit a billion rand urgently in VBS bank. 'There were indications that she wanted another two billion soon to follow. It was days before the VBS was to be placed under administration for bankruptcy,' says Ivan. In addition to the planned deposit, a commission of R1.5 million was to go to what PRASA termed the Dudu Myeni Foundation. This foundation did not exist, but those investigating the bank's downfall assumed that what was meant was the Jacob Zuma Foundation, chaired by Dudu Myeni.

Blowing the whistle on the siphoning off of PRASA funds to VBS disrupted the attempted transactions.[347]

2019

After a first round of testimonies before the Zondo Commission on State Capture, Songezo Zibi publishes an opinion piece about the good civil servants and the bad ones who replaced them.[348] 'An almost untold aspect (of the Zuma years) is the long list of victims and their stories of torment at the hands of the corrupt,' he writes. 'These are strong, ethically upstanding and committed servants of the South African public who were harassed, victimised, threatened and ejected out of state and public institutions.'

Zibi portrays Zondo witness Mathane Makgatho, the former group treasurer at the Transnet railways state enterprise, who was 'bold enough to tell (Zuma-Gupta associate) Brian Molefe, the former group chief executive, that he was enabling the looting of hundreds of millions of rands of public money' and who, after she 'fought a good fight', had to 'leave her job, fearing for her life'. He describes how good people like Makgatho were replaced by 'another corps of people, many of them black', who were of 'negotiable ethical principles and woefully out of depth'. 'When did we, as black people, lose the ability to identify clear principles and stand by them especially when our own violate those principles?' he asks and concludes that 'we have rendered invisible countless competent black professionals who were butchered during the Zuma years, and yet we now wonder why they (blacks) are not in senior leadership positions'.

Zibi asserts that the new black elite exploits real emotional trauma of racism with its 'cheap tricks', causing 'us to submit to people who are, essentially anti-black (while) at the same time competent black people are left to rot on the vine because they do not have access to the patronage system that places the incompetents above them, or they refuse to bow and scrape to low-esteemed politicians who prefer to be treated like 17th-century monarchs and overlords.'

Through the Looking Glass II

At least Tom Moyane has been removed from SARS. He has held on as much as he could all through the Nugent enquiry, with much posturing, complaining and resisting – though never once explaining or accounting – but new president Cyril Ramaphosa in the end fired him last November. In the preceding period, Moyane has reportedly assaulted his son's seventeen-year-old girlfriend and accused her of 'destroying his empire', according to the girl.[349] Seventeen she may be, but in the Moyane mind witches will get at you even with your own concrete bunker in the garage, stark empty tree-less no man's land, and armed with guards next to red carpets.

A whole empire, destroyed by a little girl.

So many in this story have styled themselves emperor, chief, king and blesser, or commander-in-chief as Julius Malema does, all in charge of their respective imagined kingdoms of peace and happiness. Most have left only rubble behind, like Mavuso Msimang's Ozymandias with his shattered face, still with a 'sneer of cold command,' lying somewhere in a desert.

Who else do they blame but witches? Powerful forces must be behind their downfall: enemies with magic, witches, a cabal, a rogue unit, white monopoly capital, or, as the red-eyed fanatics' social media also increasingly scream, Stratcom, the erstwhile secret service disinformation agency of the apartheid regime.

The choir does tend to mix up its enemies. When former Zuma puppet and state security minister Bongani Bongo, who succeeded David Mahlobo, and who is now an MP and under investigation for corruption[350] falls ill, he says he believes Pravin Gordhan caused it. RET Twitter, all witch-minded, goes full blast on how 'Pravin' poisons people now. A tweet to investigative journalist Adriaan Basson attacks his 'opinion which is orchestrated by the witchcraft of the Stratcom cabal.'[351] 'It's probably the rogue unit again,' tweets Songezo Zibi when the SARS-CoV2 coronavirus breaks out in China. And lo and behold, a few months later, with the virus now unleashed globally, the RET choirs' Mzwanele Manyi and Piet Rampedi float the conspiracy theory that white monopoly capital representative Bill Gates, out to 'depopulate the continent', is wilfully infecting Africans with the virus, together with Cyril Ramaphosa and – remarkably – comedian Trevor Noah.[352]

Poor former apartheid mercenary Steve Burnett, who killed himself, had believed that alien reptiles were the secret power that was behind everything bad in the world.

In opposition to all that is rogue and evil, new public protector Busisiwe Mkhwebane has become the champion of righteous RET. The last remnant of the Zuma empire, she got her foot in the door before it went down, and is determined to do what she can for its resurrection.

Mkhwebane absolves the former administration from crucial pending cases such as the ones on state capture and the Gupta's Free State dairy farm,[353] and instead issues investigation after report after decree after instruction against Pravin Gordhan and the SARS 'rogue unit.'[354]

Julius Malema, who once called Busisiwe Mkhwebane Zuma's puppet, now shows much love for her. He supports all that the new public protector does about Pravin and the rogue unit, even goes to court to present affidavits for her. 'She must take on Praveeeeen!' he shouts. 'Praveeen must answer!' Increasingly, he doesn't even call him Pravin (or Praveeen) anymore, but Jamnadas, his second name, openly dog whistling Gordhan as an Indian alien with a funny name. It is reminiscent of the tactics once used by Nazis when they portrayed French resistance fighters from Eastern European and Jewish background as suspicious aliens, too. 'Black with beard and night, dishevelled, threatening (...) With your names hard to pronounce,' as Louis Aragon's classic poem 'l'Affiche Rouge', after the blood-red poster portraying the Nazis' alien enemies, goes.

I think of 'l'Affiche Rouge' every time someone misspells the SARS 'rouge' unit.

The tactic still works. All over social media, there is jeering at Jamnadas, repeating that name gleefully, shouting it over Pravin Gordhan's real identity and the man's historical record as a resistance fighter. Meanwhile, the same social media fan base worships Busisiwe Mkhwebane; one follower even photoshops her in Wonder Woman's golden bikini.

Mkhwebane doesn't seem to object to a bit of adulation. At one point publicly stating that no one can remove her because she has been put in her position by God, she shortly afterwards recites Mandela's speech from the dock, made when he was facing death by hanging for fighting apartheid: 'It is an ideal which I hope to live for and achieve, but also an ideal for which I am prepared to die.' Busisiwe Mkhwebane, forever etched in my mind in her much favoured, high-heeled designer shoes and a golden bikini, is one of the strangest faulty characters Jacob Zuma ever found.

If Julius Malema, the flip-flopping demagogue, is now number one among the prominent members of the RET brigade, Piet Rampedi comes a good second. Once aspiring to be an investigative journalist, Piet now studiously ignores all facts that contradict his preferred views:

for example that it was the very white monopoly capital PR firm Bell Pottinger in London that thought up the entire Radical Economic Transformation narrative in the service of the Gupta brothers,[355] or that it was the equally white imperialist KPMG and Bain who so eagerly helped Zuma's kitchen cabinet to capture the state. White monopoly capital has never had a problem partnering with kleptocrats, white or black. The collapse of a country never harmed it either.

But instead of thinking about that, Piet now lists fellow journalists as 'cabal members' in his tweets, eventually including practically every other journalist in South Africa.[356] After a while, some still-overlooked colleagues start tweeting Piet asking to be listed, and there is also boasting with regard to their ranking on the list. 'Are you only on thirty-one? I am twelfth!' A friend jokes that 'soon, the cabal will be so big that we will all be united in it'. The strategy of excluding people from your own side to such an extent that the other side gains in number is the exact opposite of what the ANC's once was.

The RET brigade, with their talk of taking wealth and the land from white monopoly capital, often remind me of the youngster who had once told Kogie he would have her fridge. 'They confuse capital with income,' says Ivan. 'Yes, you can take the capital. Then you finish it. Then what?' Then the donors will come in, I think, like in Cameroon and Zambia and Mozambique. They will continue to take your gold and copper and seafood, and keep you on an IV drip with just enough money for you and your friends to have nice houses and cars and holidays. Maybe the RET brigade is not mad. Maybe that is precisely what they want. For Sinterklaas to come and look after them, and never mind the rest.

Hehehehe. Black Piet.

Also funny is how the RET crowd mirrors the Trumps, Bolsonaros, Putins, Modis, Orbáns and Wilders of this world. In Europe and the USA, they target brown and black people, while here in South Africa the enemies are projected as white, or puppets of whites. But it is similar: it's us and them, all over. Remove 'them', and 'we' will be fine.

March 2020

When the coronavirus pandemic breaks out, populist authoritarians everywhere desperately seek to safeguard their strong man images. In Brazil, Bolsonaro parades as if no virus can touch him; Orbán scapegoats his favourite enemies; Putin sets up figureheads to take any foreseeable blame, and Trump starts peddling fake cures from chloroquine to bleach.[357] In tandem, Mzwanele Manyi's *WMC Leaks* Facebook page and Zuma-ites generally jump from fake to faker news. Mzwandile Masina, the loudmouth mayor of Ekurhuleni and Zuma stooge, announces that he personally will get his citizens a non-existent vaccine from Cuba. A pro-Zuma bishop in KwaZulu-Natal calls his flock together to pray because 'the virus is Satan trying to stop us Christians from going (out) to praise God as we wish'.[358]

We imagine Jacob Zuma still in power in South Africa now, and once more feel deeply grateful that he is not.

Cyril Ramaphosa even starts to look really good. He says all the right things; his tone and body language communicate concern, gravitas and leadership. Emergency plans – sensible emergency plans – are announced. Sage presentations by experts are aired to the public. There are projects for field hospitals: the NASREC centre, the place of Ramaphosa's victory over Zuma, is the first to be converted into one. Lockdowns to prevent the virus spreading are put in place. Yes, lockdowns are terrible when you live with eight in a shack and you can't get to shops or even get to water, and soldiers beat you up if you try, but they work to keep the pandemic's curves flattish for a while, buying time to manage the dreaded peak.

The contrast with the insanity in the US and other places is so striking that the South African government, in particular Ramaphosa and Health Minister Zweli Mkhize – fully absolved from anything he may have had to condone as the ANC treasurer under Zuma – receive lavish praise from all quarters, and the RET brigade shuts up for a while. In wider society, health workers and activists organise hand sanitiser, protective masks, food parcels, permits for spaza shops. They campaign for shelters for homeless, help at food kitchens. Supermarket staff, electricity workers and other essential service workers brave infection risks. Nurses, doctors and cleaners prepare hospitals for the first few hundred sick. People make their own masks, wash hands, distribute health information, shop for the elderly.

Resilience, creativity. It is how Liberian nurses fought Ebola, by making masks and gloves out of rubbish bags. Africa can do it, underlies the tone of many a proud African in the media, often beside snide remarks to the fake cure and strongman policies elsewhere: take that Trump, you *poes*.[359]

But then a doctor's desperate calls for help with testing a set of possibly infected persons go unanswered. A provincial bureaucrat in Limpopo locks two other doctors in forced quarantine 'because they are infecting my people'. A hospital in the Eastern Cape cries out that they have coronavirus patients but no training, equipment, let alone protective masks or gowns. It then turns out that almost all hospitals in the province share the same predicament. Chris Hani Municipality in the former Transkei, where my ANC Ezibeleni branch is located, is particularly hard hit. Health personnel report getting infected in Durban and Johannesburg too; some clinics close before they have even admitted one COVID 19 patient. Minister Mkhize dispatches officials to intervene to address the various emergencies, but what can they do, without staff, management, expertise or resources in places that have languished without these for decades?

Johannesburg Correctional Centre, dubbed Sun City by inmates, proclaims it has a corona strategy, but it turns out that the wardens only wear their much-advertised masks once, during a minister's visit. Hand sanitiser dispensers at the facility are found to contain plain water.[360] A month into the crisis, and in spite of the new and fiercely named Coronavirus Command Council, overall management of the emergency remains erratic. Who banned the sale of sanitary pads and baby clothes as non-essential goods, not to mention jerseys and blankets now that winter is approaching? Why is a man fined for trying to get diabetes medication at a pharmacy? Who stopped public transport from and to a clinic that is overcrowded with mothers who have just given birth and now can't get home with their babies?

The lack of coherent state capability, recognised by Cyril Ramaphosa himself as the prime challenge for the country in an address last January,[361] stands in the way of fighting the virus. A group of one hundred African intellectuals publicly denounces the same in an open letter about the pandemic to all the continent's leaders. 'Like a tectonic storm, the COVID-19 pandemic threatens to shatter the foundations of states and institutions whose profound failings have been ignored for too long,' the group writes.[362] Among these failings, they list 'chronic under-investment in public health and fundamental research, limited achievements in food self-sufficiency, the mismanagement of public finances, and the prioritisation of road and airport infrastructures at the expense of human well-being.'

African governments may be advised by the best experts, and adopt the best health and social distancing policies, but if wishes were horses, as they say, beggars would ride.

In South Africa, entire provinces have not even begun to order health equipment, prepare quarantine sites or fill health personnel vacancies. There is no money for essential services 'because some people (at the top) are appointed at maximum salaries – classic cronyism' in the words of a Limpopo opposition politician.[363] The practice of 'poorly qualified people being parachuted into positions of authority through political patronage,' cited by President Ramaphosa in his January address shows itself everywhere in all its devastation. Pictures on social media show municipal councillors loading state-funded food parcels into their own private vehicles. Others are reportedly charging the state over R2,000 per parcel, in turn delivering little more than a bottle of cooking oil and a cabbage for every poor family on their list. The much-advertised coronavirus Solidarity Fund, filled with generous donations from businesses and the wealthy – and even more generous donations from citizens with modest incomes – has been allocated a board of individuals whose names are unknown, a fact that by itself sows fear. 'Can we audit this already please,' asks Twitter, and a response comes to say that that would be a good idea 'because I saw the names'.

The awareness that food parcel contracts and other such tenderpreneurial opportunities may not be the best way to galvanise new state action dawns on government after a while. Child welfare and other income grants are raised, allowing relief money, albeit a pittance in comparison to what is needed, to reach families in need.

When a picture of Communications Minister Stella Ndabeni-Abrahams is posted showing her at lunch in the ostentatious mansion of ANC MP Mduduzi Manana during the initial and most severe lockdown,[364] a storm of criticism ensues. It is difficult to say what has irked South Africans most: the breach of the lockdown, the fact that she is publicly seen to be close with Manana, who is a convicted woman abuser,[365] or Manana's house itself: a bizarrely grandiose place filled with crystal chandeliers and crystal staircase, shoe cupboards, satin-clad bedrooms, maids with feather dusters and a private gym. As testimony to what must be a completely tone-deaf nouveau riche complex, Manana, who has no record of achievement either as the deputy minister of education he was under Zuma, or as an ANC NEC member, which he still is, has just posted a video of his house on Twitter – him slowly walking down his elaborate staircase, exercising in his gym and contemplating his shoes – which is why everyone now knows him as an inexplicably rich, violent, nincompoop.

'For every politician, official, business et cetera, who looted money for health, water, housing, education, for every one of you who mismanaged, you are the reason the poor are more vulnerable to the effects of coronavirus,' tweets broadcaster and author Redi Tlhabi. 'And you are trash.'

The modestly increased grants do little to ward off the risk of starvation in many areas, where people lose jobs, homes and small businesses. 'If you don't have food, you must phone the social development agency SASSA,' a government communication exhorts, but SASSA, now headed by Totsie Memela – she is great but she is also facing terrible odds after years of Bathabile Dlamini in the post of social development minister – responds that it is already getting three thousand calls per hour.

Meanwhile, police rage through the townships. It is doubtful whether current Police Minister Bheki Cele is an improvement on Nathi Nhleko at all, as he remains silent when a man is shot in the leg looking for food and has to have his leg amputated, and when an entire street reports prolonged beatings by a police contingent with whips. Taken to task at a media conference, the minister, wearing his customary cowboy hat – a change from the magical goat skin bracelet Nhleko wore, but what is it with South African police ministers and remarkable accessories? – he answers questions about these and many more such instances of police brutality, blustering and grinning, with a remark to the effect of: You ain't seen nothing yet.

True, that. In the following weeks, a man is beaten to death[366] by soldiers in his own yard while shack dwellers in the Cape and Gauteng are evicted, forced to stay outside in streets and on fields, even though this is in violation of the government's own decrees saying that there will be no evictions during the lockdown.

'You can only clobber people on the head for so long. As with all enforcement, you have to make it possible for them to stick to the rules,' says Ivan. It is the same philosophy that the erstwhile SARS adhered to. Don't just punish people. Make sure they can comply: have your offices open and be client friendly, communicate in all languages, explain, assist. In the COVID-19 pandemic the principle means ensuring there is water, food and soap, and that people can access isolation facilities. Ivan works with Sri,[367] and Yolisa Pikie on the development of a compliance strategy to fight the pandemic in a way suitable for countries with high concentrations of poor people.[368] They send it to civil society and ANC contacts, hoping it will do some good. The *Daily Maverick* and ZAM publish it.

And as a new, still small, citizens' movement starts to grow in the pandemic, old and new names of comrades and organisations come to the fore. The Treatment Action Campaign and Section27, which fought for appropriate health care during the HIV/AIDS pandemic take up the cudgel again and lead efforts to bring resources where needed. Brave journalists report from the townships and their lockdown horrors of starvation and repression. Social justice lawyers take up cases of evictions and security force abuse. The Ahmed Kathrada Foundation forms community action networks in Gauteng. Businesses help to obtain, inter alia, protective equipment for health personnel from mining and agriculture companies.

Old struggle veterans once more participate, too. Mac Maharaj sends out an audio message calling activists in and outside the ANC to mobilise. Maisy – yes, we are in touch again – scouts around for hand sanitiser and shelter for those who need it in Soweto. Kieran – the same Kieran who helped get Mac and Gebuza over the border at the start of Operation Vula and is now a travel writer – helps edit the ex-SARS officials' COVID-19 strategy paper. Ntombenhle Nyawose,[369] educating and advocating in Pietermaritzburg, has sent a message 'Yes we must mobilise! It's the only way!' I get a bit teary when I notice that she has changed her profile picture to an image of her assassinated mother, Jabu Msomi.

There is a certain Dad's Army feel about all this. We are old now, stiffer and slower and more vulnerable as we bumble through the unknown, as we always have. But it is still a good feeling.

Epilogue

The rogue unit charges against Ivan Pillay and his former colleagues Johann van Loggerenberg and Andries Janse van Rensburg were withdrawn on 7 February 2020. The intelligence report on the same matter, that was drawn up under Zuma's reign, was set aside by the North

Gauteng High Court on 8 June that year. Johann van Loggerenberg's application to do this was unopposed by the newly incumbent Inspector General of Intelligence.

The *Sunday Times* returned the awards it had won for some of its smear campaign stories. It is a lesson for all of us not to reward the sensational too easily.[370] It was a rather empty gesture, since the prizes were cash, awarded not to the media house but to the reporters, and Wa Afrika and friends will hardly start paying up. But at least it has been said, in the words of editor Bongani Siqoko: 'There was clearly a parallel political project aimed at undermining our democratic values and destroying state institutions and removing individuals who were seen as obstacles to this project. We admit that our stories may have been used for this purpose.'

At present, the only authority still pursuing Ivan, Pravin Gordhan, Oupa Magashula and other SARS investigators – and Robert McBride – is the public protector, Zuma-era appointee Busisiwe Mkhwebane. Yolisa Pikie likens her to the Japanese Second World War soldiers who were found in jungle trenches in the '70s and '80s, unaware that the war they were still fighting was long over. Undaunted after four of her reports have been set aside or taken on judicial review, or after having been called 'irrational and reckless' and 'ignorant of law' by many, including the courts and the deputy speaker of Parliament, Lechesa Tsenoli, she has vowed to continue in her position even in the face of ongoing parliamentary proceedings to remove her. Mkhwebane maintains that, just like a judge, she has 'decisional independence' and that she is 'going nowhere'.

The values of the elders

The elders who were once the north star, like Tambo and Mandela, Helen Joseph and Kathrada and Walter and Albertina Sisulu, are long gone.

Lucia died of cancer, on 22 November 2018. In pain and thin as a matchstick, she had to live through the white monopoly capital and rogue unit smears. Klaas is in Amsterdam, but one-eyed and now walking with a crutch, he heard it there, too.

When Zuma wanted to give him a medal, also in 2018, he initially refused. He only accepted because comrades said he should, that it could weigh as a victory on the side of good. On a previous occasion, Lindiwe and Ntombenhle, Pat and Jabu Msomi's daughters, had spent a few awkward minutes with Zuma when their parents – Ivan had written the recommendations – got their posthumous medal. They say Uncle Jacob just giggled when they talked about the olden days and Ivan.

Maybe, either in the emergency or afterwards, the values of the elders will be learned anew. Perhaps stock will be taken of the enormous battles waged, not by kings and blessers and emperors and strange women who think they are Jesus, but by good people who remain points of shelter for their communities and colleagues in the midst of chaos. Perhaps there will be new recognition of those seeking truth and justice; those now seeking to repair, in the face of great odds, the damage done to their institutions and this country.

Perhaps the north star can be dusted off. It may be a bit grimy, but it has not disappeared. So many comrades still carry it within, carry on simply because it is there.

This book is for them.

Meanwhile, we still look at the world and its reflections, Ivan and I, as we did once in a theatre in Amsterdam, thirty years ago. Together and separately, looking at the same things from different angles. 'You dance around each other,' says Vani.

***

After this lifetime, the struggle will not end any time soon. It will always go on, a luta continua as they say, because you can only overcome the demons of the past if you carry on, keep walking in the dark past the veldfires as Joe and Ivan had once done, keep connecting, moving, squirreling, taking stock, finding a next step, climbing hills and taking stock again. It's much like the MacGyver story the little Mauritian boy told us long ago in Lusaka.

That story did not have an end either.

The little boy had been quite alright with that.

Where they are now

This is a list of those mentioned in the book who participated in the ANC's freedom struggle together with Ivan. They are listed under the place where they were first introduced.

The list excludes high-profile individuals (the reader is invited to Google), deceased comrades whose deaths are mentioned in the book, those whose current whereabouts are mentioned in the book, those named in footnotes, and those given changed first names or pseudonyms

Merebank and Chatsworth

- Coastal (Khamba) Govender, now retired, still organises comrades in the community.
- Spider Juggernath, retired, the same.
- Janey Juggernath and Ish Ramkissoon are retired and live in Johannesburg.
- Joe Pillay lives in Canada with his wife Barbara whom he met in Mzimpofu, Swaziland. They have two adult children, Patrick and Vanessa.
- Jenny Govender looks after her now 82-year-old mother Pushpa (Sister) in Chatsworth, who remains badass.
- Kogie and her husband Dhavan Moodley live in Secunda, where Dhavan works at SASOL.
- Prani Raidoo is principal of a primary school in Johannesburg.

Wider Durban

- After editing *Reflections in Prison,* a collection of essays by former Robben Island prisoners in 2002 and being the subject of Padraig O'Malley's *Shades of Difference*: *Mac Maharaj and the Struggle for South Africa* in 2007, Mac Maharaj now manages the South Africa in the Making exhibit, a memorial centre for the years of struggle at Moses Mabhida stadium in Durban, together with Sunny Singh.
- After serving as a colonel in the new South African Police Force, Sunny Singh is now retired. He dedicates himself to the South Africa in the Making museum project and general work in the community.
- Moe Shaik is a consultant. He recently published *The ANC Spy Bible* (Tafelberg, 2020), a book on his many years in ANC and South African intelligence circles.
- Shirish Soni was South Africa's ambassador to Kazakhstan, Qatar and Italy. He is now back in South Africa.
- Vuso Shabalala worked at SARS, then at the department of justice, then in the office of President Jacob Zuma as one of his many advisers. He is now an adviser in the office of the premier in the province of KwaZulu-Natal.
- Rae (Rajaluximi) Pillay is retired.

Johannesburg

- Thabisile Masia lives in Boksburg, where she remains active in the community.
- Dipuo Mvelase still works at SARS.
- Anwa Dramat is retired.
- Pete Richer is retired.
- Yolisa Pikie works as a consultant with Ivan.
- Adrian Lackay works as a media officer at the Public Investment Corporation.
- Riaz Saloojee works in the private sector.

Lusaka

- Ntsiki Memela-Motumi (Nombulelo) works in the SADF as a brigadier.
- Cassius Motsoaledi is retired and lives in Mzimhlophe, Soweto.
- I was sadly unable to establish the current whereabouts and

conditions of Lizo Semane (Zeph Mothopeng) and Dugmore Mthimkhulu (Morris).

Swaziland

- Totsie Busisiwe Memela is the CEO of the South African Social Security Agency.
- After returning from Swaziland, Baba Nsibande lived on the East Rand. He has since died.
- Siphiwe Nyanda is a businessman and a member of the group of Veterans and Stalwarts in the ANC and MK.
- Phumla Williams is acting CEO of the Government Communications and Information Service (GCIS).
- Sidney Moodley still works for local government in Johannesburg.
- Bee (Bhabhalazi) Bulunga works in the private sector.
- Barbara de Leeuw and Rens Trimp are retired but remain active as progressives in their community in Heerlen, the Netherlands.
- University lecturers (in York and Leeds respectively) Fred and Marianne Lubben are retired.
- Michael Stephen is deceased. June Stephen worked for Oxfam in London, until struck by illness several years ago.
- David Manyatsi taught at the University of Swaziland until his death in 2019.
- Kieran Meeke is a freelance travel writer based alternately in Canada and Spain.
- André Ravesloot is retired and lives in Spain.
- Archie Whitehead is now South Africa's ambassador in Namibia.

London/UK

- Tim Jenkin continues as a writer, documentary maker, activist and expert internet consultant. The movie *Escape from Pretoria*, an Australian-UK production based on Jenkin's 1987 and 2003 books, with Daniel Radcliffe playing Jenkin, is set for release in 2020.

Amsterdam

- Bart Luirink is the editor-in-chief of ZAM, www.zammagazine.com. He has authored several books, including *Moffies: Gay Life in South Africa*, with Madeleine Maurick, which was published in South Africa.

- Conny Braam has authored many books, including one on the Dutch assistance to Operation Vula and one on Namibian freedom fighter Hendrik Witbooi. Several of her books have been published in South Africa.

Postscript by Ivan Pillay

This book narrates, among other things, some of my experiences in and around SARS. For those interested in public administration, below are some notes on the lessons we learned.

1. THERE IS MUCH TO LEARN

Apartheid not only caused much suffering. It also excluded most of us from state power and governance. Only those who had collaborated with apartheid were allowed to participate in the upper echelons of public administration and did so as junior partners at best. We have, therefore, a lot to learn and a lot to do. We only start learning when we acknowledge that there is much that we do not know. Conspicuous consumption and lavish lifestyles will not make up for the deprivation that apartheid caused in us. Learning will definitely help.

2. THERE SHOULD BE A PLACE FOR ALL IN OUR INSTITUTIONS

Some of us in the senior management of SARS were cadres tested in the national liberation struggle. The Freedom Charter, although adopted long ago, in 1955, was (and is) a living document for us. Drawn by its aspirations and driven by its values, we were determined to make SARS an effective institution and a resource for the new South Africa. We also believed that there was a place in SARS for all patriots: a home for anyone prepared to work hard to make the country succeed. Only recalcitrant racists and free riders were not welcome.

We valued the institutional knowledge of those we found in SARS. We stopped giving voluntary retirement packages, since all these did was to encourage the most capable and confident to leave. I still find it difficult to understand why white employees should be driven out or discouraged. Surely the best way to compensate for the effects of apartheid was to harness the very persons who had benefited from separate education and job reservation and to cause them to work sincerely and effectively in the interests of a new South Africa. Besides the practical argument, it is an age-old value of the ANC that we should work with all who embrace our ideals of a non-racial and non-sexist, just society, leaving the die-hard racists to isolate themselves.

We worked hard to bring people onto the side of the new South Africa. We knew that, among whites, there were persons who were critical of apartheid as it applied to them. These were employees who were side-lined by the 'Broeders': usually they were women, gay people, English-speaking people and the young, as well as some of the better educated individuals. We engaged these segments of the SARS staff and we won most of them over to the new South Africa. We also promoted and empowered black colleagues. SARS was 80 per cent black by 2013.

3. The Constitution demands us to be fair and ethical

The letter and the spirit of the Constitution should be integrated into our lives and our work. At SARS, we understood that the state, the political party and the individual were not to be conflated. The party-political affiliation of a SARS colleague was of no importance: his or her behaviour was what counted. Likewise, as a taxpayer or client, your political affiliation, gender, colour or class gave you no advantage when you interacted with SARS. Some funders of the ANC were confused when their track record of donations received no brownie points from us. We suspected in many instances that the very donations were recycled from tenders: money that ultimately came from taxpayers and customs clients.

This, in hindsight, is what led to our downfall. Our efforts to be fair and ethical caused certain tax and customs delinquents to claim that we were targeting them because they were black, or a competitor to some businesses we favoured or because they were donors or supporters of Jacob Zuma. Eventually, we became akin to a foreign virus that had to be driven out.

4. Leaders must provide the models for acceptable behaviour

While every person is different, in a society like ours only a small proportion always lives according to sound ethical values – the operative word being 'always', in any situation. There is also probably a small proportion of people who are the opposite: such individuals are out to take only for themselves. The vast majority of people are in between. They usually act according to their understanding of what is proclaimed and practised in their environment and take the path of least resistance.

It takes many decades, even generations, to build and consolidate norms and standards in a society. Because of our late start as a democracy, and the legacy of apartheid, leaders must define and demonstrate, over a relatively short time and at every opportunity, what is and what is not acceptable. Politicians, public servants, business people and members of civil society must be mindful that they contribute either to strengthening or weakening our norms and standards.

The real question then is who determines what is proclaimed and provides the model of acceptable behaviour. If it is the ethically challenged, as during the Zuma presidency, then we will be in trouble once again. Over time, ethical leaders must succeed in increasing the proportion of persons who wish to and indeed do the right things. We need pace-setting leadership and management that deliberately seeks to integrate appropriate behaviours into every activity.

We tried to achieve this in SARS by aiming for a leadership that practised what it preached. It is, after all, not what you say, but what you do that matters; there is a reason why most of us set little store in what most politicians trot out about fighting corruption. An example was our no-gifts policy. No SARS official, no matter who, could accept even coffee or a soft drink. In situations where it would offend to refuse gifts, for example in the case of visiting dignitaries or representatives from foreign revenue services, such gifts were surrendered to the SARS Ethics Office and recorded in a register. Once a year, at a national event, these gifts were auctioned and the proceeds donated to a worthy cause.

We also endeavoured to be fair in all situations, even where it was tempting to use a heavy hand or shortcut. We were mindful that the end very rarely justifies the means; the means, on the other hand, usually shape the ends.

5. ALL MUST BE ASSESSED ON VALUES, BEHAVIOUR AND EXPERIENCE

When appointing an individual, that person's values and the pattern of his or her behaviour is of utmost importance; not the behaviour in this or that moment but the consistent pattern over time and in varying situations. Reliable tools to assess values and patterns of behaviour exist and can be helpful. If, for example, the person under consideration is not eager to learn and grow, then placing him or her in a complex environment will only frustrate both of you. Another example would be persons who like to work in a stable environment. They will be suited to steady state operations where the policies, norms and standards, and operating procedures are very clear.

Likewise, not all personalities are suited to be managers. Those whose personalities are characterised by a need for friendship, or affiliation, as it is called in relevant textbooks, will not make good managers. They may, however, be suited to tasks that require good communication skills. SARS assessed the different capabilities and allocated employees accordingly.

In addition to values and behaviour, there is no substitute for learning from work.

6. RISKS OF CORRUPTION CAN BE REDUCED

In South Africa there is no shortage of information peddlers, corruptors, influencers and fixers (real or con artists). How to blunt the impact that such people would have? At SARS, in addition to the no-gifts policy, the following is perhaps worth noting:

- We kept our lives simple.
- We avoided social and work situations where we knew there would be persons who would try to take advantage of our presence. When meeting taxpayers, we did so at the office and were accompanied by a fellow employee.
- There was an independently operated phone line to receive alerts about corruption. There was also a suspicious-activity reporting system which alerted us, inter alia, to attempts to influence us.
- A new operating model created dedicated front offices to interact with the public, thus insulating our processing and enforcement personnel who managed accounts, assessed tax liabilities and audited.
- All tax advisors had to be registered with SARS. Dedicated centres to interact with tax advisors were established.
- To avoid bias, auditors and investigators were not allowed to select or

initiate cases. Case selection became an independent function.
- Access to taxpayer records was controlled and we improved our technology systems such that any query would leave footprints.

7. ANNOUNCING BIG PLANS IS NOT MANAGEMENT

Many of our managers and leaders are not systemic. We are mainly event- and transaction-driven interventionists. By continuous non-systemic actions and instructions, we invariably break existing systems. There is little analysis, generation of options, objective selection of these options, sufficient design and realistic planning. We usually just make announcements. When that does not succeed – and it often does not, because we have broken the delivery mechanisms – we make even more announcements. From land distribution to fighting crime, the more we fail, the louder and more strident we become.

In addition, the announced plans are often variations of some or other preferred action or tool, like a new special project, or structure, or label. In this regard I like to quote the person who said 'Don't just do something – stand there!' Don't rush to action. Study the situation. Slow down so that the rational self comes to the fore. Wishful thinking and loud announcements of one or other big solution rarely have any connection with root-cause analysis, data-based evidence, design thinking and a plan.

8. WE NEED TECHNICAL COMPETENCE

Almost all present crises in South African state institutions result from the displacement of technical competence in the core business and in the management of its operations. Instead, state institutions have hired and promoted layers of generalists. Many of these generalists are not systemic and have no desire to learn the core business.

9. EFFECTIVE PEER MANAGEMENT IS ESSENTIAL

All institutions are part players in bigger value chains. Even the part of a value chain that lies within a particular institution requires seamless collaboration from different divisions within that same institution. Thus, modern organisations are complex. Yet, the capability to manage the horizontal (peers), as opposed to vertical command and control, is rare in our public service. The result is further fragmentation within institutions and in processes across the state. An appropriate example is how poor statement-taking in a charge office of a police station impacts on the efficiency of the whole criminal justice system of police, prosecutions, judiciary and prisons and the legal profession generally.

10. Corruption and dysfunctionality feed on each other

Dysfunctionality in institutions and state systems creates an increased vulnerability to abuse, theft, fraud and corruption. Collusion between corrupt and self-serving internal and external interests becomes easier and will meet only limited resistance from the remaining pockets of integrity and governance in the institutions.

11. Hero leaders do not advance institutions

'Hero leaders', who individually resolve specific incidents, cases or transactions, or defeat a real or perceived enemy, undermine service delivery. Consistent service to citizens comprises standardised daily routines that are achieved by an institution in its entirety. When every person and case is an exception, to be resolved personally by a 'big man', the majority of citizens will suffer.

With standardisation we streamline processes; we become efficient and predictable. We can then scale up or down, initiate a new product or new service using the proven stable production base.

12. 'I am accountable to you'

For some unfathomable reason, the South African government tends to concentrate its efforts on post-management governance. There is a plethora of reports about the failures of management systems and actions. Year after year, we learn about what went wrong, when it has already gone wrong.

In SARS we were not driven by the desire to avoid accountability. We wanted to account. Accordingly, we focused on upfront governance by:
a. Creating a dedicated governance unit that interacted with internal audit, the auditor general and any other governance structure. This unit understood all the issues, developed appropriate plans with the SARS divisions concerned, then monitored the implementation of corrections. It reported regularly to the EXCO.
b. Embedding and strengthening three lines of checks and balances into the institution:

- the normal vertical line of control;
- the use of shared objectives among peers to create constructive tension (horizontal), and
- resourced internal audit, such that gradually the auditor general could place greater reliance on its work and shift its focus from the mundane.

c. Empowering individuals and reducing the role of committees in decision making, so that there was clear accountability of individual managers.

d. Developing a useful rule of thumb that distinguished between usual, unusual and exceptional situations. For the usual decisions, you would need three signatures: the proposer, the proposer's manager who will recommend (or not) and finally the manager of the recommender. For the unusual, one more signature from an even higher level (the approver's boss) would be required. Exceptional situations could be dealt with by a committee under the authority of the most senior manager. This enabled us to apply clear rules to categories of risk, rather than flounder from transaction to transaction. The point is that everything, unique or not, has to be governed by a system of checks and balances.

13. Plans for big change need a base line

Where policies, processes, procedures and practices are broken, when technical know-how has been ejected and incompetents are in charge, we yearn for rapid change. Sadly, no matter how desperate we are to move forward, I do not believe big change can immediately happen. To develop a change plan, it is important to know precisely from what and where you depart. When an institution is dysfunctional, one doesn't have the required base line to do this; any planning then becomes wishful thinking.

There is, therefore, a phase of fixing and stabilising systems to achieve a base line. The good news is that just fixing processes and procedures and stabilising the institution will already result in considerable improvements as compared to the period of dysfunctionality. Once stability and predictability have been achieved, successful big change becomes possible and easier to achieve.

14. Delivery requires improving the whole

Delivery is the operations arm of an institution. It is the most predictable part of a business since it works, or should work, according to standard operating procedures. It is supported by divisions such as human resources and financial management.

In the beginning, when we sought to improve productivity at SARS, we focused on operations, working faster and pushing ourselves harder. However, reaching our limits and making no further impact, we realised we could improve on pre-implementation phases such as analysis, design and planning. We found that results were often already pre-determined in the solutioning and planning, and, therefore, we needed to pay attention to the whole value chain, including rethinking solutions.

Delivery, in other words, could not do without the enabling by experts and thinkers who focused on the whole. This 'enabling' part of SARS performed analytics, designed solutions and formulated operational policy and procedure. This way of understanding SARS helped with placement of staff. As noted above, we developed a battery of assessments to indicate the suitability of employees for delivery, enablement and support roles.

15. Citizens' compliance can be achieved

The task of building compliance, that is, to move citizens to fulfil either tax or other obligations, is a huge and complex one. In SARS we built an effective regulatory regime with robust systems that brought greater transparency to transactions and relationships; made regulation effective and cheaper in time; and actively drew the majority of taxpayers into this well-defined environment. As a result, hard enforcement actions (like investigations) could be focused on the small categories that remained outside the regulatory regime or in the margins, shepherding them into the known.

Much of this we learned from countries that had effective tax and customs institutions. The compliance model guiding tax authorities such as those of the Scandinavians, the Dutch, Canadians and Australians was extremely useful.

The model works as follows:
a. Explain and educate continuously so that the citizen understands what are 'the right things' to do.
b. Make it easy to do those right things through simple, easy-to-follow, procedures.

c. Make it difficult to infringe and misbehave.
d. Then – and only then – initiate fair and proportional enforcement responses to any breaches.

Generally, the above is grouped into three streams:
- Education
- Service
- Enforcement

In my view the model applies to building compliance in general and not only to tax and customs. It could, for example, apply to building norms and standards with regard to traffic control, fighting crime in general, or mobilising the population in the face of a pandemic. True and effective management of compliance is the opposite of the empty authoritarian response that we often see from leaders who blame citizens for problems in society, then govern almost exclusively by punishing these citizens.

16. Even limited resourced enforcement can be effective

Hard enforcement actions must focus on people who actively look for opportunities to beat the system. Since enforcement capability will always be limited when compared to the universe of active non-compliance, the challenge is how to do more with limited resources. The enforcement model SARS developed comprises three elements that sought to make the best use of limited capacity and knowledge.

- Broad coverage

The interactions of the tax authority with the public should be of such a ratio that it creates the perception that most individuals have an equal risk of drawing enforcing attention, like requests for clarifications, checks, inspections and desk audits. These soft-touch activities can be standardised and staff can be trained thoroughly. It is thus possible to carry out a large number of these actions across the tax base.

- Depth

The soft-touch actions may disclose serious non-compliance by perpetrators who are well resourced and determined to block, obfuscate and divert the authorities. The tax authority must show equal determination to go wherever it needs to go, as deep as is necessary, through every twist and turn.

The depth, as we called it, also applies to illicit activities such as:
- smuggling of drugs and tobacco products
- trade in protected species
- value-added tax and excise tax fraud

There must be a continuous process to try to standardise aspects of the depth work where possible. Such aspects could then be moved to the broad coverage responses.

- Leverage

This includes smart communications, harnessing of influencers (individuals and institutions), working with self-regulatory structures of standing like professional institutions and housing associations, and concentrating activity on a particular segment. Good examples here are the SARS projects to improve compliance in the importation and sale of electronic goods and among the banks.

17. PUNISHMENT IS NOT THE GOAL

The purpose of penalising those who deliberately infringe is not simply to punish. If the process is a fair one, it establishes once again what is acceptable and what is not acceptable to everyone. It also reassures those who comply that their compliant actions are recognised and endorsed. Penalties should lie on a continuum, which rewards willingness to comply and penalises unwillingness to comply.

18. INSTITUTIONS ARE MORE IMPORTANT THAN WE THINK

It seems to me that we are born with little more than a basic operating system. We interact with and absorb from our family, our neighbourhood, our employment, our religious and civil society organisations, our schools and other state structures. When our environment is functional and healthy our development as individuals and communities is boosted. Breaking processes, procedures and institutions to steal and defraud in the short term has long-term implications for the whole country and all our people. It impacts our present and could destroy our future.

Notes

1. He transported weapons across borders, was arrested, then escaped, and found refuge in the Dutch embassy in South Africa. He was returned to Holland in 1987 in a prisoner exchange. See: https://www.washingtonpost.com/archive/politics/1987/09/08/prisoners-returned-in-4-way-swap/b7eedec0-f046-4308-8559-3fc1dad55840/.
2. Hassen Ebrahim, in *From Marabastad to Mogadishu*, Jacana Media, 2019, mentions that he was inspired to join MK and the ANC underground because of what Solomon Mahlangu did. He also states that he 'could not get over how senseless the death (of the young fighter) was', asking if there 'could not have been better planning'. Nevertheless, the fact that Ebrahim went on to build several very successful political-military units inside apartheid South Africa does underline that Mahlangu himself was right when he made the statement on death row that his 'blood (would) nurture the tree that bears the fruits of freedom'.
3. See 'Statement on attempted poisoning of Ms Connie [sic] Braam in Harare in September 1987' here: www.justice.gov.za/trc/hrvtrans/welkom/welkom4.htm.
4. See Conny Braam, *Operation Vula*, Jacana Media, 2004.
5. See Legacies of the South African Chemical and Biological Warfare Programme, by Kathryn Smith, Chandré Gould and Brian Rappert, on www.poisonedpasts.co.za.
6. Name has been changed.
7. Name has been changed.
8. Twenty years from now I will wonder if then president Jacob Zuma,

every time he speaks disparagingly of formal education and mocks 'clever blacks', realises how much he is following in the footsteps of apartheid masters in this regard.

9   In *From Marabastad to Mogadishu*, Hassen Ebrahim, then underground in Botswana, expresses similar uncertainty felt at the time. 'I had so many questions ... but no one was available to answer these. ... There was no leadership. ... I was uncertain as to what the risks (of going home) were. Until then I was a target for assassination. What changed?'

10   A report in the *Daily Maverick* of 8 June 2018 commemorates the event: 'Fifty years later – revisiting Robert F. Kennedy's "Ripple of Hope"' by David Reiersgord. See: www.dailymaverick.co.za.

11   See https://www.sahistory.org.za/people/winnie-madikizela-mandela.

12   See https://www.theguardian.com/world/2018/apr/02/winnie-madikizela-mandela-dies-aged-81.

13   See 'No country for old spies', 17 July 2019, https://www.groundup.org.za/article/no-country-old-spies/.

14   This form of execution and torture, called necklacing, was often meted out to suspected police informers in the townships.

15   On the occasion, Zuma made a specific 'dog whistling' accusation against white ANC veteran Derek Hanekom. Hanekom sued him for libel and won.

16   Also known as the Zondo Commission of Inquiry or Zondo Commission, a public inquiry launched by the Cyril Ramaphosa government in August 2018 to 'investigate allegations of State Capture, Corruption, Fraud and other allegations in the Public Sector Including Organs of State,' as Wikipedia puts it.

17   He sadly passed away on 9 November 2019. For a fitting obituary, see 'Poet and storyteller who burned with anger and love and hope' by Ruby Marks, on the *Daily Maverick* website.

18   *Die Suid-Afrikaan* features in the book *Afrikaanse Filosofie, Perspektiewe en dialoe* by Pieter Duvenage, African Sun Press, 2016.

19   See https://en.wikipedia.org/wiki/Affiche_Rouge.

20   For example, Swimming Federation head Morgan Naidoo and Non-Racial Soccer Federation chairman Norman Middleton, and Paula Ensor and Tim Dunne of NUSAS, the National Union of Students.

21   Like Sam Ramsamy, who from 1976 chaired the South African Olympic Committee (SANROC) that campaigned to exclude whites-only sports from the Olympics; Manikum M.N. Pather, a talented tennis player and the secretary of the South African Council of Sports (SACOS); and Cape cricket administrator Hassan Howa, a fearless campaigner against whites-only cricket with his non-racial South African Cricket Board of

Control. Pather would become the first South African to address the United Nations on the issue of apartheid sports, an act that resulted in South Africa being denied entry at every level to the international sporting arena.

22 In what may have been the first case of anti-government litigation ever carried through by a non-white community, they would eventually achieve much lower prices and residents were now able to buy their homes.

23 Formed by Mohandas Gandhi, the Natal Indian Congress (NIC) in 1895, and later the Transvaal Indian Congress (TIC) in 1903, preceded the formation of the ANC in 1912. Since racism – first in the form of a colour bar under the British Empire and from 1948 under formal apartheid – dictated the lives of all South Africans, most political formations were organised along racial lines. However, the non-racial principle in the Freedom Charter, which asserted that 'South Africa belongs to all who live in it', was embraced by the above organisations during the Defiance Campaign and the movement around the adoption of the Freedom Charter in the fifties. The Coloured People's Congress and the (white) Congress of Democrats also joined what was now called the Congress Alliance. The ANC – among other organisations – was banned in the early 1960s. While the NIC and TIC escaped that fate, large numbers of their senior leaders were imprisoned, exiled or individually banned, rendering their organisations moribund. After their revival in 1971, the NIC and the TIC played leading roles in the resurgence of activism and the mobilisation and organisation of people around political and civic issues. When the United Democratic Front (UDF) was formed in 1983, the NIC and TIC would be founder members. A few years later the UDF, and later COSATU, would adopt the Freedom Charter as well. The ANC opened its doors to all races in 1985 at its last Congress in exile in Lusaka.

24 On this issue, see, for example, the Black Consciousness article in the O'Malley Archives on the Nelson Mandela Foundation website: https://omalley.nelsonmandela.org/omalley/index.php/site/q/03lv02424/04lv02730/05lv03188/06lv03193.htm.

25 He describes what happened and the nightmares that followed him ever since, here: https://journals.co.za/docserver/fulltext/rujr/2004/24/rujr_n24_a7.pdf?expires=1574941364&id=id&accname=guest&checksum=4F7AB3219E2CD8D753D7A0C68A834FB1.

26 https://theconversation.com/mandelas-lawyer-bram-fischer-a-man-who-paid-the-ultimate-price-116436.

27 https://www.sahistory.org.za/people/joe-slovo.

28 Msomi was his clan name, which he used at BAWU; Pat's actual surname

was Nyawose, the name by which his and Jabu's children are now known.
29   Nomzamo Nyawose sadly passed away after a brief illness in 2003.
30   See the report 'Reform vs Oppression: the impact of the Wiehahn Commission on labour relations in South Africa'. https://intelliconn.wordpress.com/2012/11/02/reform-vs-oppression-the-impact-of-wiehahn-commission-on-labour-relations-in-south-africa/.
31   An affiliate of the Trade Union Council of South Africa, TUCSA; see https://www.sahistory.org.za/article/trade-union-council-south-africa-tucsa.
32   See the O'Malley Archives: https://omalley.nelsonmandela.org/omalley/index.php/site/q/03lv03445/04lv03996/05lv04011.htm for details.
33   See https://www.sahistory.org.za/people/billy-nair.
34   In contrast to the ANC's general silence on Operation Vula, Nelson Mandela publicly embraced its operatives on 22 June 1991. See the press statement he released here: https://omalley.nelsonmandela.org/omalley/cis/omalley/OMalleyWeb/03lv03445/04lv03996/05lv04005.htm.
35   Published by Jonathan Ball in 2009.
36   In earlier years Mbeki, according to Gevisser, still thought that mass insurrection, rather than guerrilla war, could bring down the regime, but Mbeki's later stance became almost completely focused on bringing the ANC into (shared) power through a 'charm offensive' towards the white rulers. See the chapter titled 'The Seducer' in *The Dream Deferred*.
37   The reporter was Subri Govender, of the *Daily News*.
38   Among them were Menziwe Mbewu, Muntu Myeza, Mosiuoa Terror Lekota, Strini Moodley, Saths Cooper and Aubrey Mokoape.
39   Walter Sisulu's daughter; later a minister.
40   Six South African protesters who were on trial for the murder of a deputy mayor in 1984.
41   There is now a Krishna Rabilal Road close to Hubli Place.
42   Name has been changed.
43   See the article in the *Mail & Guardian* on this at the time: https://mg.co.za/article/2013-12-20-zuma-impressed-by-venda-women-bowing-down-to-him.
44   https://www.sahistory.org.za/people/stephen-jc-dlamini.
45   This is the phonetic script of the name; Ivan has never seen it in writing, nor do we know any of Pattan's living relatives. Based on a search of Zambian names, it could be Pattern, or Potani.
46   See the book I wrote about this later, *Incorruptible*, 2018, distributed by Jacana Media.
47   It will occur to us later, at the time when dealmaker par excellence Donald

Trump is president of the United States, that he might see the world like this too.
48   The name of the editor has sadly faded from my memory; after so many years I am also not sure if the man I spoke to was the editor-in-chief or a bureau chief.
49   See his obituary in the UK Guardian: https://www.theguardian.com/world/2011/jun/19/frederick-chiluba-obituary.
50   https://www.tambofoundation.org.za/event/the-luthuli-detachment/.
51   Hassen Ebrahim, passing through the same camp two years later in 1979, describes the place as equipped with running water, so that had improved in the meantime.
52   Jacob Dlamini, *Askari: The Story of Collaboration and Betrayal in the Anti-Apartheid Struggle*, Jacana Media, 2015.
53   The comrade, George Molebatsi, would later be arrested and jailed for MK operations in Silverton and Soekmekaar. See: https://www.sahistory.org.za/article/silverton-and-soekmekaar-trial.
54   The story is derived from *In 't Hooge Nest* by Roxane van Iperen, Lebowski, the Netherlands, 2019: https://www.goodreads.com/en/book/show/42816183-t-hooge-nest.
55   Ivan would meet X again in South Africa much later, when both worked in the South African Security Services. X has since died.
56   A shoulder-fired missile weapon that launches rockets.
57   He worked with Ravi Pillay – now MEC of finance for KZN.
58   Baskie Desai, a medical doctor and a member of the Providence unit led by Pravin Gordhan.
59   I will meet General later as part of a group that joins the National Party and is part of its election drive in 1994; see also later in this book.
60   The escape is narrated in the book *Inside Out: Escape from Pretoria Prison* by Tim Jenkin, Jacana Media, 2005.
61   Vish Sewpersadh and Yusuf Vawda.
62   Barbara de Leeuw, Rens Trimp and Fred and Marianne Lubben, from the Netherlands, Ann Sanders from the UK and Alice Armstrong, a lecturer from the USA, all assisted with transport, shelter and storage. Nuns and a priest at the Mzimpofu Mission helped hide goods and people, too. They, and some others, drew a line at assisting with the military – weapons transports and so on – but Michael and June Stephen, socialists from the UK, who had been asked to resettle in southern Africa for the ANC, helped with that. They hosted Ronnie Kasrils when he visited Swaziland and moved in and out of South Africa in a camper with bunk beds, with their child sleeping on hidden arms caches. Another Londoner from activist circles, Peter Smith, was similarly active; Ivan

remembers laughing because the name 'Peter Smith' sounded so much like an underground alias. Dutch Jaap Geldof and André Ravesloot later also came to help.

63   Trying to contact David Manyatsi in 2019, Ivan and I were told that he was recently deceased.

64   Though the ANC kept to its tenet that it was not at war with the Swazi nation, and no one ever came forward to claim the assassination, it was perhaps not surprising that such retaliation would occur.

65   A disinformation unit in the apartheid police, see: https://ewn.co.za/2020/04/27/stratcom-what-it-actually-was-and-means.

66   https://www.iol.co.za/sundayindependent/two-lives-cut-short-in-their-prime-1711250.

67   See the reference to Petrus and Jabulile Nyawose, their formal names, here: https://www.iol.co.za/news/politics/pics-zuma-bestows-national-orders-1957444.

68   Fezeka and Beauty would be supported throughout by a small group including Ivan and Redi Tlhabi. Fezeka's life story is contained in the book *Khwezi*, by Redi Tlhabi, Jonathan Ball, 2017. Tlhabi donated proceeds of the book to the Kuzwayo family.

69   Zuma had an indirect role concerning the southern Natal underground Mandla Judson Kuzwayo (MJK) unit, which was coordinated by Ivan until his departure to Zambia. The unit was then handed over to Ebrahim Ebrahim and later, after Ebrahim's kidnapping from Swaziland, to Zuma. Since underground operative Moe Shaik, who was key to the unit in South Africa, did work that was going to be important to Vula – he had, inter alia, recruited a high-ranking member of the security police – Mac Maharaj would later request for the unit to report to the Vula Command. This was authorised by O.R. Tambo.

70   Over time, outside cadres Jabu Shoke, Rayman Lalla, Ronnie Kasrils, Dipuo Mvelase, Charles Ndaba and Susan Shabalala were infiltrated. Vuso Shabalala, who was already in South Africa, was linked up later. Operatives who were part of separate projects – Janet Love, Charles Nqakula, Max Ozinsky and Christopher 'Bricks' Manye, Totsie's husband – were incorporated into Vula as well. There were also many internally based comrades who became part of Vula structures. Among them were the members of Providence, members of the MJK unit, Jabu Sithole, Mbuso Shabalala, and Mpho Scott.

71   Later, another Dutch couple, Ineke and Lynx, came to live with Lucia in the same house to assist as the messages grew in number. Archie joined the Lusaka team too, as did Cassius Motsoaledi and KwaZulu-Natal comrade Tees Misthry.

72 Ivan still has pictures of 'fit for purpose' call boxes.
73 Thanks to some of her family living in Swaziland, Totsie had a Swazi passport.
74 TRC amnesty application AC/2001/099 on page 256: https://www.justice.gov.za/Trc/decisions/trc-adt-2001.pdf.
75 Ivan's brother Joe moved from Swaziland to Canada in 1985, emigrating to that country with his Canadian teacher wife Barbara Baer, whom he had met at Mzimpofu.
76 It has not been taken care of to this day.
77 The Griqua, people of mixed KhoiKhoi and European ancestry, occupied the region of central South Africa just north of the Orange River. They were guaranteed some degree of autonomy by a treaty with the British governor of South Africa in 1848. See: https://www.britannica.com/topic/Griqua.
78 The apartheid government allowed the 'black homelands' to be used for activities forbidden and/or frowned upon in South Africa, like gambling and striptease shows; in the bantustans you could also legally indulge in sexual relations across the colour barrier.
79 See, for example, http://www.thepresidency.gov.za/profiles/minister-jackson-mthembu%3A-profile.
80 https://en.wikipedia.org/wiki/Tokyo_Sexwale.
81 To our surprise, Ivan and I found out during the preparation for this book that the father of Ivan's later colleague at SARS, Johann van Loggerenberg, was the producer of the programme *Wielie Waalie* as well as the originator and producer of its theme song. Van Loggerenberg senior died in 2014, just before Ivan, Johann and others would be branded a rogue unit and removed from SARS.
82 See the record of the TRC hearing into the Piet Retief case here: https://www.justice.gov.za/trc/media/1999/9907/p990726b.htm.
83 See Harber's account of that event here: https://www.zimbabwesituation.com/old/sep22_2003.html.
84 Name has been changed.
85 Name has been changed.
86 Names have been changed.
87 Name has been changed.
88 https://www.news24.com/news24/MyNews24/Let-us-not-allow-Aids-to-ruin-our-dreams-20130402
89 They were active in the Providence ANC unit led by Pravin Gordhan. He, together with Yusuf Vawda and Vish Sewpersad, formed the leadership of the unit. Other key members were Baskie Desai, Baker Aboobaker, Rajin Pillay, Aroomugam Moodley, Tees Misthry, Rajenthren 'Jimmy' Sewpersad

and Logie Naidoo, who would later serve as deputy mayor in Durban.
90 An article in the *Mail & Guardian* in 2002 would raise hard-hitting questions about the recently deceased Mokaba's integrity, mentioning inter alia his 'deep-pocket taste in cars and clothes', his 'Viva Comrade Mengistu' speeches, and his apparently self-confessed close relations with the security police: see https://mg.co.za/article/2002-06-14-two-faces-of-mokaba.
91 See the report in the O'Malley Archives: https://omalley.nelsonmandela.org/omalley/index.php/site/q/03lv03445/04lv04015/05lv04154/06lv04181.htm.
92 https://www.dailymaverick.co.za/article/2016-03-29-cabals-and-cliques-the-roots-of-the-politics-of-influence/.
93 https://city-press.news24.com/Voices/indian-cabal-narrative-is-to-protect-the-looting-project-20181119.
94 See, for example, https://www.iol.co.za/news/politics/effkznrally-malema-attacks-indians-over-domestic-workers-salaries-20069101; https://www.timeslive.co.za/sunday-times/opinion-and-analysis/2018-11-25-we-must-find-the-courage-to-stand-up-to-the-racist-bully-julius-malema/; and https://citizen.co.za/news/south-africa/1979906/malema-says-hes-not-racist-brings-up-gordhans-indian-cabal/.
95 https://www.bbc.com/news/world-africa-22513410.
96 Victor Molefe, whose real name was Johannes Mnisi, had returned to his birth place, Mamelodi township near Pretoria, with a demobilisation gratuity. He later worked for the army, but at some point became unemployed. Klaas de Jonge kept in touch with him until 2001, but then lost contact. He notes hearing much later, shockingly, that Victor died 'in extreme poverty' in 2007.
97 Berning Ntlemeza, see later in this book or here: https://citizen.co.za/news/south-africa/1699128/five-things-you-probably-didnt-know-about-berning-ntlemeza/.
98 Names have been changed.
99 See Hilda Bernstein's 1991 interview with Mac Maharaj in the O'Malley Archives: https://omalley.nelsonmandela.org/omalley/index.php/site/q/03lv03445/04lv03996/05lv04011.htm.
100 *Vrye Weekblad* editor Max du Preez would recount the story in his book *Of Tricksters, Tyrants and Turncoats*, Penguin Random House, 2009.
101 See the article, 'Marx and the Dutch East India Company', by Pepijn Brandon: https://portside.org/2019-06-30/marx-and-dutch-east-india-company.
102 Name has been changed.

103 Name has been changed.
104 Name has been changed.
105 Both the children's names have also been changed.
106 Shell House is the Johannesburg building where the ANC located its headquarters in 1990; the party later moved to another building which it baptised Luthuli House after its legendary leader Chief Albert Luthuli.
107 See a report on the exercise: https://www.sahistory.org.za/dated-event/motsuenyane-commission-finds-african-national-congress-anc-guilty-abuse-its-camps.
108 'The rock that crushes' is the name commonly used for the ANC's security department. See: https://en.wikipedia.org/wiki/Department_of_National_Intelligence_and_Security_(South_Africa).
109 https://www.iol.co.za/news/south-africa/gauteng/pretoria-jail-named-after-mampuru-ii-1498632.
110 Name has been changed.
111 Contrary to many media reports.
112 See www.blacksash.org.za.
113 https://www.sahistory.org.za/people/ruth-heloise-first.
114 Name has been changed.
115 Its claim to fame is that the Treaty of Vereeniging that ended the Anglo Boer War (1899–1902) was negotiated there.
116 A practitioner of traditional African medicine.
117 The RDP was instituted to make a start with redress for the dispossessed black majority, allocating all black households below a certain income limit a basic housing grant.
118 Name has been changed.
119 The name of the school has been changed.
120 See https://www.sahistory.org.za/article/south-africas-key-economic-policies-changes-1994-2013.
121 The court case record can still be found here: http://www.elaws.gov.bw/desplaylrpage.php?id=1626&dsp=2.
122 See *Apartheid Guns and Money* by Hennie van Vuuren, Jacana Media, 2017.
123 *Incorruptible*, 2018.
124 See Terry Crawford-Browne's reports here: http://pmg-assets.s3-website-eu-west-1.amazonaws.com/docs/2001/submissions/offsets/ECAAR.htm.
125 As reported in the book *The Mini-Nuke Conspiracy* by Steve McQuillan and Peter Hounam, Viking, 1995. It must also be said that none of the men ever informed me of any particular secret projects, but over time I came to understand what some that later entered the public domain were about.
126 Johann van Loggerenberg has recently published a book about this period

127 in his life titled *Cop under Cover*, Jonathan Ball, 2020.
127 In the Dutch tradition, Black Pete is portrayed by a white person with shoe polish on his face, which, of course, makes the entire custom even more offensive.
128 Name has been changed.
129 Name has been changed.
130 Name has been changed.
131 Name has been changed.
132 The incident is described by Mark Gevisser in *The Dream Deferred*.
133 See https://www.news24.com/News24/White-media-slammed-over-Mbeki-20010506.
134 See https://www.independent.co.uk/news/anc-accused-of-purging-broadcasters-1091262.html.
135 See https://health-e.org.za/2000/10/27/zackie-achmat-openly-gay-hiv-positive-humanitarian-intensely-private/.
136 *After the Party* by Andrew Feinstein, Jonathan Ball, 2007.
137 See *The Dream Deferred*, p. 313.
138 Ibid., p. 164.
139 In 'A Legacy of Liberation', also by Mark Gevisser, the 'projection' of that 'image' is described as a conscious effort by the ANC Department of Information and Publicity to convince the rest of the world that the ANC was ready for power. But Mbeki's distrust of the armed struggle, and later dismissiveness of the underground and even of civic democratic structures seem to indicate that he had started believing in his own propaganda and had come to think that he and his officials were indeed going to take care of it all. See: https://www.sahistory.org.za/sites/default/files/archive-files/mark_gevisser_a_legacy_of_liberation_thabo_mbekbook4me.org__0.pdf.
140 See the report on the South African arms deal and the UK by the UK Campaign Against Arms Trade: https://www.caat.org.uk/resources/countries/south-africa/2003-06.caat.the-south-african-deal.pdf.
141 In *The Dream Deferred*, Mark Gevisser notes that Mbeki was always particularly sensitive to criticism from Slovo and other white comrades.
142 The letter is contained in Dolny's book *Banking on Change*, Penguin, 2001, pp. 234–8.
143 Six years on, Thabo Mbeki's cabinet will call for criminal charges to be laid against those implicated in questionable loans, but an audit report in late 2007 (https://mg.co.za/article/2007-11-11-officials-siphoned-off-farmers-billions) intended to underpin such charges would stay with the cabinet 'for study', while an investigation by the National Prosecuting Authority went nowhere. Only in 2008, the Ministry of Finance brought

in Treasury employee Phakamani Hadebe to bring the Land Bank back on sound footing, which he did. A charge laid by Hadebe for fraud against his immediate predecessor, acting head Philemon Mohlahlane, finally resulted in the conviction of Mohlahlane and two accomplices in 2018. However, this case only concerns a single case of looting of an agricultural fund in 2007/2008; the rest of the disastrous management of the post-Dolny era remains unpunished. See https://www.businesslive.co.za/fm/fm-fox/2018-02-02-corruption-buster-phakamani-hadebes-next-big-challenge/?platform=hootsuite; and https://www.news24.com/citypress/News/sabc-board-rocked-by-resignation-20171116. Also see https://www.farmersweekly.co.za/archive/lulama-you-lied-axed-land-bank-boss-stands-up-to-meddling-minister/.

144 See https://www.news24.com/news24/mynews24/Boetman-is-die-bliksem-in-20140728.
145 See https://www.zammagazine.com/chronicle/chronicle-0/9-dulcie-hani-lubowski-a-story-that-could-not-be-told.
146 See http://www.armsdeal-vpo.co.za/articles11/liar.html.
147 We were still able to take Sunday's two children across the border with only a note from their mother, then. The situation now is quite different.
148 From *Time is not the Measure* by Vusi Mavimbela, Real African Publishers, 2018.
149 Ibid.
150 *After the Party*, 2007, p. 169.
151 See the relevant news report on the News24 website: https://www.news24.com/SouthAfrica/Tshwete-claims-ANC-rebels-in-plot-to-oust-Mbeki-20010424.
152 Through ANC contacts, I had found then police commissioner Tim Williams willing to allow me to peruse the docket.
153 UK-based secret service expert James Sanders told me that MI6 head Anthony Rowell was 'the only foreign secret service head who had Mbeki's personal phone number'.
154 *The End of Apartheid: Diary of a Revolution*, Biteback Publishing, 2001.
155 It is remarkable that when the UK had sent a few respected members of its anti-terrorist police branch to help South Africa resolve the Hani murder case, the British squad focused on limiting the case to the two right wingers, and refused to look at any other evidence. Chris Hani's widow Limpho told me angrily that the British investigators refused outright to examine a cooldrink can and cigarette butts – presumably left there by someone besides Janusz Waluś – in and around the yard where her husband had been shot.
156 See https://www.theguardian.com/world/2001/apr/26/chrismcgreal.

157 See on this matter the Shabir Shaik judgment by Judge Hillary Squires: https://omalley.nelsonmandela.org/omalley/index.php/site/q/03lv03445/04lv04015/05lv04148/06lv04149.htm.
158 Zuma, in the aftermath of the conspiracy allegation against Ramaphosa, Sexwale and Phosa, issued a press statement titled 'Attempts to destabilise the ANC,' dated 3 April 2001, saying he had no ambitions to become president. Sadly, I could not find a web link, but it is quoted in *The Dream Deferred*, p. 363.
159 See Moe Shaik's book, *The ANC Spy Bible*, Tafelberg, 2020.
160 Investigations found no evidence of any influence exerted by Mac Maharaj to allocate this tender to Shaik's company. See, https://mg.co.za/article/2003-08-15-maharaj-cleared-of-corruption-but-reputation-tarnished.
161 This will later also be confirmed by Sam Sole. See: https://wikileaks.org/gifiles/docs/10/1083369-africa-south-africa-thabo-s-boys-vs-vula-s-boys-the-sequel-.html; and https://mg.co.za/article/2008-09-16-master-of-information.
162 A lower profile politician, ANC MP Tony Yengeni was jailed in March the same year for accepting a discount on a very expensive car. See: https://mg.co.za/article/2003-03-19-yengeni-gets-four-years-in-prison.
163 This may have been considered acceptable at that time, but was clearly unacceptable later. That said, there is also a difference between being helped by someone who has own money to do so, and abusing state resources (as long a such abuse does not happen as a result of having been gifted something).
164 Published by Jacana Media in 2012.
165 See https://mg.co.za/article/2007-01-12-arms-deal-who-got-r1bn-in-pay-offs. Of course corruption, also in minor amounts, is always unacceptable. But the point is that the Scorpions, instead of investigating the arms deal, really only considered themselves with some minor targets, probably because these were Mbeki's enemies.
166 David Bruce, for the Institute for Security Studies, would argue in 2008 that 'if it is true that investigative mechanisms have been subject to political manipulation, the key problem has then not been that Shaik, Zuma and others have been subjects of investigation, but that high level political officials obstructed other investigations that should have gone ahead. (…) If the ANC indeed wishes to prevent this type of abuse it should motivate government to adopt and enforce guidelines regulating the relationship between senior political officials and the leadership of investigative and prosecutorial agencies, in order to discourage and

	prevent this type of political interference.' Bruce did not, however, specify the type of guidelines or their preferred legal status; such guidelines have also not materialised in any form since. See: https://issafrica.org/01-jun-2008-sacq-24/01-jun-2008-without-fear-or-favour-the-scorpions-and-the-politics-of-justice-david-bruce.
167	Name has been changed.
168	Published by Jonathan Ball in 2018.
169	See Frantz Fanon, *The Wretched of the Earth* (1963), Grove Press, USA, 2005.
170	See Van Vuuren, *Apartheid Guns and Money*.
171	The successor of the anti-apartheid *Weekly Mail*.
172	See https://mg.co.za/article/2011-12-15-thabos-boys-vs-vulas-the-sequel.
173	Headman Khona reflected something that had been remarked upon by one or two Western academics as well: 'The greatest enemy of knowledge is not ignorance, but the illusion of knowledge', a quotation attributed alternatively to physicist Stephen Hawking and US historian Daniel Boorstin.
174	See https://mg.co.za/article/2010-08-13-the-nine-lives-of-wa-afrika. The business owner, travel agent Soraya Beukes, was eventually convicted for her role in the R13-million scam.
175	As, obviously, in the case of this book.
176	See excerpts from chapter three of *The Wretched of the Earth* here: https://www.marxists.org/subject/africa/fanon/pitfalls-national.htm.
177	Years later, a personal account will appear in *City Press* of a black farming family losing its land to locally powerful ANC members. See: https://www.news24.com/Columnists/GuestColumn/who-will-protect-you-when-the-anc-comes-for-the-land-20180819-2.
178	In *The ANC Spy Bible*, Moe Shaik reveals that Mac Maharaj informed Thabo Mbeki of their suspicions against Ngcuka and their plan to go public before they did so. According to Shaik, instead of advising against the move, the president simply said, 'Do what you have to do', thereby setting them up for defeat in the Hefer Commission.
179	See the Hefer Commission report here: https://www.justice.gov.za/commissions/comm_hefer/2004%2001%2020_hefer_report.pdf.
180	See Vusi Mavimbela, *Time is not the Measure*, Real African Publishers, 2018.
181	See https://www.sahistory.org.za/dated-event/vanessa-brereton-former-human-rights-lawyer-admits-she-was-apartheid-spy.
182	His article can be found here: https://mg.co.za/article/2018-10-05-00-my-role-in-sorry-saga-ofsarsrogue-unit.
183	The same Pearlie Joubert who had written about the Third Force operative João Cunha in Yeoville.

184 Then public protector Lawrence Mushwana issued a damning report about this: https://www.news24.com/SouthAfrica/News/Ngcuka-hands-in-resignation-20040724. Andrew Feinstein mentions the possibility that Mbeki simply wanted to get rid of the rival Zuma, but not really prosecute him, perhaps because of a fear that Zuma would spill the beans on other parts of the arms deal (page 230 in his book *After the Party*).

185 The South African Revenue Service is legally compelled to uphold the confidentiality of taxpayer's information, except under specific legal circumstances.

186 The story of this murder is meticulously described in Mandy Wiener's book *Killing Kebble*, Pan Macmillan, 2012.

187 On Porritt, see: https://city-press.news24.com/Business/fourteen-years-to-get-tigon-fraudsters-to-court-20190607.

188 Because of the indemnity given by the NPA to Kebble killers Mikey Schultz, Nigel McGurk and their alleged direct handler Clint Nassif, SARS found itself unable to institute tax cases against them with the NPA. The tax agency eventually opted for civil procedures, which resulted in sequestration of Schultz and McGurk and a claim of over R24 million, pursued in an insolvency inquiry, against Nassif.

189 The Ginwala Commission found that Pikoli should be reinstated; however, a protracted fight ensued and eventually this did not happen. See file:///C:/Users/Gebruiker/Downloads/2008_ginwala.pdf; and https://mg.co.za/article/2009-02-17-pikoli-removed-from-office-vows-to-fight-back.

190 See https://www.dailymaverick.co.za/article/2019-02-06-npa-blames-mbeki-government-for-failure-to-prosecute-trc-cases/.

191 See https://www.theglobeandmail.com/news/world/nelson-mandela/mandela-arrived-late-to-the-fight-against-hiv-aids/article548193/.

192 Kebble (senior) commited suicide in 2015.

193 See https://www.dispatchlive.co.za/news/2016-12-14-poison-plots-browse-moles-and-drug-mules--some-of-sas-oddest-spy-blunders/.

194 Pronounced Sahzje.

195 Named after anti-apartheid activist, political prisoner and politician Ahmed Kathrada, the Ahmed Kathrada Foundation promotes non-racialism and the principles within the Freedom Charter and the South African Constitution.

196 See Fanon, *The Wretched of the Earth*.

197 The report we produced can be seen here (in French): http://archive.niza.nl/docs/200607301109542605.pdf.

198 Name has been changed.

199 For a report on the impact of the series of investigative reports published during 2007 in the *Daily Dispatch* see https://impact.gijn.org/case-studies/why-freres-babies-die-south-africa/.

200 For a report on Malema's connections to tender fraud in Limpopo, see: https://mg.co.za/article/2011-08-05-how-julius-malema-pulls-tender-strings.

201 For a transcript of the calls, see: https://mg.co.za/article/2009-04-06-mpshe-reveals-contents-of-ngcuka-mccarthy-tapes.

202 The verdict by Judge Nicholson in the matter, its later overturning, and the protracted dithering by the NPA remained a contentious issue in South Africa's justice circles, up to the point when Zuma was finally charged in 2018.

203 Name has been changed.

204 Name has been changed.

205 https://www.businesslive.co.za/bd/national/2019-04-17-johan-booysen-tells-inquiry-he-was-ordered-to-drop-probe-into-thoshan-panday.

206 See, for example, https://www.dailymaverick.co.za/article/2018-01-17-analysis-the-rise-and-fall-of-richard-mdluli-a-man-who-damaged-our-society/.

207 A court case against the dissolution of the Scorpions resulted in the pronouncement that the new Directorate for Priority Crime Investigations, aka the Hawks, might take over these functions, but must not be part of the police and must remain independent. See: https://mg.co.za/article/2014-11-27-concourt-hawks-not-sufficiently-independent.

208 https://mg.co.za/article/2012-05-17-brown-envelope-journalism-rears-its-head-again.

209 https://www.news24.com/SouthAfrica/Politics/Mdluli-Paper-denies-police-bribes-20120517.

210 See the report here: https://successfulsocieties.princeton.edu/publications/reworking-revenue-service-tax-collection-south-africa-1999-2009.

211 In the FAIR network, we described how this happens all over Africa; see the following examples from Kenya and Mali: https://www.zammagazine.com/perspectives/blog/875-the-associates-mali-money-like-water; and https://thinkprogress.org/kenyan-officials-bite-back-after-a-report-reveals-purchase-of-85-pens-220f489552cf/.

212 See: https://www.sars.gov.za/AllDocs/SARSEntDoclib/Ent/SARS-Strat-10%20-%20SARS%20Strategic%20Plan%202013-14%20to%202017-18.pdf.

213 See, for example: https://www.news24.com/SouthAfrica/News/

exclusive-the-damning-evidence-against-julius-malema-the-npa-chose-to-ignore-20191201.

214 See, for example: https://mg.co.za/article/2010-02-26-mike-peega-the-man-behind-dossier/.

215 For an intelligence panel report on this, see: https://www.gov.za/sites/default/files/gcis_document/201903/high level-review-panel-state-security-agency.pdf. Also see: https://www.timeslive.co.za/politics/2020-02-19-zuma-dlomo-turned-ssa-special-ops-into-parallel-intelligence-security-unit/ ; and https://www.dailymaverick.co.za/article/2019-11-06-disappeared-crucial-documents-fingering-ssa-spies-who-infiltrated-sars/; and https://www.dailymaverick.co.za/article/2019-10-15-ssa-rogue-actors-constitute-clear-and-present-danger-to-our-democracy/.

216 The quotation is contained in the book *The President's Keepers* by Jacques Pauw, Tafelberg, 2017.

217 https://www.fin24.com/Economy/former-sars-exec-mandisa-mokwena-not-guilty-of-fraud-corruption-20170926.

218 https://citizen.co.za/news/south-africa/courts/2177137/highway-hennie-delport-sars-back-in-court-over-r264m-false-claims/.

219 Because of the indemnity given to Agliotti by the NPA, SARS continued to battle for a long time to act against the man, whom they believe acted as a conduit for and recipient of the bulk of stolen moneys from businesses associated with Brett Kebble. Eventually, as in the cases of the Brett Kebble killers, SARS obtained a civil judgment for R60 million against Agliotti, on the basis of which it sequestrated him.

220 First within SARS, later publicly: https://www.fin24.com/Economy/Plot-to-discredit-Gordhan-with-Zuma-20150225.

221 Ibid.

222 Nene recounted this incident to Ivan much later.

223 See https://citizen.co.za/news/south-africa/963742/arrow-still-aimed-at-rogue-unit/.

224 Johann van Loggerenberg and Adrian Lackay, *Rogue: The Inside Story of SARS's Elite Crime-busting Unit*, Jonathan Ball, 2016.

225 See https://mg.co.za/article/2014-03-20-big-tobacco-in-bed-with-sa-law-enforcement-agencies; and Johann van Loggerenberg's *Tobacco Wars*, Tafelberg, 2019.

226 See *The President's Keepers*; and https://www.thetimes.co.uk/article/russian-tycoon-sent-zuma-jet-full-of-money-pw7vd6bnv.

227 https://www.sars.gov.za/Media/MediaReleases/Pages/7-February-2013---SARS-Enforcement-and-Customs-Operations-for-January-2013.aspx.

228 https://www.pressreader.com/south-africa/the-witness/20140219/281479274319728.
229 https://www.timeslive.co.za/politics/2020-02-19-zuma-dlomo-turned-ssa-special-ops-into-parallel-intelligence-security-unit/.
230 https://www.news24.com/SouthAfrica/News/Ministers-wife-in-drug-scandal-20090315.
231 https://www.bbc.com/news/world-africa-13310034.
232 https://www.dailymaverick.co.za/article/2018-01-23-scorpio-the-curious-case-of-anc-benefactor-robert-huang-a-never-ending-investigation-and-billions-owed-to-sars/.
233 Moe Shaik's affidavit before the Zondo Commission https://sastatecapture.org.za/site/files/documents/202/PP_1._R_Shaik_-_Affidavit.pdf.
234 https://www.politicsweb.co.za/party/report-on-inquiry-into-oupa-magashula.
235 Ibid.
236 https://www.timeslive.co.za/sunday-times/lifestyle/2013-07-14-the-drug-lord-who-took-oupa-down/.
237 See https://en.wikipedia.org/wiki/Gupta_family; and also later in this book.
238 Mba never got the job.
239 https://www.news24.com/SouthAfrica/News/black-girls-in-tears-at-pretoria-school-hair-protest-20160829.
240 Makhene, now late, and her husband's connections to the State Security Agency's Special Operations rogue unit feature in this article: https://www.news24.com/SouthAfrica/News/exclusive-how-ssa-spooks-kidnapped-one-of-their-own-20170924.
241 This meant that Siyabonga Cwele was removed from this powerful position, but Mahlobo was hardly an improvement. Cwele remained a minister too, albeit in the less important portfolio of telecommunications and postal services.
242 https://www.news24.com/Analysis/malusi-gigaba-and-state-capture-a-short-history-of-eskom-transnet-and-home-affairs-20181105.
243 https://www.timeslive.co.za/news/south-africa/2018-09-27-bathabile-dlamini-was-reckless-and-grossly-negligent-says-concourt-as-it-orders-her-to-pay-up/.
244 See, for example: https://www.iol.co.za/news/opinion/not-the-first-time-muthambis-character-is-in-the-spotlight-7199813.
245 https://www.news24.com/SouthAfrica/News/nkoana-mashabanes-bizarre-interview-a-spectacular-mess-20160530.
246 See https://www.news24.com/Archives/City-Press/Sex-Sars-and-

246 rogue-spies-20150429; and https://www.pressreader.com/south-africa/citypress/20140810/281479274574885.
247 See https://mg.co.za/article/2018-09-26-illicit-tobacco-trade-team-targeted-fellow-sars-employees.
248 See https://www.timeslive.co.za/news/south-africa/2014-08-10-love-affair-rocks-sars/.
249 Having been accused of a conflict of interest when he, while working at SARS, started a relationship with a representative of a tobacco company, Johann emphasises that he did not know of Belinda Walter's Carnilinx ties at first; and that he, when he discovered these, presented her with a choice: either she was to break off with him, or with Carnilinx. In the book *Rogue*, Johann describes how this fact, from his own affidavits and confirmed by Walter, was ignored in the Sikhakhane report. More detail on the matter can be found in his subsequent book *Tobacco Wars*.
250 See https://www.dailymaverick.co.za/article/2016-11-29-reality-check-how-rogue-unit-allegations-weakened-sars-and-undermined-its-authority/.
251 See also later in this book.
252 A remarkable complaint, considering that a Griqua leader had told Bart and me during our tour guide research that they wanted to remain undetected by the government.
253 This may have been the intention of Gayton McKenzie's Patriotic Front in 2014 as well, Ivan thinks, and also more recently at the 2019 elections the purpose of Black First Land First, the aptly called ATM, African Transformation Movement, and Hlaudi Motsoeneng's African Content Movement or ACM.
254 See https://mg.co.za/article/2015-11-20-00-zumas-deal-with-cape-gang-bosses.
255 *Nothing Left to Steal*, Penguin Random House, 2014.
256 See, for example: https://mg.co.za/article/2014-12-30-fearless-corruption-buster/; and https://www.thejournalist.org.za/the-craft/in-search-of-the-truth.
257 See https://www.pressreader.com/south-africa/sunday-times-1107/20141012/281479274659278.
258 www.zammagazine.com.
259 https://www.zammagazine.com/perspectives/the-contrarian/169-it-s-not-poverty-that-is-to-blame-for-the-weak-african-responses-to-ebola-but-bad-leadership.
260 For that story, see: https://www.zammagazine.com/images/pdf/documents/African_Oligarchs.pdf.
261 https://www.news24.com/Archives/City-Press/Zuma-scolds-clever-

blacks-20150429.
262 See https://www.pressreader.com/south-africa/cape-times/20190702/281706911230123.
263 See https://mg.co.za/article/2011-06-17-timing-of-eskom-shakeup-questioned; and https://mg.co.za/article/2016-03-24-00-the-gupta-owned-state-enterprises.
264 https://www.timeslive.co.za/politics/2019-05-07-it-was-a-sophisticated-operation-popo-molefe-on-how-transnet-was-captured/.
265 See Saloojee's testimony to the Zondo Commission: https://www.news24.com/SouthAfrica/News/mantshas-appointment-as-denel-board-chair-seen-as-continuation-of-takeover-saloojee-20190320.
266 https://city-press.news24.com/News/denel-lost-r30bn-in-deals-due-to-gupta-bribes-20191125.
267 https://www.news24.com/Books/extract-paper-tiger-soon-a-purge-of-senior-staff-began-at-independent-newspapers-20191027.
268 See Maseko's statement, first made in the ANC enquiry into the Guptas, as contained in former public protector Thuli Madonsela's State of Capture report: https://www.gov.za/sites/default/files/gcis_document/201611/stateofcapturereport14october2016_1.pdf.
269 See, for example, https://www.news24.com/SouthAfrica/News/Hawks-boss-named-in-rendition-drama-20131013.
270 https://mg.co.za/article/2016-09-15-crib-notes-why-everyone-is-burning-ntlemeza.
271 https://citizen.co.za/news/south-africa/state-capture/2180390/newspaper-reports-were-used-to-cast-suspicion-on-dramat-sibiya-zondo-hears/.
272 Koko Matshela's charge that he paid Wa Afrika to make a bad story go away was still with the Hawks in 2019. See, https://www.iol.co.za/news/politics/sunday-times-editor-subpoenaed-as-hawks-investigate-koko-bribe-claims-30001778. Information in the Pule case has it that Wa Afrika did attend a private meeting with Pule on behalf of a businessman, Jomo Sono, who was in the running for a contract at her ministry. See, https://mg.co.za/article/2013-04-28-jomo-sono-thrown-into-pules-blackmail-fray. In a third case, Public Investment Corporation head Dan Matjila stated before an enquiry that he had a private meeting with Wa Afrika in 2017, in which he 'convinced' the journalist that a story about an alleged use of state funds for a girlfriend 'was untrue'. Wa Afrika, Matjila stated, accepted this and said he would not publish it for that reason. See, https://www.justice.gov.za/commissions/pic/trns/2019-07-10-PICC-Transcript-Day52.pdf.
273 Until a change of management in 2016.

274 See, for example: https://mg.co.za/article/2011-04-08-spy-boss-alerted-zuma-about-plot and https://mg.co.za/article/2012-04-22-crime-intelligence-unit-spent-r5m-on-mdluli-family.
275 See https://mg.co.za/article/2016-10-27-how-ethical-concerns-over-gordhan-pursuit-lead-to-a-hostage-drama-at-sars.
276 The early retirement charges against Ivan, Oupa Magashula and Pravin Gordhan were withdrawn after the incident.
277 Sikhakhane's finding had probably been based on the National Strategic Intelligence Act, which forbids, as pointed out by legal expert Pierre de Vos and others, the covert gathering of intelligence relating to 'threats to the national security and stability' of the country by anyone but the official secret services. But as long as there is no suggestion that the unit investigated 'potential threats to national security', De Vos writes, the claim that the so-called spy unit breached the National Strategic Intelligence Act 'would be a legal nonsense'. The SARS investigators only investigated tax offences, which, De Vos also points out, is allowed by the act. It says any state department can 'gather departmental intelligence, and (…) evaluate, correlate and interpret such intelligence for the purpose of discharging such function.' See, https://constitutionallyspeaking.co.za/hawks-not-authorised-to-investigate-establishment-of-sars-rogue-unit/.
278 The Nugent Commission later accepted that there was such a basis. See https://www.fin24.com/Economy/reminder-what-the-nugent-commission-said-about-the-sars-rogue-unit-20190705.
279 As quoted in the report of the Nugent Commission of Inquiry, 2018. See the full report here: http://www.thepresidency.gov.za/download/file/fid/1466.
280 Pete Richer was not excluded from cover, but his costs, in the aftermath of the Labour Court case, were lower since he was not charged.
281 https://witsvuvuzela.com/2015/03/31/sadtu-story-wins-investigative-journalism-award/.
282 On Lepelle also see https://mg.co.za/article/2015-02-12-water-wars-expose-a-rotten-system-bleeding-cash/.
283 See https://mg.co.za/article/2015-05-21-peers-fear-upright-water-affairs-official-was-assassinated; and https://specials.zammagazine.com/southafrica/in-the-trenches-of-the-corruption/.
284 See https://www.timeslive.co.za/news/south-africa/2018-10-18-twitter-gobsmacked-at-sars-it-bosss-testimony-at-nugent-commission/.
285 https://www.pressreader.com/south-africa/sunday-times-1107/20150503/281505044775977.
286 The Zondo Commission subsequently heard a lot more about Ntlemeza,

from consorting with underworld figures in the so-called North West gang and threatening and intimidating IPID employees, to concocting cases against Robert McBride and other individuals perceived as obstacles, to protecting close associate Richard Mdluli from murder investigations.

287 See https://mg.co.za/article/2019-04-15-kgamanyane-wasted-no-time-restructuring-ipid-in-mcbrides-absence.

288 See https://mg.co.za/article/2014-05-29-new-skeleton-leaps-out-of-npa-cupboard.

289 See https://www.news24.com/SouthAfrica/News/Proud-moment-for-Maritzburg-Best-qualified-for-the-NPA-jobGreat-stepping-stone-for-me-20150618.

290 During this period, the Hawks also charged Oupa Magashula, Pravin Gordhan, Ivan, Johann van Loggerenberg and Andries Janse van Rensburg of SARS; Robert McBride, Matthews Seseko and Innocent Khuba of IPID; Anwa Dramat, Shadrack Sibiya and Leslie Maluleke of the Hawks. All these charges have been dropped except the one against Leslie Maluleke, which remains inactive.

291 Once again the *Sunday Times* led the charge: https://www.timeslive.co.za/news/south-africa/2016-11-14-denel-ceo-takes-golden-handshake/.

292 The Nugent Commission of Inquiry into SARS was established in May 2018 by newly installed President Cyril Ramaphosa.

293 https://www.dailymaverick.co.za/article/2018-10-05-the-bain-files-part-1-massone-knew-in-advance-moyane-would-become-sars-head-and-bain-would-get-restructuring-contract/.

294 https://www.timeslive.co.za/politics/2019-03-24-did-thuli-madonsela-help-prep-jacob-zuma-for-top-job/ and https://select.timeslive.co.za/ideas/2019-03-27-analysis-the-big-state-capture-questions-zondo-must-get-answered/.

295 It was very concretely detailed that all employees of SARS should receive labels varying from 'positive sponsorship' to 'watch out' to 'neutralize.' Testimony before the Nugent Commission later also revealed that Moyane had a hit list of officials he wanted removed. See, https://www.businesslive.co.za/bd/national/2018-09-28-hlengani-mathebula-says-tom-moyane-had-a-hit-list-of-sars-staff/.

296 SSA spy, tobacco lawyer and rogue unit smear source Belinda Walter consulted for KPMG with regard to the tobacco industry from 2009 to 2014. This apparently was not considered a conflict of interest impacting on KPMG's investigation of the rogue unit: https://www.fin24.com/Companies/controversial-attorney-and-alleged-spy-belinda-walter-

was-a-consultant-for-senior-kpmg-manager-20180430. A few months into their investigation, KPMG was also appointed by tobacco firm BAT, itself a player in the murky industry, as its external auditors: https://www.dailymaverick.co.za/article/2017-10-03-sars-wars-kpmg-report-the-firm-the-lawyers-the-auditor-and-the-blame-game/.

297 See https://www.pressreader.com/south-africa/business-day/20180307/281487866856699.

298 Chabane's family raised suspicions that the accident had something to do with an ANC conflict. Family member Thembani Chabane stated that the truck driver who caused the accident told inmates in the police cells that he had been paid R15,000 by a provincial executive member of the ANC to do what he did. However, when the ANC laid a charge of defamation against him, he retracted, saying that 'the content of my (earlier) statement was not guided by factual or concrete evidence but only rumours that were flying in the streets'. The ANC then dropped the charges against Thembani Chabane. The truck driver was sentenced to six years' imprisonment. See, https://www.iol.co.za/news/anc-denies-chabane-was-assassinated-1835673.

299 https://mg.co.za/article/2015-02-12-exposed-scary-details-of-secret-russian-nuke-deal.

300 https://www.theguardian.com/world/2013/nov/29/jacob-zuma-accused-corruption-south-africa.

301 https://www.iol.co.za/news/politics/sars-will-deal-with-nkandla-tax-issue-da-1670613.

302 https://mg.co.za/article/2018-09-28-judge-kroon-backtracks-on-ruling-that-rogue-unit-was-unlawful.

303 The Gupta's ANN7 TV, *New Age* and associated websites cannot be called 'media' and are therefore not included here.

304 An image of the complaint is included in this article: https://www.biznews.com/leadership/2017/09/15/sars-wars-moyane-gordhan.

305 See the reports on these curious developments by Marianne Thamm in *Daily Maverick*.

306 https://www.politicsweb.co.za/news-and-analysis/sars-this-is-the-inside-story--adrian-lackay.

307 Name has been changed.

308 See http://www.thepresidency.gov.za/download/file/fid/1466.

309 The weblink to the Press Council came, mystifyingly, with a virus warning when I tried, but it is https://www.presscouncil.org.za/johann-van-loggerenberg-vs-sunday-times-2874/. A media report on the verdict can be found here: https://www.news24.com/SouthAfrica/News/press-ombudsman-slams-sunday-times-for-unfair-sars-reports-20151216.

310 https://citizen.co.za/news/south-africa/2017511/why-i-refused-to-sign-off-on-nuclear-deal-despite-zuma-pressure-nene/.
311 https://www.news24.com/SouthAfrica/News/i-didnt-want-to-be-part-of-unethical-and-immoral-practices-ex-sunday-times-journalist-20151201.
312 https://www.bbc.com/news/world-africa-35093552.
313 https://www.politicsweb.co.za/documents/project-spider-web-the-full-document.
314 https://twitter.com/SongezoZibi/status/1046001596981743616.
315 https://www.defenceweb.co.za/security/national-security/feature-communications-interception-device-bust-highlights-the-world-of-non-government-spying/.
316 An exercise to collect state capture testimonies in 2017 by the South African Council of Churches was much more successful, as well as revealing. See, http://sacc.org.za/news/sacc-report-church-public-unburdening-panel-process-regina-mundi-church-soweto-may-18-2017/.
317 https://city-press.news24.com/Voices/zuma-the-ozymandias-of-the-south-20160325.
318 https://www.kathradafoundation.org/download/letter-to-the-president/.
319 https://issafrica.s3.amazonaws.com/site/uploads/PolBrief64.pdf.
320 https://www.saferspaces.org.za/blog/entry/political-assassinations-taking-a-hold-on-the-2019-elections.
321 https://www.news24.com/SouthAfrica/News/we-got-certain-things-wrong-sunday-times-on-sars-rogue-unit-stories-20160403.
322 Wa Afrika stopped doing that again in years to come, though, when both he and Piet Rampedi moved to the pro-Zuma kingdom of the remarkably named Independent Newspapers.
323 Mkhize is now minister of health and Mantashe minister of mineral resources in Cyril Ramaphosa's government; Jessie Duarte is once again deputy secretary-general of the ANC.
324 With the appointment of Richard Mdluli, Crime Intelligence had been the first state institution placed completely under Zuma's control, as far back as 2009.
325 https://www.politicsweb.co.za/documents/why-we-were-targeted--robert-mcbride-ivan-pillay--.
326 http://www.wachizungu.com/139207955.
327 See https://www.dailymaverick.co.za/article/2016-11-29-reality-check-how-rogue-unit-allegations-weakened-sars-and-undermined-its-authority/. KPMG was later exposed for having copied and pasted findings written by lawyers hired by Tom Moyane as own conclusions

in their draft report: https://constitutionallyspeaking.co.za/was-there-a-mutually-beneficial-symbiosis-between-sars-and-kpmg/. Amid much embarrassment, KPMG will withdraw the findings, recommendations and conclusions in September 2017: https://www.timeslive.co.za/politics/2017-09-15jh-kpmg-cans-sars-rogue-unit-report-apologises-to-gordhan/.

328 https://mg.co.za/article/2016-10-11-breaking-gordhan-summoned-for-fraud.
329 https://specials.zammagazine.com/.
330 See https://www.enca.com/south-africa/for-the-sake-of-our-future-stalwarts-call-for-renewal-of-anc.
331 https://www.youtube.com/watch?v=Fnyue-D6LeM.
332 https://www.youtube.com/watch?v=eQbfX1Si6wE.
333 The exact line is from 17th-century English poet John Dryden, paraphrasing Horatius.
334 As narrated here: https://mg.co.za/article/2013-04-10-a-culture-of-service-and-tolerance-lessons-from-chris-hani/
335 See this among many other enlightening quotes here: https://www.enca.com/south-africa/i-ve-got-to-be-honest-to-the-people-of-south-africa-zuma-in-quotes.
336 A report in 2019 will show that rapes of female fellow soldiers, the practice Ntsiki/Nombulelo had come home crying about in 1994, still happen in the South African National Defence Force. See, https://beta.mg.co.za/article/2019-11-22-00-sandf-sexual-abuse-and-exploitation-exposed/.
337 Activists still have some work to do here.
338 https://www.gupta-leaks.com/.
339 https://www.timeslive.co.za/politics/2017-10-05-justice-ministers-attack-on-former-constitutional-court-judge/.
340 Ironically, Cyril Ramaphosa owes his victory to D.D. Mabuza, who threw in his constituency with the Ramaphosa faction in a surprise move just before the conference, possibly precisely because he was eyeing the deputy presidency.
341 'Skollie' suffered a few tragedies in his family in 2007 besides losing his son to brain cancer. His mother died in a car crash on the night that life support for the little boy was switched off. He had also lost his first wife to a car accident a short time before. The traumatic events caused his departure from SARS in 2008.
342 The NPA decided to prosecute a Malema-connected company in the case, On Point Engineering, in December 2019. See, https://citizen.co.za/news/south-africa/courts/2205922/npa-to-prosecute-on-point-

engineering-and-a-dead-man-but-not-malema/.

343 https://www.timeslive.co.za/politics/2018-12-04-malema-welcomes-batohis-appointment-as-npa-boss/.

344 See Motau's report here: https://www.resbank.co.za/Lists/News%20and%20Publications/Attachments/8830/VBS%20Mutual%20Bank%20-%20The%20Great%20Bank%20Heist.pdf.

345 Also see https:/ww.dailymaverick.co.za/article/2018-11-21-vbs-bank-heist-effs-family-ties-and-moneyed-connections/.

346 Their work resulted in a declaratory order court instructing the Hawks to act with regard to the theft and corruption. A civil judgment overturned an over R3-billion contract for unsuitable locomotives. See: https://mg.co.za/article/2019-07-12-00-prasa-eyes-iced-company-for-its-billions.

347 PRASA's chief financial officer, Yvonne Page, who had refused to sign off on the payments, had eventually lost her job. See https://www.groundup.org.za/article/vbs-scandal-prasa-employee-hailed-her-role-saving-r1-billion/.

348 See the article here: https://www.news24.com/Columnists/GuestColumn/recover-blackness-butchered-during-zuma-years-20190708.

349 https://www.pressreader.com/south-africa/sunday-times-1107/20180527/281517931791346.

350 https://mg.co.za/article/2019-11-21-former-minister-bongani-bongo-arrested-on-corruption-charges.

351 https://twitter.com/lestsoalo/status/1152965741009936384.

352 See, for example, https://www.thesouthafrican.com/news/offbeat/atm-bill-gates-trevor-noah-tennis-match-vaccine-africa/; and https://twitter.com/ntsikimazwai/status/1247208020527976448.

353 https://www.news24.com/news24/SouthAfrica/News/more-than-r330m-in-less-than-2-years-massive-extent-of-gupta-plundering-at-estina-revealed-20190213.

354 The office she leads issued statements saying that there was no such focus and that it has 'handled over ten thousand cases in one year', but in practice, the only (former) state officials who find themselves continuously in trouble are Pravin Gordhan, Ivan, Johann van Loggerenberg, Yolisa Pikie, Oupa Magashula and President Cyril Ramaphosa himself. Ivan had to spend weeks replying in affidavits to six or seven rehashed pension and rogue unit cases. See: https://www.dailymaverick.co.za/article/2019-12-19-the-fixers-2-pravin-gordhan-hitting-a-dead-end-as-fightback-takes-a-toll/.

355 https://www.timeslive.co.za/news/south-africa/2017-09-04-report-fingers-bell-pottinger-in-white-monopoly-capital-campaign/.

356 Mzilikazi wa Afrika escapes such listing, together with – unlikely

	companions if ever there were – the old white editor of the gossip magazine, who continues to harp on about all things Vula and rogue and has been abundantly congratulated by the EFF for doing so.
357	See, for example, https://theintercept.com/2020/04/24/quack-chief-donald-trump-asks-bleach-injections-tanning-cure-covid-19/.
358	https://www.timeslive.co.za/sunday-times/opinion-and-analysis/2020-03-22-surprise-surprise-the-fly-in-ramaphosas-covid-19-ointment-is-a-zuma-flunkey/.
359	Best to Google this one.
360	https://www.timeslive.co.za/sunday-times/news/2020-04-12-sun-city-accused-of-staging-covid-19-preparedness-act-for-lamola/.
361	https://ewn.co.za/2020/01/20/ramaphosa-govt-has-prioritised-task-of-building-capable-state.
362	https://www.aljazeera.com/indepth/features/open-letter-african-intellectuals-leaders-covid-19-200417140154396.html.
363	See https://www.dailymaverick.co.za/article/2020-04-15-phophi-ramathuba-a-health-mec-out-of-touch-and-out-of-place/; and https://www.news24.com/SouthAfrica/News/covid-19-mkhize-furious-with-eastern-cape-health-mec-and-team-sends-reinforcements-20200423.
364	She later apologises and also earns herself a two-month suspension, see https://mg.co.za/article/2020-04-08-stella-ndabeni-abrahams-out-jackson-mthembu-takes-over/.
365	See https://allafrica.com/view/group/main/main/id/00055286.html.
366	See https://www.dailymaverick.co.za/article/2020-05-15-collins-khosa-ruling-judge-slams-police-and-army-lockdown-deployment/.
367	And with Sri's professor at a business school, where he is now working on a PhD, Dr Tarun Kumar Singhal, Symbiosis Centre for Management Studies, Noida, India.
368	https://www.dailymaverick.co.za/article/2020-04-24-covid-19-needs-a-strategic-war-effort/.
369	Ntombenhle Nyawose contracted COVID-19 in July 2020 and spent harrowing days in ICU. At the time of writing of this book, she was slowly recovering.
370	https://www.news24.com/SouthAfrica/News/sunday-times-to-return-prizes-money-for-discredited-reports-20181014.

Index

A

Abrahams, Shaun 323, 348, 352, 358
African Investigative Publishing Collective (AIPC) 307, 320, 343
African National Congress (ANC) 103, 126, 166, 302, 339, 359, 360
　Internal Political Reconstruction Committee (IPRC) 90, 91, 100, 102
　NASREC conference 359
　peace negotiations *see* democratic transition
　political underground 77, 85, 89, 91, 99
　Polokwane conference 265
Agliotti, Glenn 245, 247, 283, 300, 308
ANC in exile
　Angola 14, 15, 19, 21, 90, 92, 167
　Botswana 87, 88
　Cuba 31
　Mozambique 84, 85
　Swaziland 76, 77, 88, 98, 100, 101, 102, 107
　USSR 30, 31
　Zambia 18, 20, 28, 102, 106
ANC/IFP/Third Force violence 21, 59, 69, 71, 73, 76, 125, 126, 151, 167, 198, 199
Ansell, Gwen 233, 252, 254, 274, 306
Anti-Apartheid Movement of the Netherlands (AABN) 9, 11, 13, 31, 41, 127, 132, 155, 181
anti-Indian sentiment 25–26, 139, 140, 142, 366
armed struggle 15, 16, 58, 59, 77, 88, 90, 97, 99, 100, 102
arms deal 159, 191, 215, 221, 226, 231, 238, 242, 269, 278, 361, 398, 400, 402
arms trade 196, 197, 199, 219, 220, 221, 223, 227, 250, 251, 252

B

Back to the Future 12, 17, 35, 43
Bain & Company 324–25, 367 *see also* Project Phoenix
Biko, Steve 48, 53, 62, 87
Black Allied Workers Union (BAWU) 52–54, 62–64, 78

Black Consciousness Movement 25, 27, 48, 52, 53, 62, 63, 68
Black People's Convention 48
Booysen, Johan 276, 311, 324, 361
Border Management Authority (BMA) 286–89
Botha, Pik 123, 152, 188, 196, 250, 252
Braam, Conny 9, 11, 15, 17, 18, 31, 34, 38, 44, 56, 61, 96, 106, 109, 115, 378
Brown, Lynne 297, 298, 326
Browse Mole 255
Bulunga, Bee Bhabhalazi 195, 200, 229, 232, 307, 377
Burnett, Steve 196, 197, 263

C

cabal allegations 139, 142, 279, 362
Chetty, Roy 48, 52, 57
civil society action 15, 101, 259, 266, 350, 353, 357, 372
Commission on the Cabal 139, 140
community organising 47, 52, 63, 68, 69, 101, 137, 139, 166, 354
Conference for a Democratic South Africa (CODESA) 139, 143, 144, 156
Cook, Colleen 61, 66, 132, 133
Cook, Jasper 61, 160, 162, 167
corruption 216, 217, 226, 229, 236, 244, 247, 264, 267, 290, 308, 310, 320, 328, 338, 351, 359, 362, 363, 364
Crime Intelligence 276, 311–312, 342
Cwele, Sheryl 287
Cwele, Siyabonga 285, 288, 290, 405

D

De Jonge, Klaas 14, 18, 35, 36, 37, 41–44, 56, 109, 373, 396
De Leeuw, Barbara 113, 129, 377, 393
democratic transition 16, 22, 103, 104, 144, 154, 167, 168, 169, 170, 171
peace negotiations 59, 60, 108, 109
Dikeni, Sandile 44, 48, 49, 56
dossiers and disinformation 221, 225, 238, 239, 240, 241, 244, 247, 250, 251, 255, 256, 279, 280, 283, 285, 286, 291, 297, 304, 314, 334, 336, 341, 346, 356
Dramat, Anwa 277, 311, 318, 323, 324, 336, 340, 361, 376, 409
Duarte, Jessie 190, 191, 212, 221, 271, 272, 322, 329, 336, 341, 357, 360
Duarte, John 271, 322, 349

E

education transformation 205, 212, 236, 237

F

Forum for African Investigative Reporters (FAIR) 233, 235, 251, 252, 258–61, 258, 272–77, 307, 342
Fourie, Charl, 238, 263
Freedom Charter 12, 47, 56, 63, 68, 379, 391, 402

G

gender-based violence 69–71, 146, 169, 182, 183, 184, 252–55, 355, 365
good civil servants 235, 300, 340, 362, 364
Gordhan, Pravin 54, 59, 68, 69, 94, 139, 141, 143, 144, 195, 200, 224, 227, 232, 243, 247, 269, 271, 278, 279, 282, 285, 298, 302, 314, 324, 328, 334, 335, 339, 347, 352, 356, 361, 362, 365, 366, 373, 393, 395, 408, 409, 413
Govender, Coastal 23–25, 46, 47, 57, 62, 67, 86, 129, 143, 245, 249, 375
Govender, Elvis 92, 93, 129, 130, 190, 271

Govender, Jenny 29, 33, 37, 80, 86, 95, 102, 130, 245, 375
Govender, Pushpa (Sister) 26, 27, 29–30, 32–33, 37, 79, 95, 102, 130, 156, 173, 174, 245, 350, 375
Groenink, Evelyn
  investigative journalism, 13, 32, 81, 152, 196, 198, 199, 219, 220, 223, 228, 233, 234, 235, 250, 252, 258, 264, 272, 275, 307, 320, 343, 351
Groenink/Hommes family
  Groenink, Fred 13
  Groenink, Maarten 112, 113
  Hommes, Mirjam 111
  Meersschaert, Helena (Oma Lenie) 13, 161, 162
Growth, Employment and Redistribution policy (GEAR) 202, 203
Gupta family 290, 291, 298, 309, 327, 338, 351

H
Hani, Chris 18, 41–44, 88, 101, 126, 127, 138, 144, 154, 156, 167, 220, 222, 223, 252, 354, 399
Hawks 277, 311, 315, 318, 323, 341, 342, 347, 348, 357, 403, 407, 409, 413
Hefer Commission 239, 240
HIV/AIDS epidemic 210, 213, 214, 216
Hofstatter, Stephan 276, 296, 335, 340
Hogan, Barbara 61, 65, 144, 222, 269, 356
Holomisa, Bantu 17, 43, 44
Hopkins Street house 61, 62, 65, 121, 133
hostel violence 69, 71–73

I
impimpi panic 16, 38, 39, 49, 101
Independent Police Complaints Directorate (IPID) 183, 323, 341, 358
Inkatha 54, 57, 71, 146, 150
international solidarity 11, 12, 13, 17, 30, 31, 69, 95, 106, 113, 155

J
Jacobs, Bheki 167, 221, 222, 225
Janse van Rensburg, Andries "Skollie" 263, 361, 372, 409
Jenkin, Tim 93, 106, 377
Jiba, Nomgcobo 323, 358
Joubert, Pearlie 150, 151, 243, 297, 312, 334, 335, 340, 401
journalism 49, 123, 126, 228, 234, 251, 260, 264, 272, 276, 307, 357
Juggernath, Janey 127, 129, 375
Juggernath, Spider 129, 375

K
Kasrils, Ronnie 45, 254, 345, 393, 394
Kathrada, Ahmed 339, 350, 354
  funeral 353–56
Kebble, Brett 244, 246, 250, 252
Kemp, Stephanie 146, 349
Kesavan, Sri 272, 311, 312, 344, 343, 347, 371
King, Dave 282, 283, 304
KPMG 317, 324, 344, 345, 366, 409, 410, 411, 412
Kriegler, Judge Johann 341, 356
Kuzwayo, Beauty 95, 104, 253, 288, 348
Kuzwayo, Fezeka 95, 104, 252, 253, 254, 255, 289, 349
Kuzwayo, Judson 67, 94, 95, 101, 105, 117, 129, 253, 254, 394

L

labour movement 52–54
Lackay, Adrian 272, 280, 285, 303, 321, 330, 343, 376, 404
Land Bank 216, 217, 236, 398, 399
land reform 216, 217, 236
Lebelo, Luther 291, 311, 313, 320
Lombard, Helgaard 263
Louw, Chris 44, 45, 49–52, 181, 182, 217, 271
Lubowski, Anton 197, 219
Luirink, Bart 11, 34, 49, 61, 113–21, 128, 137, 138, 147, 152, 153, 160, 162, 175, 306, 318, 342, 344, 345, 377, 406

M

Maake, Cassius 90, 102
Mabaso, Clifford 54–55, 69, 86
Magashula, Oupa 271, 282, 284, 290–91, 290, 313, 323, 346, 372, 408, 409, 413
Maharaj, Mac 35, 58–61, 76, 106–107, 113, 126, 127, 140, 142, 145, 150, 151, 224, 225, 226, 231, 233, 235, 240, 252, 269, 271, 326, 328, 371, 376, 394, 396, 400, 401
Mahlobo, David 296, 336
Maintenance Court 175–78
Maisy 69–71, 133, 138, 145, 149, 152, 158, 160, 162, 165, 167, 183, 189, 271, 343, 371
Makwakwa, Jonas 262, 320, 325, 328, 346
Malema, Julius 141, 143, 236, 265, 279, 280, 284, 299, 345, 351, 361, 365
Mandela, Nelson 108, 144, 292
Mandela, Winnie 36–39, 71, 91, 151, 219
Mandla 157, 163, 164, 175, 185, 187, 193, 202, 204, 207, 208, 209, 221, 231, 236, 237, 238, 263, 271, 394
Mantashe, Gwede 337, 340, 349
Manuel, Trevor 202, 269, 296, 335, 349
Manye, Christopher 131, 132, 394
Maphumulo, Shadrack 67, 77–79, 92, 94, 95, 100, 102, 104, 117, 249
Masia, Philip 63–64, 66, 72–73, 75, 79, 82, 84, 85, 87, 117–21, 134, 143, 159, 160, 162, 167, 171, 180, 201, 202, 218, 271
Masia, Thabisile 63–64, 66, 75, 376
Mastenbroek, Rudolf 220, 242, 280, 329, 332–33
Mbeki, Thabo 60, 127, 141, 144, 202, 212, 217, 222, 226, 231, 238, 239, 242, 244, 248, 250, 256, 259, 265, 267, 360, 401
Mbokodo 166, 188
McBride, Robert 129, 322, 323, 325, 337, 339, 342, 359, 360, 372, 409
Mdluli, Richard 276, 277, 310, 357, 409, 411
Meeke, Kieran 107, 371, 377
Memela, Totsie Busisiwe 14, 15, 101, 102, 107, 108, 131, 132, 143, 169, 189, 216, 217, 370, 377, 394, 395
Memela-Motumi, Ntsiki 14, 20, 21, 35, 169, 376, 412
Ministry of Intelligence 287, 289, 290, 296, 336, 364
Mkhize, Zweli 341
Mkhwebane, Busisiwe 351, 164, 365, 372
Modise, Joe 154, 159, 167, 197, 224
Mokaba, Peter 139, 141, 143
Moodley, Kogie 95, 102, 127, 128, 130, 301, 302, 366, 375
Morris *see* Mthimkhulu, Dugmore
Motsoaledi, Cassius 132, 376, 394

Index

Motsuenyane Commission 166
Moyane, Tom 290, 314, 315–17, 320–21, 321, 329–31, 331, 334, 344, 361, 363, 364
Msomi, Jabu 52–53, 57, 63, 66, 67, 79, 95, 99, 104, 139, 249, 371, 373
Msomi, Pat 52–53, 57, 63, 67, 76, 78, 79, 84, 86, 89, 90, 92, 95, 97, 98, 99, 104, 139, 373
Mthimkhulu, Dugmore 14, 15, 19, 20, 21, 35, 36, 40–41, 43, 169, 377
Mvelase, Dipuo 143, 200, 376, 394

N

Naicker-Pillay, Dhanam (Dhanabaikamal) 27, 29, 33, 37, 47, 130, 178, 179
Naidu, Lenny 102, 127, 128
Natal Indian Congress (NIC) 47, 54, 57, 139, 144
National Intelligence Agency (NIA) 172, 188, 197, 249
National Peacekeeping Force (NPKF) 167, 168, 169
National Prosecuting Authority (NPA), 240, 247, 248, 249, 256, 314, 322, 341, 357, 360, 371
  Priority Crimes Litigation Unit 361
Ndaba, Charles 59, 109, 394
Ngcuka, Bulelani 238, 239, 240, 244
Nhleko, Nkosinathi 296, 336, 357
Nkoli, Simon 137, 138
Nombulelo *see* Memela-Motumi, Ntsiki
non-racial sports 46, 47
non-racialism 13, 47, 48, 57, 103, 143, 353
Nsibande, Baba 93, 100, 101, 377
Ntlemeza, Berning 310, 317, 322, 341, 356, 396

Nyanda, Siphiwe ("Gebuza") 100, 106, 107, 132, 225, 349, 377
Nzima *see* Msomi, Pat

O

Operation Vula 9, 12, 17, 30, 45, 55, 58–61, 94, 101, 102, 106–9, 109, 132, 140, 141, 156, 236, 394
  Vula Boys allegations 224, 225, 231
Oppelt, Phylicia 280, 303, 333, 336

P

Pahad, Aziz 32, 241
Pahad, Essop 141, 142, 221, 222
Pamela 134, 158, 162, 163, 165, 167, 173, 180, 182, 183, 184, 185, 186, 188
Pauw, Jacques 284, 298, 299, 300, 303, 306, 356, 404
Peega dossier *see* Project Snowman
Peega, Mike 280, 284, 300, 333
Pikie, Yolisa 38–39, 272, 38–39, 11, 312, 315, 316, 329, 343, 344, 347, 362, 371, 372, 376, 413
Pikoli, Vusi 248, 249
Pillay, Devi 4, 153, 154, 156, 157, 158, 160, 162, 163, 164, 165, 167, 170, 171, 172, 174, 175, 179, 180, 183, 184, 185, 188, 189, 193, 202, 204, 205, 206, 207, 218, 219, 221, 256, 257, 262, 265, 266, 270, 272, 292, 304, 313, 342, 343, 344
Pillay, Dharma 32
Pillay, Joe 24, 26, 27, 30, 57, 67, 77–80, 89, 95, 97, 98, 102, 129, 153, 375
Pillay, Kisten 26, 27, 153
Pillay, Loga 26
Pillay, Rae Rajaluximi 104–5, 111, 112, 113, 114, 130, 145, 148, 376
Pillay, Suggie 26, 46, 79, 80, 102, 153
Pillay, Vadivaloo 26, 27, 32, 33

Pillay, Vani 194, 195, 199, 201, 203, 204, 208, 210, 221, 236, 262, 270, 271, 272, 291, 292, 304, 312, 319, 342, 373
Pretorius, Torie 151, 219, 220, 226, 247, 360
Project Phoenix 323, 324
Project Spiderweb 335

R

Raadschelders, Lucia 20, 34, 36, 106, 108, 127, 266, 372, 394
Rabilal, Krishna 67, 76, 77, 86, 87, 88, 89, 97, 98, 104, 129, 141, 152, 228, 392
Rabkin, Sue 254
Radebe, Jeff 31, 297
Radebe, Leonard 282, 283, 284, 303
Radical Economic Transformation (RET) 307, 308, 309, 326, 364, 366
Raidoo, Prani 95, 102, 127, 375
Ramaphosa, Cyril 144, 222, 307, 352, 357, 358, 367, 368, 390, 413
Ramkissoon, Ish 127, 128, 375
Ramlakan, Vijay 129
Rampedi, Piet 295, 326, 334, 339, 364, 365, 366, 411
Ravele, Gene 279, 281
Ravesloot, André 107, 377, 394
Reconstruction and Development Plan (RDP) 195, 202, 397
Renwick, Robin 223
Richer, Pete 312, 313, 316, 318, 322, 325, 330, 376, 408
Roberts Construction 68, 77, 86
rogue unit allegations 299, 303, 304, 305, 326, 335, 336
    Broken Arrow 283
    criminal charges 360
    KPMG report 344

Kroon board 328–29
pension payout allegations 313, 314
Project Snowman 280, 284
Public Protector investigation 365
Sikhakhane report 315, 328–29

S

Saloojee, Riaz 308, 323, 376
Scorpions 220, 224, 225, 231, 241, 256, 265
    arms deal investigation 224–226
Sedibe, Glory ("September") 88, 102
Selebi, Jackie 226, 239, 246, 247, 248, 283
Semane, Lizo 14, 15, 19, 20, 21, 35, 36, 39–40, 39, 43, 75, 83, 169, 308, 377
Sentinel, The 24, 25, 63, 67, 68, 129, 131
September, Dulcie 13, 32, 81, 196, 198, 219, 355
Sewpersadh, Vidhu 139
Sewpersadh, Vish 139, 393
Sexwale, Tokyo 154, 173, 222, 307
Shabalala, Mbuso 59, 109, 394
Shabalala, Vuso 200, 376, 394
Shaik, Moe 126, 224, 238, 239, 288–89, 329, 376, 394, 401
Shaik, Shabir 224, 225, 226, 231, 233, 238, 242, 244, 400
Sibiya, Shadrack 310, 323, 360, 409
Sikhakhane, Muzi 316 *see also* rogue unit allegations: Sikhakhane report
Singh, Sunny 22, 58, 66–68, 76, 90, 97, 117, 142, 376
Sinterklaas 201, 202, 203, 205, 311, 331, 349, 366
Sister *see* Govender, Pushpa
Slovo, Joe 60, 106, 123, 127, 144, 216
Sole, Sam 225, 230, 231, 232, 245, 400

Soni, Shirish 115, 131, 200, 376
South African Broadcasting
    Corporation (SABC), 121–26,
    213, 297
South African Revenue Services
    (SARS) 199–201, 219, 228, 230,
    242-47, 262–63, 271–72, 278–82,
    279, 283-85, 289, 290, 295, 299,
    303, 306, 316, 344, 346, 379, 387,
    395, 404
    anti-corruption 246
    building SARS 195, 200, 201,
       227, 228, 230, 232
    customs 285–88
    High Risk Investigations Unit
       (HIRU) 284, 316
    tax evasion 282, 283
    the dismantling of SARS 295,
       296, 324, 325, 330, 331, 339
    transformation 262
state building 83, 104, 195, 202, 203,
    230, 232, 236, 241, 278, 301 *see
    also* democratic transition
state capture 345, 358
    capture of law enforcement 248,
       256, 296, 310, 314, 317, 322,
       323, 331, 340, 341, 346, 347,
       360
State Security Agency (SSA) 288–89,
    295, 351, 356
    infiltration of SARS 280, 281,
       285, 290, 300
    Special Operations Unit (SOU)
       298
Sunday 100, 157, 160–66, 170, 171,
    174, 175, 177, 180, 184-88, 193,
    201-04, 207, 209, 211-16, 223,
    231, 232, 237, 261, 263, 271, 320,
    343, 344, 347, 357, 360
Sunday Times 234, 276, 277, 278, 280,
    290, 299, 303–06, 309–11, 310,
    313, 316, 322–23, 323, 328, 333,
    334, 335, 336, 341, 372
    Press Ombudsman 331–33
    retraction and apology 339
Symington, Vlok 314, 347

T
Tambo, O.R. 16, 59, 60, 88, 106, 108,
    154, 167, 354, 394
Thandi 138, 157, 163, 164, 170, 184,
    185, 193, 202, 204, 206, 207, 221,
    238, 266, 271, 343
tobacco industry 284, 295, 298, 299,
    300, 307
tourism in the new SA, 113–21, 116
Transitional Executive Authority
    (TEC) 167, 168, 199
trauma 19, 20, 21, 37, 38, 39, 49, 88,
    105
Trimp, Rens 113, 129, 377, 393
Tshwete, Steve 114, 191, 222

U
uMkhonto we Sizwe (MK) 12, 14,
    15, 16, 17, 18, 58, 77, 78, 85, 88,
    89, 90, 92, 97, 99, 100, 102
unions, 54, 176, 262, 317, 391 *see also*
    labour movement
United Democratic Front (UDF) 15,
    69, 101, 140

V
Van Loggerenberg, Johann 196–199,
    228, 244, 246, 272, 297, 296, 298,
    300, 305, 311, 315, 317, 329, 333,
    334, 339, 360, 362, 371, 372, 395,
    397, 404, 409, 413
Van Rooyen, Des 289, 332, 333
VBS 361, 362, 413

W
wa Afrika, Mzilikazi 233, 234,

276–77, 295, 303–306, 310–11, 313, 322, 326, 334, 339, 414
Walter, Belinda 300–01, 312, 316
Whitehead, Archie 90, 94, 101, 160, 162, 189, 343, 377, 394
Williams, Mark-Anthony 318–19, 318
Williams, Phumla ("Flo") 102, 143, 309, 377

X

Xaba, Nyameka 314, 341, 346–47
xenophobia 266–67

Z

ZAM 306, 307, 371
Zeph *see* Semane, Lizo
Zibi, Songezo 335, 336, 363, 364
Zuma, Duduzane 290, 337, 345
Zuma, Edward 285, 298
Zuma, Jacob 39, 70, 91, 106, 142, 144, 224–26, 238, 242, 244, 250–256, 265–67, 269, 276, 280, 284–85, 288, 296, 299, 301–02, 353, 355, 358, 360, 362, 372, 373

Previous titles by Evelyn Groenink

'Tussen Township en Tafelberg', a tour guide to South Africa (with Bart Luirink, Odyssee, Amsterdam, 1992)

Wonderland (Atlas, Amsterdam, 1998)

Dulcie (Atlas, Amsterdam, 2001)

Bij de blanken is het beter (It's better where the whites are), Atlas, Amsterdam, 2013

Incorruptible: The story of the murders of Dulcie September, Anton Lubowski and Chris Hani (South Africa, 2018).

We thank the following for their support in publishing this book:

Arthur Goldstuck
Ashwin Moyene
Ben Williams
Beverley Naidoo
Carolyn Raphaely
Catriona Jarvis
Corinne Rosmarin
Denis Hirson
Dianne Stewart
Gill Bolton
Glen Impey
Graeme Friedman
Helen Douglas
James Bissett
Karin Pampallis

Kevin Ritchie & Associates
Louis Gaigher
Maeve King
Mamma Jacqui
Mary Burton
Michelina Giacovazzi
Moira Levy
Roger Southall
Rona V van Niekerk
Ryan Childs
Sebastian Seedorf
Steven Dubin
Sue Grant-Marshall
Trisha Cornelius